CREATING
COMPOSITIONS

Creating Compositions

HARVEY S. WIENER
Coordinator of Writing
LaGuardia Community College
City University of New York

McGRAW-HILL BOOK COMPANY
New York St. Louis San Francisco
Düsseldorf Johannesburg Kuala Lumpur
London Mexico Montreal
New Delhi Panama Rio de Janeiro
Singapore Sydney Toronto

1234567890MUMU79876543

This book was set in Trump and Trade Gothic by Progressive Typographers. The editors were David Edwards and David Dunham; the designer was Emily Harste; and the production supervisor was Tom Lo Pinto. The drawings were done by Eric G. Hieber. The printer and binder was The Murray Printing Company.

Library of Congress Cataloging in Publication Data

Wiener, Harvey.
    Creating compositions.

    1. English language—Rhetoric. I. Title.
PE1408.W5819   808'.042   72-10208
ISBN 0-07-070146-6

Acknowledgments

William Carl Bondarenko, "The Girl's Banana." Reprinted from *American Vanguard*, edited by Don M. Wolfe. Copyright 1948 by Don M. Wolfe. Reprinted by permission of Don M. Wolfe.

Claude Brown from *Manchild in the Promised Land*. Copyright © 1965 by Claude Brown. Reprinted by permission of The Macmillan Company.

Pearl S. Buck, from "The Frill," copyright 1933 by Pearl S. Buck. Renewed. Reprinted by permission of Harold Ober Associates Incorporated.

Malcolm N. Carter, "Anatomy of an Accident," *The New York Times*, December 19, 1971. Copyright © 1971 by The New York Times Company. Reprinted by permission.

Thomas J. Cottle, "In the Car Shop," *Saturday Review*, June 19, 1971. Copyright 1971, Saturday Review, Inc. Reprinted by permission of *Saturday Review* and the author.

Eugene N. Doherty, "Proud Words," from *American Scene: New Voices*, edited by Don M. Wolfe. Copyright © 1963 by Don M. Wolfe. Reprinted by permission of Don M. Wolfe.

G. S. Ferdin, R. C. Peck, and R. S. Coppin, from "The Teen Aged Driver" in *Highway Research Record #163*. Reprinted by permission of the Highway Research Board.

Germaine Greer, from *The Female Eunuch*. Copyright © 1971 by Germaine Greer. Reprinted by permission of the publisher, McGraw-Hill Book Company.

Langston Hughes, "Brass Spittoon" from *Fine Clothes to the Jew*. Copyright 1927 by Langston Hughes, renewed. Reprinted by permission of Harold Ober Associates.

Maude White Katz, from "End Racism in Education: A Concerned Parent Speaks." Reprinted from *Freedomways Magazine*, vol. 8, no. 4 (fourth quarter), 1968.

Paul W. Kearney, from *Highway Homicide*. Copyright © 1966 by Paul W. Kearney. Reprinted by permission of the publisher, Thomas Y. Crowell Company, Inc.

John Oliver Killens, "The Stick Up" from *The Best Short Stories by Negro Writers*. Copyright 1967 by John Oliver Killens. Reprinted by permission of International Famous Agency.

William Leigh, Jr., "Six O'Clock," from *The Freshman and His World* by Don M. Wolfe, Ruth A. Firor, Thomas L. Donahue. Copyright © ·1954 by Don M. Wolfe, Ruth A. Firor, and Thomas L. Donahue. Reprinted by permission of Don M. Wolfe.

Mary E. Mebane, "An Open Letter to Gloria Steinem." Appeared in *The New York Times*, October 29, 1971. Copyright © 1971 by the New York Times Company. Reprinted by permission.

Edna St. Vincent Millay, "Lament," from *Collected Poems*, Harper & Row. Copyright 1921, 1948 by Edna St. Vincent Millay.

National Safety Council for permission to use material from "Traffic Accident Facts," 1970 edition.

The New Merriam-Webster Pocket Dictionary, copyright © 1971 by G. & C. Merriam Co., publishers of the Merriam-Webster Dictionaries. Entries reprinted by permission.

The *New York Times Encyclopedia Almanac, 1970*, from "Environmental Pollution" and charts from "Travel and Transportation." Copyright © 1970 by the New York Times Company. Reprinted by permission of the New York Times Company.

Jeffrey O'Connell and Arthur Meyers, from *Safety Last: An Indictment of the Automobile Industry*. Copyright © 1966 by Jeffery O'Connell and Arthur Myers. Reprinted by permission of Random House, Inc.

George Orwell, from *Such, Such Were the Joys*. Copyright 1953. Reprinted by permission of Harcourt, Brace Jovanovich, Inc. and Mrs. Sonia Brownell Orwell.

John R. Regan, "My Room at the Lilac Inn," from *The Purple Testament*, edited by Don M. Wolfe. Copyright 1946 by Don M. Wolfe. Reprinted by permission of Don M. Wolfe.

Roget's International Thesaurus. Copyright 1946 by Thomas Y. Crowell Company. Entries under the work "humorist," #844 reprinted by permission of the publisher.

Philip Roth, from *Portnoy's Complaint*. Copyright © 1967, 1968, 1969 by Philip Roth. Reprinted by permission of Random House, Inc.

Carl Sandburg, "Mag," from *Chicago Poems*. Copyright 1916 by Holt, Rinehart and Winston, Inc. Copyright 1944 by Carl Sandburg. Reprinted by permission of Holt, Rinehart and Winston, Inc.

Margaret Sloan, "What We Should Be Doing, Sister." Appeared in *The New York Times*, December 8, 1971. Copyright © 1971 by The New York Times Company.

Betty Smith, from *A Tree Grows in Brooklyn* (hardbound edition). Copyright 1943, 1947 by Betty Smith. Reprinted by permission of Harper & Row, Publishers, Incorporated.

Thomas Wolfe, from *Look Homeward Angel*. Reprinted by permission of Charles Scribner's Sons. Copyright 1929 by Charles Scribner's Sons; renewal copyright © 1957 by Edward C. Aswell, Administrator, C. T. A. and/or Fred W. Wolfe.

Thomas Wolfe, from *You Can't Go Home Again*. Copyright 1934, 1937, 1938, 1939, 1940 by Maxwell Perkins; renewed 1968 by Paul Gitlin. Reprinted by permission of Harper & Row, Publishers, Incorporated.

The World Almanac and Book of Facts 1971, charts on auto thefts and mileage records. Copyright © 1970 by *The World Almanac*. Reprinted by permission.

TO DON MARION WOLFE
whose ideas take on new power with each generation
of young writers

AND TO MY STUDENTS
who illustrate with every theme they write the
eternal freshness of those ideas

CONTENTS

PREFACE

If even the idea of writing a composition turns your hands cold and sweaty and sets your stomach flipping, this book is for you. If even after an essay is assigned you never have anything to write, this book is for you. If you do know what to write about but after a few sentences you run out of things to say, this book is for you. And this book is for you if you know that you make mistakes in writing but you just cannot make sense out of complicated rules of grammar.

Creating Compositions affirms that if you live by feeling and looking and hearing and responding, then, you can write. Today, more than ever, college students have experiences so rich and special that they are the perfect and logical source to provide meaningful writing activities. Your experiences—the countless moments of pleasure and sorrow and surprise that fill each day—make the best compositions. After you develop through this book the skills that will sharpen your ability to recreate your experiences in written words, then you can move easily into the world of abstract ideas where details other than those based upon experience are often needed to support a written assignment. But this book always stresses the individual's life as the most important resource for creating compositions of any kind.

Furthermore, *Creating Compositions* moves gradually into the formal college "essay" by focusing first upon the well-developed paragraph. In Part I your early practice in composition will be with the one-paragraph theme. You will have a new view of the paragraph, too: instead of a unit of four or five sentences (typical of many newspaper and magazine styles), the one-paragraph composition you write will develop more fully and at greater length the details you need to support ideas. Part II deals specifically with the four-paragraph essay and shows clearly the relationship between the one-paragraph theme and the longer theme.

Each chapter of *Creating Compositions* is organized around a topic whose meaning your own life experiences can dramatize: family moments, high school memories, noisy afternoons on a summer street, the role in your life of the liberated woman, to name just a few. In most of the chapters, after the introduction you will find activities designed to involve you in the topic. In class you will discuss your ideas about the quality of your own experiences, about photographs that catch a worthy moment, and about other materials that explore your own responses to life. In that way, and well before actual writing begins, you will have a chance to share ideas and to listen to the ways that other people think about a topic.

Early in each chapter you will have an opportunity to build up strengths in vocabulary that will be helpful for the writing assignment; you can use in your paragraph or essay some of the new words you have learned. To simplify the difficult (and often unpleasant) process of learning vocabulary, words are presented clearly and easily; as a result, you can try to figure out definitions without always having to look first in a dictionary. Finally, all correct definitions appear in the back of the book as a ready check for the definitions you have attempted.

A section in each chapter called Building Composition Skills explains different techniques in the construction of a paragraph or essay and gives you an opportunity through clear exercises to experiment with these techniques before you need to use them in your compositions. You will learn several methods of paragraph construction—comparison-contrast, description, narration, among others—as you investigate the specific parts of a paragraph. You will learn about and practice with different kinds of details you need for support—from details so alive with the senses that you can recreate an experience easily to details built upon statistics and quotations you have selected from reliable sources. This section includes activities designed to help you improve your sentence structure. When you work with the essay itself, you will learn about introductions and conclusions and will be given some handy suggestions for developing the main body paragraphs.

The section named Solving Problems in Writing looks at some particular areas of written communication that have long troubled students of composition. There you find, just to name a few, the run-on error, the sentence fragment, problems with subject and verb agreement, special punctuation skills, and problems with pronouns. In all the explanations the stress is upon clear presentation. Charts and clearly marked model sentences illustrate principles by example more often than by rule. The often confusing language of grammar is avoided; when grammatical terms are necessary, definitions are simply written so that you can understand them without difficulty. And the exercises that allow you to try out what you learn require that you apply each skill in the language of your own sentences. You probably will not need to do all the exercises and you can probably leave out those activities which deal with skills that you and your instructor agree you already know. Perforated pages make it possible for your instructor to collect the work you do directly in the book.

In each chapter a section called Writing the Paragraph offers specific goals for the writing exercise. Before you have to write your own composition, you will read some examples of what other students wrote in response to the same assignment. The questions that appear after these student models suggest directions for your own writing; so does the checklist of goals that remind you of the specific skills you are trying to build. Suggested topics will give you additional ideas for your own themes.

The section The Professionals Speak gives you writing samples from the works of important authors. These samples illustrate how professionals deal with the same kinds of materials you are asked to treat in your writing. And to provide a special challenge either through review or through more practice in composition, there is at the end of each chapter a section called Reaching Higher. At the end of the text itself appears A Minibook of Special Skills that presents briefly several important areas of communication which you may need for successful work in a variety of college classrooms. There you will find techniques for improving your spelling and vocabulary. And you will learn how to write a business letter, how to prepare footnotes and bibliography, how to take notes and write a summary, and several other skills.

You might like to know that students in composition classes prepared several of the illustrations and took some of the photographs that open the chapters. These, along with the themes written by students, are promises of what you will be able to do. Your work will improve upon the models that appear here. In writing about your own experiences and comparing them with those other students write, you develop a whole new sense of your own way of life. You think through the moments that have built your character and personality; the insights you gather help mold in many ways your own development for the future.

Many people deserve thanks for their help in the preparation of this book. From Don Marion Wolfe, my teacher and friend (and to whom I have dedicated this text), comes the whole philosophy of sensory language and the need for exploring individual moments in order to write with meaning. His too are the ideas for using model paragraphs as the heart of any composition program and for using activities in language that require the student to call upon his own resources in communication. To Don Wolfe my gratitude is limitless. To my wife Barbara Koster Wiener go thanks for her patience during the preparation of the materials and for her skills as a teacher of reading which made her assistance invaluable. To my colleagues at the Basic Skills Department at Queensborough Community College for encouraging me to begin and develop this book and to my colleagues at LaGuardia Community College for urging me to press toward its completion I owe many thanks. I extend my appreciation to Professor Joan Poloff and Robert Baylor whose suggestions I welcomed but did not always faithfully follow. And without Bernice Linder's careful preparation of the manuscript I could not have managed at all. Finally it is to the students in my composition courses who proved each term anew the infinite resources of their own lives and their ability to commit those vital elements into words—it is to them I offer deep gratitude.

Harvey S. Wiener

CREATING
COMPOSITIONS

part I

PARAGRAPHS

chapter 1

A NEW PLACE, A NEW LOOK: DESCRIPTION IN ACTION

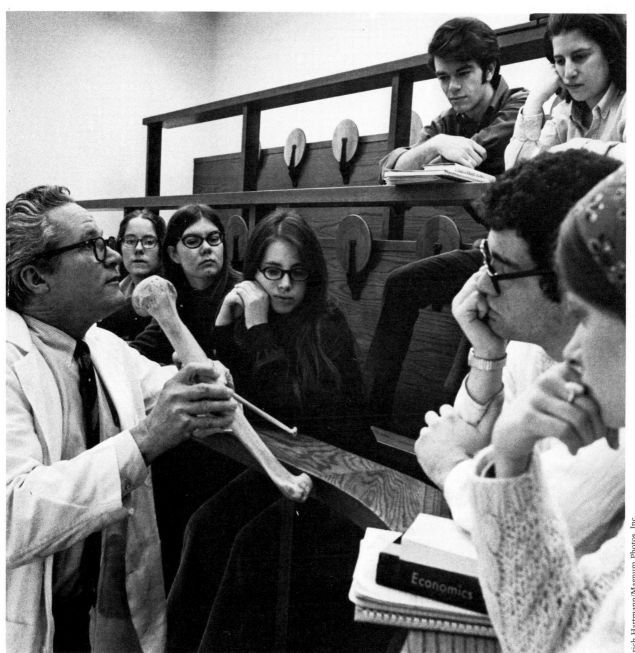

INTRODUCTION

The classroom in which you now sit is a new place for you, a place filled with colors and noises and the actions of people you do not know. This room itself and the people in it will be the focus of your first theme. When you experiment with this one-paragraph assignment, you are going to make this place come alive. You will call upon your sense impressions of sound, color, smell, touch, and action to illustrate your major reaction to the class-room situation. Before you write you will read what other students before you have written in response to the same assignment.

VOCABULARY

Step 1. Words to Describe Situations.   These words specify reactions you may have to the classroom. You may find them helpful in writing about your room. Write definitions on the blank lines. For any words you do not know, check a dictionary or Appendix A.

1. dynamic_____

2. tiresome _____

3. frantic _____

4. tranquil _____

5. intense _____

6. boisterous _____

7. dismal _____

8. indifferent _____

9. effervescent _____

10. lax _____

Step 2. Applying Vocabulary.   After you are sure of the meanings of the above words, write:

1. a word to describe a gloomy place _____

2. a word to describe a room that bubbles with excitement _____

3. a word to describe rough noisiness _____

4. a word that means peaceful _____

5. a word that shows lack of tension _____

6. a word to indicate something boring _____

7. a word to show the presence of strong emotion _____

8. a word to describe wild excitement _____

9. a word to show energetic activity _____

10. a word to indicate a lack of preference _____

Step 3. Words That Name Sounds.   Read each sentence. Copy the itali-cized word into the blank space in Column I. Try to develop a definition from the way the word is used in the sentence, and write your definition in the blank space in Column II. Then, check the definitions you have written with the actual definitions from a dictionary or from Appendix A. Write the correct definition in the blank space in Column III.

Example:	I	II	III
1. He *guffawed* at the jokes, his whole body shaking with delight.	*guffawed*	*laughed strongly*	*laughed in a loud burst*

2. Such a *din* arose from the apartment upstairs that surely another rock session had begun.
3. A car engine *whined* like a crying cat.
4. She spoke so low that her words were *inaudible*.
5. When the dog wandered into the classroom, the class *erupted* into shrieks of laughter.
6. The vibrations of a bell *resounded* through the empty hall.

BUILDING COMPOSITION SKILLS

Sensory Language

Step 1. Listening Well. Listen a moment to your "silent" classroom. Write three sentences that tell sounds you hear. Use a word that reveals the sound clearly.

Example: I hear the clink and jangle of keys.
Someone coughs and clears his throat.

1. _____

_____

2. _____

_____

3. _____

_____

Step 2. Action and Color. Look around. Write three sentences that show some action in the room. Use a color in each sentence.

Example: *An old yellow window shade blows in the air.*
            Next to me a girl scratches her long black hair.

1. _____

   _____

2. _____

   _____

3. _____

   _____

Step 3. What You Feel.   Touch your desk, your shirt or sweater, your pen, or your wristwatch. Write a sentence that includes a word to show what you feel. Use a color or a sound as well.

Example: *I hear the tick of my watch as I touch its cool glassy surface.*
            My brown wool sweater is warm and scratchy.

1. _____

   _____

2. _____

   _____

3. _____

   _____

The practices above demonstrate an important technique in writing: *concrete sensory detail. Concrete* means specific, solid; *sensory* means relating to any of the senses. The highly specific pictures that result are called *images.* Notice in the two columns below how the images in Column I are general and have little sensory appeal, while those in Column II are concrete because they appeal strongly to the senses.

I	II
1. an old book	an economics book with yellowed pages and a torn binding
2. a pen	a smooth pen that clicks when I push the silver top
3. the wall	a high white wall, its plaster chipped and cracked
4. the desk	_____
5. the floor	_____
6. a shirt	_____

Step 4. Concrete Details.   In the blank spaces under Column II, write concrete sensory details for the general pictures in Column I.

Topic Sentences

The key to a good paragraph is its topic sentence. For your purposes at this point, the topic sentence should always come as the first sentence of the paragraph. The chart below will help you recall the function of the topic sentence.

A TOPIC SENTENCE REMINDER

Good Topic Sentences:	*Why:*
1. Introduce the topic immediately.	So your reader knows what you will write about. So you know what you will write about.
	Hint: Do not surprise the reader. Tell him immediately what you want to write about.
2. Limit the topic.	So you will not have too much to write about. So you will have enough to write about. It helps limit the topic to only one major feature or point.
3. Give an opinion or an attitude or a reaction or an impression that the writer has about his topic.	It gets the reader interested in the topic: he will want to find out why you feel the way you do about your subject. It introduces a key word which will help you relate all your supporting ideas to one dominant impression.

Here are two effective topic sentences which are successful because they introduce a limited topic clearly *and* give the writer's opinion about that topic. Each is explained for you.

1. Everyone in my writing class this Monday morning seems nervous and uncomfortable.

   Topic The people in the writing class
   Opinion Nervousness

2. An atmosphere of eager activity surrounds the people and things in my writing class on a late September afternoon.

   Topic People and things in the writing class at one specific time
   Opinion Eager activity

The writer of sentence 1 above would need to show in each sentence that follows his topic sentence why he feels everyone is nervous.

The writer of sentence 2 above would need to show the details which make him sense eagerness and activity.

Step 1. Determining Topics and Opinions. From the following topic sentences on a variety of subjects write the topic and the opinion or attitude on the blank spaces. Follow the examples given above.

1. Most college freshmen are shocked at complex registration procedures.

Topic _____
_____
_____

Attitude _____
_____
_____

2. Our kitchen on a Sunday night reflects Mother's love for cleanliness and order.

Topic _____
_____
_____

Attitude _____
_____
_____

3. I'll always regret the day I decided to play hooky in my high school senior year.

Topic _____
_____
_____

Attitude _____
_____
_____

4. To me, professional baseball is the dullest sport imaginable.

Topic _____
_____
_____

Attitude _____
_____
_____

5. Television for the preschool age groups is a valuable aid to mothers.

Topic _____
_____
_____

Attitude _____
_____
_____

Step 2. Improving Topic Sentences. These topic sentences need to be improved by the introduction of key opinion or attitude words which will help limit and specify the topic. Rewrite the sentences in the space provided. You may wish to change the idea of some of the sentences as you introduce opinion words. Try to avoid those too general opinion words like *good, nice, pleasant, enjoyable* by using some of the vocabulary on p. 4.

Example:

1. I have a collection of old coins. *My collection of old coins is the envy of my Uncle Dave.*

2. My younger brother goes to nursery school. _____
_____

3. There are many forests in New York State. _____
_____

4. One day the principal called me into his office. _____
_____

5. Soldiers undergo training before they can fight. _____
_____

6. I took the six o'clock train to Philadelphia one December evening.
_____
_____

7. Pete Seeger plays the guitar for children on *Sesame Street.* _____
_____

8. College students are required to buy their own books. _____
_____

9. W. C. Fields is a humorist. _____
_____

10. A large number of working people eat all meals in restaurants. _____
_____

Step 3. Clearing up Topics. The topic sentences below fail to specify the topic to be developed in the paragraph. Many lack key opinion words. Others give important details but fail to clarify exactly what the topic will be. Rewrite the sentences in the space provided. Strive to make them more clear and effective topic sentences.

Example:

1. It all happened one day last spring. *On a day last spring I finally learned how to relax.*

2. On a cool May morning my friends and I went to the park. _____

_____

3. There was a rainbow of blue and red spread across the sky. _____

_____

4. A small puppy crossed the street when the light turned red. _____

_____

5. Narcotic addicts may use dirty needles to inject drugs into the blood.

_____

_____

Step 4. Predicting Topics.   A good topic sentence predicts for the reader some of the details to be found in the paragraph. For each topic sentence below, write two kinds of information you might expect to find in the paragraph. The first one is done for you.

1. Owning a summer home in the country presents many problems.

1. *a. problems of keeping the house in order during winter months*

   b. problems of unwanted guests.

   _____

2. Sundays for me are days of relaxation and pleasure.

2. *a.* _____

   _____

   b. _____

   _____

3. John F. Kennedy's assassination brought deep sorrow to the hearts of most Americans.

3. *a.* _____

   _____

   b. _____

   _____

4. In this complex society, there are many vital reasons to explain why adult males turn to alcohol.

4. *a.* _____

_____

_____

b. _____

_____

5. Eighteen-year-olds certainly do deserve the right to vote!

5. *a.* _____

_____

b. _____

_____

_____

6. The welfare systems in today's urban centers are disgraceful.

6. *a.* _____

_____

b. _____

_____

Step 5. Topic Sentences. The most effective way to construct your sentence is to decide beforehand those details you wish to discuss. Suppose you wanted to write a paragraph on pollution and you wanted to discuss these two issues:

1. Machines such as cars and trains and lawn mowers as major pollutants
2. Humans as careless destroyers of our air and water

Here is a topic sentence that would permit the writer to discuss the two details he wishes:

Both machines and human beings share the awful guilt of polluting our air and waters.

The topic is clearly stated. Which words give the opinion or attitude? If the topic sentence were:

Pollution is a terrible problem.

the writer would have presented too broad a topic for treatment in a composition of limited length. There are just too many possibilities for the writer to consider with such a topic sentence, and he would tend to treat too quickly many points without examining closely two or three points that are especially important.

For each group of details in Column I, write a topic sentence (including opinion and limited topic) in Column II.

I

1. Dogs are good company for lonely people.
   Dogs are affectionate and devoted.
   Dogs protect property.

2. My uncle donated a large collection of books to the library.
   He gave $1,000 to the American Cancer Society.
   He gave twenty brand-new shirts to the local hospital.

3. My fifth-grade teacher always made fun of me.
   A junior high school math teacher accused me of cheating.
   My senior homeroom teacher always thought I was talking.

4. On our trip to Cape Cod we got lost three times.
   We got two blowouts at the same time.
   My dad lost his wallet.
   The motel clerk never received our reservations.

II

1. _____
   _____
   _____
   _____
   _____
   _____

2. _____
   _____
   _____
   _____
   _____
   _____

3. _____
   _____
   _____
   _____
   _____
   _____

4. _____
   _____
   _____
   _____
   _____

Step 6. Topic Sentence and Details. For each topic in Column I, write a limited topic sentence including an attitude or opinion word in Column II.

Then write two details you might expect to find in the paragraph under Column III.

I	II	III
Example:		
1. Books	*Reading for enjoyment is certainly not a popular activity with teenagers.*	*Television and movies as more exciting and lively forms of entertainment* *Reading-skills problems for many teenagers.*
2. Fathers		
3. Free colleges		
4. Week-night dating		

Step 7. More Topic Sentence Practice.   Let us change the method slightly. Before you write the topic sentence, note two details in Column II which you wish to develop in a paragraph suggested by the topic in Column I. Write the topic sentence in Column III.

I	II	III
Example:		
1. Diets	*A crash diet I went on aways left me hungry. It made me very sick. I gained back all the weight I lost anyhow.*	*I learned from a crash diet I foolishly followed for two weeks that serious problems may result from an unwise eating program.*

I	*II*	*III*

2. Smoking

3. The two-year college

4. Credit cards

5. Campus football

6. Blind dates

Getting It All Together

Transitions I. In a composition that is basically descriptive, the writer moves clearly from one feature of the description to another by using certain types of *transitional expressions*. A transitional expression is a connector; it is a bridge, a hookup, between statements and ideas in paragraphs. Here are some transition words which can relate ideas in a paragraph that describes a place; they will be helpful as you write your classroom theme.

there	next to
behind	in the rear
up above	in front of
to the left	up front
to the right	over
nearby	around
below	surrounding

at the _____   near the back
beside   forward
far off   through the _____
inside   from the _____
alongside

Step 1. Seeing Transitions at Work.   Examine the sentences in Column I below. The ideas seem unrelated and unclear. By adding transitional expressions in the blank spaces in the same sentences under Column II, make the relationship between ideas clearer. You may want to add a word or two after the transition as well.

I	II
The classroom in my old public school stood empty when I arrived early for the spring open-school night to see my sister's teacher. I saw the same kind of creaky wooden desk my own teacher used. The blackboard looked clean and freshly washed and I was tempted to write some nasty thing on it in big white letters. I could see the open wardrobe; twenty-five black hooks, each numbered in red ink, hung empty without a coat or hat. I saw a rolled-up map and an empty water basin. As I walked a cool refreshing breeze blew. I heard the sound of someone laughing. Perhaps it made fun of me for standing alone; I decided I'd better not wait.	The classroom in my old public school stood empty when I arrived early for the spring open-school night to see my sister's teacher. _____ I saw the same kind of creaky desk my own teacher used. _____ the blackboard looked clean and freshly washed and I was tempted to write some nasty thing on it in big white letters. _____ I could see the open wardrobe; twenty-five black hooks, each numbered in red ink, hung empty without a coat or hat. _____ I saw a rolled-up map and an empty water basin. As I walked _____ a cool refreshing breeze blew _____. I heard the sound of someone laughing. Perhaps it made fun of me for standing alone _____. I decided I'd better not wait.

SOLVING PROBLEMS IN WRITING

The Mirror Words I

The following exercises focus upon five groups of words that are especially difficult to spell because they look and sound so much like other words with different meanings.

---

it's, its it's: it is it has	*It's* raining. Tell us if *it's* true. When *it's* noisy, I leave. *It's* been a long time since we met.

Hint: You must be able to use the words *it is* or *it has* whenever you want to use *it's*.

---

its: possession or ownership by some non-human thing	The cat hurt *its* paw. In a quick breeze the tree lost *its* leaves. The desk was old, but *its* surface shone. **Hint:** If you can use *his* or *her* and the sentence gives a sense of ownership, you can use *its*. The tree lost *his* leaves. *His* gives the sense of ownership; since trees have no male or female qualities, *its* should be used.

Step 1. *It's* or *Its*. Write the correct word, *it's* or *its*, in the blank space below.

1. _____ hard to learn touch-typing.

2. While _____ not essential to brush a dog daily, the animal should

   have _____ fur cleaned at least once a week.

3. Whoever sees him knows that _____ his strong personality that earned him reelection.

4. The hat fell on the ground, and a layer of dust covered _____ surface.

5. _____ not the sound of the rattlesnake that disturbs me as much

   as _____ ugly, slimy shape.

---

two   too   to

two: the number 2

too: 1. One meaning is *very, more than enough, excessively,* or *in a great degree.*
        She is *too* thin.
        That shop is *too* expensive.
     2. *Too* means *also* as well.
        Let me go *too.*
        Will the mayor, *too,* speak at the luncheon?

to: 1. *To* is used to show direction. It means *toward, for,* or *at.*
        Throw the ball *to* Steven.
        It's unimportant *to* me.
     2. *To* is used as part of the infinitive. An infinitive is the starting point of any verb used in a sentence. In the sentence "He likes food," *likes* is the verb whose infinitive is *to like.* All infinitives are preceded by the word *to.* These two sentences use infinitives correctly: notice the word *to.*
            [infinitive]
        They like to fish in a stream.

> To run in track meets, you must begin to train your legs.
> [infinitive]   [infinitive]

Step 2. *To, Two, Too*. Fill in the blanks in the paragraph below with the correct form: *too, two,* or *to.*

Running _____ school one icy day, the _____ of us fell on the stairs that lead _____ our writing class. Although the steps were _____ slippery, we could have been more careful _____ . We agreed _____ walk _____ class thereafter, starting earlier by _____ minutes so we would not be _____ late for the professor _____ start the lesson.

Step 3. Using *To, Two, Too* Correctly. Follow directions.

1. Write a sentence that uses *too* to mean *very.* _____

_____

2. Write a sentence that uses *to* as an infinitive. _____

_____

3. Write a sentence using the word *two.* _____

_____

4. Write a sentence using *too* to mean *also.* _____

_____

5. Write a sentence that uses *to* as a direction word. _____

_____

there   their   they're
there: a place   Was it *there?*

Hint: *There* often starts a sentence. It is sometimes followed by *are, were, is,* or some other verb.

   There are three birds.
   There was a good movie at the Rialto.
   There sat two children playing.

their: ownership for a group   It's *their* books.
                                   Was it *their* house that burned?

> they're: they are
>
> **Hint:** If you can say *they are,* you can use *they're.*
>
> *They're* late again!
> If *they're* tired, they should sleep.

Step 4. *Their, They're, There*. Circle the correct word from parentheses.

1. (Their, There) stood five buildings.
2. (They're, There) not buying more food.
3. (There, Their) opinions are important.
4. (There, They're, Their) was a sudden noise.

> your   you're
> your: ownership. It means *belonging to you.*
> Is that *your* car? Give *your* theme a lively title.
> you're: you are
>
> **Hint:** If you can say *you are,* you can use *you're.*
>
> *You're* late.
> When *you're* out of town, call.

Step 5. Listening for *Your* and *You're*. Read the brief paragraph below, noting the use of *your* and *you're.* Then cover it with a sheet of paper and write it as your instructor dictates.

Before you're too far advanced in your first semester at college, it's a good idea to spend some time in your college library. By getting to know your way around the large steel shelves and the rows of books in red and black and green, you're sure to lessen the pains that usually come when your first term paper is due. At an early visit look at the card catalog under a topic in which you're interested. Pick out a book that will hold your attention. If you can't find it on the shelves yourself, your librarian will give you all the help you need.

_____

_____

_____

_____

_____

_____

---

who's   whose

who's: the contraction for *who is* or *who has*

   Who's at the door?
   Tell him *who's* on the phone.
   Who's been to New York?

Hint: If you can say *who is* or *who has,* you can use *who's.*

whose: possession. It asks a question (*Belonging to whom?*) or it refers to some
        person or thing named earlier in the sentence.

   Whose dime is that?
   The man *whose* briefcase was lost offered a reward.

Step 6. Sentences with *Who's* and *Whose*. Complete the following sentences so that they make sense.

1. Who's _____?

2. My teacher, whose _____, arrived late.

3. When you see who's _____, tell him my mother is not at home.

4. I am eager to learn whose _____.

5. I am eager to learn who's _____.

The Run-on Error

Before you begin learning about the run-on error, study the Sentence Review Chart.

SENTENCE REVIEW CHART

1. To be a sentence, a word group must contain a subject and a verb and must express a complete thought. In the following sentences, the verb is underlined twice, and the subject once.

Our <u>teacher</u> <u>gave</u> us an assignment.
The <u>men</u> <u>work</u> hard.

Hint: To find a verb, try these tests.
      A. Put *yesterday, today,* or *tomorrow* in front of the sentence. Whatever word changes is the verb, because only verbs show tense—time change.

      The men *work* hard.
      Yesterday the men *worked* hard.
      Work changed to *worked* with the word *yesterday.* Only verbs change in this way. *Work* is the verb.

Tomorrow the men *will work* hard.

Work changed to *will work* with the word *tomorrow*. Only verbs change this way. *Work* is the verb.

B. When you have the word you think is a verb, put *he, she, we, it, you, I*, or *they* in front of the word. If you've created a word group that makes sense, you have a verb.

Word	*Test*	
work	I work, they work	Verb
sings	he sings, it sings	Verb
frankfurter	I frankfurter, they frankfurter	No verb
is	she is, he is	Verb
seldom	I seldom, you seldom	No verb

2. Some sentences have verbs made up of more than one word.

Our teacher had given us an assignment.
Those men should have worked hard.
They were laughing aloud.

3. Some sentences have more than one verb for the same subject.

Those men worked and laughed.

4. Some sentences have several sets of subjects and verbs joined together.

Those men worked, but because they laughed, the job was finished late.

5. Some word groups, although very brief, are grammatically correct and are considered complete sentences because they express complete thoughts.

He ran.
It fell.

You might logically say, "We do not know who *he* is nor what *it* is. Aren't those sentences incomplete?" However, from a grammatical point of view, these word groups, because they contain subjects and verbs and express complete thoughts, *are* sentences. You might need more information to understand fully the correct meaning the sentence tries to offer, but often that information appears in sentences that come earlier or later on.

6. Some sentences have more than one subject for the same verb or verbs.

My mother and father drove to New York.
Mr. Jones and Mr. Smith arrived late but had dinner.

7. Some sentences express complete thoughts, although the subject does not actually appear in the sentence.

Walk!
Go down the steps quickly!

In both of these sentences, the subject is understood to be the word you.

Run-on sentences are word groups which mistakenly push two or more sentences together as one:

They <u>arrived</u> late to class the <u>teacher</u> <u>looked</u> angrily at them then <u>he</u> <u>turned</u> his head away.

HOW TO FIX THE RUN-ON ERROR

1. The easiest way to fix the run-on is to use a correct end mark between sentences: a period, a question mark, or an exclamation mark. *A comma is not an end mark. It does not separate complete sentences.* If you read aloud the run-on sentences above, listen to the sound of your own voice. Where your voice stops and drops, use a period.

   <u>They</u> <u>arrived</u> late to class. The <u>teacher</u> <u>looked</u> angrily at them. Then <u>he</u> <u>turned</u> his head away.

   [Period] [Capital letter] [Period]

   Of course, you need to use a capital letter to start the new sentences. If you had used a comma after *class* or *them* in the sentences above, you would have incorrectly separated two complete sentences (the subjects and verbs are underlined for you to help you see how the standards for completeness are met). Some composition teachers like to call the run-on error which uses a comma to separate complete thoughts a *comma splice*. A *comma splice* is merely two or more sentences run together with a comma between them.

2. When two run-on word groups, each complete with subject and verb, are very closely related in meaning, these word groups may be separated by a semicolon. A semicolon (;) does what a comma cannot do: the semicolon can separate complete thoughts. If you choose to use a semicolon, always begin the word group after the semicolon with a small letter.

   They arrived late to class. The teacher looked angrily at them; then he turned his head away.
   [Semicolon] [Small letter]

   A semicolon could not sensibly come after the word *class*, because the next word group contains a different subject and therefore gives no close relationship in meaning to the first word group.

   Hint: A subject and a verb must come both before and after the semicolon.

3. Instead of keeping complete word groups apart, we may join them together with suitable joining words (*conjunctions*) and proper punctuation.

   a. When the two sentences have equal importance in your mind, use one of these joining words: *and, but, or, for, nor.* Use a comma before the conjunction.

   They arrived late to class, and the teacher looked angrily at them. Then he turned his head away.
   [Comma] [Conjunction]

   They arrived late to class. The teacher looked angrily at them, but then he turned his head away.
   [Comma] [Conjunction]

---

b. You may also join the run-on sentences by making one complete word group less important than the other (see pp. 93–94). Many different conjunctions perform that function. Here are a few: *because, while, although, since, when, if, as.* Use a comma after you complete the word group that begins with one of these joining words. Sometimes you need to add a new word or two, take away words, or change the position of words when you correct the run-on with one of these conjunctions.

    [Less important word group]   [Comma]

As they arrived late to class, the teacher looked angrily at them. Then he turned his head away.

      [Less important word group]   [Comma]

Because they arrived late to class, the teacher looked angrily at them. Then he turned his head away.

          [Less important word group]

They arrived late to class. Although the teacher looked angrily at them, he then turned his head away.   [Comma]
[Position of words changed]

Step 1. One Error, Many Corrections. Here are two complete sentences run on as one:

There are not so many students in the college classroom it is not as crowded as in high school.

Fix this run-on error on the blank lines below. The words and the punctuation will tell you which of the three methods you have just learned is the best to use in correcting the run-on.

1. There are not so many students in the college classroom; _____

    _____

2. Because _____ , _____

    _____

3. There are not so many students in the college classroom, _____

    _____

4. There are not so many students in the college classroom. _____

    _____

5. Since _____ , _____

    _____

How to Find Run-on Errors

Repairing the run-on mistake is easy, once your teacher points out the error by writing in the margin of your paragraph RO for run-on or CS for comma splice. The trick is, of course, to find the run-on errors yourself.

1. Here are some simple hints to help you find run-on sentences:

    Read your paragraph aloud: When your voice stops and drops, use a period.

    Read your paragraph from the last sentence to the first sentence. That will help you keep apart complete thoughts.

    Count your sentences. In this way, you will be looking for end marks, and you will be aware that a small number of sentences probably means a run-on or two are in your paragraph.

2. But the best way to recognize the run-on is to learn carefully two groups of *run-on stop signs.* These words, used at the start of complete-thought word groups, mean trouble to you, because they cause freshmen to make run-on errors more frequently than any other words. Each time you write one of the words in either group, you must stop to think if there is a possibility that you may be writing a run-on sentence.

RUN-ON STOP SIGNS: GROUP I

then	there
now	consequently
however	moreover
finally	therefore
suddenly	

Hint: These words are not conjunctions. They do NOT join sentences correctly. If they open complete-thought word groups, they must be preceded by a period or a semicolon. At times, a conjunction and a comma work as well.

In this word group, the run-on stop sign starts a complete sentence, and must have either a semicolon or a period before it:

[Run-on
stop sign]

We drove for a long time. However, we rested afterward.
We drove for a long time; however, we rested afterward.

In this word group, the run-on stop sign is used correctly in the middle of the sentence and it does NOT start a complete-thought word group:

We drove, however, for a long time.

Step 1. Correct Punctuation for Run-ons. Correct the run-on errors below by inserting correct punctuation or changing incorrect punctuation. One sentence is already correct.

1. We were impatient, finally they arrived.
2. I dislike white bread, however, I like rye bread.
3. I do research in the library there is no noise there at all.
4. You must attempt, then, to speak in a clear voice.
5. She cooked yesterday, therefore, I'll cook today.

Hint: Check for subjects and verbs to test sentence completeness.

RUN-ON STOP SIGNS: GROUP II

it	we	
she	he	**Hint:** Although these words are frequently used in the middle of sentences, they are also used as sentence openers. If one of these words opens a sentence, the word must be preceded by a period or a semicolon.
you	they	
I		

Step 2. Rewriting the Run-on. Fix the run-on errors below by rewriting the word groups correctly on the blank lines. Use any of the methods explained on pp. 21–22. All the run-on mistakes are caused by Group II *stop signs*. One sentence is correct as it stands.

1. Suddenly we heard a loud bang it was only the garage door. _____

   _____

   _____

2. When I finally made college, I was excited beyond belief. _____

   _____

   _____

3. College freshmen are adventurous, they will try anything once. _____

   _____

   _____

4. Creeping quietly, my little brother sneaked out the door, we saw him

   anyway. _____

   _____

   _____

5. The engineers finally finished the bridge, they did a marvelous job it

   is obvious that they enjoyed their work. _____

   _____

   _____

Use the two brief run-on review charts below to help you complete steps 3 to 7 correctly.

RUN-ON REVIEW CHARTS

Run-on Finder

1. Read word groups aloud. At stop and drop of voice, use a period.
2. Read word groups from last complete thought to the first complete thought. Look for subject and verb to test completeness.
3. Count sentences.
4. Recognize run-on stop signs:
   a. Group I: *then, now, however, finally, there, consequently, moreover, therefore.*
   b. Group II: *it, she, you, I, we, he, they.*

Run-on Fixer

1. Use end marks between complete sentences. Use capital letter for next word after period.
2. Use a semicolon. Start next word with small letter.
3. Use a conjunction:
   a. with one of these use a comma directly before: *and, or, nor, but, for.*
   b. with one of these, use the comma after the whole word group is completed and when the word group opens a sentence: *because, since, while, although, as, when.*
4. Never use a comma alone to separate complete sentences.

Step 3. More Run-on Errors.   Rewrite correctly the run-on errors in the blank spaces below. These sentences contain the vocabulary you learned at the beginning of the chapter.

1. The movie was quite intense therefore the youngsters enjoyed the cartoons that followed. _____

_____

_____

2. The driver erupted, he discovered a dent in the fender. _____

_____

_____

3. Soft tones are not apparent in modern music, however, many people enjoy resounding rhythms. _____

_____

_____

4. Frantically, the dog barked I attempted to stop him finally he lay down and kept silent. _____

_____

_____

5. Indifference may deprive a man of friends, moreover he may prefer it
that way. _____

_____

_____

Step 4. Avoiding the Run-on Mistake. Follow directions given in each
statement below.

1. Write two sentences about the weather. Start the second sentence with
the word *it.* _____

_____

_____

_____

2. Write two complete thoughts about watching television, separating
them with a semicolon. Open the second sentence with the word *however.* _____

_____

_____

_____

3. Write a pair of sentences about winter sports, opening the second sentence with the word *there* or *now.* _____

_____

_____

_____

4. Write two sentences to tell what you do on a Saturday morning. Start
the second sentence with the word *then.* _____

_____

_____

_____

5. Write three sentences about transportation. Use the word *it* to start the
second sentence. Use the word *moreover* to start the third sentence.

_____

_____

_____

_____

_____

_____

_____

Step 5. Stop-sign Words in Sentences. Use correctly in the blank space the *stop sign* that appears in parentheses before each set of word groups. Correct any faulty punctuation. Use capitals when needed.

(however)   1. We knew, ——————, that hope was lost.

(then)   2. A black car drove up —————— the mayor stepped out.

                3. As soon as his followers spotted him,
(they)   —————— waved excitedly.

(there)   4. All alone he stood —————— without a friend in the world.

(however)   5. I prefer short stories ——————, novels often hold my interest.

(finally)   6. It was a long and difficult trial ——— the jury delivered a verdict.

                7. No one stood on the beach or swam in
(there)   the water —————— were only two gulls near the shoreline.

                8. The check arrived after three o'clock;
(consequently)   —————— I could not deposit it in the bank.

(I)   9. Let me tell you why I came here ——— am looking for a job in the neighborhood.

                10. Many college students need large sums
(therefore)   of money to help meet expenses ———, they take part-time jobs.

Step 6. Correcting Sentence Errors. In the blank lines below these run-on errors, rewrite the sentences correctly in any way you wish. Some sentences are already correct.

1. Poetry is still in style for young people much of their poetry is accompanied by music. _____

   _____

   _____

2. To be enjoyed, coffee should first be sniffed it has a wonderful aroma.

   _____

   _____

3. Along the ground the cat moved quietly however the sparrow sensed his presence and flew quickly away. _____

   _____

   _____

4. Most progressive senators believe, moreover, that job opportunities must sharply increase. _____

   _____

   _____

5. My brother attended a junior college then he completed two more years of work for his B.A. _____

   _____

   _____

6. Since the recession set in, many high-paid executives lost their jobs it is hard for these older men to find new work. _____

   _____

   _____

7. We waited for a very long time, counting the seconds carefully as the clock ticked slowly on however, no one arrived. _____

   _____

   _____

8. Formerly the whole family took trips together now everyone goes his own way. _____

   _____

   _____

9. What did you say the doctor is sick too? _____

_____

_____

10. Ernest Hemingway wrote a number of important novels he used to rewrite each page many times his patience never wore thin. _____

_____

_____

Step 7. Run-ons in Paragraphs. Correct the run-on errors by changing some of the punctuation in the paragraph below. Capitalize the first letter of any words that start sentences. You may add words if you wish.

The New Comic Books

Comic books attract as many young people today as they did years ago, however, the material presented is much different now the stories that were once so innocent often have political themes. Long ago, our favorite characters worried only about dates and clothes, they were occupied with simple social situations moreover, no one ever thought of political goals today comic-book characters are involved in elections, demonstrations, and sometimes riots. We can expect Betty to be less interested in Archie as a potential date than as a politician, and Jughead's hat will surely be covered with countless pins with political slogans I don't think it's wrong but it does seem strange to me each time I glance at my younger sister's comics.

WRITING THE PARAGRAPH

Your first assignment is to write a paragraph of twelve to fifteen sentences that brings this classroom to life. Read the paragraph below, written by a student in response to the same assignment. When you finish reading it, write the answers to the questions about the topic sentence and about concrete sensory detail in the blank lines below.

The Gloom Room

On this dreary October afternoon in my writing class here on the second floor of Boylan Hall at Brooklyn College, a shadow of gloom hangs over the people and things that surround me. The atmosphere is depressing. There is an old brown chair beside the teacher's desk, a mahogany bookcase with a missing shelf, and this ugly desk of mine filled with holes and scratches. As I rub my hand across its surface, there is a feeling of coldness. Even the grey walls and the rumble of thunder outside reflect the atmosphere of seriousness as we write our first theme of the semester. When some air sails through an open window beside me, there is the annoying smell of coffee grounds from a garbage pail not far off. My class-mates, too, show this mood of tension. Mary, a slim blonde at my right, chews frantically the inside of her lower lip. Only one or two words in blue ink stand upon her clean white page. David Harris, slouched in his seat in the third row, nibbles each finger of each hand. Then he plays inaudibly with a black collar button that stands open on the top of his red plaid shirt. There is a thump as he uncrosses his legs and his scuffed shoe hits the floor. A painful cough slices the air from behind me. I hear a woman's heels click from the hall beyond the closed door and a car engine whine annoyingly from Bedford Avenue. If a college classroom should be a place of delight and pleasure, that could never be proved by the tension in this room.

— Harry Golden

Step 1. Understanding the Selection. Follow the instructions.

1. Copy out the topic sentence. _____

   _____

2. What key word (or words) shows Mr. Golden's opinion of the subject

   he is writing about? _____

3. There are two things in particular that Mr. Golden will discuss about his writing class and he announces them both in the topic sentence. What are they?

   a. _____

   b. _____

4. Copy out three groups of words that contain sounds.

   a. _____

   b. _____

   c. _____

5. Copy out three word groups that paint a picture because they employ color.

   a. _____

   b. _____

   c. _____

6. Write in your own words two bits of action you see in Mr. Golden's theme.

   a. _____

   _____

   b. _____

   _____

7. Copy out a sentence that appeals to the sense of smell. _____

   _____

8. Copy out a group of words that include a word that appeals to the

sense of touch. _____

_____

9. Which word picture, in your opinion, is most vivid? _____

_____

10. Why do you think Mr. Golden mentions the time of year and time of

day in the first sentence? _____

_____

_____

Step 2. Another Student Theme.   Underline the topic sentence in the next student theme. Circle any words that appeal to color, sound, smell, or touch. Put a check in the margin next to the line that you think contains the best word picture in the paragraph.

A Few Minutes To Go

Sitting here in this basic English class on a rather warm Monday morning, my fellow prisoners probably feel the tension of doing their first writing. The free people on the outside of the classroom are shuffling about rather aimlessly as the period is coming quickly to a close; but inside there is much tension. On my left sits Rocco, tapping his polished chrome pen nervously on his red and yellow notebook. A look of blankness and fear sits on his face. When his eyes meet mine they drop quickly down to his empty sheet of theme paper. On my right I can see Barry in a dark blue shirt. He holds a tight sweaty grip on his pencil and tries to get in a few inspired sentences before the time allotted for the period expires. Suddenly an amusing smell lightens our discomfort as it disturbs my trend of thought. A passerby ambles in front of the door with a cupful of golden French fries from the truck that sells them near the main gate of the college. Taking a quick look at the clock on the wall, I see the hands have almost reached their destination with only a few minutes to go. The ruffling of papers becomes more pronounced, in fact, deafening to this supposedly silent classroom. My mind goes blank as all these distractions seem to be growing and growing in strength. Consequently, I will put a period at the end of this sentence to end my misery.

—Lawrence Skibicki

1. What one word in the closing sentence goes back to the attitude as ex-

pressed in the topic sentence? _____

2. How does the description of Rocco go back to the topic and opinion of

the topic sentence? _____

_____

3. This theme uses some interesting vocabulary. What do you think the

word *ambles* means in line 13? _____

What do you think the word *distractions* means? _____

Manuscript Form

A manuscript is the final copy of an author's created work; it should be carefully prepared before it is submitted. Mess up your *first* copy all you like. Draw arrows. Cross out words. Draw pictures. Use purple ink or crayon or pencil. Use a scissors to cut out words and sentences. Paste the words in new positions where they make more sense. Rip up pages you don't like and start again. But here are some suggestions for good manuscript preparation for the copy you submit to your instructor.

1. Leave wide margins (1 to 1½ inches) on all four sides.
2. Write in ink on one side of each page only. Use regulation theme paper if you write by hand. If you type, use sturdy bond 8½ by 11-inch typing paper. Do not use onionskin. Use blue or black ink: nothing fancy.
3. Make sure your name, class, date appear where your instructor asks for them.
4. If you write by hand, print all your capital letters (this makes them easier to read). Leave large spaces after each end mark. Make periods firm and clear.
5. Check your theme by proofreading (look ahead to pp. 114–115) for careless errors.
6. Errors may be easily changed with a good ink or typewriter eraser. Avoid crossing out or writing over words. If there are too many scratchouts on your theme, take a few moments to recopy it.

IF YOU WRITE THE COMPOSITION IN CLASS

1. Do not plan on rewriting: you will not have time.
2. Think for several minutes about the topic. Spend a minute or two examining the topic sentence you write.
3. Jot down some ideas on scrap paper. If an outline helps you, draw one up quickly.
4. You are still responsible for errors. Check your theme by proofreading (see pp. 114–115) for careless mistakes. Save at least five minutes at the end of the session to proofread.
5. Most instructors encourage you to use a dictionary and thesaurus even when you write your composition in class. Check with your teacher, and if it is all right with him, look up words to check spelling errors. See pp. 461–462 for reminders on using the dictionary and thesaurus.

Requirements

Make your theme lively, vivid, and well organized by following carefully the directions given in the chart below. Reread the two student themes before you begin writing; use those themes as models for your own paragraph.

A Checklist of Requirements: Theme 1

1. Write a topic sentence that includes an opinion and mentions what your topic will be. Make sure the topic is properly limited.
2. Mention time and place as early as possible in the paragraph.
3. Use at least three words that appeal to the sense of sound. See pp. 5–6 for some new "sound" vocabulary.
4. Use at least three colors in different places throughout the theme.
5. Mention two of your classmates by name. If you don't know the name of a person you want to write about, ask him! Show each classmate you mention performing some action: Mr. Golden says that Mary chews the inside of her lip.
6. Give the reader an idea of your surroundings by describing parts of the room. Try to make the details fit in nicely with the opinion word you state in the topic sentence.
7. Use at least one group of words to appeal to the sense of *touch,* and one group of words to appeal to the sense of *smell.*
8. Give your paragraph a title. *A title is not a topic sentence. If you can use part of the topic in your title, you must still repeat the topic in the topic sentence.*
9. *a.* Write one sentence that uses the semicolon correctly. See p. 21.
   b. Use at least one of the *run-on stop signs* to open a complete thought word group. See p. 23.
   c. Try to use one or two vocabulary words from those introduced at the beginning of the chapter.
10. Check your theme for errors, especially for run-ons and for the spelling problems noted in this chapter.
11. Don't jump too quickly from one item to another within the room. As you mention a person or a thing within the classroom, take two or three sentences to show clearly what you see before you move on to another object.
12. Use words like *up front, to my left, nearby, across the room, far away, above, beside, in the corner* to help you move from one thing you wish to describe to another.

Follow-up

When your instructor returns your graded composition:
1. Check your paper to make sure that you understand his writing and any correction symbols he may have used.
2. Correct all errors in mechanics.
3. Rewrite the entire paper if you are urged to do so. Correct any problems in content and thought development.
4. Enter on the Individual Spelling List (p. 459) all the words you misspelled.

5. Enter on the Theme Progress Sheet (Appendix B, p. 483) the total number of errors you made in each category listed on top of the page. In that way you can see before you write the next theme just what kinds of mistakes you usually make.

THE PROFESSIONALS SPEAK

The details of a room are essential parts of good fiction. Writers know that to make a firm impression on the reader's mind, they must give lively sensory images so that the scene may be easily visualized.

Step 1. A Vivid Kitchen.   Read the selection below from *A Tree Grows in Brooklyn* and answer the questions on sensory language.

SOME WORDS TO KNOW BEFORE YOU READ

contend: to struggle in opposition
recessed: set back
mantelpiece: the shelf around a fireplace
hearthstone: a stone forming the place where fire can be made
partition: something that divides
rubbly: rough
inflexibly: in a way that is rigid
welt: a swelling on the surface of the body
perpetual: happening all the time

The Kitchen

The kitchen was living room, dining room, and cooking room. There were two long narrow windows in one wall. An iron coalrange was recessed in another wall. Above the stove the recess was made of coral-colored bricks and creamy white plaster. It had a stone mantelpiece and a slate hearthstone on which Francie could draw pictures with chalk. Next to the stove was a water boiler which got hot when the fire was going. Often on a cold day, Francie came in chilled and put her arms around the boiler and pressed her frosty cheek gratefully against its warm silveriness. Next to the boiler was a pair of soapstone washtubs with a hinged wooden cover. The partition could be removed and the two thrown into one for a bath tub. It didn't make a very good bath tub. Sometimes when Francie sat in it, the cover banged down on her head. The bottom was rubbly and she came out of what should have been a refreshing bath, all sore from sitting on that wet roughness. Then there were four faucets to contend with. No matter how the child tried to remember that they were inflexibly there and wouldn't give way, she would jump up suddenly out of the soapy water and get her back whacked good on a faucet. Francie had a perpetual angry welt on her back.

— Betty Smith
A Tree Grows in Brooklyn

1. Copy out two pictures you see clearly because they identify colors.

   a. _____

   b. _____

2. Copy out two verbs that tell a sound.

   a. _____

   b. _____

3. Underline the one sentence you think shows the liveliest action.
4. Sentence 7 contains four words that appeal to touch. Copy them here:

   a. _____ b. _____ c. _____ d. _____

   What other sentences use touch words?
5. Circle any words that show transition.

REACHING HIGHER

Step 1. Photo into Words. Look at the photograph on p. 3. Decide what kind of room it shows; then, decide on your own attitude toward the room as it is represented. Write a topic sentence. In a paragraph of fifteen to twenty sentences, support the opinion in your topic sentence with lively sensory details. Use words to show color and action. Imagine the sounds you might hear and some of the touch sensations you would experience: include these as well in the paragraph. Identify people you see.

Step 2. A Room You Remember. Describe with concrete detail some memorable room you have had the opportunity to observe recently. Read the student theme below by Yudis Resnick, looking for sounds, colors, and actions.

SOME WORDS TO KNOW BEFORE YOU READ

dexterity: skill in using hands or body
askew: off to a side
synchronize: to make things happen at the same time
scurry: to move quickly, in a hurry
hubbub: loud, confused noise

A Rush-hour Lunch

At exactly twelve o'clock every afternoon the wide glass doors of Deli City open and large numbers of people rushing in from Thirty-fourth Street push into the store. As if they had synchronized their watches, the waiters and waitresses swing into action at exactly the same moment. With speed and dexterity the chefs take orders, fill plates, and pocket money. A short squat attendant, his white apron flying, scurries from table to table hurriedly refilling the relish containers. Behind every counter, stacked high with spicy salami and roast beef, stand four serving men in white, a spoon or a fork in one hand. They stand with their arms in mid-air until, on receiving an order, they swiftly dish out the food. Waitresses rush back and forth trying to clear dirty tables. Their soft rubber shoes skimming over the dingy gray linoleum sound like the squish of wet sneakers. People all around me push and pull to get their food and find seats. Men and women moving in lines in front of the counters stand squashed together, like the atoms and molecules in a solid block of ice. An elderly lady, clutching her pocketbook desperately, her hat askew and eyes in a glaze, is swept along with the crowd. Looking for a seat I feel the clammy hand of the person next to me as he brushes past with his tray. Two women, ahead of me on the line, sputter angrily at each other and before I know it they are wildly waving their hands and screaming, because another lady got ahead of them. The din overshadows everything. Everywhere people shout at each other from across tables and counters. Red hamburgers patted into neat mounds sizzle on a greasy, blood-spattered grill. I hear the boisterous guffaws of a big jolly gentleman sitting next to me. His clothing, a flashy plaid suit, a bright pink shirt, and a wild tie, perfectly complements his personality. Voices of the men behind the counters boom out orders five seconds apart. Adding to the hubbub, a group of Spanish women converse in their native tongue, everyone talking at once. The physical atmosphere also reveals hustling activity. Alongside, the long picture windows are foggy with mist; I can see little droplets of water trickling down and in the reflection of the hazy glass I see masses of people swarming all about. The air, too, is heavy with vapor and the moist grimy feeling of my neck, face, and hands makes me shudder. I struggle to the doorway and push the heavy swinging doors open. With a sigh of relief, I step outside into the crisp, empty street, a welcome relief from the noise of Deli City.

—Yudis Resnick

Step 3. Your Own Photo Essay. With an Instamatic camera or a Polaroid, take several pictures of your writing classroom during a normal class session. Try to take pictures that will convey *one* dominant impression you have about the room. You may want to show that the room is a *lively* place or one that is *tense, happy, dull,* or *spirited.* When you get the pictures back, mount them and present them to the class. Can your fellow students determine the impression you are trying to create from your pictures?

chapter 2
RELATIVES AND PERSONALITY: TELLING A STORY

Burt Glinn/Magnum Photos, Inc.

INTRODUCTION

As you grow more mature, your view of your relatives takes on a new quality. Maybe your mother still can make you angry by telling you what time to go to sleep, or your uncle knows how to annoy you by starting a conversation just when you are watching television. As you more and more use your independence, however, you can see your relatives more and more as people with problems, with strong personality points, with shortcomings. Maybe if your father isn't around anymore, you come to understand how hard it has been for your mother to keep the family together and running smoothly. Maybe too many cousins and brothers and sisters constantly prevent the privacy you want. Or is it that too many responsibilities fall your way and you feel that you are being cheated of fun and good times? Perhaps you are pleased, on the other hand, of the role you play in the family structure and take pride in working after school just to help out with the money problems. Maybe your mother in recognizing your maturity acts more like a friend than a commander in chief. Maybe an older cousin or a younger brother is a special comfort when you feel rotten. Perhaps your father, usually strict and unwilling to let you move out to things on your own, suddenly looks the other way when you come home just before dawn or rush off before cleaning up your room. Or maybe he shouts you down louder than ever as you show that you want to break away from the family rules.

These moments when your relatives show themselves as real people and not as the angels and devils you pictured when you were younger are the subjects you will look at for your next theme. The paragraph you write will narrate a brief event which shows some aspect of a relative's personality. Because your story will be about one moment, you are going to learn how to limit your topic sentence in a new way, by specifying time and place right in the opening sentence of the paragraph. Furthermore, you will learn to tell the event in the order in which the details occurred so that the reader clearly understands the way things happened.

VOCABULARY

Step 1. Words to Describe People.   These words are helpful in describing people, what they do and what they say. Check a dictionary and write in the definitions in the blank spaces. See Appendix A for more help.

1. scowl _____

2. wilted _____

3. pious _____

4. brute _____

5. introvert _____

6. rage _____

7. disenchantment _____

8. extrovert _____

9. mutter _____

10. gnarled _____

Step 2. Using New Vocabulary. Fill in the blank with a word from the above list so that the sentence makes sense.

1. In a voice so low we couldn't understand her, she _____ her answer.

2 Her _____ behavior was obvious when she crossed herself and looked up to God.

3. He is surely an _____ because he loves talking to people and being in crowds.

4. A child experiences _____ when he learns his parents are not perfect.

5. In the August heat he flopped into a chair, his shirt all _____ from perspiration.

6. An _____ is satisfied to sit alone and think.

7. With an obvious _____ on his face, the driver grabbed his ticket for speeding from the policeman and drove away, cursing.

8. From years of labor his _____ fingers moved slowly and with pain.

9. In a _____ the entertainer stamped his feet and screamed angrily at the crowd, "Now shut up or I leave!"

10. In crowds people act like _____, pushing and shoving like animals.

Step 3. How People Do or Say Things. The following words, all ending in -ly, are good to help show how people do or say things. Check them in the dictionary and write in the definitions. For more help, see Appendix A.

1. succinctly _____

2. quizzically _____

3. sullenly _____

4. limply _____

5. irritably _____

6. painstakingly _____

7. precariously _____

8. intently _____

9. jovially _____

10. solemnly _____

Step 4. Seeing Opposites. Each word or group of words below is an antonym (a word whose meaning is the opposite of another word) of one of the words above. Write in the space the word from above that you think best suggests an *opposite* meaning.

1. in a good-humored way _____

2. unhappily _____

3. in a manner without danger _____

4. in a long and drawn-out way _____

5. firmly and forcefully _____

6. in a patient manner and without anger _____

7. with no great concentration _____

8. carelessly _____

9. joyfully _____

10. without any strangeness _____

Step 5. Vocabulary in Sentences. Follow directions.

1. Write three sentences about an aunt or uncle you really like. Use two or more of these words: *extrovert, jovially, intently.*

_____

_____

_____

2. Write three sentences about someone in your family who has personality traits you dislike. Use two or more of these words: *irritably, sullenly, solemnly, mutter.*

_____

_____

_____

3. Write a few sentences about someone who does a very difficult job. Use two of these words: *painstakingly, precariously, wilted, gnarled, intently.*

_____

_____

_____

4. Write a sentence in which you use correctly *disenchant, disenchanted,* or *disenchantment.*

_____

5. Write three sentences about someone you have observed who was angry. Use two of these words: *brute, rage, sullenly, irritably.*

_____

_____

_____

6. Explain in the space provided the meaning of each word group below.

   a. spoken *succinctly* _____

   b. stood *limply* nearby _____

   c. introverted behavior _____

   d. a *pious* look _____

   e. glanced *quizzically* _____

BUILDING COMPOSITION SKILLS

Finding the Topic

One of the best ways to get ideas on any topic is to talk about and listen to the ideas of the people around you. You get to air out your own thoughts and see how they sound before you begin to put them on paper. You also get ideas about your own life when you hear the ideas your friends may have.

Step 1. Talking about the Topic.   Pick any word group below and read it aloud, adding your own ending. Then, in a few more sentences, explain what you said. Or, if your instructor suggests, write down in a few brief sentences your completion for any of the statements. At the bottom of this exercise are the answers some other freshmen gave.

   1. My mother gets mad when _____

   _____

2. My aunt understood when _____

_____

3. I like when my father _____

_____

4. A beating I'll never forget came _____

_____

5. My mother never lets me _____

_____

6. My mother makes me glad when _____

_____

7. One thing my mother and I always fight about is _____

_____

8. When I'm ready to go on a date, my father always _____

_____

9. My mother always forces me to _____

_____

10. I wish my father would _____

_____

Here are some freshman responses:

One thing my mother and I always fight about is watching my younger brothers and sisters on weekends. I know my mother is entitled to a day away from the kids, but I also have other things I'd rather do than baby-sit.

— Mary Colby

I wish my father would let me drive the car just once without his saying, "Now be careful!" when he hands me the keys.

— Robert Wilson

My mother makes me glad when she lets me do the cooking on Thursday nights. That way I get a chance to make what I like.

— Caren Simon

I like when my father slips me an extra ten bucks so my mother shouldn't see when I'm going to spend more than I should on a date or a new attachment for my car.

— Steve Maspeth

A beating I'll never forget came when my uncle hit me once when I was sixteen. I talked fresh to my mother. I told her to shut up because she kept nagging me about my haircut and he smacked me clear across the living room!

— John Geramel

My mother always forces me to tell her where I'm going, who I'm going with, and when I'll be home every time I leave the house on a Friday night.

— Paula Bunin

Expanding the Opener

An effective topic sentence is nicely limited when it mentions a topic specifically and gives your opinion about the topic that you want to discuss. (If you need a quick review, see Chapter 1.) But you can further limit the topic sentence—when you write a paragraph that tells a story—by showing where and when the event you are writing about takes place. By *where* we mean the room, the outdoor setting, the physical location in which the moment happened. By *when* we mean not the date, but the season or month of the year, the part of the day, the day of the week. Sometimes a word of color or sound or touch helps the *when* and *where* details come to life. Here are two topic sentences, made from the statements you talked about on pp. 41–42, which give the topic and opinion, tell when or where, and use a sense word.

Example:

    [Time]   [Place]   [Opinion]   [Sound]

One winter evening in our kitchen my mother surprisingly screamed in anger when I refused to run downstairs on an errand.

Topic: Refusing to run an errand.

   [Opinion]   [Color]

I always feel great when my father lets me drive the family in our blue

          [Place]   [Time]

Ford down the freeway every Sunday morning.

Topic: Driving with the family.

Step 1. Expanding a Topic Sentence. Add details of time or place or both to the topic sentences listed in Column I and rewrite them under Column II. If possible, use a sound, color, or touch word.

Example:

I

1. My mother feels happy when I play the piano.

II

On weekday evenings near Christmas my mother feels happy when I sit down to play at our brown and battered piano.

2. My father understood when I needed more money.

3. I didn't like it when my mother gave me orders in front of my friends.

4. My uncle still likes playing basketball with my brother and me.

5. My grandmother always looks tired after a hard day's work in the house.

6. My father is the worst driver I know.

Step 2. Writing Sentence Openers. In each item in Column I below there is a subject mentioned. For each write a topic sentence that includes time and place, gives an opinion, and appeals in some way to one of the senses. Try to put the words that tell *where* or *when* right at the beginning of the sentence. There are two examples for the first one.

I	II
1. helping with house chores	Every Saturday morning I hate dragging myself out of bed to carry a heavy bag of dirty clothes to the laundry on Macon Street.
	The weekend chore I dislike most is scrubbing clean the gray kitchen linoleum.
2. going to work with mother or father	

3. an afternoon out with the family

4. buying clothes with a parent

5. being punished by a relative

6. watching a younger brother or sister

Step 3. Analyzing the Topic Sentence. Turn to p. 7. Look at the topic sentences numbered 1 and 2. What words tell the time of the event? Why did both of these topic sentences have to tell *place?*

Turn to p. 8. Pick out the one sentence in Step 1 that mentions time and place.

Using Chronology

Whenever you relate a moment, the events are easily understood when you write of them in the time order in which they happened. The arrangement of details or events according to time is *chronology*. The sentences on the right below present the events in their order of occurrence, while those on the left jump around without logic from event to event.

Confused

On Sundays the whole family has a good time. We usually eat lunch of fried chicken and French fried potatoes at a diner on Route 17. My father and I wash the car after breakfast so it looks new and shiny when Dad zooms our blue Chevy down the street to the Garden Parkway. My mother and sister

Chronological

On Sundays the whole family has a good time. After a lazy breakfast, my father and I rush downstairs to wash the car while my mother and my sister clean up the house. After an hour or so we go upstairs, change our clothes because we're sweaty, and then the whole family piles into the clean blue clean up the house first, and then we're off driving in the sun. Of course, we change our clothes because after an hour of car washing we're all sweaty. When we finally get home, we're all exhausted!

Chevy. Dad zooms down the street to the Garden Parkway; we're off driving in the sun. Later we stop at a diner on Route 17 for a bucket of fried chicken and French fried potatoes. When we get home, we're all pleasantly exhausted!

Step 1. Chronology. Write four sentences in chronological order about each subject named below.

1. combing your hair

    a. _____

    b. _____

    c. _____

    d. _____

2. preparing for a date

    a. _____

    b. _____

    c. _____

    d. _____

3. looking for a job

    a. _____

    b. _____

    c. _____

    d. _____

4. sitting at the breakfast table

    a. _____

    b. _____

    c. _____

    d. _____

5. registration at college

    a. _____

    b. _____

    c. _____

    d. _____

Step 2. Telling the Order. Here is a good topic sentence that calls for a paragraph through *chronological order.* Write six or seven sentences beneath it in which you tell details in the order in which they might have occurred.

On cold February mornings walking my dog is an awful job. _____

_____

_____

_____

_____

_____

_____

Sentence Variety

To make sure that the sentences in your paragraph are not dull, start one or two of them with a word that ends in -*ly*. You have a number of these words in your vocabulary already (*swiftly, slowly, annoyingly, suddenly*). Step 3 on pp. 39–40 introduces some new and more difficult -*ly* words.

Step 1. -*ly* Words for Variety. Make an -*ly* word based upon the definitions in Column I and write it in Column II. Then, in Column III, write a sentence that starts with the word you have written in II.

Examples:

I	II	III
1. in a tired way	*tiredly*	*Tiredly my mother drags her packages up the stairs.*
2. in a firm way	*firmly*	*Firmly my brother shook my hand.*
3. in an instant		
4. all of a sudden		
5. in a hurry		
6. in a dramatic manner		

7. with great danger   _____   _____

                                                 _____

                                                 _____

8. without getting tired   _____   _____

                                                 _____

                                                 _____

9. in a way without hap-   _____
   piness
                              _____   _____

                                                 _____

                                                 _____

10. in a clumsy manner   _____   _____

                                                 _____

                                                 _____

Step 2. Two -*ly* Openers.   A very effective technique for opening sentences is to use *two -ly* words at the beginning. Separate the -*ly* words either with a comma or with *and* or *but*. Don't use two -*ly* words that mean exactly the same.

Slowly, annoyingly, the actor's voice filled the theatre.

Strongly and cautiously the lion stalked his prey.

Write a sentence about each subject indicated below, starting each sentence with two -*ly* words. Check the vocabulary on pp. 39–40 for some new words. Use a separate sheet of paper.

1. a tree blowing in the wind
2. a snow storm
3. coming home from work
4. a child playing
5. a jet in flight

SOLVING PROBLEMS IN WRITING

Using Quotations Correctly

One way of adding life to a composition is to use the words spoken by a person who plays some part in your paragraph. It's usually more realistic and more lively to use the person's specific words rather than a statement which summarizes what was said. Look at the difference.

1. My mother said that I shouldn't stay out too late because I had to go to work early in the morning.
2. My mother muttered, "Don't stay out too late, hear, because the alarm's going off early and you'd better be able to get up for work!"

Sentence 2 has more force because it lets the reader hear the person's words. Now of course, if you are writing about a moment that occurred a while ago, it's impossible to remember *exactly* what a person said. Still, if you recall the general idea of the person's words, construct your sentence so that the reader hears it as a quotation.

Correct punctuation of quotations—exact words—is sometimes tricky. Remember that most quotation sentences have two parts: one part tells who is talking and how the person says his words; another part tells what is being said. These parts must be separated by punctuation. Study the charts below.

I. EXACT WORDS AT THE END [Quotation marks]

[Capitalize first spoken word]

My mother shouted, "Don't stay out too late, hear, because the alarm's going

[Comma]   [End mark inside: period, question mark, or exclamation point]

off early and you'd better be able to get up for work!"

[Quotation marks]

Hint: If the same person speaks another sentence—without being interrupted—right after his first one, DON'T use another quotation mark. Put the last quotation mark after the very *last* word any one person speaks.

My mother shouted, "Don't stay out too late, hear, because the alarm's going off early and you'd better be able to get up for work. I won't be able to wake you!"

Step 1. Correct Quotations. Put in the correct punctuation for these sentences.

1. The teacher said quietly there will be no class tomorrow.
2. Alan Shephard said after his flight to the moon we have had a terrific flight. It's just been completely super all the way around.

II. EXACT WORDS AT THE BEGINNING

[Quotation marks]

"Don't stay out too late, hear, because the alarm's going off early and you'd

[Capital letter]   [Quotation marks]   [Small letter]   [Period]

better be able to get up for work," my mother shouted.

[Comma, question mark, or exclamation point: no period]

Step 2. Writing Quotations. Put in the correct punctuation for these sentences.

1. More funds must be found to assist the urban poor replied the senator.
2. A poorly addressed envelope may get lost in the Christmas rush the postman reminded us.

III. EXACT WORDS BROKEN UP

[Quotation marks]   [Close quotes]   [Small letter]   [Open quotation again]

"Don't stay out too late, hear," my mother shouted, "because the alarm's

[Capital]   [Comma]   [Comma]   [Small letter (A sentence is *continued*.)]

going off early and you'd better be able to get up for work."

[End mark]   [Close quotes]

Step 3. Punctuating Quotations.   Punctuate these sentences correctly.

1. I want to know she said why you do such ridiculous things
2. Did you hear the joke the comedian asked about the old lady who had a young husband

Hint: The question mark goes at the end of the complete question.

Step 4. Practice with Exact Words.   In Column I write five sentences you have heard spoken on campus recently. In Column II, rewrite each sentence with correct punctuation to show who did the talking. Sometimes a word like *shouted, muttered, whispered,* or *cried* is more vivid than *said.* In other sentences, *said* is adequate because the quotation itself tells the tone the speaker is using with the words he says. In two sentences use the spoken words at the beginning; in two others use the spoken words at the end. In one sentence break up the spoken words as in Chart III. One of each appears in the examples below.

I

Examples:

1. "Who's got a smoke?"

2. "Hey, we'd better move or we'll be late for class."

3. "This cafeteria coffee is poisonous!"

4. _____

_____

_____

_____

5. _____

_____

_____

_____

II

My friend Steve yelled, "Who's got a smoke?"

"Hey, we'd better move," someone insisted, "or we'll be late for class."

"This cafeteria coffee is poisonous!" gasped a tall boy with a frown.

_____

_____

_____

_____

_____

_____

_____

_____

6. _____   _____
   _____   _____
   _____   _____
   _____   _____

7. _____   _____
   _____   _____
   _____   _____
   _____   _____

8. _____   _____
   _____   _____
   _____   _____
   _____   _____

Sentence Fragments: Phase I

The *fragment* is an incomplete part of a sentence used as though it were a sentence itself. Here are some fragments that are easy to recognize.

1. Over the curb and into the street
2. Rushing noisily through the trees
3. Just to play his radio quietly
4. Usually dressed in a blue woolen sweater

None of the above makes any real sense. Since a sentence contains a complete thought and has a subject and a verb (see the Sentence Review Chart, pp. 19–20), the word groups above are not sentences.

Sentence 1 has no subject or verb. *What* is being done over the curb and into the street? *Who* is doing it?

Sentence 2 has no subject (*Who* does the shouting?) and only a part of a verb—the word *shouting.*

Sentence 3 has no subject (*Who* plays the radio?) and only part of a verb—the words *to play.* (You may recall that when *to* is used like this, what results is merely the starting point of the verb: it is not a verb itself.)

Sentence 4 has no subject (*Who* dressed in a woolen sweater?). It might—depending upon its meaning in a paragraph—also need a word like *is* in order to be complete.

Each fragment, 1, 2, 3, 4 above, separated from the sentences that come before it, is easy to recognize because it really makes no sense. But now look at the fragments as they appear as parts of paragraphs and read the explanations alongside.

Fragment	Explanation
1. *a.* In a square of pavement down the block a small dog played with a rubber ball, but it rolled out of his reach. *b.* He rushed after it. *c.* Over the curb and into the street.	Here a student might think that the subject *he* and the verb *rushed* in sentence *b* would also serve as subject and verb in word group *c.* But that is not the case. Word group *c* is a fragment because it lacks its own subject and verb. The capital letter in *over* and the period after *street* indicate that the writer thought the sentence a complete one.
2. *a.* A winter day like today is never pleasant. *b.* Everywhere I can hear the howl of the wind. *c.* Rushing noisily through the trees. *d.* There is also too much snow along the streets.	Here, a student might think that the word *wind* in sentence *b* would serve as the subject in word group *c.* But word group *c* must have its own subject. Furthermore, the word *rushing* is not a verb: if *is* or *was* appeared before it, or if the word were *rushed* instead of *rushing,* it would be a verb. But as it stands, word group *c* is also a fragment because it lacks a verb.
3. *a.* It is important to understand that teenagers often require privacy. *b.* For an hour or two a boy wishes to be left alone in his room. *c.* Just to play his radio quietly.	Here, it is possible that an inexperienced writer would imagine the word *boy* in sentence *b* to serve as the subject in word group *c.* But word group *c* must have its own subject to be complete. In addition, *to play* is no verb. We need to add a word such as *wants* or *likes* before the infinitive. Sometimes the infinitive can be changed to a verb: *plays, played,* or *is playing.* But as it stands, word group *c* is also a fragment because it lacks a verb.
4. *a.* John Callahan, six feet seven inches tall, is easy to recognize on campus. *b.* He towers over everyone around. *c.* Usually dressed in a blue woolen sweater. *d.* John braves the cold without an overcoat.	Here, the writer gives no subject in word group *c.* Furthermore, *dressed*—as it is used—is only a part of a verb. It must have *is* or *was* or some such word before it. So, word group *c* is also a fragment because it lacks a verb.

Fixing the Fragments. Knowing that sentence fragments lack subjects, complete verbs, or both, you should not find this kind of sentence error difficult to correct.

1. Add a subject and a verb to make the sentence complete.

Correct This Fragment
Over the curb and into the street.

This Way [Added subject]
The dog jumped over the curb and into the street. [Added verb]

Rushing noisily through the trees.

[Subject]
It is rushing noisily through the trees.
[Word added to make verb]

It rushes noisily through the trees.
[-ing word changed to verb]

Just to play his radio quietly.

[Subject]
He just wants to play his radio quietly.
[Word added to make verb]

He just plays his radio quietly.
[Infinitive changed to verb]

Dressed in a striped woolen sweater.

[Subject]
He is usually dressed in a striped woolen sweater.
[Word added to make verb]

Step 1. Completing Sentences. The last sentence in each word group below is a fragment. Rewrite the fragment in the space provided and add a subject, a verb, or both in order to make the sentence complete. You may wish to change an *-ing* word or an infinitive to a verb; or you may wish to add a new verb as a helper.

1. I was secretly thrilled when I took my first puff of the cigarette. Knowing I was not allowed to smoke.

_____

_____

_____

2. Man grew concerned about pollution when he went fishing in a river and found all the fish he wanted. Destroyed at the bottom of the river.

_____

_____

_____

3. Tests are important. Progress is easy to measure and test scores, therefore, help the students. Also the instructors.

_____

_____

_____

4. Man has always wanted to explore new places. To walk on Mars and on Venus.

_____

_____

_____

5. Students today may choose any course of study. Choose engineering, a career in nursing or drafting, or a life dedicated to the arts.

_____

_____

_____

2. Another way to fix the fragment is to connect it to the sentence that comes before it or after it. In that way you legitimately give the fragment the subject and verb it needs by using words of another sentence.

Notice how the last two sentences in a, b, and c on p. 52 may be joined together to eliminate the fragment:

Correct the Fragment

This Way

He rushed after it.
Over the curb and into the street.

He rushed after it over the curb and into the street.
[Small letter]
[No period]

I can hear the howl of the wind. Rushing through the trees.

I can hear the howl of the wind rushing through the trees.
[No period]
[Small letter]

For an hour or two a boy wishes to be left alone in his room. Just to play his radio quietly.

For an hour or two a boy wishes to be left alone in his room just to play his radio quietly.
[No period]
[Small letter]

3. A fragment may be effectively corrected by attaching it to the sentence that comes after it.

Correct the Fragment

This Way

Usually dressed in a striped woolen sweater. John braves the cold without an overcoat.

Usually dressed in a blue woolen sweater, John braves the cold without an overcoat.
[Comma]

Here is another example:

Correct the Fragment

This Way

Hearing the photographer talk about his travels through Alaska. Audiences responded with enthusiasm.

Hearing the photographer talk about his travels through Alaska, audiences responded with enthusiasm.
[Comma]
[Small letter]

Hint: When you open a sentence with a fragment that contains an -*ing* verb part or an -*ed* verb part, follow the fragment with a comma.

Step 2. Correcting the Fragment. Each of these groups contains at least one fragment. Correct the error by adding the fragment either to the sentence that comes before or to the sentence that comes after. Write your new sentence in the blank spaces alongside.

Hint: Make sure that the new sentence you have written makes sense.

1. My eyes, blinded by the smoke, see a figure. Lying in pain and nearing death. The man remains in my sight despite the confusion and noise.

_____

_____

_____

_____

2. People complain all the time that talent and genius are dead. But this is not true.

_____

_____

The raw materials of genius are everywhere. On our city streets, in our ghettos, in our small towns.

3. A vacation in Atlantic City is wonderful. Swimming in the ocean all day and watching men make fudge at night. I never get tired of the place!

_____

_____

_____

_____

4. In the midst of the street is an old, battered Cadillac. Never to reclaim its once proud standing as America's status symbol.

_____

_____

_____

5. Everyone at a college basketball game is charged with excitement. Especially the spectators. They clap wildly and give spirit to the team.

_____

_____

_____

Finding the Fragments. Here are some suggestions for learning to recognize sentence fragments of the type described in this chapter.

1. Read your paragraph aloud. Learn to tell the difference between pauses between words and stops between sentences. A pause often requires a comma. A full stop requires a period or one of the other end marks, a question mark or an exclamation point. A semicolon may also be used to indicate a complete stop between sentences.
2. Read the sentences of your paragraph from the last to the first. In that way you'll be listening for complete thoughts that make sense.
3. Look for an -ing word used incorrectly as the verb in a sentence.
4. Make sure every sentence has its own subject and its own verb. (See item 7 on the Sentence Review Chart, p. 20, for "understood" subjects.)
5. Make sure every sentence expresses a complete thought by itself.
6. Watch out for these *Fragment Stop Signs: Group I* because they are expressions which often open word groups that fail to include subjects and verbs.

Fragment Stop Signs: Group I

just mainly	especially
for instance	for example
such as	like
also	

If you open a sentence with one of these words or word combinations, be sure a subject and verb come later on in the sentence.

Study the review chart below before moving on to the next steps.

A FRAGMENT FINDER	A FRAGMENT FIXER
1. Read aloud. Listen for incomplete thoughts.	1. Add subject, verb, or both.
2. Look out for -ing words, especially when they start sentences.	2. Add fragment to sentence that comes before or sentence that comes after. Make sure final sentence makes sense.
3. Look for subject and verb in each sentence.	3. Change an -ing word to a verb by using is, was, are, were, am in front of it. Or, change -ing word to a verb.
4. Read paragraph from last sentence to first. Stop after each sentence and ask: Is it a complete thought?	4. If you put an -ing fragment or another "verb-part" fragment in front of a sentence, use a comma after the fragment.
5. Know Group I of the Fragment Stop Signs. just mainly especially for instance for example like also such as	5. Change an infinitive to a verb by removing "to" and using the correct form of the verb. Or, put one of these verbs before the infinitive: like(s), want(s), plan(s), try (tries), is, was, were, are, am.

Step 3. Eliminating Fragments. Each set of sentences below contains one *or more* sentence fragments. Correct the fragments by using any of the methods you learned so far. Cross out words, add words, change or remove punctuation. One set of sentences is correct: mark it C. Use separate paper.

1. Blankly I looked into the mirror. Blinking my eyes to erase the image. I couldn't believe anyone could look so awful. Not even I.
2. When men leave their desks, they leave behind their chains of struggle for another time. Leave behind a closed door many problems for tomorrow.
3. Just a word about business. Have we renewed your subscription under the correct address? If not, your magazine may not arrive in time.
4. There are many new and positive features on city streets. First of all, the storefront schools. The local health department with programs against lead poisoning. Also the community centers.
5. The crowd broke swiftly at the sound of the sirens. In the middle two boys rolled over each other, punching wildly and kicking their feet against the pavement.
6. Some people don't mind noise when they read, but others must have absolute silence. For example, my mother. Even the soft sound of the radio in the next room keeps her from concentrating. Instead of relaxing her.

7. Dad is doomed to failure in his personal relations with his family. He is always trying to be nice. Trying all the time to please everyone. He only succeeds in making somebody unhappy.

8. Many television programs can be called failures because they have little educational value. But commercial TV stations show more and more interest in "teaching" programs and have added a number of shows which help youngsters learn. One being *Mister Rogers' Neighborhood.*

9. In order to accent his point the speaker made wild gestures with his hands. Like an actor in a very dramatic moment of a play. He banged his hand on the table to emphasize one particular sentence. To show the audience his real concern for the important issues.

10. Many moments of tension face the would-be college athlete. For many reasons. He must be willing to practice for long hours. Frequently missing good times with his friends and giving up many hours of study. He can look forward to aching muscles and poor grades.

Step 4. Avoiding the Fragment Error.   Use each of these word groups to open a sentence of your own. Write the sentence in the space provided.

1. Raising his hand

_____

_____

2. Not allowed to attend classes after dark

_____

_____

3. Selecting his fellow candidate

_____

_____

4. Arriving at registration late

_____

_____

5. Irritated by the smell of cigarette smoke

_____

_____

WRITING THE PARAGRAPH

Your assignment for this theme is to write a paragraph of at least twelve to fifteen sentences to show one moment in which you reveal some aspect of a relative's personality.

WHAT IS A "MOMENT"?

1. A "moment" is a memorable instance in your life that illustrates some opinion or idea you want to write about.
2. A "moment" is limited as much as possible in time; it is a brief span of minutes which you recall sharply.
3. You must make this "moment" as vivid for your reader as it was for you when you experienced it. In order to do this, you need to fill in details of the moment with concrete sensory language. Remember that you create pictures (images) by using colors and sounds and smells that will let the reader share your experience.
4. What kinds of details do you need to make the moment come alive? Show some images of the setting (where the moment occurred) through color, smell, touch, and sound; describe the people who participate in the moment (show their faces and actions); use bits of important dialogue that people speak as the moment develops.

Step 1. Reading Samples. Read the paragraphs below written by students in response to the same assignment. When you finish reading each paragraph, write the answers to the questions on expanded topic sentences, sensory language, chronological order, and sentence variety.

The House Didn't Catch Fire

Because of my grandmother's bravery, the September night our brown wood house in a New Jersey forest didn't catch fire is one night I will never forget. I remember those moments clearly. There was a full moon outside my window, floating on white clouds in a blue velvet sky, an unusually quiet and chilly night. I sat spellbound by the fire in the fireplace; it cracked and popped as it burned the wood. And the orange, red and blue colored flames danced in the darkness of my room. Suddenly, precariously, my window lit up from an enormous fire a few miles away. The moon no longer floated on its puffy clouds. When flames danced up the trees and caused the wood to crackle like the fire in my fireplace, I screamed for my grandmother from the next room. She rushed in and quickly took my hand and we ran out of the house. I held tightly to her as she stood looking at the fire and felt the soft cool flannel of her yellow gown. Grandmother looked up into the flaming sky as though she was praying to God, while lines of worry and fear grew deep in her dark brown skin. The fire looked as if it sped in our direction as my grandmother dashed around the side of the house. I felt cold and afraid standing in front there all alone. Soon grandmother returned with two wooden pails of water from the water tubs. When she threw water on the house and dashed back to the tubs, I ran to the water also, grabbed a handful and threw it on the house, because I was seven and too small to carry a wooden water pail. We threw water on the house and the earth nearby until they were completely soaked. By now the fire had grown closer and nearly encircled the house. We ran inside to wait for the fire either to die down, or to kill us; the heat outside was too much to bear. My grandmother held me close to her again. As the night grew into day, I grew tired and went to sleep. I awoke to find the fire had stopped within yards of our home, leaving the earth burnt and bare for miles around. But my grandmother's courage and quick thinking kept our house standing.

—Odessa Harris

1. What is the key word that shows the writer's opinion in the topic sentence? _____

2. Which words in the topic sentence tell time? _____

   _____

   Which words tell place? _____ Which words in the topic sentence give a picture by using a color as an example of sensory language? _____

3. The topic sentence indicates that the paragraph will contain information about *two* related aspects of the topic. What are they? _____

   _____

4. Copy out three word groups that tell sound.

   a. _____

   b. _____

   c. _____

5. Copy out a sentence that begins with two *-ly* words.

   _____

6. Copy out two word groups that use color.

   a. _____

   b. _____

7. Copy out two word groups that indicate some lively action.

   a. _____

   b. _____

8. What words indicate some sensation of touch? _____

   _____

Jungle Boy

A suppertime conversation one fall evening several years ago shows how both my parents can join forces to make me feel worse than I already do. My mother slammed the knives and forks upon the table with a startling clatter and stormed back to the sink. A bright yellow tablecloth with red roses did nothing to counteract the tension that hung about our usually cheery kitchen. Quizzically my father glanced at me but I lowered my eyes quickly and labored at my grapefruit until I squeezed it dry. My brother solemnly leaned over his lamb chops and string beans. The large black, yellow and blue marks on his arm stood out, the result of a fight with me that afternoon. Again mother stalked to the table, her brown eyes moist, the glass salt shaker clenched in her hand. She let loose her rage in a violent burst of words. "Are you crazy? Do you want to break your brother's arm?" I slouched lower in my chair, taking a piece of broiled meat in my mouth but unable to swallow it. My father looked at me through steel grey eyes. "I told you never to raise your hands in anger in this house," his voice boomed. The words echoed in my head as I felt my face warm. My mother shrieked at the top of her voice, "Why can't you get along with your brother the way your cousins do. They laugh together and play together, but not you, not Allen of the jungle, you have to fight and punch your brother." Quietly, sternly, my father said, "I've never hit you, Allen, without first discussing the situation with you like civilized people, have I?" I stirred uncomfortably in my chair and murmured an acknowledgment. My father's words weakened the wall that I built to fight my mother's assault. "I've brought you up to respect your brother and him you. We won't speak about this again, but in the future you'd better think before raising your hands." Feeling ashamed for my childish behavior, I excused myself from the table and tramped off sullenly to my cave.

—Allen Zuckerman

1. Which word group, in your opinion, gives the picture you see most

   clearly? _____

2. What is the topic of this paragraph? _____

3. What is Mr. Zuckerman's attitude toward his topic (check the topic

   sentence!)? _____

   _____

4. Copy out the quotation sentence that you find most realistic, a sentence
   that includes words you think a person might really say in the situation.

   _____

   _____

5. Why is the use of color in the sentence about the tablecloth so effective?

   _____

   _____

   Where else is color effectively used? _____

   _____

6. Do you think the title is a good one for this paragraph? Why? _____

   _____

7. What do you think the word *stalked* means? _____

Check the dictionary for a more accurate definition and write it here.

_____

Why do you think the author uses *stalked to the table* to tell how his mother arrived instead of *came to the table* or *walked to the table?*

_____

_____

Requirements

Follow these suggestions before you write a one-paragraph theme that in some way reveals the personality of one of your relatives. Reread the samples on the preceding pages before you begin.

A CHECKLIST OF REQUIREMENTS

1. Write a topic sentence that states a limited topic through some opinion or attitude word.
2. Tell of *only one moment* in which your relative revealed his personality.
3. Try to include time and place in the topic sentence. If you find this impossible, tell time (month, part of the day, or season) and place (a special room, some street whose name you mention) as soon as possible.
4. Use several colors in various places in the paragraph. Mr. Zuckerman says "steel grey eyes"; Miss Harris writes "our brown wood house."
5. Show the relative about whom you are writing as he or she performs some action. Use a lively verb. Odessa Harris shows a vivid picture of her grandmother dashing from the water tubs to the house.
6. Show your relative's face as he responds to the situation you're writing about: "lines of worry in her dark brown skin"; "her brown eyes moist." The eyes are particularly easy to write about if you combine color with another sense like touch (*moist, hard, soft,* etc.).
7. Use several word groups that appeal to the sense of sound. "Jungle Boy" includes "slammed the knives and forks upon the table with a startling clatter."
8. Show details of the scene in which the moment occurs; use a detail of *touch* and one of *smell*.
9. Start one sentence with an *-ly* word. Start another sentence with two *-ly* words separated by a comma or *and.*
10. Write one quotation sentence which gives someone's exact words. Check the Review Charts on pp. 49–50 for correct punctuation.
11. Tell your story in clear chronological order. See pp. 45–46.
12. Use at least two of the new vocabulary words on pp. 38–40.
13. Check your theme for errors, especially the fragment mistake explained earlier in this chapter, and the run-on error, explained in Chapter 1. See also your Theme Progress Sheet (p. 483) and your Individual Spelling List (p. 459).
14. Give your paragraph a lively title. See pp. 197–199 for some help if you need it.

Some Topics to Think About

In case you have some trouble finding a moment about which to write, perhaps one of these titles will give you an idea.

1. My Mother's Temper
2. A Good Uncle
3. My Father's Bad Mood
4. Working For My Father
5. When I Appreciated My Brother
6. When My Mother Made Me Mad
7. An Unjust Moment
8. My Sister, the Pest

9. Family Battle
10. An Unforgettable Beating
11. My Father and My Date
12. My Father Understood
13. Asking For Money
14. My Father, the Boss
15. Grandmother Butting In

For some more topic ideas, turn back to p. 41 and reread the sentences in Step 1.

THE PROFESSIONALS SPEAK

Strong moments between parents and children are important parts of many novels and stories. Professional writers work from the same kinds of materials you have been asked to write from in this theme.

Step 1. Reading Two Professional Samples. Read the excerpts below and answer the questions after each selection.

Ben's Shoes

Ben bought a new pair of shoes. They were tan. He paid six dollars for them. He always bought good things. But they burnt the soles of his feet. In a scowling rage he loped to his room and took them off.

"Goddam it!" he yelled, and hurled them at the wall. Eliza came to the door.

"You'll never have a penny, boy, as long as you waste money the way you do. I tell you what, it's pretty bad when you think of it." She shook her head sadly with puckered mouth.

"O for God's sake!" he growled. "Listen to this! By God, you never hear me asking any one for anything, do you?" he burst out in a rage.

She took the shoes and gave them to Eugene.

"It would be a pity to throw away a good pair of shoes," she said. "Try 'em on, boy."

He tried them on. His feet were already bigger than Ben's. He walked about carefully and painfully a few steps.

"How do they feel?" asked Eliza.

"All right, I guess," he said doubtfully. "They're a little tight."

He liked their clean strength, the good smell of leather. They were the best shoes he had ever had.

Ben entered the kitchen.

"You little brute!" he said. "You've a foot like a mule." Scowling, he knelt and touched the straining leather at the toes. Eugene winced.

"Mama, for God's sake, Ben cried out irritably, "don't make the kid wear them if they're too small. I'll buy him a pair myself if you're too stingy to spend the money."

"Why, what's wrong with these?" said Eliza. She pressed them with her fingers. "Why, pshaw!" she said. "There's nothing wrong with them. All shoes are a little tight at first. It won't hurt him a bit."

But he had to give up at the end of six weeks. The hard leather did not stretch, his feet hurt more every day. He limped about more and more painfully until he planted each step woodenly as if he were walking on blocks. His feet were numb and dead, sore on the palms. One day, in a rage, Ben flung him down and took them off. It was several days before he began to walk with ease again. But his toes that had grown through boyhood straight and strong were pressed into a pulp, the bones gnarled, bent and twisted, the nails thick and dead.

"It does seem a pity to throw those good shoes away," sighed Eliza.

— Thomas Wolfe,
Look Homeward Angel

1. Because this scene comes from a novel where situations grow one from the other, it lacks the kind of topic sentence—one right at the beginning of the moment—that you have been asked to write. Which of these sentences would *best* serve, in your opinion, as a topic sentence for the selection you just read?
   a. Misers cause a lot of trouble.
   b. It happened when he was much younger.
   c. Eliza's stinginess about a pair of shoes aroused anger and discomfort.

   Why did you pick the one you did? _____

   _____

2. Which words paint the best picture, the one you find easiest to see in your mind? _____

3. Wolfe has used several excellent action words. Guess at the meaning of each italicized word and write it in Column I. Then, checking a dictionary, see how close you came. Put the correct definition in Column II.

	I	II
He *loped* to his room.	_____	_____
With *puckered* mouth.	_____	_____
Planted each step *woodenly*.	_____	_____

4. Notice the effective use of quotation sentences. Why does the writer have Eliza say *again* at the end of the selection a line just like this one she says earlier: "It would be a pity to throw away a good pair of shoes."

   _____

   _____

5. The events in the selection you read follow a strict chronological arrangement. Below several important details from the selection are listed. But

they appear in the wrong time sequence. Put number 1 in front of the first event that occurred; number 2 in front of the second, and so on.

_____ Ben begged Eliza not to let Eugene wear the shoes.

_____ Eliza scolded Ben for wasting money.

_____ Ben bought a new pair of tan shoes.

_____ Ben said he never asked anyone for anything.

_____ Eugene's toes were bent and twisted, the nails thick and dead.

In the following selection, Mr. Lindabury is the president of the insurance company that employs the writer's father. "King Kong" Charlie Keller is an outfielder for the New York Yankees.

My Father

I remember—to go back even further in this history of disenchantment—I remember one Sunday morning pitching a baseball at my father, and then waiting in vain to see it go flying off, high above my head. I am eight, and for my birthday have received my first mitt and hardball, and a regulation bat that I haven't even the strength to swing all the way around. My father has been out since early morning in his hat, coat, bow tie, and black shoes, carrying under his arm the massive black collection book that tells who owes Mr. Lindabury how much. He descends into the colored neighborhood each and every Sunday morning because, as he tells me, that is the best time to catch those unwilling to fork over the ten or fifteen measly cents necessary to meet their weekly premium payments. He lurks about where the husbands sit out in the sunshine, trying to extract a few thin dimes from them before they have drunk themselves senseless on their bottles of "Morgan Davis" wine; he emerges from alleyways like a shot to catch between home and church the pious cleaning ladies, who are off in other people's houses during the daylight hours of the week, and in hiding from him on weekday nights. "Uh—oh," someone cries, "Mr. Insurance Man here!" and even the children run for cover— the *children,* he says in disgust, so tell me, what hope is there for these niggers' ever improving their lot? How will they ever lift themselves if they ain't even able to grasp the importance of life insurance? Don't they give a single crap for the loved ones they leave behind? Because "they's all" going to die too, you know—"oh," he says angrily, "'they sho' is!'" Please, what kind of man is it, who can think to leave children out in the rain without even a decent umbrella for protection!

We are on the big dirt field back of my school. He sets his collection book on the ground, and steps up to the plate in his coat and his brown fedora. He wears square steel-rimmed spectacles, and his hair (which now I wear) is a wild bush the color and texture of steel wool; and those teeth, which sit all night long in a glass in the bathroom smiling at the toilet bowl, now smile out at me, his beloved, his flesh and his blood, the little boy upon whose head no rain shall ever fall. "Okay, Big Shot Ballplayer," he says, and grasps my new regulation bat somewhere near the middle—and to my astonishment, with his left hand where his right hand should be. I am suddenly overcome with such sadness: I want to tell him, *Hey, your hands are wrong*, but am unable to, for fear I might begin to cry—or he might! "Come on, Big Shot, throw the ball," he calls, and so I do—and of course discover that on top of all the other things I am just beginning to suspect about my father, he isn't "King Kong" Charlie Keller either.

Some umbrella.

> —Philip Roth,
> *Portnoy's Complaint*

1. The word *disenchantment* (see p. 39 for definition) is the key word of the opening sentence. Why is the writer disenchanted with his father's ball-playing efforts? _____

_____

2. Although Roth sets the reader in time in the first sentence, he changes the chronology by relating events that occurred before father and son began their game. Where has the father been earlier in the morning?

_____

_____

3. *a.* The writer's father gives the impression that his job of selling insurance is an important service to poor blacks. What words show, however, that he has no respect for the people with whom he deals?

_____

_____

   b. How are we supposed to feel about the writer's father after he speaks in imitation of black dialect, "they sho' is"? _____

_____

   c. How could the father's attitude toward the people who buy insurance from him also be a source of *disenchantment* to the son? _____

_____

4. What words, by appealing to the sense of sight through color, give a picture you find easy to see? _____

_____

5. What words appeal to the sense of touch? _____

_____

6. In order to understand the last line, "some umbrella," you need to re-read the last sentence of the first paragraph. What does the sentence mean by the word "rain"? _____

_____

What does the sentence mean when it uses the words "decent umbrella"?

_____

_____

In what ways is the writer's father also no decent umbrella? _____

_____

REACHING HIGHER

Step 1. Photo into Words. Look at the photograph on p. 37. Write a paragraph of at least fifteen sentences which explains the parent-child moment you see. Use details of color, of sound, of touch, of smell to make the scene come alive.

Step 2. Observing Someone You Know. Read this selection and then write a brief paragraph in which you describe some relative *you* observe close up. Show the person's eyes, hands, and face. Use a comparison as vivid as Miss Esposito's below: "large hands like shovels." Use lively verbs like *quivered, slumped, chuckled, wilted, muttered.* Check your dictionary for any you do not understand.

Grandma

   On a rainy night in front of the TV, the roar of a Boeing 707 and the pitter of rain echoed in my ears: in her heavy red fireside chair sat Grandma, intently watching the lit screen. The glow from the table lamp beside her shined softly in her heavy blue eyes, glaring through her thick-rimmed spectacles. Her gray hair, pulled back tightly in a bun, touched the back of her neck. As she sat smiling at a cigarette commercial, her wrinkles deepened and her dimples quivered as she chuckled. Her large hands like shovels sat folded serenely in her lap and her elbows rested on the wooden armrests. A spacious chair surrounded her thin, slumped frame. As an old movie, *The Diary of a Young Man,* unfolded, her head nodded and her spectacles slid down and rested precariously on the tip of her nose. On the table before her, a plate filled with orange wedges, dry and wilted, sat waiting. And as she snored loudly, her heavy breath fluttered the handkerchief in the pocket of her worn tan sweater. Then, as I lifted her head onto a downy pillow, she sleepily muttered, "Graci."

— Patricia D'Esposito

Step 3. Review. Read this freshman paragraph for the kinds of errors you have learned about so far. Correct the mistakes directly on the page. The following list tells the kinds of errors and how many of each there are.

Run-on: 5
Fragment: 5

Quotation: 2
Errors with *there-their-they're:* 1
Errors with *it's-its:* 1
Errors with *to-two-too:* 4

Undeserved Treatment

The time my father caught me smoking without his permission when I was twelve was the first time he treated me like an adult however I didn't deserve such treatment. At the P.S. 219 schoolyard one Saturday morning in May I stood under a bent basketball hoop and puffed wildly on a shriveled white butt that I had found near the curb on Clarkson Avenue. I felt like a big shot. Knowing I wasn't supposed to be smoking because I was to young. Suddenly I spotted my father's Chevy squeaking too a halt at the curb therefore I threw away the cigarette. Hoping Dad hadn't seen it. I watched him jump out of the car and rush toward me. Suspiciously, firmly, he asked were you there smoking just now? I lied when I said, "No," but he ordered me into the car anyway. He must have noticed the odor of smoke, it made him ask if he could smell my breath then I confessed. Better late than never. Dad was to angry to speak as he drove. Their he sat at the wheel with his lips closed tightly and his harsh blue eyes looking in anger from the road too me and back to the road again. I knew he wanted to do something. To smack me or maybe just to shout one of his usual lectures. Consequently I pushed myself as close to the car door as possible, I still remember the feel of it's cold steel handle. Digging into my side. However, instead of lecturing, Dad only said, "It's your life." "If you want to risk losing it, go ahead and smoke." I felt rotten not because he caught me doing something he didn't like, but because he treated me in a manner I don't think I earned.

chapter 3

STREET SCENES AND SANDLOTS:
GATHERING MEMORIES

INTRODUCTION

Each of us builds up unforgettable memories from childhood. These memories are built from experiences in school, from weekend rides on buses or subways, from days in the country sun, or from nights on the city streets. Some of the moments are filled with delight and laughter; others, through fear or pain or anger, still leave a bitterness in the mouth. Maybe for you, like for Claude Brown, the author of *Manchild in the Promised Land*, the best part of going to school was playing hooky, and you had a friend like Danny who made hooky a game, who taught you to break into the mailbox for the yellow absence postcard so your father wouldn't beat you with a razor strop. Perhaps like Mark Twain in his *Autobiography* you remember from a Mississippi boyhood every single detail of the tree fruit on the farm: how peaches and pears look piled in pyramids, how your teeth ache if you bite a frozen apple from a cellar barrel in winter, how an apple looks sizzling in a fire, and how the fruit tastes with sugar and cream. Perhaps like Jim Burden in Willa Cather's *My Antonia* you recall prairie things: how gophers run up and down plowed ground, how queer red bugs move in and out of the earth, how you must never walk the garden without a knife or a hickory cane with a copper tip just in case a rattlesnake moves along the ground. Maybe you remember your first day in this country after a long journey; perhaps you recall the sting the first time someone cursed your race or made fun of your religion; or do you remember the first time you sneaked a cigarette in the back row of a movie house? The scars and the joys of your younger days will be the substance of the next theme.

To recall experiences like these in writing you certainly might want to use the *narrative* (see p. 58); the telling of one moment through lively sensory images makes the strongest impression upon the reader. In this chapter you will learn further how to develop the paragraph by using *several* examples. Since each example will be built upon an incident from your own life, you will again use concrete sensory detail (see pp. 5–6), but not with as much completeness as you can achieve in a paragraph that narrates one single event. If you use several examples, you will need to move the reader smoothly from one instance to another; therefore, you will examine further some transitional devices.

VOCABULARY

Step 1. Meanings from Sentences. Each underlined word below appears later on in the chapter in a similar way. Try to determine the meaning of the word from the way it is used in the sentence. Circle the letter next to what you think is the best definition. Check in Appendix A.

1. Such an unusual <u>phenomenon</u> as space walking was denied to men of all centuries before ours.
   a. trip   *b.* space ship   *c.* event   *d.* discussion

2. Through the <u>dingy</u> windows drifted only one beam of light.
   a. dull   *b.* opened   *c.* dignified   *d.* cracked
3. He <u>flicked</u> the bug that landed on his girl friend's shoulder.
   a. picked up eagerly   *b.* threw off with a quick motion
   c. ignored   *d.* gently lifted with two fingers
4. The old man held a faded <u>bandana</u> by one corner.
   a. bandage   *b.* record   *c.* sweet yellow fruit   *d.* handkerchief
5. That <u>episode</u> seriously changed his outlook, for he learned then the true value of hard study.
   a. homework   *b.* incident in life's experiences   *c.* teacher
   d. severe mistreatment
6. Such a <u>startling</u> crash arose from the basement that the janitor leaped out the door and rushed down the stairs.
   a. surprising   *b.* noisy   *c.* beginning   *d.* foolish
7. A <u>melancholy</u> look crossed his face as he lowered his eyes and sighed.
   a. joyous   *b.* sneaky   *c.* militant   *d.* gloomy
8. A <u>burly</u> oak stood unmoved by the lashing wind and rain.
   a. tiny   *b.* dead   *c.* sturdy   *d.* dry
9. The stricken dog lay upon the earth; it <u>quivered</u> suddenly; then it died.
   a. barked softly   *b.* kicked its paws   *c.* screeched
   d. trembled slightly
10. "Just <u>liberate</u> that fifty dollars from the drawer when no one is looking," he muttered playfully.
    a. steal   *b.* make change for   *c.* spend   *d.* pay out
11. Held back by excessive <u>rotundity</u>, the dog could barely lift himself over the steps as he climbed up the long stairway.
    a. tiredness   *b.* starvation   *c.* plumpness   *d.* itchiness
12. If you are <u>compelled</u> to perform some task, it may seem difficult.
    a. asked   *b.* shown how   *c.* forced   *d.* told
13. She opened her purse and with <u>grudged</u> fingers counted out three dirty pennies for spending money.
    a. unwilling   *b.* wrinkled   *c.* swollen   *d.* gracious
14. Such a <u>conviction</u> cannot be challenged by even the clearest statements of fact and logic.
    a. statement   *b.* lie   *c.* idea   *d.* strong belief
15. The gull <u>hovered</u> above the water; but with one swift leap he caught his prey.
    a. walked   *b.* hung suspended   *c.* laughed softly
    d. shook hungrily
16. Although what is received <u>illicitly</u> may at first bring extreme delight, later consequences often erase all early pleasures.
    a. unexpectedly   *b.* childishly   *c.* unlawfully   *d.* unwillingly
17. Certain worthwhile goals in life are <u>unattainable</u>.
    a. not able to be reached   *b.* not able to be taught
    c. not having any value   *d.* not able to be seen

18. The boat <u>cleaved</u> a white path through the rough green waves.
    a. cut   *b.* made   *c.* covered   *d.* elevated
19. Only the <u>elect</u> know the joys of carefree life.
    a. nominated   *b.* officials   *c.* very rich   *d.* chosen few
20. A <u>lanky</u> cat stretched its long legs and then stepped clumsily across the road.
    a. tall and thin   *b.* lazy and tired   *c.* spotted   *d.* ugly

BUILDING COMPOSITION SKILLS

Finding the Topic

Step 1. Getting Ideas. Complete any word group below by reading it aloud with your own ending. Then, in a few more sentences, explain what you said. Or, write down in a few brief sentences your completion for any of the statements and then read aloud what you have written.

1. One teacher I (liked) disliked was _____

   _____

   _____

2. When I returned to my old neighborhood, I _____

   _____

   _____

3. I got in trouble when _____

   _____

   _____

4. One Christmas I'll never forget was _____

   _____

   _____

5. At school, my friend and I always _____

   _____

   _____

6. When I played hooky, I _____

   _____

   _____

7. I was embarrassed when _____

_____

_____

8. I could always annoy my teacher by _____

_____

_____

9. The things that frightened me as a child were _____

_____

_____

10. I first learned about death when _____ _____

_____

_____

Here are some freshman responses:

1. I almost got in trouble with the police when my friend and I threw M-7's up and down our street. Those firecrackers made plenty of noise! But when we spotted a police car we had enough time to dump our matches and the rest of the stuff into an open garbage pail. So, the cops just drove on by.
— John Farrell

2. I was embarrassed when my wig popped off in my high school English class. There I sat with my real hair in dozens of ugly pink curlers, the whole class laughing.
— Shelly Broidy

3. One teacher I liked was an old history teacher in junior high school. He always took a personal interest in me. Once, when the class went to a museum to see a new American Indian display, I didn't have the money, so he treated me.
— Cary Wiggins

Paragraph Unity: Using Subtopic Sentences

It's often helpful, especially when you use several examples to support your point, to remind the reader of the topic in several places in the paragraph. The subtopic sentence serves that function.

Here is a topic sentence that will obviously introduce a paragraph which uses several instances to support the topic:

When I was seven years old and the family moved from a small village in Puerto Rico to Manhattan, everyday city occasions frightened me.

This topic will deal with selected events of city life; the writer's opinion is that these events were frightening. The very next sentence would present the first subtopic:

The traffic noises scared me.

The word *scared* repeats the opinion of the topic sentence; *traffic noises* introduce one specific aspect of the topic for discussion. The next three or four sentences would explain how the traffic noises were frightening. Images filled with sensory language in these sentences would support this first unit of thought. After the writer finishes this thought group, he would write another subtopic sentence:

I also didn't like the people I saw on the streets.

The words *people I saw on the streets* introduce another part of the topic for the writer to discuss. The words *didn't like* refer back to the opinion in the topic sentence. The next few sentences would illustrate the point of the subtopic with colors and sounds and actions. After this thought unit ends, another subtopic sentence would appear:

And every new thing I saw in Manhattan looked oversized and ugly.

The words *every new thing I saw in Manhattan* refer the reader back to the original topic; the words *oversized and ugly* repeat the writer's opinion toward what he will discuss. In this way the paragraph achieves unity—all the sentences will build on the main idea.

SUBTOPIC SENTENCE CHART

Subtopic Sentence	*Why*
1. Introduces one *aspect* of the topic you want to discuss	So it's clear to the reader what proof you will use at a given point in the paragraph So it's clear to you what part of the topic you are treating at a given point in the paragraph
2. Uses a word similar to the "opinion" word in the topic sentence	So the reader is reminded of your position on the topic So that you remember that you're trying to prove only a certain feature about the topic So that the details in the sentences that follow the subtopic sentence all try to support the key impression you have given about the topic in the topic sentence

---

Step 1. Writing Subtopic Sentences. For each topic sentence below, write subtopic sentences as indicated.

Hint: Each subtopic sentence:
a. Introduces some aspect of the topic that can be discussed in a few sentences;
b. May repeat some idea of the opinion word.

Example:

1. At Springfield Gardens High School trouble and I were never far away from each other!

Subtopic sentence 1: Once I "borrowed" my homeroom teacher's key for a practical joke.

Subtopic sentence 2: To protest the awful cafeteria food, I caused a commotion.

Subtopic sentence 3: The Dean of Boys summoned me when he learned I cut history eighteen times.

2. Two important events in my life make the summer of 1972 outstanding in my memory.

Subtopic sentence 1: _____

_____

_____

_____

Subtopic sentence 2: _____

_____

_____

3. I was always a poor student in secondary school.

Subtopic sentence 1: _____

_____

_____

_____

Subtopic sentence 2: _____

_____

_____

Subtopic sentence 3: _____

_____

_____

_____

4. My first day at Santa Monica High School was filled with surprises.

Subtopic sentence 1: _____

_____

_____

_____

Subtopic sentence 2: _____

_____

_____

_____

Subtopic sentence 3: _____

_____

_____

_____

5. Practice with our local baseball team is more fun than work.

Subtopic sentence 1: _____

_____

_____

_____

Subtopic sentence 2: _____

_____

_____

_____

Subtopic sentence 3: _____

_____

_____

_____

6. Job hunting as a teen-ager still in high school is a depressing experience.

Subtopic sentence 1: _____

_____

_____

_____

Subtopic sentence 2: _____

_____   _____

_____

_____

Subtopic sentence 3: _____

_____

_____

_____

Hint: There is no set number of subtopic sentences to use for each paragraph. If you write only two subtopic sentences, each subtopic (thought unit) will need to be developed in greater detail. Write three subtopic sentences and you will need to use fewer details for each thought unit.

Even paragraphs that do not give several incidents can benefit from subtopic sentences. Paragraphs of description (Chapter 1) and narration (Chapter 2) achieve unity too when subtopic sentences introduce major blocks of thought. Each subtopic sentence needs several sentences of support for whatever aspect of the topic the writer introduces. Here a topic sentence introduces a paragraph that narrates:

I never expected my father to save my life one August afternoon when I was eight.

Here are two subtopic sentences:

Subtopic sentence 1: Innocently I stepped into the shallow end of the public swimming pool.

Subtopic sentence 2: Suddenly my father shouted my name.

Step 2. Understanding Subtopics. Answer these questions about the topic and subtopic sentences above.

1. What kind of information would you expect to find in the seven or eight

   sentences after subtopic sentence 1? _____

   _____

2. What kind of information would you expect to find in the seven or eight

   sentences after subtopic sentence 2? _____

   _____

3. *a.* What is the opinion expressed in the topic sentence? _____

   _____

   b. What word in subtopic sentence 1 reminds the reader of the opinion?

   _____

c. What word in subtopic sentence 2 reminds the reader of the opinion expressed in the topic sentence? _____

Step 3. Finding Subtopics. Reread "The Gloom Room" on pp. 29–30.

1. Copy out the first subtopic sentence, the sentence that introduces the one aspect of the topic that the writer will discuss first. _____

   _____

2. Copy out the second subtopic sentence. _____

   _____

3. What details does Mr. Golden use to support the first subtopic sentence?

   _____

4. What details does he use to support the second subtopic sentence?

   _____

   _____

   Reread "A Rush-hour Lunch" on pp. 35–36.

1. What is the first subtopic sentence? _____

   _____

2. Copy out the second subtopic sentence, the sentence that tells the reader that the discussion of waiters and waitresses is over but that a discussion of other rushing people will begin. _____

   _____

3. What sentence serves as subtopic sentence 3 because it tells that the writer will now show how sounds at the restaurant contribute to the atmosphere of rushing? _____

   _____

4. What details support Miss Resnick's fourth topic sentence, "The physical atmosphere also reveals hustling activity"? _____

   _____

Step 4. Subtopics and a Single Narrative Moment. For each topic sentence below, write two subtopic sentences.

Hint: Each subtopic sentence should introduce in general terms the one part of the topic the writer will discuss.

1. The frantic pace of life in a gas station is a trying experience for worker and customer alike.

Subtopic sentence 1: _____

_____

_____

Subtopic sentence 2: _____

_____

_____

2. *Peaceful* is the best word to describe the inside of Lady of Lima Church on a Sunday morning.

Subtopic sentence 1: _____

_____

_____

Subtopic sentence 2: _____

_____

_____

3. A friendly game of stickball in front of Mrs. Belson's house didn't end as friendly as it started!

Subtopic sentence 1: _____

_____

_____

Subtopic sentence 2: _____

_____

_____

4. Every Saturday morning is my turn to tackle the unpleasant task of shopping at our local supermarket.

Subtopic sentence 1: _____

_____

_____

Subtopic sentence 2: _____

_____

_____

5. One Friday night in an empty shopping-center parking lot my friends and I drank wine for the first time.

Subtopic sentence 1: _____

_____

_____

Subtopic sentence 2: _____

_____

_____

Sometimes a writer wishes to mention a larger number of instances to support his topic sentence in a paragraph. In that case, each instance is not highly developed—it is told in just a sentence or two—and a subtopic sentence to introduce each example is unnecessary. The paragraph below uses several instances to support the attitude in the topic sentence, but does not need subtopic sentences. The unity in the paragraph comes from repetition of key words (see pp. 83–84).

SOME WORDS TO KNOW BEFORE YOU READ:

downs: a low area of land in South England
cricket: a popular English game; it is played by two teams, the ball hit along the ground with a kind of bat toward a goal
sixpence: an English coin worth a little more than a dime
newt: a salamander, a small lizardlike animal

Memories of Crossgates School

I have good memories of Crossgates, among a horde of bad ones. Sometimes on summer afternoons there were wonderful expeditions across the Downs, or to Beachy Head, where one bathed dangerously among the chalk boulders and came home covered with cuts. And there were still more wonderful midsummer evenings when, as a special treat, we were not driven off to bed as usual but allowed to wander about the grounds in the long twilight, ending up with a plunge into the swimming bath at about nine o'clock. There was the joy of waking early on summer mornings and getting in an hour's undisturbed reading (Ian Hay, Thackeray, Kipling and H. G. Wells were the favourite authors of my boyhood) in the sunlit, sleeping dormitory. There was also cricket, which I was no good at but with which I conducted a sort of hopeless love affair up to the age of about eighteen. And there was the pleasure of keeping caterpillars—the silky green and purple puss-moth, the ghostly green poplar-hawk, the privet hawk, large as one's third finger, specimens of which could be illicitly purchased for sixpence at a shop in the town—and, when one could escape long enough from the master who was "taking the walk," there was the excitement of dredging the dew-ponds on the Downs for enormous newts with orange-coloured bellies. This business of being out for a walk, coming across something of fascinating interest and then being dragged away from it by a yell from the master, like a dog jerked onwards by the leash, is an important feature of school life, and helps to build up the conviction, so strong in many children, that the things you most want to do are always unattainable.

—George Orwell
Such, Such Were the Joys

Arrangement by Importance

In telling about an event, you know that the clearest way to present the moment is to give the details in chronological order—the order in which things occur. If you write a paragraph that gives several instances or examples to support the topic sentence, you can certainly write about them in the order in which they occurred. But another method is to tell the details in the order of their importance: tell about the least important thing first and the most important thing last. In this way you build up to the proof that has the most significance.

Suppose you wanted to write a paragraph for this topic sentence:

All through high school my friend Larry made me seem like the class troublemaker.

Let's assume that you would develop these three incidents as illustrations in the paragraph:

1. the time I almost got suspended because he gave *my* name and class when some teacher caught him cutting and wandering outside the school building;
2. the time Larry flattened a math teacher's tire and left nearby a book with my name on it;
3. the time he accidentally threw my English homework into a puddle.

From these incidents, although item 1 might have occurred first in time, because it seems to be the most important it would best be discussed last in the paragraph. Item 3 seems least important so it could be the first event discussed.

Step 1. Making the Order Count. In Column I jot down three instances you might discuss for each of these topic sentences. In Column II, arrange the details in order of importance.

I
I always loved living in a big city.

	II Order of importance
a. _____	1. _____
b. _____	2. _____
c. _____	3. _____

The guidance counselor in my high school helped me more than anyone else.

a. _____	1. _____
b. _____	2. _____
c. _____	3. _____

Step 2. Arranging Details by Importance. Instead of writing in more detail about two or three instances, you can mention seven or eight instances, each in just a sentence or two. In Column I, list seven events that could be written to support the topic sentence as given. In Column II, arrange the details according to importance as *you* see it.

I

1. At our last assembly in my senior year, our principal, Mr. Epstein, made several startling announcements.

II Order of importance

a. _____

b. _____

c. _____

d. _____

e. _____

f. _____

g. _____

1. _____

2. _____

3. _____

4. _____

5. _____

6. _____

7. _____

2. Many new "freedoms" must be granted to high school students of today.

a. _____

b. _____

c. _____

d. _____

e. _____

f. _____

g. _____

1. _____

2. _____

3. _____

4. _____

5. _____

6. _____

7. _____

Getting it All Together

Transitions II. In Chapter 1 you learned about bridging thoughts through transitions—idea connectors—that move the reader from place to place. But you can also join ideas by means of other types of connecting words.

Connecting through Time

later on	suddenly	former
afterwards	now	latter
years ago	some time later	in the first place
earlier	in the first place	in the next place

before	once	further
next	often	furthermore
first	yesterday	meanwhile
second	today	previously
third	tomorrow	when
	then	at last
	in the past	
	thereafter	

Hint: These words help refer the reader to the idea that came directly before. The words suggest that the ideas are numbered.

Step 1. Using Time Connectors. Here are several ideas that could be used in a paragraph. They are not sentences. Using these details, connect the ideas with some of the time transitions above and write complete sentences in a paragraph.

movies always a form of amusement to me
liked *Sound of Music*
details of mountainside and vast blue skies
jingling tunes and cheerful voices of children
tastes changed
went to see only adventure films
was excited by *The Longest Day* and *Ben Hur*
saw *Easy Rider* and *Midnight Cowboy*
realized film not only for amusement
make serious comments on today's world

_____

_____

_____

_____

_____

Connecting through Coordinators
and, but, for, or, nor, yet

You learned that these words could join sentences together. They also serve to connect ideas in separate sentences. Notice how the sentence on the left below—a correct sentence grammatically—may be written as two sentences, the second of which makes a powerful transition to a new thought group.

He tried everything he could to make me like him, but I just could not bear the way he treated my mother.	He tried everything he could to make me like him. But I just could not bear the way he treated my mother.

Hint: *And, but, for, or, nor, yet* may be used at the beginning of a sentence. Make sure a complete thought follows the coordinator. Make sure the sentence before is logically related to the sentence that follows the coordinator. Don't open more than one or two sentences for each paragraph in this way.

Step 2. Coordinators as Transition Words. Use a coordinator that makes sense as a sentence opener in each blank space below.

1. A teen-ager in today's world may choose to struggle in the job market.

   _____ he may put off working by attending college, in the hopes of better employment later on.

2. A woman may not wish to be liberated from the home. _____ this is a very good thing for a number of young children who need a mother's guidance.

3. Cancer is still a deadly and horrible disease. _____ there have been many promising advances in recent years which indicate that a cure may not be far off.

4. Read the selection before you answer the questions. _____, to do it another way, look over the questions first.

Connecting through Repetition

Sometimes the repetition of a word or two either at the beginning or in the heart of the sentence helps join ideas together. Notice the repetition of the words *I know* in this series of ideas:

Boyhood Farm Days

As I have said, I spent some part of every year at the farm until I was twelve or thirteen years old. The life which I led there with my cousins was full of charm, and so is the memory of it yet. I know how the wild blackberries looked, and how they tasted, and the same with the pawpaws, the hazelnuts, and the persimmons; and I can feel the thumping rain, upon my head, of hickory nuts and walnuts when we were out in the frosty dawn to scramble for them with the pigs, and the gusts of wind loosed them and sent them down. I know the stain of blackberries, and how pretty it is, and I know the stain of walnut hulls, and how little it minds soap and water, also what grudged experience it had of either of them. I know the taste of maple sap, and when to gather it, and how to arrange the troughs and the delivery tubes, and how to boil down the juice, and how to hook the sugar after it is made, also how much better hooked sugar tastes than any that is honestly come by, let bigots say what they will. I know how a prize watermelon looks when it is sunning its fat rotundity among pumpkin vines and "simblins"; I know how to tell when it is ripe without "plugging" it; I know how inviting it looks when it is cooling itself in a tub of water under the bed, waiting; I know how it looks when it lies on the table in the sheltered great floor space between house and kitchen, and the children gathered for the sacrifice and their mouths watering; I know the crackling sound it makes when the carving knife enters its end, and I can see the split fly along in front of the blade as the knife cleaves its way to the other end; I can see its halves fall apart and display the rich red meat and the black seeds, and the heart standing up, a luxury fit for the elect; I know how a boy looks behind a yard-long slice of that melon, and I know how he feels; for I have been there. I know the taste of the watermelon which has been honestly come by, and I know the taste of the watermelon which has been acquired by art. Both taste good, but the experienced know which tastes best. I know the look of green apples and peaches and pears on the trees, and I know how entertaining they are when they are inside of a person. I know how ripe ones look when they are piled in pyramids under the trees, and how pretty they are and how vivid their colors. I know how a frozen apple looks, in a barrel down cellar in the wintertime, and how hard it is to bite, and how the frost makes the teeth ache, and yet how good it is, notwithstanding. I know the disposition of elderly people to select the specked apples for the children, and I once knew ways to beat the game. I know the look of an apple that is roasting and sizzling on a hearth on a winter's evening, and I know the comfort that comes of eating it hot, along with some sugar and a drench of cream.

— Mark Twain
Autobiography

Step 3. Finding Connectors. Read "Memories of Crossgates School" on p. 79. Circle the words repeated at the beginning of several sentences, words that help connect ideas through repetition.

Connecting through Pronouns

he	you	its
she	who	our
it	whom	their
we	his	your
they	her	whose

A pronoun takes the place of a noun. When you use a noun in one sentence, a pronoun that occurs later on in another sentence automatically refers the reader back to the original noun. In that way, you can help ideas move smoothly from one to the other.

Step 4. Pronouns as Connectors. Circle the pronouns that help connect the sentences in this paragraph.

The Tailor Arrives

Almost instantly there was the sound of soft steady footsteps through the open doors, and from the back of the house through the hall following the manservant there came the tailor. He was a tall man, taller than the servant, middle-aged, his face quiet with a sort of closed tranquility. He wore a long robe of faded blue grass-cloth, patched neatly at the elbows and very clean. Under his arm he carried a bundle wrapped in a white cloth. He bowed to the two white women and then squatting down put his bundle upon the floor of the veranda and untied its knots. Inside was a worn and frayed fashion book from some American company and a half-finished dress of a spotted blue-and-white silk. This dress he shook out carefully and held up for Mrs. Lowe to see.

—Pearl S. Buck
"The Frill"

Step 5. A Brief Paragraph with Pronoun Connectors. Write five sentences to describe the person sitting next to you in class or someone you know. Mention the person's name in the first sentence. Connect the ideas in each succeeding sentence by using pronouns to bridge each complete thought. Use a separate sheet of paper.

Hint: It must always be clear to the reader just which noun the pronoun replaces. In this sentence:

The mother held the baby and she laughed at her

we don't know—because the pronouns are unclear—just who did the laughing at whom.

Sentence Variety: Coordination and Subordination

Read these sentences about Miss Walters and write on the blank space your first reaction to the way the sentences sound.

(1) I remember my fourth grade school teacher. (2) My memories of her are bad. Her name was Miss Walters. (3) She knew her subjects well. (4) She didn't treat all her students in the same way. (5) The girls were her favorites. (6) She showered them with attention. She stroked their long hair. (7) She straightened the backs of their blouses. (8) We boys giggled at her sweet talk to the girls. (9) She always yelled at us. (10) We did our homework. (11) She never approved. (12) We stood on line quietly. She frowned and yelled anyhow.

Did you write *choppy* or *childish?* If you did, you probably sensed that some of the sentences needed to be joined in some way. Although very brief statements as sentences are often effective in writing, there are several other ways of structuring sentences for a clear development of ideas.

Using Coordination Wisely

The words

and, but, or, for, nor, and the semicolon (;)

are coordinators and may be used to correct run-ons. Even if you don't write run-on sentences, you will want to know how to use these words correctly because they do help thoughts flow smoothly in a paragraph. Coordinators join two complete thoughts together so that they both are equal in importance and strength.

What They Mean	*How to Use Them*	
and The information that follows in the second complete thought is true along with, in addition to, the related information in the first complete thought.	The boys sat in the school-yard with their shirts off, (and) they enjoyed sunning themselves.	This part of the sentence tells what the boys do in addition to sitting in the schoolyard with their shirts off.
but The information that follows in the second complete thought is something you would not expect to happen based upon your information in the first complete thought. Idea two tells an *exception* to idea one.	I wanted to see the *Mod Squad* on television, (but) I had too much homework.	You wouldn't expect someone who wanted to watch the program (as stated in the first part of the sentence) to miss it.
for The information in the second complete thought tells why the events in the first complete thought happened or should happen.	We were not permitted to visit the baby, (for) we both had colds.	This tells why the visit (stated in the first thought) could not occur.
or The information in the second complete thought is an alternative—another possibility—to the information in the first. *Or* suggests that only one of the two ideas will be possible.	You must arrive on time, (or) you will miss the first part of the examination.	This will occur only if what is told in the first part of the sentence does not occur.
nor *Nor* continues into the second complete thought some negative idea begun in the first. The semicolon indicates close relationship between both complete thoughts.	[This word begins the negative idea] He never ate candy, (nor) did he miss the taste of sweetness.	This continues the negative idea.
	It was time for a new car(;) even his father agreed to that.	This thought depends for its sense on the thought before the semicolon.

Hint: Remember to use a comma whenever you use a conjunction to connect two complete thoughts.

Notice how well sentences 1 and 2 in the paragraph on Miss Walters (p. 85) may be coordinated.

I remember my fourth grade school teacher, *but* my memories of her are bad.

Similarly, sentences 5 and 6 may be united:

The girls were her favorites; she showered them with attention.

What other sentences might be coordinated effectively?

_____

_____

_____

Three Important Hints:
1. Too many coordinated sentences in a paragraph are poor. Use coordination sparingly.
2. Don't coordinate more than two complete sentences with conjunctions. Your paragraph will be just as dull as if you had not used any coordinators. Sometimes semicolons may be used effectively to coordinate *three* complete thoughts, or a combination of semicolon and conjunction: *We drove carefully through the strange neighborhood; all of us watched the street signs, but nothing looked familiar.*
3. Make sure that the two complete thoughts you coordinate make sense together.

Step 1. You Pick the Coordinator.   Here are five coordinated sentences written by professional writers. The coordinator in each case is left out. Circle the best coordinator from the choices given on the right, and write it into the blank space.

1. The big patch of shadow might be a hut cer-

    tainly, _____ it might be a cave lead-   for   ;   but
    ing down into the very depths of the earth.
                                    —Leo Tolstoy

2. A breeze must have blown outside, _____   or   for   nor
   the net on the basket moved . . .
                                    —Philip Roth

3. Now and then pigeons flutter _____   but   ;   for

birds glide in and sing gay songs _____   but   ;   nor
both birds and pigeons are drinking from the
beautiful fountains.
                        —Woodie King, Jr.

4. At my father's funeral I had nothing black to

wear, _____ this posed a nagging prob-   for   but   and
lem all day long.
                        —James Baldwin

Step 2. Completing Sentences. Based upon the coordinator used below, add a complete thought to the sentence that appears. Make sure that your final sentence makes sense. Look at the example.

1. Jimmy found five dollars, but *he was warned not to spend it.*
2. A college student must often give up after-school employment, for

_____ .

3. Suddenly thunder filled the air; _____ .
4. A person should never drive a car without sufficient practice, nor

_____ .

5. Women have in the past been overlooked for job advancement, but

_____ .

6. I can deliver the package personally, or _____ .

Step 3. Coordinators in Your Sentences. Using any of the methods of coordination, write a sentence about the topics listed below. Use each type of coordinator at least once.

Hint: Make sure a complete thought (containing subject and verb) follows each coordinator.

1. Saturday _____

_____

2. books _____

_____

3. the street _____

_____

4. lunch _____

_____

5. basketball _____

_____

6. rock music _____

_____

7. days _____

_____

8. money _____

_____

9. newspapers _____

_____

10. department stores _____

_____

SUBORDINATION FOR MATURE STYLE

Another way to join thoughts in paragraphs is to set up a relationship between two thoughts, a relationship in which one of the two ideas is stressed more than the other. Let us join sentences 8 and 9 in the paragraph about Miss Walters on p. 85 so that one of the thoughts gets more emphasis:

a. Because we boys giggled at her sweet talk to the girls, she always yelled at us.

The words "she always yelled at us" express a complete thought and, as such, give the part of the sentence that is most important.

The words "because we boys always giggled at her sweet talk to the girls" are not a complete thought and, therefore, get less emphasis than the rest of the sentence. Those words give "background information": they tell *why* the teacher yelled. But clearly, it is the yelling of the teacher that the writer wants to stress, and he shows that the boys' giggling made the teacher react in the way she did.

Now look at the sentences joined together in another way:

b. Because she always yelled at us, we boys giggled at her sweet talk to the girls.

Here, the words "we boys giggled at her sweet talk to the girls" are the most important part of the sentence because they can stand alone as a complete thought.

The words "Because she always yelled at us" are not a complete thought. As "background information," they tell *why* the boys giggled. But it is the giggling of the boys that this writer wants to stress, and he shows that the teacher's yelling made the boys react in the way they did.

The technique that makes one part of a sentence less important than another is *subordination*. Only the writer himself can decide which part of the sentence is less or more important. Completely different meanings are achieved by subordinating different word groups within a sentence: this is clear in sentences *a* and *b* above.

It's obvious that the word *because* is the word that brings about the subordination in sentences *a* and *b*. It is one word among many which are called *subordinators*. Although all subordinators connect the less important part of a sentence to the part that gets the emphasis, they explain different things about the emphasized part of the sentence.

If you want to show *why* the stressed part of the sentence occurred, use one of these to subordinate:

as
since
because
in order that
so that
as long as

[This tells *why* the visit to the doctor occurred.]

Example: Since I had a sore throat, I went to the doctor.

[This is the stressed part of the sentence. It tells a complete thought.]

Step 1. Subordination to Tell Why. Make up a correct subordinate part to tell *why* for each of these complete thoughts. Use one of the subordinators above. Be sure a subject and a verb come after the subordinator:

1. _____, I studied for more than ten hours.

2. _____, we always enjoyed visiting our neighbor, Mrs. Davis.

If you want to show *when* the stressed part of the sentence occurred, use one of these to subordinate.

after	whenever
as	while
as soon as	until
before	once
since	provided
when	

[This tells *when* the wish for popcorn occurred.]

Example: After the movie began, we decided we wanted popcorn.

[This is the stressed part of the sentence. It tells a complete thought.]

Step 2. Subordination to Tell When. Make up a correct subordinate part to tell *when* for each of these complete thoughts. Use a subordinator from the chart above. Be sure a subject and verb follow the subordinator.

1. _____, there is no one who can help you with the paint job.

2. _____, he straightened his tie and cleared his throat.

3. _____, the reporters rushed to the telephones to call their newspapers.

If you want to show *where* or *how* the stressed part of the sentence occurred, use one of these to subordinate:

wherever   if
where   how   as if
                      as though

                [This tells *where* forces of
                    good work.]

Examples: Wherever evil appears, the forces of good will work against it.

                             [This stressed part of
                        the sentence is a complete
                            thought.]

        [This tells *how* John rushed out.]

  As if he never heard her call his name,
John rushed out the door.

  [The stressed part of the
  sentence: a complete
  thought.]

Step 3. Completing Subordinated Sentences. Write the stressed part of the sentence for each subordinated word group below.

1. Wherever he went, _____.
2. As though a sudden voice cried out to remind him to be home at six,

_____.

If you want to show *under what condition* the stressed part of the sentence occurred, use one of these to subordinate:

although   unless
if   provided
though   once

[You would not expect a
  tired person to run.]

Although I was tired, I ran the ten blocks home.

[This tells *under what condition*
    the ads will be read.]

Once you buy the newspaper,
I can look at the want ads.

  [This, a complete thought, is
  what the sentence stresses.]

Hint: *Although* introduces an idea that you would not expect to happen based upon the information in the stressed part.

Step 4. Subordinates Tell Conditions. Complete the sentences below by adding a subordinated section that tells under what conditions the main part of the sentence occurred. Use the subordinator as indicated.

1. Although _____, his parents still try to help him.

2. Unless _____, our baseball team will lose the pennant again this season.

3. If _____, in most cases the problem of poor spelling can be overcome.

Hint: Always use a comma after the subordinate part of the sentence when the subordinate part comes first.

[Subordinate
   part]

As she arrived, we left.
               [Comma here]

Step 5. Subordinating Your Sentences. For each topic below, write a sentence that uses subordination at the beginning of the sentence. Use as many subordinators as you can from the four groups above. Don't forget commas after the subordinated part. The first is done for you.

Example:

1. telephone *While I wash the dishes, my sister talks on the telephone.*

2. houses _____

_____

3. shoes _____

_____

4. your mayor _____

_____

5. the newspaper _____

_____

6. your relationship with a parent _____
_____

7. trains _____
_____

8. snakes _____
_____

9. parties _____
_____

10. Mars _____
_____

Subordinated portions like the ones you've been writing may also appear at the end of a sentence. Don't use a comma before the subordinated section if it comes at the end.

Example: I watched the moon landing because I am interested in space programs.

Step 6. Subordination to Join. Each item in Column *I* below contains two brief sentences. Subordinate one of the two sentences, and rewrite your new sentence in Column *II*. Then, subordinate the other sentence, and write the new sentence in Column *III*. Look at the example.

I	*II*	*III*
1. I heard the mailman. I opened the door.	*As I heard the mailman, I opened the door.*	*As I opened the door, I heard the mailman.*
2. Everyone was quiet. The senator spoke.		
3. We had to go shopping. It started to rain.		
4. I sent him a Valentine's		

Day card. He sent me a
gift.

_____ _____

_____ _____

_____ _____

5. An ambulance sounded in
   the street. My father
   woke up.

_____ _____

_____ _____

_____ _____

6. That man owns a hard-
   ware store. He does not
   know about electric
   drills.

_____ _____

_____ _____

_____ _____

Hint: If the subordinated part—placed at the end—starts with *though* or *although,* use a comma.

Example: We read the whole book, though we were bored.

[Comma]

Step 7. More Practice. Several subordinated sections are listed below. For each one write a complete sentence that uses the subordinate part at the end. Look at the example.

when they bought a new car
although I couldn't understand it
whenever I get the chance
before I clean up my room
provided he brings his guitar
as long as he watches television

1. *He will never get that report done as long as he watches television.*

2. _____

3. _____

4. _____

5. _____

6. _____

If you want to describe someone or something you have mentioned in the stressed part of the sentence, use one of these to subordinate:

who
whose   that
which

Hint: The word *which* is never used to refer to a person, only places and things. Wrong: Those people which eat fast will be ill. Correct: Those people $\begin{Bmatrix} who \\ that \end{Bmatrix}$ eat fast will be ill.

The meat *which* we ate was tasty.

[This identifies the woman.]

1. The woman whose purse was stolen called the police.

[This identifies the book.]

2. We bought the book which had the most pictures.

[This identifies the man.]

3. The man who enjoys his work does the best job.

4. The Empire State Building, which is in New York, is no longer the tallest building.

A HINT ABOUT COMMAS

Sentences 1 to 3 do not use commas around the subordinate part because the subordinating sections identify some subject. Without the words *whose purse was stolen*, we have no way to identify the woman. Without *which had the most pictures*, we cannot identify the book in sentence 2. Without *who enjoys his work* we have no idea of which man is being identified. *Subordinate sections that identify the subject don't need commas.* However, when information is added in a subordinate section to describe further a subject already identified, you need to use commas as in sentence 4 above.

[Comma]   [Comma]
Professor Barton, who teaches here, is ill.
[This *adds* information; the person is already identified.]

The book that fell in the puddle is ruined.
[This identifies the book: no commas.]

I love Lena Horne's voice, which is lively and strong.
[Comma]   [This *adds* information; the voice has already been identified.]

Step 8. Practice with *Who, Whose, Which, What, That*. Add words to complete the subordinate section in each sentence below. Use commas where necessary.

1. The boy *who* _____ lost his license.

2. Those two school buildings *whose* _____
   have just been opened for students.

3. Kennedy Airport *which* _____ receives
   hundreds of complaints each week.

4. He is the one man *who* _____ .

5. Most students prefer courses *that* _____ .

Step 9. Writing Sentences that Subordinate. For each of these subordinated sections, write a complete sentence that makes sense. Put the subordinated part in the middle or at the end of the sentence; remember to put in commas, when necessary. Use a separate sheet of paper for this activity.

1. who complains all the time
2. whose car is parked illegally
3. that appeared suddenly
4. that starred the Beatles
5. who enjoys biology
6. that crashed
7. which he lost
8. who never forgets my birthday
9. whose speech was dull
10. which disturbed our sleep.

Step 10. Rewriting Coordinated Sentences. Although coordination is often effective, subordination of ideas allows for much greater sentence variety. Most students use coordination too frequently. Change each coordinated sentence below to a sentence that uses subordination.

1. I read the book, but I did not like it too much.

Example:

Although I read the book, I did not like it too much.

2. I looked out the window, and I saw how hard it was raining. _____

   _____

3. The workers demonstrated, for they disapproved of conditions in the

   factory. _____

   _____

4. One little child danced in the circle, and the other children sang a song.

   _____

   _____

5. My friend must work after school, or he cannot pay for his courses.

   _____

6. It is not easy to get an apartment in a large city, and it is not always possible to furnish inexpensively. _____

   _____

Step 11. Rewriting a Paragraph.   On a separate sheet of paper, rewrite the paragraph about Miss Walters that appears on p. 85. Use coordination and subordination to vary the sentence length and structure. Use coordination only once; use subordination at least three times.

SOLVING PROBLEMS IN WRITING

Sentence Fragments: Phase II

The technique of subordination you learned earlier in this chapter is an essential characteristic of effective writing style. Used incorrectly, however, subordination gives rise to another type of *sentence fragment*. It's important to use the subordinating word group only when it can join on to a complete sentence, a word group that can make sense standing alone. These fragments appeared on freshmen papers because students forgot that subordinators must *join* ideas together:

1. **When** an empty shopping <u>cart</u> <u>soared</u> down the aisle.
2. **Who** really <u>looked</u> ridiculous.
3. **Unless** our food stamp <u>program</u> <u>receives</u> much more publicity.

The words in boldface are *subordinators*. Each one indicates that a major and complete idea will be expressed either earlier or later on in the sentence.

In number 1, the reader wants to know *what has happened* **when** that empty shopping cart soared down the aisle.

In number 2, the reader wants to know **who** *it is that* looked ridiculous.

In number 3, the reader wants to know *what will happen* **unless** the food stamp program receives more publicity.

It is true that each of the word groups does contain a subject and a verb (they are underlined in each case). However, the use of the *subordinator* means that connection to a complete thought must be made for a correct sentence.

But those subordinator-fragments are easy enough to recognize in isolation. Now look at them as they appear in parts of paragraphs.

Fragment

a. (1) Parents should leave their children at home when shopping must be done. (2) One afternoon at the A&P I stood minding my own business at the corn counter. (3) *When an empty shopping cart soared down the aisle.* (4) I knew some little brat was to blame.

b. (1) All the children in the third grade danced in snowflake costumes on the auditorium stage. (2) Over to the left stood my fat cousin Tyrone. (3) *Who really looked ridiculous.* (4) He was covered with a big white sheet and he moved more like a hippo than a snowflake.

c. (1) The government's latest attack on hunger is doomed. (2) *Unless our food stamp program receives much more publicity.* (3) In every ghetto countless people will go on starving.

Explanation

The word *when* here is a subordinator. It must connect all the words that follow it to a complete sentence. Since word group 3 is standing alone, and *not* connected to a complete thought, it is a *fragment*. The reader needs to know, within word group 3, what happened *when an empty shopping cart soared down the aisle.*

The word *who*, as it is used here, is a connector. It must join all the words that follow it to a complete sentence. In addition the sentence that uses the word *who* must also identify the person that *who* refers to. It's not enough to use *Tyrone* at the end of sentence 2. Since word group 3 is standing alone, and not connected to a complete thought, it is a *fragment*.

The word *unless* is a subordinator. It must connect all the words that follow it to a complete sentence. Since word group 2 is standing alone, and not connected to a complete thought, it is a *fragment*. The reader needs to know, within word group 2, what will happen *unless our food stamp program receives much more publicity.*

FIXING THE SUBORDINATOR FRAGMENT

1. Join the fragment to the sentence before. In a above, join 2 and 3.

One afternoon at the A&P I stood minding my [No period] own business at the corn counter when an [Small letter] empty shopping cart soared down the aisle.

In b above, join 2 and 3.

Over to the left stood my fat cousin Tyrone, [Small letter] [Comma] who really looked ridiculous.

In c above, join 1 and 2.

The government's latest attack on hunger is [Small letter] doomed unless our food stamp program receives [No period] much more publicity.

Hint: A comma may be required when a subordinate word group is added at the end of a complete sentence. See pp. 94–95.

Step 1. Adding Fragments On: I.   Correct the selections below by adding the fragment onto the sentence that comes before it.

1. Many reference books are important aids to knowledge. A dictionary is a particularly helpful text. Because it tells how to pronounce words as well as how to spell them.
2. Coretta Scott King will always be remembered as a woman of courage. A woman who tried to continue the important work her husband started.

FIXING THE SUBORDINATOR FRAGMENT

2. Join the fragment to the sentence after.
In c, p. 98, add 2 and 3.

Unless our food stamp program receives much
[Comma]
more publicity, in every ghetto countless people
[Small letter]
will go on starving.

In a, p. 98, add 3 and 4.

When an empty shopping cart soared down the aisle, I knew some little brat was to blame.
[Comma]

Hint: When a subordinate word group comes first in a sentence, use a comma between it and the complete sentence that follows.

Step 2. Adding Fragments On: II.   Correct the two selections below by adding the fragments to the sentences that follow them.

1. We can go anywhere in the world by way of the television screen. While we could only use our imagination with the radio. The TV takes us to places through pictures in addition to words.
2. After my uncle heard the news. He broke out in tears. It was the first time I had ever seen a man cry.

Hint: In trying to decide whether to add the fragment to the sentence before or after, first decide which way makes more sense. Add the fragment to the sentence to which it is most closely related in meaning.

FIXING THE SUBORDINATOR FRAGMENT

3. Add a new subject-verb word group to the fragment.
In a, p. 98.

When an empty shopping cart soared down the
[Added word group]
aisle, I had to jump out of the way. I knew some
[Subject]   [Verb]
little brat was to blame.

Step 3. Adding Words to Fragments. Add the necessary words to these fragments and rewrite the correct sentence on the blank lines below. Remember punctuation.

1. Whoever arrives late. _____

_____

2. Until the police arrived. _____

_____

FIXING THE SUBORDINATOR FRAGMENT

4. Sometimes you can take out the subordinator and some accompanying words in order to correct the fragment.

In a, p. 98.

[Remove coordinator]

When An empty shopping cart soared down the aisle.   [Capital letter]

Sometimes it is necessary to add a new word which will serve as the subject.

In c, p. 98.

[Added word; subject of *looked*]

He
Who really looked ridiculous.
    [Remove subordinator]

Step 4. Dropping the Subordinator. Correct these fragments by removing the subordinator. Add a subject when necessary. Use a capital letter to start the correct sentence.

1. Since most people like smoking.
2. A table that broke into a million tiny pieces of glass.

Hint: Use this method only when all others fail. It's best to incorporate the fragment into a complete sentence. In that way you will be improving your writing style by using subordination.

FINDING THE FRAGMENT

You can see that the only way to spot the subordinator fragment is to be thoroughly familiar with the list of subordinators you were asked to experiment with earlier in this chapter. Here again are most of the subordinators, this time in Stop Sign warning charts. If you memorize these words, you'll know what causes most freshmen to write fragments.

FRAGMENT STOP SIGNS

I		II	
as long as	how	what	whoever
after	provided	which	whomever
although	if	who	whatever
as	since	whose	
as if	so that	that	
as soon as	though		
because	unless		
before	until		
whenever	when		
once while	where		
	whether		

Hint: Remember, do not avoid using these words. When used correctly, they add variety and clarity to your style.

REVIEW CHARTS: THE SUBORDINATOR FRAGMENT

A Fragment Finder

1. Learn the list of subordinators that frequently give rise to fragments (see above).
2. Read the sentences aloud; do not confuse a pause for breath (which may or may not be indicated by a comma) with a complete stop (indicated by a period, a semicolon, or some other end mark).
3. Read your sentences from the last one to the first, stopping after each sentence to see if a complete thought has been expressed.

A Fragment Fixer

1. Join the fragment to the sentence that comes before.
2. Join the fragment to the sentence that comes after.
3. Add a new subject and verb word group.
4. Remove the subordinator. Add any new words.

Step 1. Correcting Fragments. Most of the selections below contain fragments of the subordinator type. Correct the fragments in any of the ways you learned. If the selection is correct, mark the sentence C.

1. Many doctors refuse to say marijuana is harmless. Because the results of certain tests are still not known. _____

_____

2. A new addition to the rock movement was Joan Baez's baby Gabriel. Who made a public appearance at his mother's recent concert at Carnegie Hall in New York. _____

_____

_____

_____

3. A complete checkup is considered essential. Whenever a man starts a new job. His health should be excellent, especially if the job is physically difficult. _____

_____

_____

4. Many awards were given to the New York *Times.* The newspaper that tries to report the news carefully. That doesn't distort things. _____

_____

_____

5. Pollution creates an unhealthy atmosphere for breathing. In some cases for people who inhale these fumes constantly a lung problem. _____

_____

_____

6. The automobile is a machine that man produced to get himself from place to place. Which it does. But this machine is destroying all the air we must breathe. _____

_____

_____

7. Until I decided to go to college, my plans for the future were unsettled. After I got into school, however, I knew that nursing was for me. ____

_____

_____

8. My brother enlisted in the army last month. Since he didn't know what to do by way of a profession. Maybe the service is good for someone like him. _____

_____

_____

_____

9. He doesn't seem to be very smart. I've heard him talk and his opinions seem to be ridiculous. Although he says he reads a large number of books and magazines that he takes out of the library every week. I doubt it.

_____

_____

10. The truth about Henry David Thoreau, who went to jail for refusing to pay taxes to a slave state, is that he knew what would happen to him. If he didn't pay the money to the tax collector. But he was willing to

face the consequences. _____

_____

_____

_____

_____

_____

Step 2. More Practice with Fragments. Study the fragment review charts on pp. 56 and 101. Then follow directions.

1. Write two sentences which tell something you see on your way to college every day. Use the words "as I come to school every day" in

one of your sentences. _____

_____

_____

_____

2. Write one complete thought about a person you know who always looks tired. Use the words "who always looks tired" in your sentence.

_____

_____

3. Write two sentences that tell what you like to do after an exam is over. Open one of your sentences with one of these word groups:

When an exam is over
After I take an exam

_____

_____

_____

4. Write a sentence that tells what you do when you have to wait for someone. Start your sentence with one of these words: *when, if, while.*

_____

_____

5. Write a sentence or two about summer sports you enjoy. Use the words *to swim* or *to stay out late* or *to rest in the sun* somewhere in your sentence. _____

_____

_____

6. Write a sentence that tells your opinion of some course that you were forced to take in high school or college. Use the words "which is required" in your sentence. _____

_____

_____

7. Write two sentences about types of foods you enjoy. Open the second sentence with the words *for example.* _____

_____

_____

_____

8. Write three sentences about people you know. Use one of these word groups in *each* sentence:

who loses his temper easily
who always says hello every day
whom I have known for a long time

_____

_____

_____

_____

_____

_____

9. Write a sentence describing the face of one of your friends. After filling in the blank space, use this word group in your sentence: *whose eyes are always* _____. _____

_____

_____

10. Write a sentence or two about some change in your habits or behavior as a result of your coming to college. Use one of these word groups somewhere in your sentence: *because I came to college* or *since I came to college.* _____

_____

_____

_____

11. Write a sentence which tells of some outdoor summer activity you can do even if there is no sun. Use this word group somewhere in your sentence: *whether or not the sun shines.* _____

_____

_____

12. Write a sentence or two about people who run in order to catch a bus or a train. Start your sentence with these words: *While running for a bus.* _____

_____

_____

_____

13. Write a sentence whose first word is *whoever.* _____

_____

_____

14. Write two sentences, each one telling a kind of movie you like. Start the second sentence with *also.* _____

_____

_____

_____

15. Write two sentences about a book you would recommend. Use this word group to open the second sentence: *A book that everyone should read.* _____

_____

_____

_____

16. Write two sentences about a teacher you had in elementary school. Use this word group correctly in either sentence: *a former teacher of mine.* _____

_____

_____

_____

17. Write two sentences of advice you'd give about treating colds. Open the second sentence with these words: *to keep down a fever.* _____

_____

_____

_____

18. Write two sentences about a truck on a highway. Use this word group correctly in either sentence: *racing down the highway.* _____

_____

_____

_____

19. Write two sentences to tell what you'd do if you suddenly found a thousand dollar bill. Open one of the sentences with the word *if.* ____

_____

_____

_____

20. Write a sentence that begins with *although*. _____

_____

Step 3. Complete Sentences. In the space provided make complete sentences of the fragments in the following word groups. Some of the vocabulary you've learned is used here. If you've forgotten the meaning of the word, check the definitions in Appendix A.

1. With a taciturn smile the youngster sneaked to the edge of the curb. Precariously jumped into the street to tease his mother. But when he

   heard the thud of tires he jumped back on the sidewalk. _____

   _____

   _____

   _____

2. Living in a basement apartment, we are always dissatisfied. Our rooms are often dismal because of too few windows. Although a good strong

   light helped cheer things up a bit. It is still not a good place to live. ___

   _____

   _____

   _____

3. He rushed through the door. With an angry shout. Imagine our intense

   surprise! _____

   _____

   _____

4. It is not necessary always to use a great number of words in order to convince someone of the merit of some point of view. Anyone can learn

   to speak succinctly. If he really wants to. _____

   _____

   _____

   _____

5. Few people I know are as melancholy as our mailman. A man who always has a frown. Whenever he sees me. _____

_____

_____

_____

_____

Writing Plurals

Although the usual method of plural formation involves the addition of an -s, there are several variations. Study the review charts below which show examples and state rules.

Regular Plurals

Add -s to the singular for most plurals

boy + -s = boys
pencil + -s = pencils
tree + -s = trees

Words Ending in Y

1. If a consonant comes before the y, change the y to i and add -es.

   cit(y) + -s = cities
   part(y) + -s = parties
2. If a vowel comes before the y, add only -s.

   day + -s = days
   key + -s = keys

Words Ending in F

1. Most words ending in -f form plurals by adding s:

   roof — roofs
   chief — chiefs
2. Some words ending in f change to v and add -es:

   leaf — leaves   wife — wives
   elf — elves   self — selves
   wolf — wolves   half — halves

Plurals that Add Syllables

If another syllable is added when you pronounce the plural, add -es. Word ending in s, ss, ch, sh, tch, x, z add another syllable and therefore add -es.

fox + -es = foxes
church + -es = churches
glass + -es = glasses

Words Ending in O

1. Add -s to most words ending in -o.

   piano + -s = pianos
   radio + -s = radios
2. Exceptions

   echoes   heroes   mulattoes
   potatoes   Negroes   mosquitoes
   tomatoes   torpedoes   mottoes

-en Plurals

Some words add -en to make plurals

ox — oxen
child — children

Inside Plurals

Some words show plural by changing letters within the word:

mouse — mice
man — men

Words Ending in F (continued)

   knife – knives   calf – calves

   shelf – shelves   loaf – loaves

Plurals that Stay the Same

Some words are the same in plural and singular:

cattle	series
deer	sheep
bass	wheat
corps	means
cod	dozen
	swine

one deer, many deer

a series, three series

Inside Plurals (continued)

louse – lice

foot – feet

tooth – teeth

goose – geese

foot – feet

Foreign Words

Some foreign words still keep the plural of the language from which they originated:

alga	algae
oasis	oases
alumnus	alumni
alumna	alumnae
parenthesis	parentheses
thesis	theses
basis	bases
bacterium	bacteria
medium	media
phenomenon	phenomena
axis	axes
criterion	criteria
radius	radii
fungus	fungi

Combination Words

1. If a word is formed by combining two or three words, make a plural of the main word.

   son-in-law = sons-in-law   man-of-war = men-of-war

   editor-in-chief = editors-in-chief

   commander in chief = commanders in chief

2. If the combination is written as one word, add *-s* or *-es* to the end.

   suitcase = suitcases

   cupful = cupfuls

Hint: Check the dictionary for plurals of combination words.

Step. 1. Plurals.   Write the plurals of these words:

1. policeman _____
2. kiss _____
3. hero _____
4. deer _____

5. louse _____
6. criterion _____
7. belief _____
8. turkey _____

9. patient _____

10. fee _____

11. birch _____

12. tomato _____

13. alumnus _____

14. passerby _____

15. series _____

16. tablespoonful _____

17. century _____

18. child _____

19. calf _____

20. roof _____

21. mosquito _____

22. crisis _____

23. bush _____

24. auto _____

25. soprano _____

Step 2. Selecting Plurals.   Change the word in parentheses to a plural and write it in the space provided.

1. Both (woman) _____ used their (knife) _____ carefully.

2. Those (lady) _____ were (alumna) _____ of Eastern College where they sang (solo) _____ in the school play.

3. (Turkey) _____ taste better than (goose) _____, but I could never eat (deer) _____.

4. My (brother-in-law) _____ both serve as (chief) _____ in bread (bakery) _____ where (man) _____ bake dozens of (loaf) _____ daily.

5. The (hero) _____, chased by (wolf) _____, injured them(self) _____ in the (bush) _____.

WRITING THE PARAGRAPH

Select some memories from your childhood as the basis of this written assignment. In fifteen or more sentences of at least three hundred words express your recollections through details of people, places, and actions. You may choose—as your instructor directs—to develop your paragraph by presenting several instances to support your topic sentence, as Julius Passero does on the next page. Or, you may wish again to relate one moment from your past, expanded through details of color and sound and touch like those in the theme by Twyla Boardley on p. 112.

Step 1. A Paragraph About Teachers.   After you read the following paragraph answer the questions.

Horrors and High School Math

 I will never forget my math teachers because I disliked most of them through-out my high school years. I remember my eleventh year math teacher vividly. She was a short, dumpy woman with a straight nose on which a pair of gold-rimmed glasses sat tightly at the end. Before each lesson began, she compelled me, her worst student, to erase the long white columns of algebraic figures from the chalk-boards. Each day she gave pages of homework, expecting us to hand in our assign-ments during the very next class. I hated those pages of math, so I just ignored them. In the end, of course, my reward was a *fifty* in red on my report card. Next, my geometry teacher stands out in my mind. Although Miss Carpenter was no more than twenty-five, she acted like an old witch of a hundred. She wore the same dingy green dress each day. Sloppily, mousy brown hair hung in her eyes, and throughout every lesson she scooped strands and curls off her forehead. Her voice, high-pitched, would screech across the classroom and down the hall. "Julius," I can still hear her squeak, her lips pinched in a little pink circle, "if you don't know about diameters, I'll have to fail you." Everything about that teacher was awful! But of all my math teachers, I disliked most the one who taught me algebra. A tall, lanky man weighing a mere hundred-or-so pounds, this teacher had an angry temper that kept most of us from asking questions. Once a short girl in the last row asked timidly, "Will you explain that again please?" As Mr. Gilian's face grew scarlet, he plunged his hands in his black pants pockets. "Try paying attention," he barked, "and then you won't have to bother me with ridiculous questions." From my past unpleasant experiences with math teachers I have grown to dislike them all automatically; is it any wonder that my math grades never rise above C's and D's?

—Julius Passero

1. What is the topic as announced in the topic sentence? _____

 _____

 What attitude does the writer express? _____

 _____

2. Underline the three subtopic sentences. Circle the specific words in the subtopic sentences that refer the reader back to the topic sentence.

3. Put a check in the left-hand margin next to each line that shows an action or a color. Put a check in the right-hand margin next to each line that uses a word to appeal to the sense of sound.

4. Draw brackets ([ ]) around any three sentences that make transitions (see pp. 84–85) through pronouns. Circle the pronouns that help move one idea into the next.

5. Are the details arranged in chronological order or in order of impor-tance? How do you know? _____

 _____

 _____

Step 2. A Student's Memories of Brooklyn. Write answers to the ques-tions that come after this theme.

The Watermelon Man

The most pleasant memory of my youth in the slum section of Bedford-Stuyvesant in Brooklyn is the scene of the watermelon man and his crew when he drove into our neighborhood on a summer Saturday. His horse would turn first onto Tompkins Avenue. Straining under the weight of many green-striped melons, the horse chewed on its leather bit and heaved the wagon forward slowly, each step an effort. The straw hat it wore shaded its sad brown eyes. Its skin, a dirty brown and white, rippled with the stress of animal work like waves slapping some muddy shore. Patched leather straps that served as reins ran over its hide and flicked at lazy green flies; the insects buzzed in the air or hovered over the shining sample of melon, its pits winking in the sun like a thousand brown eyes. The driver and his friends too are unforgettable. The hands that held the reins were calloused and coarse, yet these overly large hands with square dirty nails held the reins with an almost regal gesture. The veins and muscles in the hands and arms of this kingly watermelon man looked like the ropes on an old homemade swing. He wore a dirty vest, a torn undershirt, and melon-splattered jeans, emblems of his trade. Suddenly, his sons and nephews in the back of the wagon laughed and grinned and started the chant, "Melon, melon, watermelon." The watermelon man, his grey hair moist with sweat, his wide mouth showing a perfect set of teeth, now took up the melody. Red bandanas and gaudy handkerchiefs waving in slight breezes, these fine men sang and hummed the chant. Finally, a transaction began. A woman from a brownstone window across the street called, "Hey, them melons fresh?"

"Yes, ma'am," cried the figures in the wagon.

"Well bring me up one," she snapped from above. "No, not you ugly. You, yeah, the cute one."

"Anything else you wants 'sides a melon, honey?" replied the "cute" one, winking at his companions in the wagon who heckled and howled at this.

"Just a melon!" screamed the hoarse voice of a man from the same window above.

I, standing in front of Jack's Candy Store on the corner of Madison Street, must have snapped that scene firmly in my mind, for I still can hear the cry of the watermelon man as it struts and dances in my ears: "Melon, melon, watermelon. Git de fresh watermelon. Melon. Melon."

—Twyla Boardley

1. This scene may be roughly divided into three thought units: (a) the horse, (b) the driver and his friends, (c) the scene of purchase between a customer and the watermelon men. Copy out the subtopic sentence that introduces each of these units of thought.

    a. _____

    b. _____

    c. _____

2. Underline each picture you find easy to visualize because of color or sound words.

3. Draw brackets around the sentence that uses a semicolon. Is the semi-

colon used correctly? How do you know? _____

_____

4. Why does Miss Boardley mention the place of the moment in the topic

sentence? _____

_____

Why is the time, "a summer Saturday," important to mention in the

topic sentence? _____

_____

5. What does the dialogue contribute to the paragraph? _____

_____

Requirements

Follow these suggestions before you write a one-paragraph theme that in some way reveals some memorable feature of your youth. Read the samples on pp. 111–112 before you begin.

A Checklist: What To Do In Theme #3

1. Decide, with your instructor's help, whether to write a paragraph about *one* specific moment in your childhood or a paragraph which employs two or three instances to show something about your youth.
2. Write a topic sentence (see p. 7) that announces the subject of the paragraph and gives your attitude toward the subject. If you tell about one moment only, mention time and place in the topic sentence.
3. Use subtopic sentences (see pp. 72–74) to introduce each new aspect of the topic. Notice how Miss Boardley (p. 112) and Mr. Passero (p. 111) —both writing different kinds of paragraphs—use subtopic sentences to tell in general terms the one specific part of the paragraph that will follow.
4. Use colors. Miss Boardley says "lazy green flies."
5. Use words that tell sounds like *squeak, screamed,* or *snapped.*
6. Use words that show lively actions: Miss Boardley says the horse "chewed the leather bit and heaved the wagon forward. . . ."
7. Use at least one line of someone's spoken words. Which spoken sentence in Mr. Passero's theme is most original?

Hint: See pp. 48–50 for punctuating quotations.

8. Show details of the scene; use a touch word and a word that appeals to the sense of smell.

9. Use effective transitions to tie your sentences together: see pp. 81–85.
10. Arrange your details either in chronological order or in order of importance, whichever suits your paragraph best.
11. Use at least three of the new vocabulary words on pp. 69–71.
12. Open one sentence with a word that ends in *-ly*.
13. Start at least three sentences with different subordinators given on pp. 90–92.
14. Use a semicolon correctly (see p. 86).
15. Proofread your paragraph (see below), looking especially for run-on errors, sentence fragments, and errors in writing plurals.
16. Give your paragraph a lively, effective title (see pp. 197–199).

Some Topics to Think About

In case you have trouble finding a topic, reread some of the sentences on pp. 71–72. Here are some other topics you might wish to write about:

1. when you played hooky
2. how you used to get in trouble at school
3. your first date
4. the fun you had with a local team or gang
5. the first job you ever had
6. the ways you would help out at school
7. a teacher or some teachers you liked (or disliked)
8. three of the worst rules you had to obey in high school or junior high school
9. the time(s) your mother had to come to school
10. how a special teacher taught you some important lessons
11. your first disappointment
12. the fear(s) you had as a child
13. getting arrested
14. the early heroes you had as a child
15. the first time(s) you did something you knew was wrong or bad

Proofreading

Proofreading is the act of rereading your final theme copy to look for errors. The suggestions below will help you locate careless mistakes.

TIPS FOR BETTER PROOFREADING

1. Read *slowly*. This is not a job done by skimming. Look at — and read aloud, if necessary — every word. Don't let your eyes move too swiftly from one word to the next.

---

2. Use a ruler or a blank sheet of paper below each line; this will help you locate spelling errors by cutting off later words from your line of vision. Block any words that may distract you on the line you are checking. The fewer words you examine at a time, the easier it is to find spelling errors.

3. Examine each syllable of each word. Touch each syllable of difficult words as you proofread.

4. Be aware of your own usual errors. A glance at your Progress Sheet (p. 483) before you do any written work puts you on your guard. If you're a chronic run-on writer, know the run-on Stop Signs. If you write fragments, know the fragment Stop Signs. If you usually confuse *its* and *it's* and you have used one of those words in your paragraph, stop for a second to analyze the spelling you've chosen.

5. If you are writing in class, cross out errors neatly or erase them neatly. Some students like to skip lines so they can insert any words or ideas they leave out through carelessness. If you've left out a word or words, draw a caret (‸) be-

low the line and insert what was omitted. Do it this way:

went
So we awakened early and ‸ to the beach

6. You can't look up every word to check spelling, but you do know which words you are unsure of. *Look them up in the dictionary.* And keep a record of the words you usually spell wrong (see "Your Own Demon List," p. 459).

Step 1. Practice with Proofreading.   Correct the errors in the excerpt from a student sample below by following the suggestions above.

Even when i was in the forth grade of public school 235, I was insecure and unsure of of myslef. Once I had to in front of the class to read a composition. Its frightening to stand in front of other childrens. All I could thing about was was my squeaky voice I was scarred my friendes would laug at me even thought they new me. So many brown a blue eyes starring at me made it worser. Atlhough my Teacher kept shouted, "speak up, Ellen!" I just remained quite.

THE PROFESSIONALS SPEAK

The amusing story below builds upon youthful experiences in a school setting. Notice the appeals to the senses of color and sound. Also, notice how short the sentences are, and be prepared to explain *why* they are so short when you answer the questions at the end.

The Girl's Banana

She was six. I was five and a half. She wore green. I wore all colors.
She was standing in the school yard. I was, too. So we met. She was peeling her banana. I watched. She leaned over to drink from the fountain. I walked up to her

and leaned over, too, and took a big bite out of her banana. She stopped drinking and screamed. I ran away.

I ran all the way home and had lunch and came back to school and walked into the classroom. Little green dress was there, and she was crying. She looked at my teacher and pointed at me. I started to run, but I changed my mind. I wanted to see what would happen, so I stayed. But I was sorry.

My teacher put her fingers around my neck and brought me down to the principal's office. Little green dress came along to tell on me. Her teacher gave me a bad look when we walked in. She was holding the banana peels.

The principal was big and fat and asked why I took a bite out of the little girl's banana. She said "little girl," but I was littler than she was. Anyway, I didn't answer. She asked me again. I didn't answer again. My teacher asked me why I took a bite. I didn't answer her. She said for me to look her in the face. I looked out the window. She said turn around to her. I looked down at my shoelaces. They were brown, and one was untied. Little green dress's teacher stuck her finger in my face and said I should talk if I knew what was good for me. I knew what was good for me. I didn't talk.

The principal took hold of my shoulder and wiggled it. She didn't hurt me, but she was big and fat and she could have. She said I should hurry up and talk and said didn't I have a tongue. I had a tongue. But it didn't want to move. She asked me if I ate lunch. I didn't answer. She asked me if I was hungry. I held my breath. She asked me if my mother fed me at home. My lips were beginning to quiver. She asked me again if my mother fed me. If she had been a smart principal, she would have known that my mother fed me. Her mother fed her. I began to cry. Everybody started to talk at once, and I was getting mad. Little green dress looked at me, and tears rolled down my cheek. And I was breathing with my throat.

The principal pushed me into a corner and said not to turn around. She said that would fix me. It was all right. But little green dress wasn't. She started to cry. The principal told her not to cry, because I was being-fixed. I wanted to turn around and tell her that I was very all right, but I didn't because if she was smart, then she would know. If she was smart.

Everybody's feet went out of the office except the principal's. Her feet walked to the desk. I could hear her breathing. She didn't breathe right, not like my mother. I wanted to tell her, but I didn't think she would breathe like I wanted her to; she was stubborn.

I stood in the corner looking. The corner turned into two corners. Then three. Then I couldn't count any more, and my head was bothering me. I was thirsty, too. I wanted to ask the principal if I could go out in the hall and get a drink of water. But I didn't. Couldn't she tell I was thirsty? If I was the principal and she was me, I would let her go and get a drink. I was getting tired, too, and I wanted to ask her if I could sit down. I wanted to ask her a lot of things, but nothing came out of my mouth. So I waited.

I got sleepy waiting, so I closed my eyes. No more corners, and I fell asleep standing up.

But I didn't wake up standing. I was straight up and down, but I was on the floor looking up. For a minute I thought the world was upside down. But it wasn't.

I got up and walked to the door and looked out into the hallway. Nobody was there. Everything was quiet. I walked back to the corner where I was supposed to wait. I waited until it got dark outside. I thought a hundred years went by. I walked out of the office and held my breath until I reached the heavy doors. Then my legs ran all the way home so fast that I was there before I even thought about running home.

I walked into the kitchen. The whole family was having supper, and they were laughing and screaming about me biting the girl's banana. I ran out of the kitchen and through the parlor and down the front steps. It was dark and lonely out. I didn't way to go crazy, so I sat down on the curb and cried.

Little green dress came by wearing a red dress. I stopped crying and stuck my tongue out at her. She stuck her tongue out at me. I stuck my tongue out at her again, and she ran away. She skipped down the block and turned the corner, and I hated her. I got up from the curb and walked across the street. I didn't know what to do with myself, so I sat down on the curb over there and looked at the lights in the windows of my house. Then I cried again. Nobody understood me. Not even me.

I looked at the moon. It was big and round and white. It looked just like a hole in the sky. I wanted to crawl right through and see what heaven was like. But I didn't do it. I wanted to stay awhile and think of little green dress's red dress. I loved her. If I knew why, I would know why I took a bite out of her banana.

—William Carl Bondarenko

Step 1. Checking on Details.   Write the answers to these questions.

1. From whose point of view is this story told? _____

   How old is the narrator? _____

2. Why has the writer used such short sentences? _____

   _____

3. Which pictures are most vivid in their appeal to color? _____

   _____

4. Underline the pictures which you think show the best action. Circle the words that give lively sounds.

5. Explain the last few sentences. How do they help to summarize the child-

   ish silliness of the entire moment? _____

   _____

   _____

Step 2. Several Examples as Support.   Read the following selection which develops a topic through several instances. Answer the questions after the paragraph.

Down South

Down South seemed like a dream when I was on the train going back to New York. I saw a lot of things down South that I never saw in my whole life before and most of them I didn't ever want to see again. I saw a great big old burly black man hit a pig in the head with the back of an ax. The pig screamed, oink-oinked a few times, lay down, and started kicking and bleeding . . . and died. When he was real little, I used to chase him, catch him, pick him up, and play catch with him. He was a greedy old pig, but I used to like him. One day when it was real cold, I ate a piece of that pig, and I still liked him. One day I saw Grandma kill a rattlesnake with a hoe. She chopped the snake's head off in the front yard, and I sat on the porch and watched the snake's body keep wiggling till it was nighttime. And I saw an old brown hound dog named Old Joe eat a rat one day, right out in the front yard. He caught the rat in the woodpile and started tearing him open. Old Joe was eating everything in the rat. He ate something that looked like the yellow part in an egg, and I didn't eat eggs for a long time after that. I saw a lady rat have a lot of little baby rats on a pile of tobacco leaves. She had to be a lady, because my first-grade teacher told a girl that ladies don't cry about little things, and the rat had eleven little hairless pink rats, and she didn't even squeak about it.

I made a gun down South out of a piece of wood, some tape, a piece of tire-tube rubber, a nail, some wire, a piece of pipe, and a piece of door hinge. And I saw nothing but blood where my right thumbnail used to be after I shot it for the first time. The nail grew back, little by little. I saw a lot of people who had roots worked on them, but I never saw anybody getting roots worked on them.

Down South sure was a crazy place, and it was good to be going back to New York.

—Claude Brown
Manchild in the Promised Land

1. After rereading the topic sentence, copy out the words that tell the topic. _____

_____

What words tell the attitude? _____

_____

2. Read aloud the examples the writer gives to develop the topic he has suggested in the topic sentence.
3. Draw two lines under each word or words that show a lively action.

REACHING HIGHER

Step 1. A Photo into Words. Look at the photograph on p. 68. Write a topic sentence that introduces the main subject of the picture and some opinion you have about the subject. Write subtopic sentences—if necessary—to introduce each aspect of the topic; add details of color, sound, smell, touch, and action to support each subtopic sentence.

Step 2. A New Paragraph Attempt. Select a topic from pp. 71–72 or p. 114 and write a paragraph which you develop through a *number* of instances instead of just two or three instances as you have already done. Reread "Memories of Crossgates School" on p. 79 to refresh your memory about this type of paragraph.

Step 3. Building Lively Quotations. A sentence that gives someone's exact words can often be expanded through action and sensory language to paint a vivid picture. Both Mr. Passero's and Miss Boardley's paragraphs are rich in lively quotation sentences. A sentence like this:

"Wake up!"

draws a much poorer picture for the reader than this:

"Hurry up!" my sister said angrily, as her brown eyes flashed and she stamped her foot on the floor.

HOW TO DO IT

A. Tell who talks:
   "Hurry up!" *my sister said.*
B. Tell how or when the words are spoken:
   "Hurry up!" my sister said *angrily.*
C. Add a detail to describe the speaker's face and/or some action or movement:
   "Hurry up!" my sister said angrily as her brown eyes flashed and she stamped her foot on the floor. [Description of speaker] [Action]

Expand each of these quotations by adding details as explained above. The first is done for you. Check correct punctuation, pp. 48–50.

1. Please sit down. *Raising her eyebrows in surprise, the speaker mumbled, "Please sit down," as the listeners jumped to their feet and applauded.*

2. Call the police! _____

   _____

   _____

   _____

3. You'd better bring your mother to school with you tomorrow. _____

   _____

   _____

   _____

4. All right wise guy. What's your hurry? _____

_____

_____

_____

5. I apologize. _____

_____

_____

_____

6. I tried the best I could. _____

_____

_____

_____

chapter 4

HIGH SCHOOL AND COLLEGE: SEEING THE DIFFERENCE

INTRODUCTION

By now you are pretty much caught up in the rush of college events: you no longer lose your way in the corridors of the strangely shaped Science Building; you can run from one end of campus to another in two minutes and still drop into your seat before the professor starts his lecture precisely at 9 A.M.; you know how to look at the instructor and nod your head, whether or not you know what he is talking about; you have found, if you are lucky, some subject that excites you, one that you want as the focus of your life's work. High school seems far behind you . . . yet not far enough from your life that you don't automatically make comparisons between what happened then and what is happening now. Is your own approach to learning different now? Are the teachers and the methods different here in college or just like those in high school? Was high school smaller and more friendly? Is college a challenge to you, a place you enjoy, or a place you dread?

One of the best ways we have to analyze, understand, and evaluate is through comparison and contrast. It is second nature for us to compare one experience with another to see points of resemblance and difference. In writing, such a process adds force to your style: the reader comes to understand the value of your experiences as you yourself put together the strands of comparison or contrast.

In this chapter you will learn a variety of methods to develop comparison-contrast paragraphs. One method separates the objects of comparison into two distinct parts in the paragraph; another method blends the two objects as you discuss their similarities or differences point by point; still another paragraph design uses both similarities and differences. You will learn how to compare two dissimilar objects in *analogy,* and you will learn in a *mood* paragraph how to compare your own inner feelings with a scene that surrounds you at a given moment. In addition, you will learn to use single-sentence comparisons in order to add more sharpness and clarity to a visual paragraph. And there will be more hints about correctness as you learn sentence agreement.

VOCABULARY

Step 1. Words for Campus Personalities. These words will make more vivid your attempts to describe people who surround you on campus. Each word is used so that you can figure out its meaning. Write your definition in Column I. Then, check a dictionary (or Appendix A) to see how close you came; write the dictionary definition in Column II.

		I Your Definition	II The Dictionary Meaning
Example:		*energetic*	*sparkling*
1. scintillating	Her *scintillating* lectures are filled with vivid examples and lively gestures.		
2. aimless	Dr. Hart's *aimless* remarks during lectures always leave me wondering what the purpose of his lessons is.		
3. cynical	Dr. Caldwell's *cynical* nature makes him always find fault with our good intentions.		
4. obnoxious	Because I object to men with very long hair, I find that fellow particularly *obnoxious.*		
5. hostile	Some campus groups are so *hostile* to anyone who disagrees with them that they have very few real friends beyond their own circles of interest.		
6. stimulating	The study of data processing is *stimulating* enough for me to want to work with computers all my life!		
7. erudite	His broad range of knowledge and his interest in intellectual activities make him quite an *erudite* scholar.		

8. egotistical   Any student *egotistical* enough to boast to everyone that he knows more than the professor is bound not to succeed.

9. perceptive   My college counselor shows that he is *perceptive* by knowing my problems before I tell them to him.

10. dedicated   Professor Coonfield is the most *dedicated* biology teacher I know: who else works so many hours in the lab and helps his students whenever they need it?

Step 2. Picking Out Meanings. Put a check next to the letter that best completes the statement.

1. If you are *aimless* you
   - *a.* cannot shoot a gun straight
   - *b.* have no clear goal
   - *c.* need no help
2. An *egotistical* person
   - *a.* shows that he believes he is best
   - *b.* performs in shows
   - *c.* is better than most other people
3. If you are *stimulating*
   - *a.* you will not bore anyone
   - *b.* you will not be bored by anyone
   - *c.* you read many books
4. A *perceptive* teacher
   - *a.* is a counselor with problems
   - *b.* knows everything about his subject
   - *c.* senses things without knowing definitely about them
5. A *hostile* act is
   - *a.* usually performed by the host or hostess
   - *b.* an unfriendly one
   - *c.* a political rally
6. An *obnoxious* person
   - *a.* offends other people
   - *b.* wears long hair
   - *c.* is always a hard worker

7. *Scintillating* conversation
   a. sparkles with life and excitement
   b. is dull
   c. usually cannot last long
8. If you are *erudite*
   a. you like to talk to people
   b. you have a great deal of knowledge
   c. you are polite
9. *Cynical* people
   a. try to please others as often as possible
   b. are easy to please
   c. find fault everywhere and deny goodness in others
10. A *dedicated* student
   a. is very interested in and concerned with his schoolwork
   b. has very little interest in his schoolwork
   c. gives everything he has to his friends

Step 3. Words for Contrasting Moods. Check the definitions of these words to describe moods. Write definitions you understand in the blank spaces (see Appendix A).

"Up" Moods	*"Down" Moods*
rapturous _____	irate _____
confident _____	depressed _____
affectionate _____	lethargic _____
serene _____	indifferent _____
magnanimous _____	callous _____

Step 4. Listening In on Moods. Each statement made below identifies a mood named in Step 3. Name the mood that the person who speaks seems to be experiencing.

1. "I just don't feel like doing anything. Man, I'm tired." _____

   _____

2. "Let me kiss you again. I love to hold you." _____

   _____

3. "If I get my hands on him, I'll kill him. I'll tear him from limb to limb." _____

4. "Oh, it was not important. Of course I forgive your mistake. You really couldn't help it." _____

5. "I feel so calm and peaceful." _____

6. "Look, I don't care one way or the other." _____

7. "I know I can do the job right." _____

8. "I'm so delighted that I'm overjoyed. What a beautiful, wonderful, sunny day!" _____

9. "I never felt so rotten in all my life." _____

10. "It's easy to ignore other people's problems. You just have to harden yourself to everybody else's troubles. Not even a hungry child bothers me." _____

BUILDING COMPOSITION SKILLS

Finding the Topic

Step 1. Talking It Over. From your seat, speak for a minute on one of these aspects of school life. Show how your specific experiences with the high school or college scene illustrates your point, as Thomas Baim does below.

1. the physical setting: high school and college
2. college and high school teachers: the main difference
3. college and high school: teachers are all alike
4. control versus freedom in school experiences
5. student rights in the school community
6. student dress
7. lectures versus class discussion: which is better?
8. college is more unfriendly than high school
9. students (should, should not) help plan courses
10. student violence versus student reason: getting things done
11. the student lounge: what high schools need too
12. the student lounge: abuse and vandalism
13. buying your own books: a great (awful) idea for high schools
14. the high school, college, and job training
15. machines can teach as well as teachers

To me lectures are worthless; group discussions make much better and more interesting class sessions. Mr. Goldman, my junior history teacher at Park Lane High, lectured to us all the time. Even though he had a lively booming voice and a good knowledge of his subject, after thirty minutes, feet would shuffle on the floor, pencils would drop, girls would whisper and yawn as the teacher turned his back to write on the board. I loved history, but I found myself staring out the window at the sky or the clouds. But Mr. Rudnicki, my psychology teacher here at State, never lectures. Sure, he contributes information to our discussions—sometimes he talks for ten minutes straight—but lots of other people talk as well. It's much more exciting to hear different voices and different opinions. We all sit around with our chairs in a circle and usually more than half the class talks at each session. I know it's much harder to learn in this kind of class because you never really know what's 'right' since there is often no definite information. But I find I'm always thinking about what went on in my psych class, and I can't wait to forget what I scribbled in my notebook during a lecture!

—Thomas Baim

Step 2. Sharing Ideas in Panels. Divide the class into groups of four or five and discuss the following subject:

While everyone should go to high school, not everyone should go to college.

Each person should try to give some illustration, experience, or factual detail to illustrate his opinion. After ten or fifteen minutes of discussion, select one person from each panel as leader to summarize before the whole class the various points discussed. A session may follow where students in the class can ask questions of the various panel leaders. Here are some points you might want to consider: add several of your own to these suggested in one class.

Pro

1. High school training gives enough education; people need no more classroom training and much more job training.

2. College requires special abilities, skills, and concentration which not everybody has.

3. We need people to do plumbing, carpentry, shoemaking, etc.; if everyone goes to college, who will perform all of those services?

Con

1. Everyone should go to college! The more learning a person gets, the better his chances of earning more money and prestige.

2. Saying "not everyone should go to college" means blacks and other minorities should not go to college. This is a racist statement, an attempt to kill open-admissions policies to keep seats in college available for white middle-class Americans.

3. Everyone should not go to high school *or* college. Some people who have no interest in book learning might do very well learning from their jobs at the age of fourteen or fifteen. Why should they have to suffer in a classroom when they could be having rewarding experiences elsewhere?

Comparisons for Clearer Pictures

An important way of adding liveliness to your written expression is to make comparisons so that the reader sees clearly some picture you are describing. Notice how the picture in Column I below is given new life in Column II by means of a comparison.

I

Her blue eyes sparkled.

II

Her eyes sparkled *like small blue circles of ice.*

By using the word *like* (or *as*) in II above, the writer compares *eyes* to *small blue circles of ice.* Such a comparison, using *like* or *as*, is called a *simile.*

A *metaphor* is a comparison that leaves out the comparing word *like* or *as*:

Her eyes were small blue circles of ice.

This kind of comparison is often very forceful because it shows that the object is so much like the thing to which it is being compared that it almost becomes that thing. Look again at the difference.

Her eyes were *like small blue circles of ice.*

Here, a woman's eyes are compared to circles of ice, and there are two distinct features of the comparison, *eyes* and *blue circles of ice.*

Her eyes *were small blue circles of ice.*

Here, the woman's eyes are said to *be* those *blue circles of ice.* It is as if the eyes and the icy blue circles were one and the same; the eyes take on all the qualities of the ice.

Sometimes, to add liveliness, a writer can give some nonhuman object living qualities. The comparison between a nonhuman object and a living thing is called *personification:*

The hot day dragged its weary feet into the evening.

In the sentence above, the *day,* a nonhuman object, is given the qualities of a person who is tired: the words *dragged its weary feet* express the human quality.

Step 1. Reading Lively Comparisons. Read aloud these comparisons by professional writers. Explain the meaning of the comparison. Which sentence lets you see most clearly what the writer had in mind? Which comparison is most original?

1. In the sky the sun hung like an apricot.

   —J. Ernest Wright

2. Life is too much like a pathless wood where your face burns and tickles with the cobwebs broken across it, and one eye is weeping from a twig's having lashed across it open.

   —Robert Frost

3. The yellow fog . . . rubs its back upon the windowpanes . . . licked its tongue into the corners of the evening . . . slipped by the terrace, made a sudden leap, and seeing that it was a soft October night, curled once about the house and fell asleep.

   —T. S. Eliot

4. Like as the waves make towards the pebbled shore, so do our minutes hasten to their end.

—William Shakespeare

5. If dreams die, life is a broken-winged bird that cannot fly.

—Langston Hughes

6. The budding twigs spread out their fan to catch the breezy air.

—William Wordsworth

7. Then, there was a crush of falling timbers nearby and Scarlett saw a thin tongue of flame lick up over the roof of the warehouse in whose sheltering shadow they sat.

—Margaret Mitchell

8. His face was white as pie-dough and his arms were lank and white as peeled sticks.

—Robert Smith

9. The faintness of the voice . . . was like the last feeble echo of a sound made long and long ago.

—Charles Dickens

10. The mysterious East faced me, perfumed like a flower, silent like death, dark like a grave.

—Joseph Conrad

Step 2. Comparisons of Your Own. Using the word groups below, write sentences that make a comparison in a vivid picture. Strive for originality, humor, beauty, clarity. Use any of the three types of comparisons you have learned so far—simile, metaphor, personification. The first is done for you in two ways.

1. a bus

The bus sputtered and coughed; then, with a loud sneeze of exhaust it shook down the street like a sick old man.

—Carl Faber

Like an old grey elephant the school bus plodded down White Plains Road.

—Carol Grosso

2. the wind

_____

_____

_____

_____

3. an old tree

_____

_____

_____

_____

4. a teacher's voice _____

_____

_____

5. youth _____

_____

_____

6. a cat _____

_____

_____

7. a smile _____

_____

_____

8. the radio _____

_____

_____

9. an old Ford _____

_____

_____

10. love _____

_____

_____

Step 3. Avoiding Trite Comparisons. When a comparison is used too frequently in language it loses its freshness, its force, its originality. Any
statement or expression that is repeated frequently is called *trite*, or *hack-*

neyed. Such expressions appear numbered from 1 to 10 below. For each one, rewrite the comparison so that is has a new and lively strength. Use separate paper. The first is done for you.

1. quiet as a mouse—quiet as a schoolyard in the gray rain of a Sunday morning
2. red as a beet
3. white as a ghost
          or
   white as a sheet
4. fresh as a daisy
5. old as the hills
6. blue as the sky
7. as different as night and day
8. warm as toast
9. strong like a lion
10. happy as a lark

Step 4. Comparisons in Paragraphs. Reread quickly the selections mentioned under I below. Copy into the space under II an example of the type of comparison mentioned.

    I   *II*

1. "The Watermelon Man," p. 112 (simile)   _____

2. "Jungle Boy," pp. 59–60 (metaphor)   _____

3. "Grandma," p. 66 (simile)   _____

Getting It All Together: Transitions III

As you may recall, certain words help one idea in a paragraph flow smoothly into the next idea. The *transition* words below, cementing together ideas so that the thoughts are related clearly, show relationships you might want to indicate in your paragraph.

Transition Words That Add One Thought to Another

		Transition Words to Compare Ideas
in addition	likewise	in the same way
moreover	nor	similarly
and	further	likewise
and then	next	
besides	last	
again		
too		
furthermore		

Transition Words to Contrast Ideas or Admit a Point

but	although
still	on the other hand
however	in contrast
nevertheless	otherwise
on the contrary	conversely
after all	while this may be true
notwithstanding	yet
even though	granted
though	in spite of

Transition Words to Show that One Idea Results from Another

as a result	accordingly
thus	therefore
because	consequently
since	then
hence	

Step 1. Transitions for Smoothness. In this paragraph, fill in each blank with a transition word that will help move one idea smoothly into the next. The comments in the margin tell what kinds of transition words you need. Make sure that the word you select makes sense in the blank.

The True Musician

[Contrast] _____ Plato believed that music played a strong part in a man's education, he did not ignore other areas of learning. Music, through rhythm and

[Add] harmony, could bring grace to the soul _____ a man educated in music

[Result] could develop a true sense of judgment; _____ he would be able to recognize quality in art and nature and could respond with praise for good things.

[Compare] _____ a man who knew music could, without having to think too

[Contrast] long, give blame to any bad artistic works. _____ any man who devoted his life only to music risked the chance of becoming too womanly,

[Result] too softened and soothed. _____ such a man would be a feeble warrior and of little use to the Greeks. Someone who practiced gymnastics,

[Contrast] _____, could fill himself with pride and spirit and become twice

[Compare] the man that he was. _____ he could develop courage for battle.

[Admit point] _____ athletics made an essential part of the educated man, Plato also knew that too much focus on physical training could make a man ex-

[Add] cessively violent and fierce. _____ he might come to hate philosophy

[Compare] and the art of persuasion in preference to battle. _____ such a man

[Result] would live in ignorance and would not be civilized. _____ Plato showed that the man who learned music and athletics in good balance was best: "He who mingles music with gymnastics in the fairest proportions . . . may be rightly called the true musician. . . ."

Transition Words That Summarize

therefore	consequently
in conclusion	thus
finally	to sum up
as a result	accordingly
in short	in brief
as I have (shown)	in other words
(said)	
(stated)	

Transition Words That Emphasize

surely	indeed
certainly	truly
to be sure	in fact
undoubtedly	without a doubt

Transition Words That Tell an Example Will Follow

for example	specifically
for instance	as an illustration
as proof	to illustrate

Step 2. Example, Summary, Emphasis: Transitions. From the three lists above, select one word that will fit in the blank as a good transition. Comments in the margin tell the kinds of transition words you need.

1. Communication between different points in New York is not always diffi-

[Example] cult. _____, at Forty-second Street passengers can board trains for any borough but Staten Island.

[Emphasize] 2. Learning does not always supply all the answers. _____ a learned man is happy if he knows enough questions!

3. More and more young men and women show a preference for the music

[Example] of the good old days. _____ many young contemporary musicians have begun reviving the tunes that their parents enjoyed long ago.

4. Modern medicine can boast of a number of extraordinary accomplish-

[Example] ments. _____ heart transplants, long thought of as impossible,

[Emphasize] are now common. _____ this achievement speaks for the remarkable advances science has made in our century.

5. Large areas of Jamaica Bay have been contaminated by pollution from a

[Summarize] variety of sources. _____ local residents have urged greater care in disposing of waste and in planning airport extensions.

Step 3. Checking More Transitions.   Read "A Vast Difference," pp. 138–139. Circle the transition words that add, compare, contrast, show result, summarize, or indicate example.

THE COMPARISON-CONTRAST PARAGRAPH

A favorite method of paragraph and essay development for most writers involves comparison-contrast. *Comparison* means showing how things are alike and *contrast* means showing how things are different. Sometimes a paragraph may be developed through illustrations of how things are *different*; other paragraphs discuss *similarities* only; still others may treat both *likenesses and differences.* The writer himself decides which approach he wishes to take.

Hint: If you are asked to *compare* two things, it usually means that you should *contrast* them as well.

Whatever approach you choose, there are several helpful patterns you can use to make the comparison effective.

Likenesses or Differences

Pattern 1.   In this paragraph pattern you discuss one of the two objects for comparison first; then you discuss the other object. But you decide on *one basic way* in which the two objects are either alike or different and illustrate your opinion with details. For instance, you might realize that comparing high school and college is really too big a job to handle effectively in a paragraph. The topic is broad, and you might have trouble putting all your ideas together smoothly. By singling out one basic difference or similarity, you can limit the general topic "comparing high school and college." For example, you might decide that high school and college are basically different in the kinds of teachers that serve at each institution. The first part of the paragraph would give some illustration about high school teachers; the next part of the paragraph would illustrate something about college teachers.

HINTS ABOUT PATTERN 1

1. The subtopic sentence (see pp. 72–73) will help you to introduce the basic difference for each object.
2. One interesting way to illustrate your point is to discuss first *one specific instance* at high school and then one *specific instance* at college. Each instance would be a dramatic moment expanded from your life. In a paragraph

---

contrasting teachers at high school and college, the first moment might show the time a high school teacher lost his temper; the next moment could show one specific time a college teacher showed patience and understanding. By using concrete sensory detail (see pp. 5–6), you would make each moment come alive with color, sound, and action.

3. If you want to use more than one instance from your experience to illustrate each part of your point, remember that each instance also needs vivid sensory language. True, you will not be able to go into great detail for each instance, but you certainly need to make the moment as lively and clear as possible. For example, if you are contrasting teachers at high school and college, you might show briefly how a high school teacher lost his temper, and how another high school teacher refused to answer questions; you might then show about college teachers how one showed patience and understanding, and how one had lunch with you just to chat and make you feel comfortable.

4. Sometimes you can combine 2 and 3 above: state briefly several instances that illustrate your point about the first object; then focus upon one dramatic moment that illustrates your point about the second object.

Step 1. A Student's Theme. Read the student sample below. Answer aloud the questions after the paragraph.

The School Lunchroom

   One way to illustrate the great difference in student freedom in high school and college is to examine the cafeteria. In the Central High School lunchroom there is great regulation and control. On any school day Mr. Travis stands behind a tall silver microphone at the front of the room and after several short blasts on his whistle, shouts out the order in which students at the various tables may join the line at the lunch counter. At the counter itself there is the choice between the usual veal in mud-brown gravy and the old standby, pasty tuna fish on rye; but a student must choose quickly because the rush is on to feed several hundred people in a forty-five-minute period. To encourage our speed, one serving woman at the hot table smacks her metal spoon on a wooden board, shouting, "Keep it moving!" And although talking and laughter among students seem to show that freedom really exists, limitations are everywhere. Five or six teachers drift between the tables reminding students to lower their voices. Singing, aimless wandering around the room, smoking, shouting across tables are all forbidden. If anyone violates these rules, he must report to one of Mr. Travis' "goons," an obnoxious senior who sits at a table up front and with a hostile look copies down the student's name in large blue letters. All these regulations make freedom really absent from the high school lunchroom. On the other hand, a visit to the Brooklyn College cafeteria shows that few limitations on freedom exist. On a December afternoon surrounding me as I eat a salad of rare roast beef and a slice of peach crumb pie (a far cry from Central High's stew) are the scintillating voices of hundreds of students. At the next table five men in purple and white fraternity sweaters play poker noisily, clinking dimes on the scratched formica tables. Sometimes a dollar bill flips like a frog to the floor, snatched up quickly by someone's fist. Down near the glass exit doors a small student combo of guitars and bongo drums beats out a stimulating number. A dozen people around the group clap in time to the music. Suddenly a shout of "Hey, Charlie" cuts through the cloud of cigarette smoke, and a girl in a short skirt rushes with open arms towards a fellow with a kinky red beard. They embrace affectionately, kiss with a loud smack, and then laugh with their arms locked; no one but me, it seems, gives them a second glance. Above all this racket indoors a student outside screams over a bull horn the date of the next rally for peace in Viet-Nam. One of his friends runs from table to table giving out mimeographed papers in red and pink and green. This kind of cafeteria activity is a striking example of what college freedom can mean and what high schools lack in the way of student liberty.

—Paul Columbo

1. What is the basic way in which the high school and college are said to differ?
2. What two moments does Mr. Columbo use to illustrate his point?
3. Why do you think the writer sets both of his illustrations in a cafeteria?
4. Which, in your opinion, are the liveliest images of action? What details name sounds? Where is color used effectively?
5. Read each of the two subtopic sentences. What key words are used in the subtopic sentences, words that have similar meanings?

Step 2. Practicing the Pattern. Assume that you would develop each subject in Column I in a comparison-contrast paragraph like Pattern 1. In Column II, write down one basic way in which the two objects are either alike or dissimilar. In Column III, tell two specific moments you could use to illustrate each object. Look at the example.

I	II	III
	Major Similarity or	*Two Illustrations*
Topic to Compare	*Difference*	*a.* time I sat through an
1. baseball and football	baseball: dull	eleven inning no-hitter
	football: exciting	*b.* time I watched the Jets and Packers at Shea Stadium
2. books and television		
3. driving and racing		

4. city and country winters   _____   _____

_____   _____

_____

_____

5. cafeteria meals and home-cooked meals   _____   _____

_____   _____

_____

_____

Pattern 2. In this comparison-contrast paragraph you discuss a few important points about the first object; then you discuss a few important points about the second. There is no basic focus of comparison as there is in Pattern 1. In a paragraph comparing high school and college in this manner, you might, for example, discuss these three points:

1. the physical appearance of your high school
2. the nature of student freedom in your high school
3. the atmosphere of friendliness in your high school.

Of course, each point would need some kind of detail to support it. After you finish your discussion of high school, you would then discuss

1. the physical appearance of your college
2. the nature of student freedom in your college
3. the friendliness in your college.

SOME HINTS ABOUT PATTERN 2

1. A subtopic sentence can help you introduce each of the two objects you are comparing.
2. You will not be able to go into too much detail for each of the points. However, make sure you can support each point with some kind of illustration.
3. Pattern 2 often tends to yield a dull paragraph because each point is repeated twice, once for each object. Lively illustrations and vocabulary that does not use the same words over and over can overcome the dullness somewhat.

Step 3. Understanding Another Approach. Assume each topic in Column I would be developed in a comparison-contrast paragraph like Pattern 2. In Column II list three significant points that you could use to illustrate each part of the topic. Look at the example.

I	*II*
Topic for Comparison	*Discussion Points*
1. city and country summers	1. traffic
	2. kinds of sports
	3. landscape
2. dogs and cats	_____
	_____
	_____
3. hamburger stands versus "fancy" restaurants	_____
	_____
	_____
4. student-planned schools and faculty-planned schools	_____
	_____
	_____
5. women doctors and men doctors	_____
	_____
	_____

Pattern 3. This pattern does not separate the two objects you are discussing. Instead, it treats both objects together as each point of comparison is mentioned. For example, in a paragraph comparing high school and college, let's assume that the writer wants to discuss these three points:

1. physical appearance
2. the nature of student freedom
3. friendliness.

After he mentions each point, the writer would discuss both the high school and college in relation to that point. He would illustrate how high school and college compared in physical appearance; he would then illustrate student freedom at both places; finally he would compare friendliness at the two schools.

Step 4. A Point-by-Point Comparison. Read the student paragraph below developed by means of Pattern 3. Answer the questions that come after it.

A Vast Difference

Queensborough Community College differs vastly in many ways from my old high school, Samuel J. Tilden. In the first place, no two institutions could look more unlike! Queensborough spreads out on a peaceful hill on an old golf course overlooking Jamaica Bay, and the air is filled with the salty smell of the sea and the creaking of gulls. Tilden, on the other hand, stands in one old building on Tilden Avenue in the heart of Brooklyn, surrounded by parked cars and traffic. The blare of a horn or the roar of truck engines frequently break in on a lesson while everyone strains to hear the teacher's words. Aside from these dissimilarities in appearance, student freedom marks another difference between the two schools. Queensborough students select their own programs, and a student may use his free time between classes in any way he likes. He can visit the cafeteria and enjoy a cup of coffee and doughnuts while a rock group sings over the radio. He can go to the student lounge in the Humanities Building, stretch out on a couch, have a coke, light up a cigarette. Conversely, at high school, free time is not really free; at lunch a student must not leave the building nor must he go anywhere but the basement cafeteria, a dreary and ugly place. If a student has a period without a class, he must sit silently in the Study Hall. Consequently, many restless students cause trouble by whistling, stamping their feet, or throwing "spit-balls" when the teacher up front drops her eyes for a minute. Another major difference between Queensborough and Tilden is the friendliness of the students. At the college, for example, everyone is informal. A blonde-haired girl I never saw before sat next to me in a new leather chair in the lounge, and in a matter of minutes we talked about teachers, dating, and homework assignments. But at high school, if a student did not belong to a clique of people, she never got to know anyone besides the few friends she had from the neighborhood. Many times I would wander through the halls between classes, and people who sat next to me in my subject rooms earlier in the day barely nodded to me as I passed. Maybe this is my own personality problem, but I never felt as if my high school was a friendly place. In conclusion, I believe the college surroundings and atmosphere are much more enjoyable; if my high school were as pleasant a place perhaps my work and grades would have shown more my true abilities.

— Marlene Kearney

1. Put a check in the margin next to each subtopic sentence: the one that introduces physical appearance; the one that introduces student freedom; the one that presents the idea of friendliness.
2. What details make you see most vividly bits of the college campus?

_____

_____

3. What details help Miss Kearney show that the high school is, physically, a different place? _____

_____

4. What details best show student freedom at college? _____

5. How does the writer compare the quality of friendliness at the two places? _____

_____

> **SOME HINTS ABOUT PATTERN 3**
> 1. Ordering details by importance (see p. 80) is usually the best plan for this pattern. You may wish, therefore, to discuss in less detail your first point or points so that you can concentrate more fully on the last point, the one that is most important to you.
> 2. The subtopic sentence helps you introduce each new point of comparison.
> 3. Transition words help you move easily from one point to the next.

Likenesses *and* Differences

Pattern 4. In this comparison-contrast paragraph, you discuss both likenesses *and* differences. You can decide on *one basic way* in which the two objects may be compared (as in Pattern 1) or you can discuss a number of points of comparison and contrast of two objects without naming some central focus (as in Pattern 2). The point here is that both similarities *and* dissimilarities appear in the paragraph. Of course, you will have to illustrate just *how* these two objects have some similar features and how they have different features. If you think the differences are more important, discuss the *similarities* first, so that you may give the reader the most important idea *last* (see p. 80 for order of details). If you think the similarities are more important, discuss the differences first.

Let us assume that you select *student freedom* as the one basic point of comparison between high school and college, and that the *difference* in student freedom at both of these places is what you think most important. The first part of your paragraph could illustrate through vivid details one or more of these similarities:

1. free expression in the classroom
2. free choice of programs
3. freedom to follow extracurricular activities.

Then, you might focus upon one or more of these differences:

1. the right of peaceful demonstration
2. the freedom to use spare time without supervision
3. the right to select teachers.

Determine the *number* of points you want to discuss by the nature of the details you wish to use. One dramatic, expanded illustration for *one* of the points would mean that fewer points would be treated in the paragraph.

SOME HINTS ABOUT PATTERN 4

1. The topic sentence should indicate that your paragraph will treat *both* similarities and differences. Coordination or subordination (see pp. 89–95) may be effectively used in the topic sentence.

   /[Subordinator]
   Although high school and college students of today enjoy a number of freedoms, I believe that the college campus has a much firmer idea of student liberty.

   It is true that a sense of friendliness and a spirit of brotherhood may be
   /[Coordinator]
   found in both the secondary school and the university, but to me the college campus is still a cold and unfriendly place.

2. Remember, if differences are more important to you, discuss similarities first; if likenesses are more important, talk first about differences. Topic sentence I below stresses the major area of difference; topic sentence II stresses the major areas of likenesses. Both sentences deal with similar topics.

I	II
Although both high school and college students of today do enjoy a number of freedoms, I believe that the college campus puts liberty much more firmly in practice.	Despite the fact that a college campus often has a firmer concept of liberty, student freedom in both the high school and the college is limited and ineffective.
This paragraph will stress the difference in college freedom and high school freedom.	*This paragraph will stress that high school and college are alike in their limited idea of freedom.*

3. Sometimes you do not need to explain both similarities and differences, even though you wish to make the point that likenesses and differences exist. You can assume that the reader understands, appreciates, or agrees with the part that you do not wish to explain. In this way you can use the entire paragraph to develop only one of the two objects for comparison. For example, in topic sentence I above, the writer could assume that his readers would agree with this part of his sentence: "high school and college students of today do enjoy a number of freedoms." He would not have to discuss these freedoms; he could move right on to illustrating the differences as he sees them.

Step 5. Understanding the Pattern. For each subject of comparison or contrast in Column I, list in Column II two or three similarities that might be expanded with details in a paragraph. In Column III, list two or three differences between the two objects, differences that might also be expanded with details in the paragraph. Look at the example.

I Topic for Comparison	*II* Some Similarities	*III* Some Differences
1. Oldsmobile and Volks-wagen	a. comfort b. safety features c. expensive on repairs	a. economy for Volkswagen b. ease of parking with Volkswagen c. smallness of Volkswagen an advantage in heavy traffic
2. listening to recorded music or listening at a live show		
3. office jobs and outdoor employment		
4. the beautiful or the intel-ligent: two types of dates		
5. mother's temper versus father's temper		

Step 6. Comparison-Contrast. Pattern 4: A Student Model. Read the student's paragraph below which discusses likenesses and similarities about one basic feature of high school and college. In the margin are explanations of the various parts of the paragraph. Write the answers to the questions that appear after Mr. Shand's theme.

Personal Concern

[Subtopic sentence: tells that discussion of likenesses will follow.]

[One similarity]

[Instances to illustrate the similarity]

Although good teachers at high school and college have many similar qualities, college teachers bring something more to their relationship with students. Certainly superior teachers appear at both places. These teachers are dedicated to their subjects and more learning through research and education. One senior teacher at my high school taught five classes each day in history and then sat through graduate school classes as a student at night so that he could finish his master's degree. Similarly my psychology teacher, Mr. Zimmerman, shuffles about the second floor laboratory after classroom hours examining mice in his experiments with sensory perception. Good teachers in addition try to make their subjects lively and exciting. Mr. Gold,

[Topic sentence:
1. Tells that similarities and differences will be discussed.
2. Tells that the *differences* are more important.]

[Another similarity (note transition "in addition" and reference to topic sentence with "Good teachers.")]

[More points to finish discussion on similarities]

[One specific moment to illustrate the difference.]

my high school English teacher, amazed the class when he spoke from memory the first scene of *Macbeth,* playing the part of each witch in a different voice. And when my college economics teacher talks about old money systems, he gets so fired up that everyone listens to him with interest. Good high school and college teachers also treat students fairly, do not lose their tempers easily, and are generally "nice guys" that anyone would not mind having as a friend. But it seems to me that the teacher on the college campus is much more concerned with his students in a personal way. Late one Tuesday afternoon last month while I waited for a conference with my writing teacher, I overheard Mr. Sadlo's conversation with another student in the class through the thin grey walls of the office cubicle. In a quiet whisper some fellow spilled out his feelings about his own family, about how he and his father never liked each other, and how the student left home several months ago. He told Mr. Sadlo that he now lived with some friends in a commune-type apartment, but that he felt depressed because he had no money or job in sight. In an instant Mr. Sadlo dialed the Student Counseling Service and set up an appointment for this fellow with someone in charge of financial aid. When he clicked down the receiver and explained the procedure to the student, I heard in his voice a deep personal interest, as if he really cared and that this was a problem that involved him, too. Then he stood up, his chair squeaking, and cleared his throat. "Here, Robert," he said softly, "take this five dollars until things straighten out." That moment strongly impressed me: the teacher really did not know the student very well and yet he was willing to involve himself personally in the student's life. At high school I never saw a teacher with the time or the office space to treat serious personal matters that troubled students. In spite of some basic likenesses, therefore, between the teachers at both schools, to me the college teacher is much more able and willing to involve himself in the student's personal welfare.

— Jeffrey Shand

[Subtopic sentence: tells that discussion of differences will follow.]

[Closing sentence:
1. Transition word "therefore"
2. Restates main idea (teachers are alike at both places but college teacher offers more to students).
3. Summarizes subtopic: teacher at college more personally involved.]

1. What is the basic feature of comparison between high school and college? _____

_____

2. Mr. Shand names five ways in which the two objects are alike, but he only gives instances to illustrate *two* of them. Write the five points in the lines below; then put checks next to the two points that are supported with illustrations.

a. _____

b. _____

c. _____

d. _____

e. _____

3. How does Mr. Shand illustrate the major difference he sees between the two objects he discusses? Is his illustration effective? Why? _____

_____

_____

4. Mr. Shand writes several concrete images through appeals to color and sound. Put a check in the margin next to the sentences in which they appear.

TWO IMAGINATIVE CONTRASTS

1. Analogy

An analogy is a special kind of comparison. It relates two things that seem to be very different on the surface by showing that there are many things these two objects have in common.

Step 1. Reading an Analogy. The paragraph sample below is developed through analogy. What does the topic sentence announce as the terms of the analogy? Which details of color and sound and touch make the comparison most vivid?

Biology Jailhouse

Professor Diedrich's biology class on the Monday morning of midterm day at Prep is a prison scene. First we convicts stand uncomfortably outside the classroom door in our dismal winter coats in brown and grey, whispering behind our hands or staring nervously down the empty hall. This is leisure time for the prisoners. Some men squat on the floor and frown; others lean against the ugly green walls near the lab; others drag deeply on stubs of cigarettes. A black film of unshaved whiskers sits like coal dust on every face. Sullenly, my friend Tony says "You wanna butt?" He pushes a pack of Lucky Strikes at me, but I shake my head no. Suddenly footsteps sound on the stairway around the bend. The warden, Professor Diedrich, marches firmly to the door and shouts, "Let's go!" We all snap to attention and, still slouching, march single file into the lecture hall. "Take every other seat. Skip two rows between you and the person in front of you. When the examination begins, there's to be no talking or smoking." I fall into my seat, thinking, "I wish I could break out of this place." But I know I'm just paying for my crime:

everyone warned me not to take biology in my freshman year. Suddenly two guards —assistant examiners—burst through the doors with cartons of test booklets and question sheets. Taking a handful of books and question pages, the guards stamp between the rows, tossing out the equipment solemnly. "Nobody writes," barks the professor, "until eight o'clock sharp!" He scribbles in yellow chalk the time the exam begins, the time it ends, and the time it is now, measuring out a life's sentence for the prisoners before him. At eight o'clock the bell howls like a siren; everyone jumps and writes a name across the first page of the examination blue book. Occasionally, nervously, someone glances up at the beady-eyed guards who watch us without a smile. But I know my parole will begin just one hour from now. If I pass this awful exam, maybe I will not be a two-time loser like most of my friends, just an "ex-con" who learned his lessons and never returned to the biology jailhouse.

—Charles Gomez

Step 2. Some Analogy Topics. Here are some other analogies you may wish to develop in a paragraph about the college or high school scene. As your teacher directs, select one of these for your theme assignment. Better yet, make up your *own* analogy to develop in a paragraph.

1. teachers are like automobiles
2. learning is a baseball game
3. homework: my private war
4. campus personalities and colors
5. college as army life
6. books as people
7. the college exam room as hospital
8. the term paper as track race
9. the principal's office as courtroom
10. a date is like a card game

2. Contrasts to Create a Mood

A richly imaginative comparison-contrast paragraph is one in which you compare and contrast one of your inner moods to the actual moment in which you were experiencing that mood. In this paragraph type you set up a contrast between your inner emotions and the world around you. You need to use a number of concrete details to make the scene rich in sensory appeal; and you need to mix in those details with the thoughts and feelings which reflect the mood you are experiencing.

A mood, as you know, is some state of feeling at a given time. Each of us lives through a number of moods each day: happiness, boredom, loneliness, fear, excitement, depression, sorrow, anger, discomfort, relaxation, tiredness. The point of this writing assignment is to set the mood in a specific place at a specific time and weave in the details of the setting with your own inner state.

Step 1. Examining a Student Paper. Read Miss Goldberg's paragraph below. Which image stands out most in your mind as an accurate description of the scene? Which words reveal best the inner feelings of the writer? What word in the topic sentence sets the mood?

Thoughts at the Supper Table

On a Tuesday evening last March, after returning home from a tiring day at school, I felt the pressure of my school life overpower me as I drifted towards the table, and slouched into my seat. My mother hastily served steaming soup bowls and took her place as the meal began. "Well, Susan, how was school today?" she questioned, trying to start a conversation. I gazed at my soup bowl sullenly, not responding to her question. As I stared at the letters, which, carelessly arranged, floated aimlessly in the red alphabet soup, I realized that the white letters revealed the awful assignments and events of that miserable day. They spoke up powerfully, taunting me with unfulfilled responsibilities. "C," one yelled, sticking forcefully between the bits of carrot. "Composition due on Thursday," it blared. Bouncing upward, another letter shoved its way foreward. "D," it thundered. "Drown! Drown! Drown! Why haven't you studied for your philosophy test? Don't be surprised if you get a D." Unexpectedly, the letter "T" surfaced in the bowl and floated steadily in the foam of the heated broth. This action proved that like the "T" I too would be forced to stretch out my hands and perform an authentic "dead man's float." "B," roared another character of the alphabet. "Burn! Burn! Burn! Why didn't you study for your sociology midterm examination? You know it's tomorrow." The smoke of the hot soup curled curiously, reminding me that burning is no easy death. Unconscious of the world around me, I imagined coarse ropes choking the tender necks of newborn infants, human flesh packaged for sale as prime cuts, and human bodies roasted like medium-rare steaks. "Susan, did you hear me?" my mother nudged, interrupting my obnoxious nightmare. "I asked about how school is coming along," she repeated anxiously. "Oh! Fine! Couldn't be better," I answered, trembling. My mother removed the soup bowls and brought in the next platter. I picked up my fork and lowered my head. There upon my plate lay one portion of my awful dream, steak broiled to a crisp medium-rare. Immediately, I dropped my fork and speedily escaped the dinner table. "I swear," my mother screeched. "I'll never understand today's crazy kids as long as I live."

—Susan Goldberg

Step 2. Another Mood Paragraph. Read Mr. Gross' theme below. Write the answers to the questions that appear underneath the selection. Use separate paper.

Waking on a Monday Morning

I hear an innocent click and then, "It's seven fifteen on a bee-yoo-tiful Monday morning here on WABC" blares out of my clock radio on my bedroom dresser; "Oh damn, it's Monday!" I think with a groan. Lifting out of bed with the grace of a sick hippo, I manage to turn the volume down. Resting my weight on my dresser, I grope for the light switch. In an instant the bulb flashes on and knocks me with its glare right back into bed. I weigh in my mind what I have to do. "Damn, I don't feel like getting up, and I don't feel like going to work, and I don't feel like going to school." I smile to myself. I'd sure hate to have to put up with me in the morning! Finally pushing my better judgment to the top, I stumble into the bathroom, banging my knee on the door. After I wash with icy water, I return to the closet for a faded pair of dungarees and an ugly old sweatshirt. "The sun is out strong," the disc jockey screams, in a rapturous voice, "and it's a perfect November morning." Ugh! I look out the window; the early morning cloudiness hangs like a grey film on everything in sight. "How the hell can anyone enjoy Mondays?" I mutter to the plastic face of the radio. It sneers at me. "Sure, what does that announcer care?" I figure to myself. "He works four hours a day and earns fifty grand a year. No wonder he's so happy!" I notice I've buttoned my shirt wrong. I do it all over again, cursing. When I move lazily into the kitchen I grab a chipped bowl and a box of Rice Krispies from the cabinet above the sink. Setting my breakfast on the table, I try to pour the cereal into the plate, but the cereal has its own thoughts and tumbles onto the tablecloth, onto my lap, onto the floor. "Damn these rice thingees! We ought to declare war on China or Japan or wherever we get rice from!" Cleaning up the mess, I return hungry to my room where the skinny white hands of my clock tell the whole story. "Seven forty-five. I'd better move it." Scooping up a fistful of change, I release the nickels and quarters into my pocket with a jingle. I snatch my jacket and pull it around me, glancing at my face in the mirror. Awful! I look at the clothes and papers and books strewn haphazardly everywhere in my room. Awful! Quickly I zoom out the front door, slamming it behind me. A cool morning breeze and the sun rising above the roof across the street suddenly make me feel better. Trapping that ugly part of myself within, I say aloud, "Okay Monday, we're on neutral grounds now. I'm ready to take you on!"

—Ronald Gross

1. What contrast does the topic sentence set up? _____

2. Which quoted words are to you most realistic? _____

3. What details of the scene best reflect the writer's mood? Where do the details *contradict* the writer's mood? _____

SOME HINTS ABOUT THE MOOD PARAGRAPH

1. Tell the major feeling in the opening sentence. Miss Goldberg says, "I felt the pressure of my school life overpower me."
2. Identify the setting as soon as possible. Mr. Gross mentions the clock radio on his bedroom dresser in order to locate the scene for the reader.

3. Show the thoughts that go through your mind as the mood develops. *At the same time,* show the details of the moment. These details of the outside world keep mixing in with your inner world of feelings. Notice how Miss Goldberg uses the letters of the alphabet soup to help identify and reflect her mood. For Mr. Gross, the voice of the disc jockey interrupts a mood.
4. Use eight or ten lively images of concrete details.
5. Use quotation sentences to identify thoughts or give spoken words like: "Composition due on Thursday," it blared.

or

"I swear," my mother screeched. "I'll never understand today's crazy kids as long as I live."
6. Use comparisons like those explained on pp. 127–129. By making the soup letters talk, Miss Goldberg uses personification. Where does Mr. Gross use simile?

Step 3. Some Moods to Write About.   Here are several moods which college and high school students have stated they have felt at some time. Perhaps one might suggest to you possibilities for a paragraph. The key in selecting a proper mood for writing is to try to remember a brief moment you experienced recently in which your feelings were all one major kind.

1. boredom in class
2. Sunday evening depression
3. fear at exam time
4. joy in being alive
5. rainy-day blues
6. excitement at a concert
7. dislike of a teacher
8. waiting for the bell
9. nervousness at a date
10. sleepiness with homework
11. alone at the beach
12. peacefulness on a walk
13. love for a parent
14. sorrow at a loss of a pet
15. pity for a drunk
16. pride at some achievement
17. fear of going mad
18. pleasure during a good meal
19. feeling important at a rally
20. anger at a friend

SOLVING PROBLEMS IN WRITING

The Mirror Words: II

Here are several more words which cause confusion because they look and sound alike.

quit: to stop. I *quit* my job last week.
quiet: silent; without noise. A *quiet* room is restful.
quite: completely; rather; entirely. He was *quite* disturbed at the accident.

Step 1. Quit, Quiet, Quite?   Fill in the blank with *quit, quiet,* or *quite* so that the word group makes sense.

1. a _____ day

2. _____ correct

3. _____ dull

4. _____ countryside

5. _____ a fool

6. _____ work at five

7. _____ willing

8. a _____ child

9. "I _____!"

10. _____ successful

---

principal: 1. a head person at a school. The *principal* speaks to the students each day.

2. a major sum of money. The *principal* he invested earned $1,250 interest.

3. a descriptive word that means *most important.* Rice is still the *principal* food for many people.

principle: a rule, a major belief, a basic idea or truth
One *principle* for success is hard work.
As a man of *principles,* he refused a bribe.
The *principle* of atoms and molecules goes back to the early Greeks.

Hint: Princip*le* and ru*le* both end in *-le*: if you use princip*le* make sure it means ru*le*.

Step 2. Using *Principal* and *Principle*.   Fill in the blank with the correct word, *principle* or *principal.* You may need the plural form.

1. He knew the _____ of geometry.

2. The _____ summoned the student's mother.

3. The _____ effect is the loss of blood.

4. A wisely invested _____ earns good returns.

5. The _____ of many religions are the same.

6. People with _____ weigh carefully any moral decision.

7. The pilot explained the _____ of airplane safety.

8. The _____ student leader is Carl Haverstrom.

9. Our _____ left town for an important conference.

10. Psychologists investigate the _____ of human behavior.

> loose: rhymes with *moose*. It means *not tight, free;* sometimes it means *set free.*
> A *loose* shoelace is dangerous.
> You should *loose* the anchor before sailing.
> lose: rhymes with *whose*. It means *to misplace* or *not to win or keep.*
> If you *lose* the registration form, you will have to pay another fee.

Step 3. *Lose* or *Loose*. Write in the correct word, *lose* or *loose,* so the word group makes sense.

1. a _____ screw

2. _____ a book

3. The handle is _____.

4. Don't _____ the race!

5. _____ an investment

6. _____ collar

7. get _____ from the chain

8. _____ a quarter

9. a _____ button

10. _____ the kites in tall branches.

> no: negative; not any
> I have *no* information about it.
> now: at this time
> *Now* you can understand his reasons.
> know: to understand, to be acquainted with
> I *know* the principles of chemistry.
> They *know* the family next door.

Step 4. *No, Now, Know* for Proper Meaning. Fill in the blank space with the correct word, *no, now, know.*

Ball Four

(1) _____ one ever expected the colorful ballplayer Jim Bouton to reveal so many secrets of America's pastime. (2) _____ many baseball players (3) _____ they should have been more careful about what they said when Bouton, with (4) _____ thoughts other than a wish for honesty, scribbled notes on locker-room talk in his pad. (5) _____ baseball player treated harshly in *Ball Four* can forgive Bouton; to (6) _____ the strange behavior of professional athletes is one thing, but why Bouton chose to tell it (7) _____ to the world (8) _____

manager, coach, or player can understand. However, the public must (9)

_____ about the private lives of their heroes, so most fans are (10)

_____ in Bouton's debt for a lively and revealing book about baseball.

> were: the past tense plural form of the verb *to be*
>
> **Hint:** *Were* rhymes with *her.*
> We *were* searching for our car.
> They *were* laughing.
>
> where: a word that tells a place or asks "in what place?"
>
> **Hint:** Pronounce the *wh* at the start of the word. *Where* rhymes with *care.*
> In the city *where* I grew up many changes now appear.
> *Where* did all that noise come from?

Step 5. *Were* and *Where* in Action. Fill in the blank with the correct word, *were* or *where.*

1. _____ six apples eaten this afternoon?

2. _____ can a hungry man go for food?

3. All the papers _____ scattered over the floor.

4. Is that _____ you work?

5. Is that the store that you _____ describing?

6. There _____ eight team members there.

7. We _____ trying to get the instructor's attention.

8. A library _____ books may be borrowed free is one of Benjamin Franklin's ideas.

9. _____ you born before 1950?

10. None of us knew _____ to wait.

> piece: a part or portion of something
>   One *piece* of glass stuck in his finger.
> peace: without war; a state of restfulness
>   *Peace* is one of man's noblest goals.

Step 6. *Piece* or *Peace*? Fill in the blank with *peace* or *piece.*

1. a _____ of pie

2. _____ on earth

3. a time without _____

4. a _____ pipe

5. a _____ of clay

6. that _____ of paper

7. The U.N. works for _____.

8. an old _____ of news

9. need some _____ and quiet

10. a _____ candidate

> then: at a certain time
> The folk singer performed, and *then* we left the party.
> than: a comparing word
> She is taller *than* her brother.

Step 7. Using *Then* and *Than*. Fill in the blank space with the letter *-e* or *-a* to make *then* or *than,* whichever the sentence requires.

1. The lyrics of Bob Dylan are softer and more mysterious th____n the lyrics of John Lennon.

2. The speaker angrily arose; th____n he stormed toward the door shouting, "When you behave better th____n a pack of wolves, th____n I can continue my talk!"

3. If you have eaten a short while ago, th____n it is wiser to select something less filling, even though the steak is tastier th____n anything else on the menu.

> lead: 1. rhymes with *weed.* It means *to show the way.*
> A good instructor will *lead* you to discover important values.
> The boy who *leads* must know the forest path.
> 2. rhymes with *fed.* It is a grayish metal.
> A *lead* pencil contains graphite and no *lead* at all.
> led: rhymes with *fed,* too. This *led* is the past tense of *lead.* It means *showed the way.*
> He *led* us through the filthy back alleys of Los Angeles.

Step 8. Making Sense with *Lead* or *Led*. Fill in the blank spaces with the letters *-ea* or *-e* to make *lead* or *led,* whichever the sentence requires.

The concern with poverty l____d public interest for many years, but today issues involving the environment l____d the list of national priorities. Although this should perhaps not be so, air pollution is indeed a pressing problem. One look at the l____d gray skies of New York tells that this city l____ds many others in its need for urgent solutions to heavy, polluted air l____ding to physical discomfort and sometimes death. New York once l____d the nation as an industrial center and entertainment capital, but now its pollution l____ds the number of its distinctions.

> knew: had knowledge about; was familiar with
> They *knew* each other from childhood days.
> new: the opposite of old
> That *new* car has all the safety features.

Step 9. *Knew* or *New* in Word Groups.   Write in *knew* or *new* so the word group makes sense.

1. that _____ desk

2. _____ the answer

3. three _____ classes

4. They _____ that story.

5. _____ the directions

6. _____ family on the block

7. _____ the family on the block

8. a _____ idea

9. _____ the assignment

10. the _____ assignment

> cloths: woven material used to make a variety of items
>   Dry the dish*cloths* before using them.
> clothes: what you wear
>   The *clothes* of today are lively and imaginative.
> close: to shut; next to
>   Please *close* the door. Stand *close* to me.

Step 10. Picking Correct Words: *Cloths, Clothes, Close.*   Underline the correct word, *close, cloths* or *clothes,* in each sentence below.

1. My interest in (cloths, clothes) is limited to what I wear on Saturday nights.
2. Various (cloths, clothes) may be used to make a warm coat or dress; often (cloths, clothes) with new textures give a special touch to either formal or informal (cloths, clothes).
3. If you remember to (close, clothes) the door in the closet, you will not need dust (cloths, clothes) to clean your (cloths, clothes, close).

Step 11. Review of Troublesome Words.   Fill in the blanks in the sentences below with the proper letters so that the words are used correctly.

1. If you stand clo____ to the princip____ you can see that he is wearing

   ____ew clo____.

2. Do not l____se that dish clo____.

3. One princip____ we w____re sure to follow was "Qu____ while you're ahead."

4. If you followed w____re the p____ce marchers l___d you, trouble would

   not have broken l___se at this qu___t demonstration.

5. Qu___ a few l___se p___ces of l___d lay on the floor.

AGREEMENT OF SUBJECT AND VERB

You probably know already that a verb can tell time, so to speak, because it indicates whether an action has already happened, will happen soon, or is in the process of happening.

The girl spoke *in a loud voice* shows, through the verb *spoke,* that the action happened in the *past;*

The girl will speak *in a loud voice* shows, through the verb *will speak,* that the action is going to occur sometime in the *future;*

The girl speaks *in a loud voice* shows, through the verb *speaks,* that the action is happening at *present.* The quality of time telling that verbs illustrate is called *tense:* past, future, and present are three of the main tenses in the English language. In using the present tense, problems in agreement arise.

AGREEMENT DEFINED

When a subject is singular, the verb must be singular.
When a subject is plural, the verb must be plural.
The girl speaks in a loud voice

    [singular   \singular verb
    subject   (-s ending)]
    (no -s
    ending)]

The girls speak in a loud voice.

    [plural   \[plural verb
    subject   (no -s ending)]
    (-s ending)]

Hint: The letter *s* is often a clue to proper agreement.

---

(1) *Singular Subjects* {Go with} *Singular Verbs* | (2) *Plural Subjects* {Go with} *Plural Verbs*

(1) *Singular Subjects (which usually do* {Go with} *Singular Verbs (which usually do end in* **s**)
not end in **s**)

A teacher works hard.
    \no *s* to show
    singular subject]

A safe driver moves carefully
    \no *s* to show
    singular subject]

Remember: Some subjects form plurals in ways other than adding an -*s* (*children, men, mice*). See pp. 108–109.

(2) *Plural Subjects (which usually do* {Go with} *Plural Verbs (which usually do end in* **s**) *not end in* **s**)

Teachers work hard.
    \no *s* to show
    plural verb]

Safe drivers move carefully
    \no *s* to show
    plural verb]

Step 1. Verb and Subject in Agreement. Select a subject from Column I and a verb that agrees with that subject from Column II. Write the words in Column III. Then write a sentence with each subject-verb combination you have made in the spaces below. Look at the example.

I	II	III	
liars	toss	*S.*	*V.*
birds	laughs	*liars*	*cheat*
child	repair	_____	_____
mechanics	fly		
trees	cheat	_____	_____
alumni	return		
person	speaks	_____	_____
soldiers	fight		
	dances	_____	_____
		_____	_____
		_____	_____
		_____	_____

1. *Most liars cheat without a second thought.*
2. _____
   _____
3. _____
   _____
4. _____
   _____
5. _____
   _____
6. _____
7. _____

PRONOUNS AND AGREEMENT PROBLEMS

A singular pronoun works with a singular verb.
   A plural pronoun works with a plural verb.
   Pronouns used as subjects do not end in **s**, so the letter **s** cannot serve as a clue to agreement as far as the subject is concerned. But because a singular *verb* in the present tense usually ends in **s**, look for an **s** at the end of the verb when a singular pronoun subject is used.

Singular Pronoun Subjects	Plural Pronoun Subjects
I it	we you
he you	they
she who	

It **crawls** along the ground.

[singular pronoun]

They **crawl** along the ground.

[plural pronoun]   [no s]

Exceptions

1. *I*, even though it is singular, is always used with a verb that does NOT have the singular **s** at the end.

   I sing   not   I sing**s**
   I run   not   I run**s**

2. *You*, even though it can be used as a singular or plural, is always followed by a verb that does NOT have the singular **s** at the end.

   You sing   not   You sing**s**
   You run   not   You run**s**

Step 2. Plural to Singular.   Rewrite each sentence below, changing the plural subject to a singular pronoun subject. In most cases you will have to change the verb too so that it agrees with the new subject. *Do not add -ed to the verb:* that will *avoid* the agreement error by shifting into past tense where there are few problems in agreement! Study the example. All subjects and verbs are underlined.

1. They often <u>want</u> dinner too early in the day.

   He often wants dinner too early in the day.

2. We <u>play</u> baseball every afternoon in July.

   _____

3. They <u>talk</u> too softly.

   _____

4. Both <u>boys</u> <u>fix</u> the automobiles easily.

   _____

5. The <u>instructors</u> <u>drive</u> to school each morning at eight o'clock.

   _____

6. They <u>go</u> to the local service station for repairs.

   _____

SOME SPECIAL PRONOUNS

Even though they may seem plural to you, some pronouns, when used as subjects, are singular and always go with singular verbs. Although people do not usually keep to this rule when they speak, formal writing still requires that you use singular verbs with these subjects.

Singular Pronouns

anybody	somebody	neither
anyone	everybody	either
nobody	someone	everything
no one	everyone	nothing
none	each	something

Examples: [singular verb (*s* ending)]

Singular ⎰Anybody believes a sincere speaker.
Subject ⎱Everyone tries hard.

                [singular verb (*s* ending)]

Step 1. Sentences of Your Own. On a separate sheet of paper write a sentence for each singular pronoun listed above. Be sure that the verb is singular (check for the **s** ending) and that the tense is present (don't add -*ed*).

Example: Each boy drifts off on his own.
              Everyone buys a newspaper.

FOUR TROUBLESOME VERBS

I *TO BE*

Singular Forms

am: Use with *I* only.
is: use with all singular subjects (except *you*)
I *am* tired today.
It *is* late.
The wind *is* blowing.

Plural Form

are: use with all plural subjects and with *you*
You *are* attractive.
The students *are* busy.
They *are* all outside.

Hint: Do not use *be* with any subject.

        It *is* late. *not* It *be* late.
        They *are* at the movies.
                not
        They *be* at the movies.

This verb has agreement problems in the past tense as well.

Past Singular

was: use with all singular subjects (including
    I) except *you*
I *was* awake early.
        not
I *were* awake early.

Past Plural

were: use with all plural subjects and with *you*
They *were* singing.
        not
They *was* singing.

He *was* seated in the rear.
     not
He *were* seated in the rear.

You *were* lucky to miss being drafted.
     not
You *was* lucky to miss being drafted.

II *TO HAVE*

Singular Form

has: use with all singular subjects except *I*
    and *you*
He *has* a cold.
The book *has* a torn page.
It *has* a bright red cover.

Hint: If the subject is singular, the verb ends in *s*.
If the subject is plural, the verb does not end in *s*.

Plural Form

have: use with all plural subjects and *I* and *you*
I *have* five dollars.
You *have* a cold.
The women *have* new cars.

III *TO GO*

Singular Form

goes: use with all singular subjects except *I*
    and *you*
She *goes* to sleep early.
The dog *goes* out before dinner.
It *goes* to its favorite tree.

Hint: If the subject is singular, the verb ends in *s*.
If the subject is plural, the verb does not end in *s*.

Plural Form

go: use with all plural subjects and *I* and *you*
I *go* to the garage daily.
Men *go* to work.
You *go* too far when you drive.

IV *TO DO*

Singular Form

does: use with all singular subjects except *I*
    and *you*
She *does* laundry at night.
It *does* not look right.

Hint: If the subject is singular, the verb ends in *s*.
If the subject is plural, the verb does not end in *s*.
Another hint: Although contractions should be
avoided in formal writing, it is important for you to
know that contractions with some of these verbs
and the word *not* cause many agreement problems for
students. To figure out the correct form of the verb,
separate the contraction into two words.

Plural Form

do: use with all plural subjects and *I* and *you*
You *do* the work!
I *do* too much driving.

doesn't; does not	Use with singular. He doesn't work. (does not)
don't: do not	Use with plurals, *I, you.* They don't work. (do not)
wasn't: was not	Use with singular (and *I*). The doctor wasn't in. (was not)
weren't: were not	Use with plurals and *you.* You weren't ill. (were not)

Step 1. Picking Correct Verbs. Circle the correct form of the verb in each sentence below. Then write the subject and the verb in the appropriate columns alongside each sentence. Look at the example.

S.　　　　*V.*

he　　*goes*　　1. As I watch him, he (go, goes) into the store to buy a pound of bacon.

_____ _____ 2. He (was, were) trying to reach us by phone, but

_____ _____ 　　he (has, have) not paid his bill in so long a time

_____ _____ 　　that all the service (was, were) discontinued.

_____ _____ 3. It (does, do) not matter whether or not a person

_____ _____ 　　(be, is, are) smart; if he (have, has) ambition, it

_____ _____ 　　(be, are, is) enough.

_____ _____

_____ _____ 4. If she (go, goes) to the dance, a girl (has, have)

_____ _____ 　　a chance to meet someone.

MORE THAN ONE SUBJECT

[Subject is plural]　　　　　[Plural verb]

A desk and an old lamp stand in the room.

　　Since *desk* and *lamp* both make up the subject, the subject is plural; therefore a plural verb is needed.

When ⎰ either . . . or 　　　⎱ join the subjects, the verb agrees with the subject that stands closest to the verb.
⎰ neither . . . nor 　　⎱
⎰ or 　　　　　　　⎱
⎰ nor 　　　　　　⎱
⎰ not only . . . but also ⎱

Either the manufacturer or the <u>driver is</u> at fault.
　　　　[Closest subject:　　 [Verb: singular]
　　　　singular]

Either the manufacturer or the <u>drivers are</u> at fault.
　　　　[Closest subject:　　 [Verb: plural]
　　　　plural]

Step 2. More than One Subject. Use the expressions indicated to open each sentence. Then use the correct form of the verb in parentheses in a sentence of your own. *Do not use the past tense:* use only the present.

Example:

1. Television or radio (to play)

Television or radio plays in my house most of the day.

2. Neither the passengers nor the driver (to be) _____

_____

3. Not only the police but also the firemen (to have) _____

_____

4. Either the two chief lawyers or the young assistant (to do) _____

_____

IS, ARE, WAS, AND WERE WITH IT, HERE, WHERE, AND THERE

To start a sentence correctly with *Here is, There is,* or *Where is,* remember that *there, here,* and *where* are not subjects: subjects in these sentences always come after the verb.

[Not the subject]   [Subject (singular)]
Here is an old *tree.*
    [Verb: singular]
[Not the subject]   [Plural]
There are dead flowers on the lawn.
    [Verb: plural]

It is followed by a singular verb, *is,* even when the word it refers to is plural.
  It is an important idea.
      [Singular]

  It is ideas like these that we need.
    [Plural]

Step 3. Special Openers. Use the words given below as the subject for each sentence. Open each sentence with *it, here, where,* or *there* and the verb that agrees with the subject: *is, are, was,* or *were.*

Example:
1. three hundred cars. *There were three hundred cars in the parking lot.*

2. an apple _____

3. several tires _____

4. many accidents _____

5. a young bird _____

WORDS THAT GET IN THE WAY

Don't be confused by singular or plural words that appear between the subject

and the verb in a sentence.

[Although this word is plural and close
to the verb, it is *not* the subject.]

The rain (on the rooftops) is causing trouble.
[Singular subject]   [Singular verb]

[Although this word is plural and close
to the verb, it is *not* the subject.]

A group (of students) was here before.
[Singular subject]   [Singular verb]

Don't be confused by certain words that join with the subject: *together with,
as well as, in addition to, along with* do not affect the subject.

[These words do not affect the subject.]

The banker, (together with his partners), was arrested for theft.
[Singular verb]

Step 4. Verbs That Agree.   Circle the correct form of the verb.

1. A plate of candles (is, are) on the table.
2. Three quarts of milk (has, have) a large quantity of vitamins.
3. A junkyard of old cars (does, do) not improve the appearance of our highways.
4. Mr. Davis, as well as his two brothers, (has, have) serious problems with income tax.
5. Someone among the visitors (was, were) guilty of taking the painting.
6. The floors, in addition to the ceiling, (need, needs) to be painted.

PLURAL WORDS THAT ACT AS SINGULAR

Some words, though they look plural, always take singular verbs:

physics
economics
civics
mathematics
news
measles

Amounts of weight, height or length, time and
money:
Three ounces *is* a small amount.
Six feet *is* very tall.
Three hours *was* not enough time.
Five dollars *is* what I am paid each day.

Economics *is* difficult.
Measles *is* a childhood disease.

Titles, though they may be plural, take singular verbs.
The Birds was a Hitchcock thriller.
Lilies of the Field is Sidney Poitier's best film.

> **Hint:** These words are always plural and take plural verbs:
>
> scissors   trousers
> glasses   means
> riches
>
> The scissors *are* on the table.

WORDS BOTH SINGULAR AND PLURAL

Words like *committee, group, team, family,* and *class* referring to an action by the group as a whole, take singular verbs.

   When you want to stress that each individual in the group does something, use a plural verb.

The committee *are* leaving the work until tomorrow.	The committee *is* leaving the work until tomorrow.
The plural verb *are* stresses individuals leaving the work.	Here you are showing that the committee acts as a whole in leaving the work.

Step 5. Verbs Singular or Plural?   Write in the correct form of the verb in parentheses.

(to be)   1. Physics _____ hard to understand in high school.

(to be)   2. Several minutes _____ all I can afford to wait.

(to have)   3. My   trousers   _____ ripped on a nail on the chair.

(to raise)   4. The class _____ hands to indicate approval of the instructor's proposal.

AGREEMENT WITH WHO, THAT, WHICH

   The words *who, that,* and *which* are singular *or* plural based upon the words they refer to.

The boy who finds the money keeps it.
   [*Who* is singular   \Singular because
   because it refers   *who* is singular]
   to *boy,* a
   singular word.]

One of the pages that appear looked badly torn.
      [*That* is plural   \Plural because *that*
      because it refers   is plural.]
      to *pages,* a
      plural word.]

Step 6. Agreement with *Who, That, Which*. Circle the correct form of the verb.

1. She is one of those girls who (is, are) always complaining.
2. This is one of the cars which (causes, cause) more accidents than any others on the road.
3. It is I who (believes, believe) that telephone rates are too high.
4. I used to live in one of the houses that (was, were) infested with rats and roaches.

Step 7. Reviewing Agreement Problems.   Finish each incomplete sentence below so that agreement is correct. Use the verbs in the columns.

is	go	warn
are	goes	warns
was	do	joke
were	does	jokes
looks	have	sit
look	has	sits
tries	laugh	feel
try	laughs	feels
want	speed	throw
wants	speeds	throws

Example:

1. An old truck and a '71 Volkswagen *speed down Rogers Avenue.*

2. Each of the astronauts _____

_____.

3. The college newspaper, together with an important magazine, _____

_____.

4. Anyone who _____

_____.

5. Either the manager or the employee _____

_____.

6. Neither the infielders nor the umpire _____

_____.

7. Mathematics _____

_____.

8. Broken scissors _____

_____.

9. Twenty-five cents _____

_____.

10. Neither of the two parents _____

_____.

Step 8. More Review. Circle the correct form of the verb.

1. Here (is, are) the famous ruins of Rome.
2. One of the unions which (has, have) been fighting for women's rights received a check for several thousand dollars.
3. *O Pioneers* (is, are) a book by Willa Cather.
4. It (is, are, be) seven weeks since I have seen you.
5. The cake or the cookies (need, needs) to be refrigerated.
6. Great riches (is, are) the aim of many men.
7. Fifty pounds (was, were) a great deal of weight to lose.
8. The bicycle (has, have) two flat tires.
9. Every day that woman (go, goes) past my house with her little dog.
10. That (is, are, be) the worst example of freedom that you could mention.

WRITING THE PARAGRAPH

Think about some of your early reactions to college life, and using any one of the several methods of paragraph development explained in this chapter, write a composition which in some way uses the technique of comparison-contrast. Read the student themes on pp. 135–136, pp. 138–139, pp. 141–143, pp. 144–145, and pp. 146–147 for a review of the approaches you may use.

Checking Your Paragraph Quality

Before you write the final copy of your paragraph, use this checklist for your composition so that you follow as many of the suggestions as possible. After you write the composition, fill in the checklist and submit it to your instructor along with your theme.

1. Did I write a topic sentence that makes clear what I wany my paragraph to deal with and that states some dominant impression I have about the subject (p. 7)?   _____

2. Did I use subtopic sentences and/or transitional expressions to help the ideas move smoothly from one to the other? (p. 73 and pp. 131–133).   _____

Here are two transitional expressions that appear in my theme.

a. _____

b. _____

3. Does my paragraph contain several word pictures that use sound, color,   _____
   smell, and touch?
   Here is one word picture that uses sound.

   _____

4. Did I use two or three comparisons (pp. 127–128) in my paragraph?   _____
5. Did I try to use several words from the new vocabulary on pp. 123–   _____

   125? Here is one word I used. _____
6. Did I check my Theme Progress Sheet and proofread my paragraph,   _____
   looking for the errors I usually make? Did I check especially for the
   run-on and fragment error?
7. Did I examine my theme for any mistakes in agreement? Have I checked   _____
   carefully for words I may have confused, like those explained on pp.
   148–155?
8. Did I look in the dictionary for any words that troubled me as I spelled   _____
   them?
9. Did I use a variety of sentence types: subordination; coordination; sen-   _____
   tences that open with -ing words; sentences that open with words that
   end in -ly?
10. Did I write fifteen to twenty sentences of 350 to 400 words?   _____

MORE SCHOOL TOPICS FOR COMPARISON

Below appear some topics, related to your impressions of high school and
college, that may be developed in comparison-contrast paragraphs. If you
still have trouble finding a topic, examine the subjects mentioned on pp.
126, 145, and 148.

1. Compare the drug situation on the high school and college campus.
2. Show how college and high school basketball (football, baseball) games
   compare.
3. Contrast your own approach to learning in high school and college.
4. Show how registration day is like a race or a battle or a roller-coaster
   ride.
5. Show your mood at the start of an eight o'clock lecture class.
6. Compare the gym facilities at high school and college.
7. Show how classroom learning compares with "real-life" learning.
8. Show how a college date compares with a high school date.
9. Compare a college teacher with some high school teacher.
10. Compare your first day at high school with your first day at college.
11. Compare government elections and college elections.

and bemoaning his fate of having to teach them. In English, another teacher pre-sumably had forsaken literature and was spending the time "making politics" as Bobby referred to it. Discussions centered about the Panthers, union organizing, what high school students can do.

"Usually, Pearson [Frederick Pearson, the English teacher] just tells us the only problem we face is just being black, but because you were here he didn't say it today," Phil explained to me. "Sometimes I don't mind all the political stuff, but sometimes it's one helluva drag. What the hell good is it this cat tellin' us we're black? If we don't know that, who does?"

"'Nother thing," Bobby went on, "is that Pearson and Mullahy and these other cats really don't like most of the guys 'round here."

"He's right," Phil nodded.

"You know, they used to have this stud Grimshaw, or somethin' like that. When you'd wise off in shop, he'd just whup you. Right in front of everyone."

"You ever see that?" I asked.

"Yeah, once," Phil replied. "Clemie Treevin's older brother, I can't think of his name, but he was messin' around right where we were at today. And old man Grim-shaw first threatens to chop his finger off on the band saw. He's goin' round saying, 'I think I'll just take the tip off this guy's little pinkie.' Showin' everybody, too. Man, you shoulda seen Treevin. Man, he was petrified silly."

"I'm getting sick just hearing about this," I said.

"You and me both," said Bobby. Phil smiled.

"I ain't kiddin' you, man. That's what he did. I saw it myself. Finally, he just gave him a couple whacks on his ass and told Treevin he'd throw him out of school if he ever did something like that again. Tom, you don't like the noise in the shop? Well, you could hear a pin drop that day. But they got rid of that guy. One month he was fired. Bam, he was gone. Just like that. Only good thing they ever done round here."

"You like the new guys, Phil?"

"Yeah, They're all right. Give you trouble once in a while, but mostly, like, it's all right."

"Yeah, it's all right," Bobby concurred. "Could be worse, I s'pose."

"But you like the machine shop, don't you?"

"Sure."

"I mean, it's . . . school's good during those hours, isn't it?"

"Yeah, you ain't kiddin'. I wish all day I could just stay down there and do my work," Phil responded.

"Yeah. That'd be a groove," Bobby said. "But then it wouldn't be school, would it?"

"Say it, brother."

"Yeah," I said, "I guess you're right. It probably wouldn't be school. Funny. . . ."

"You know you're some kind of heavy cat for a honkie," Bobby grinned at me. "Some heavy cat."

"What d'you mean?"

"Well, you know, worryin' about us that way and our school. You never went to no school like this, did you? You probably never spent that much time in a car shop before, right?"

"That's right."

"And you're worryin' about us."

"He ain't worryin', man. He's studyin' us. Ain't that right, man?"

"Yeah. I'm filming you."

"Yeah, so where's your camera supposed to be?"

"In my mind."

"I tell you, Phillie, this here's one helluva strange cat. You're a strange cat, Thomas my boy." We all laughed then and pounded one another's shoulders and arms.

"You're pretty cute yourself," I dared.

"Hey now, careful, man. We ain't that close, 'sweetie boy,'" Phil defended.

"I *knew* it," Bobby was shaking his head.

"You gonna be here tomorrow, Tom?" Phil was asking. Bobby had already started to walk away, his shoulder brushing up against the tall iron fence.

"I leave tonight. I've got to get home."

"Yeah, I figured." Overhearing us, Bobby suddenly returned.

"You gonna come back?"

"I hope so, but I don't know when."

"Hey, we should exchange addresses. You got some paper?"

"Yeah. Here. Tom, you gotta pencil?"

"Good."

"Where the hell's my ball-point pen?"

"Yeah. Good. Here, you can write on this book."

"Where? Here all right?"

"Must have left it in my locker."

"Can you read my writing?"

"Sure, fine."

"No trouble."

"Great. Here. How's that?"

"Beautiful."

"Perfect. So . . . O.K."

How many times had this scene been portrayed? It was like a train station parting. All of the political anger, the racial differences, and the age disparities vanished in the exchange, really, of autographs and people connecting, even when they know that so much of what society is and stands for keeps them distanced, keeps their unborn children distanced as well. Always the exchange of addresses and the promise to let them see a manuscript should one get written. Always the remarks like, I'll protect you by disguising your identity, and their ingenuous insistence that they want no "aliases" but, instead, seek all the fame and notoriety an article might fetch. Then they walk back into the streets, and I leave their city.

Bobby Richmond's father was killed in a car accident. He, his mother, and four sisters now live in a nearby housing project. A year ago, Yvonne, his oldest sister, was raped in the boys' locker room by a man whose identity is still not public knowledge. Some folks insist it was a teacher; others say one of the school's policemen. Soon afterward she quit school. Another sister, Arlene, withdrew from high school in the tenth grade. Her pregnancy left no doubt in the minds of the school board. What bothered her most of all was that some local social workers urged her to have an abortion. "They couldn't understand why I wanted my baby more than all the schooling in the world."

Phil Fannion never knew his father. Matthew Josiah Fannion, Jr., was dead or had disappeared—Phil continues to doubt the veracity of the death story—by the time Phil was born, the youngest son of Matthew and Louise Parker Fannion. Both of

Phil's brothers had been active members in a neighborhood gang, one of them having been seriously knifed in the groin during a fight with a member of his own gang. Three times his mother had almost died of renal failure, the last time the pains becoming so severe her cries could be heard in the Richmonds' apartment all the way across the project. In the middle of the night, two policemen came and took her in an ambulance to the County Hospital, the attendants there muttering things like, "If she makes it it'll be a miracle." Phil didn't miss one day of school. "I had no place else to go," he sighed. "I sure wasn't any good to anyone anywhere."

Neither boy feels he has any business being in school. "It just keeps me from my job," Bobby said. Both work, and school means "seven hours wasted when eight, ten, fifteen bucks are waitin' to be earned." Car shop, however, is different. The boys like their work. The clock is rarely watched, and, strangely, nothing is ever stolen from the jackets that hang from the enamel hooks as easy prey. Most of the boys prefer sports, obviously, but the car shop is a good second choice.

It's a physical world melded together by special cognitive skills and an exact, scientific language of labor, assemblage, and construction. There is music and dance and beauteous liberation in that shop. Wood is carefully touched, its straight edges lined up by eye, the timbre of metal listened for, its smoothness felt. Mouths store Phillips Screws or hold the ends of string, and pockets are filled with nails, knives, tape measures, and screw drivers.

It's like the principal says: "The kids are learning a trade. It's good for them. Can't everybody go to college, you know. But this is very important for these disadvantaged youths. You'll see what I mean when you visit down there. Andy here will show you where to go. Understand you've been talking with Richmond and Fannion?"

"Yes, sir."

"Dangerous boys. Dangerous boys. Wish we could separate them. Violent. You pick that up yet?"

"No. Not yet."

"Well, you will. Violent. Regular thing. Bad home life. No father around when the kids needed one. Always carrying knives or something. Caught Richmond last year carrying a gun. Believe that? [Absolutely not, I thought.] Fought like a bear to keep us from getting it. Had to call his mother in and everything. Trouble with these people is they don't even know what their kids are doing half the time. And if the parents can't help us out. . . . I mean they think we're running some kind of reform school here."

For a long while, I had forgotten the conversation with Anthony Maggio, the principal of "Boys Tech." "Tough Tony the Gouger," Bobby had called him. "Someday, man." Phil had smiled. I recall how our impressions of those boys had not been at all coincident. Just recently, however, our conversation became vivid again, prompted by the news that five boys from "Tech" had "turned the trick" on a filling station and were now headed for a state reform school: Beatty, John R.; Walker, Lawrence J.; Cleveland, Millard L.; Richmond, Robert E.; and Fannion, Phillip R. Car shop had saved them from the rooms and teachers upstairs. Certainly it had brought us together. It had permitted them to call me "honkie" and helped me to interpret that sound, for the moment, as a label of intimacy. But not too many schools can safeguard their students, especially those schools in which constraints are vicious and omnipresent.

The police report had described Robert Richmond as "carrying a gun and violent." He was the only one of the five charged with resisting arrest and assaulting an officer. One for "Tough Tony," zero for the social scientist. Do school personnel know their "own kind" best, or do they produce a certain kind just more easily knowable to themselves?

—Thomas J. Cottle

1. Why does the author compare the school to a prison?

_____

_____

2. Where do you find images of action, of sound, of touch, of smell? Pick out several of the most vivid.

_____

_____

3. How does the atmosphere in the car shop contrast with the atmosphere in the rest of the school?

_____

_____

4. What does the word *ambience* in paragraph 2 mean? How do you know?

_____

_____

5. Why do the boys respond so well to the activities in the car shop?

_____

_____

6. Why does the author give us personal family details about Bobby Richmond and Phil Fannion?

_____

_____

7. How would you answer the question in the last sentence of this essay?

_____

_____

REACHING HIGHER

Step 1. Pictures to Words. Look at the photograph on p. 121. Write a paragraph that compares and contrasts the scene you see with the scene at your own college. Use concrete sensory language to fill in details. Write a topic sentence that states the comparison clearly.

Step 2. Other Topics. Several other topics for comparison-contrast appear below. Write a paragraph about any one of them.

1. two movies you saw
2. summer in the city and summer in the country
3. radio and television
4. driving and racing
5. baseball and football
6. the "mini" look versus the "maxi" look
7. heroin and methadone
8. marijuana and alcohol
9. two girl friends (boyfriends) you had
10. two television comedies (dramas, "specials," movies)
11. two newspapers or magazines you read
12. summer sports and winter sports
13. telephone conversations and face-to-face conversations
14. two poems you read
15. two political leaders:
    Kennedy and Johnson
    Kruschev and Stalin
    Washington and Lincoln
16. poverty today and yesterday
17. children's toys today and yesterday
18. city ghettos and suburban ghettos
19. two concerts you saw
20. picnics and dinners at home

Step 3. Reviewing Sentence Correctness. Correct the brief paragraph below which contains six run-on errors and nine sentence fragments. Add any words or punctuation you wish in order to make the sentences right. Check the Run-on Review Charts on p. 25 and the Fragment Review Charts on p. 56 and p. 101.

Too Much Freedom

An important difference between high school and college is student freedom college students have too much freedom. For example, disagreeing with teachers. One day last week we reviewed for the psychology midterm early in November. When a student disagreed. He shouted out his opinion at the teacher, Mr. Howard. A soft spoken man with blue eyes and a friendly smile. Mr. Howard listened patiently he tried to explain his point to the student. Who would not listen. Who kept shouting, "But this is what I think!" The teacher smiled and nodded and sometimes stroked his small white beard he never stopped the student I thought the student should have been disciplined in some way. Because the rest of us just sat there while that student wasted twenty minutes of everyone's time. At high school students disagreed too, however, they usually waited for the teacher to finish talking or at least raised their hands to get the teacher's attention. Once in my reading class at East Bay High School. A boy called out an answer. That was wrong anyway. Miss Shirley glared at him and folded her arms then she said firmly, "You'd better learn to control yourself. Another outbreak like that and you'll find yourself in the dean's office!" Maybe she was too harsh with the student, but at least Miss Shirley remembered that the rest of the class had freedom too. Freedom to learn without interruptions.

Step 4. Writing about the Essay. Write a paragraph which compares and contrasts any aspect(s) of your former high school with Boys Technical High School as it is described in "In the Car Shop" on pp. 166–171.

chapter 5

"MENACE OR MARVEL?"
FACT-FINDING FOR THE AUTOMOBILE

Charles Harbutt/Magnum Photos, Inc.

INTRODUCTION

No single machine has had so strong an effect upon the lives of Americans as the automobile. People have found an answer to the dream of new freedom in the family car. A beat-up Chevrolet or a bright blue Ford is for many families the only magic light in lives of ugliness and discomfort. Distances between cities shrink; a new state, a new climate, a new neighborhood stands just around the corner. A father loads up a trunk with luggage and one family heads for a July vacation in the mountains; Spanish children in south Brooklyn clamber into a shiny red Oldsmobile for a day at Coney Island and a feast of frankfurters and French fries at a busy Surf Avenue stand; a mother on Cape Cod drives her daughter to school in the rain; a salesman speeds from New York west to San Francisco, squares of cotton and silk and wool spread out on the backseat as samples for new dresses; a high school youngster grips a steering wheel in sweaty palms as the first driver-education lesson begins.

But the automobile brings not only delight. Hospital beds and gravesites count the victims of the four-wheeled monster, child and adult alike the victim of speed and carelessness on the road. Few families indeed have not felt the pain of automobile tragedy. Increasingly producers stand criticized of displaying poor workmanship, of using faulty parts, of showing unconcern for safety. The air we breathe is a black cloud of pollution, many believe, because the automobile pumps poisonous fumes and endless streams of smoke into the atmosphere.

This theme assignment focuses upon the automobile in your life. You will be able in this paragraph once again to call upon your own experience to illustrate a dominant impression you have about some aspect of the automobile. And the language of sensory images (see pp. 5–6) will help you write the details you need to support your point of view.

However, there are other kinds of details you need to learn about, details which further help support a paragraph. While the details of your own experiences told through vivid sensory language always make a most exciting and interesting kind of paragraph, very often you write about things which have no root in your own lives. Writing about World War I in history class, about the varieties of cell reproduction in biology, about the economic status of the American Indian in sociology: for these kinds of assignments you often need some source of details other than your own experience. Aside from images—which you may indeed be able still to use—you will learn in this chapter about using statistics as details; you will also see how to use quoted material, paraphrase, and cases from reliable sources as details to support a paragraph.

VOCABULARY

Step 1. Words for Automobile Facts. These words will help you use and understand information about automobiles. Write the definitions next to the words you already know. For any words whose meanings you do not remember, check a dictionary or see Appendix A for some help.

1. vehicular _____   6. protrusion _____

2. definitive _____   7. chronic _____

3. sustain _____   8. allude _____

4. statistically _____   9. graphic _____

5. autopsy _____   10. emission _____

Step 2. Checking for Meanings. Each of the words above is used in an expression you might find in your readings. In each blank below, write a definition that you think best explains the word group.

Hint: Use the dictionary for any other words you do not know.

1. high alcohol content revealed by *autopsy* _____

2. *sustained* fractures and contusions _____

3. a *chronic* complaint about convertibles _____

4. *alluding* to unsubstantiated figures _____

5. a *graphic* illustration _____

6. *statistically* irrelevant _____

7. a *definitive* conclusion _____

8. high lead *emissions* _____

9. *vehicular* fatalities escalate during holidays _____

10. lethal *protrusions* on the dashboard _____

Step 3. *-ing* Words for Liveliness. These verbs, in their *-ing* forms, will add life to your written communication and will help you make some changes in your writing style (see pp. 192–196). Check your dictionary for any you do not know; write the definition in the blank space (see Appendix A for more help).

Hint: Look up the word in its infinitive form. Look up *wheeze*, not *wheezing*, for example.

1. wheezing _____

2. sputtering _____

3. asserting _____

4. elucidating _____

5. assenting _____

6. reiterating _____

7. lauding _____

8. intervening _____

9. brandishing _____

10. lamenting _____

Step 4. Naming the Action. From the above, write in the blank a word that would:

1. indicate sorrow or regret _____

2. show something coming between two events or occurrences _____

_____

3. indicate breathing with a whistling sound _____

4. show that someone was praising something _____

5. show someone was trying to make something clear _____

6. show someone was waving something as if it were a weapon _____

_____

7. indicate a manner of excited and unclear speech _____

8. show someone repeating something _____

9. show agreement _____

10. show someone was making a statement he thought was true _____

_____

BUILDING COMPOSITION SKILLS

Finding the Topic

Step 1. Sharing Opinions. Here are several statements made by college freshmen about automobiles. Pick out the one or two remarks with which you most strongly agree or disagree and discuss your opinions with the class.

1. Cars are not luxuries anymore; they are necessities. Any talk about limiting them, therefore, is ridiculous.
2. A car is nothing but a status symbol for many people who believe a man is as big and powerful as his car is.
3. Women drivers are the worst drivers on the road.
4. Without a car a college man doesn't stand a chance with the opposite sex.
5. Most air pollution is a result of poor automobile construction.
6. Public transportation is so undependable, unsafe, and unattractive that the automobile is the only reasonable way to get you where you want to go.
7. More severe penalties must be developed for drunken drivers.
8. People who drive are responsible for air pollution, not automobiles themselves.
9. Automobile racing at Indianapolis and at the Grand Prix competition does not encourage speeding for ordinary drivers, but it does show how skillful, intelligent, and careful a good driver can be with his car.
10. There are so many factors responsible for tragic auto accidents that safety on the roads is almost impossible.

Using Statistics and Cases

An effective way of backing up your own position on a topic is to use *statistics:* statistics may be thought of as "facts," the numbers and examples (revealed through responsible investigation) that you can use to support a point. To be believed, statistics should

1. come from reliable sources;
2. be clearly and understandably presented;
3. be honest and not omit important records which might not support the argument you present.

Step 2. Statistics Tell the Story. Here is part of a brief paragraph from a longer report on the environment prepared by the *New York Times.* Read the paragraph, developed through statistics, and then answer the questions in the spaces provided.

SOME WORDS TO KNOW BEFORE YOU READ

shroud: a cloth used to wrap dead people in before they are buried
snuffed out: extinguished quickly
fortnight: a time span of two weeks
meteorologist: weather specialist

Pollution Shroud

1   The fouling of the world's . . . air . . . is the
2   fastest spreading disease of civilization. In 1952, a
3   pollution shroud, hanging low over London, killed 4,000
4   persons within a fortnight and caused 4,000 more
5   Londoners to die lingering deaths over the following
6   three months. In 1948, a "killer smog" snuffed out 20
7   lives in Donora, Pennsylvania, and made 6,000 other
8   townspeople so sick that they probably wished they were
9   dead; however, meteorologists reported that Donora got
10   off easy. In Yokkaichi, Japan, today, schoolchildren
11   routinely wear gas masks while at play.

—*New York Times Encyclopedic
Almanac*, 1970

1. Which statistics do you find most surprising, informative, or interesting?

   _____

2. Why do you think the writer says "pollution *shroud*" in line 3 instead
   of *pollution cloud?* How is this an example of figurative language? (See

   pp. 127–129.) _____

3. What is the advantage in using "snuffed out" in line 6 instead of, say,

   destroyed? _____

Step 3. Cases Make the Point.   In the following selection from a book on
auto safety, the topic idea is developed, in part, by *cases*. A case is a specific incident from an accurate source (involving real people or events)
which supports the position you wish to develop.

The man, Gikas, named in the first sentence, is a doctor from Ann Arbor,
Michigan, who investigates auto accidents.

Answer the questions after you read.

SOME WORDS TO KNOW BEFORE YOU READ

catapulted: thrown with great force
jut: to extend beyond the main part
protruding: sticking out
uncollapsible: cannot be caved in
multiple: many

Accidental Deaths

Gikas had shown us three slides relating to one accident. One was an x-ray of
a skull, gray except for the sharply outlined shape of a car radio knob in the brain.
The second was of the bloody dashboard, where the radio knob had been. A companion knob was still there, jutting out. The third was of the header, the steel bar

that connects the roof with the windshield. It was covered with blood. A sixteen-year-old boy had been driving a fourteen-year-old girl to a party in his father's Buick. They went off the road on a curve and hit a tree head-on. The boy died against the header. (If it had been padded, he might be alive.) The girl was catapulted into the instrument panel. Instead of recessed knobs, a safety precaution that would probably have cost Detroit not one cent and only a thought about safety, the knobs jutted out, like lethal spears. She hit the radio; the knob went through her eye, inches into her brain, and she died instantly. Gikas pressed the button on his slide projector and we saw the results of another accident. A family of three, father, mother and six-year-old daughter, were driving along a road. A drunk, coming the other way, pulled out to pass and didn't make it. They crashed head-on. The mother, in the right front seat, hit the protruding instrument panel and died of a fractured larynx. The little girl, in the back seat, flew past the sandwiched front seat and hit the jutting dashboard. The slide showed the huge dent. She sustained multiple fractures of the lower jaw, her tongue lost support, and she strangled on it. The father was killed against the uncollapsible steering column.

—Jeffrey O'Connell and Arthur Meyers,
Safety Last

1. Because this selection comes from a book and the topic idea is presented in earlier paragraphs, there is no clear topic sentence. Put a check next to one of the following statements that you feel would make the best topic sentence for the selection.

   a. Automobile accidents are terrible.
   b. Young drivers and drunkards are responsible for a good number of automobile deaths.
   c. Poor construction of automobile interiors causes shocking deaths in driving accidents.

2. What two cases do the writers give to back up their position? _____

   _____

3. Why do you think the writers mention that one set of passengers was going to a party or that one of the accidents involved a six-year-old girl?

   These facts are really not important to the main idea. _____

   _____

HINTS FOR USING CASES AND STATISTICS

1. Statistics must often be read from charts or graphs. Be sure you understand what the various figures and numbers mean.
2. Don't just pile up a series of numbers as statistical information; your style will be dull and your reader will lose interest.
3. Write your statistics in a clear way. Expressions like "a pollution shroud" and "a killer smog snuffed out 20 lives" add life to the paragraph on air pollution.

> 4. In using cases, identify as much as possible the people, the events, the specific families whose experiences support your opinion in the paragraph.
> 5. Select statistics from reliable sources. You can mention your source directly in the paragraph by writing something like this:
>
>   The <u>Los Angeles Times</u> reports . . .
>
>   or
>
>   A 1969 study by the World Health Organization shows . . .

Charts, Graphs, and Numbers: Some Truths about the Automobile

Below you will find various statistics about the automobile. After you examine them, answer the questions in Step 1 about how you would use these statistics in a paragraph.

1964 Auto Thefts in Standard Metropolitan Statistical Areas with Populations Over 500,000
[A Selection]

Boston, Lowell, Lawrence	31,033
Chicago, Illinois	44,558
Cleveland, Ohio	27,119
Detroit, Michigan	33,294
Los Angeles, Long Beach, California	59,623
Miami, Florida	8,509
New York, New York	91,472
Philadelphia, Pennsylvania	20,250
San Francisco, Oakland, California	35,667
St. Louis, Missouri	20,471
Washington, D.C., Maryland, Virginia	20,686

Source: Uniform Crime Reports (FBI)

The American Motorist Drove 875 Billion Miles

The mileage traveled by the over 89,500,000 passenger cars registered in the United States in 1970 was estimated at 875 billion miles. In addition, more than 225 billion miles were driven by the nearly 19,000,000 trucks and buses in the country.

It is estimated that private passenger cars are used for 90% of all vacation and recreation trips in the United States. During 1970, some 110,000,000 Americans took to the highways within their own country for at least one vacation or pleasure trip by automobile, setting a new record. They spent 34.5 billion dollars and traveled an estimated 240 billion miles.

Source: *The World Almanac and Book of Facts: 1971*

Percentage of Drivers with Significant Blood-Alcohol Levels Revealed in Autopsies after Fatal Accidents

1. Montana: 55%
2. Nassau County, N.Y.: 50%
3. Grand Rapids, Mich.: 60%
4. Delaware: 63%
5. Nineteen California counties: average 55%
6. Baltimore: 52%
7. In New York City, of 69 drivers dead within 24 hours of an accident, more than 55% had alcohol levels of .10 to .40%

Source: *Accident Facts*, National Safety Council

Lawsuits and the Car Makers

Santa Barbara: A judge ruled $70,000 against General Motors' Corvair. Because of unsafe design, the car overturned and severed the driver's arm.

York, South Carolina: $312,000 against Ford when a girl was pierced by a protruding lever from the gear shift.

Chicago: General Motors refused to produce important facts on the Corvair in a case involving paralysis of a driver and injured family. Damages will run near $1,000,000.

Texas: Ignition switch in a Chevrolet did not shut (though the driver had taken out the key); a passenger getting out accidentally hit the gas pedal; the car took off and hit a pedestrian who was awarded $225,000 from General Motors.

Source: *Safety Last*

Automobile Registrations: 1968

State	Registrations	State	Registrations	State	Registrations
Alabama	1,445,865	Louisiana	1,318,024	Oklahoma	1,154,970
Alaska	88,687	Maine	385,633	Oregon	1,008,475
Arizona	723,840	Maryland	1,491,429	Pennsylvania	4,845,935
Arkansas	716,002	Massachusetts	2,104,396	Rhode Island	402,030
California	9,314,496	Michigan	3,734,339	South Carolina	1,020,375
Colorado	994,194	Minnesota	1,678,755	South Dakota	284,640
Connecticut	1,446,251	Mississippi	790,540	Tennessee	1,543,887
Delaware	239,269	Missouri	1,858,293	Texas	4,792,377
Dist. of Col.	235,325	Montana	303,964	Utah	448,142
Florida	3,167,146	Nebraska	664,121	Vermont	171,342
Georgia	1,870,944	Nevada	228,592	Virginia	1,724,400
Hawaii	315,289	New Hampshire	304,066	Washington	1,558,851
Idaho	321,982	New Jersey	2,983,498	West Virginia	641,122
Illinois	4,358,260	New Mexico	434,657	Wisconsin	1,693,341
Indiana	2,204,462	New York	5,647,505	Wyoming	146,735
Iowa	1,335,317	North Carolina	2,036,631		
Kansas	1,078,238	North Dakota	265,384	Total	33,698,101
Kentucky	1,330,851	Ohio	4,845,218		

World Road Accidents on the Increase

Country		Killed or injured per 10,000 population 1950–1952 average	1964–1966 average	Differ-ence, %	Country		Killed or injured per 10,000 population 1950–1952 average	1964–1966 average	Differ-ence, %
Canada	Killed	17.5	25.2	+ 44.0	Norway	Killed	4.7	10.6	+ 125.5
	Injured	384.4	766.6	+ 99.4		Injured	38.6	215.3	+ 143.0
Japan	Killed	5.3	13.5	+ 154.7	Poland	Killed	5.4	8.0	+ 48.0
	Injured	39.4	457.8	+1,061.9		Injured	22.3	63.7	+ 208.0
France	Killed	8.8	22.9	+ 160.2	United Kingdom	Killed	10.2	15.0	+ 47.0
	Injured	174.2	547.8	+ 214.5		Injured	415.8	725.3	+ 74.0
Germany (West)	Killed	23.2	27.7	+ 18.9	Yugoslavia	Killed	2.8	9.1	+ 225.0
	Injured	656.3	755.0	+ 15.0		Injured	19.7	133.4	+ 602.0
Hungary	Killed	5.6	8.8	+ 57.1	Australia	Killed	22.0	27.5	+ 25.0
	Injured	39.0	182.4	+ 367.7		Injured	476.9	675.2	+ 41.0

Cars and Highway Safety

The chances of surviving an accident are three times greater in a large, heavy car than in an imported compact, and twice as good as in a domestic compact.

   These are the inferences from preliminary findings in a study of all reported automobile accidents in the State of New York during the first nine months of 1968. There were 291,000 accidents involving 462,000 cars. The statistics below show the percentages of vehicles of various sizes that were involved in accidents in which one or more occupant was killed or injured badly enough to require hospitalization. The most extensive of its kind, the study was made by the New York Department of Motor Vehicles for the National Highway Safety Bureau.

   One distributor of foreign compacts, Volkswagen of America, Inc., contended that the figures may not tell the whole story. "Studies show that smaller cars are driven by younger drivers, are driven more miles per year, and are used more often at hours . . . when serious accidents are more likely to occur," the company said. Nevertheless, the findings seemed to confirm what many motorists have long suspected: that other things being equal, the smaller the car, the bigger the risk of an accident.

Type of Car	Average Weight (in Pounds)	Percentage of Accidents involving Death or Serious Injury
Domestic Luxury	4,800	3.1
Domestic Intermediate	3,700	4.0
Domestic Economy	3,400	5.2
Domestic Compact	2,800	6.4
Foreign Compact	1,900	9.6

Source: World Health Organization Statistics Report, 1968

High School Driver Training by Violations and Accidents

Driver Training Status	Males			Females		
	No.	Average Violations (mean)	Average Accidents (mean)	No.	Average Violations (mean)	Average Accidents (mean)
Total	3,878	0.541	0.162	2,786	0.169	0.075
School offered driver training class	3,198	0.522	0.157	2,296	0.164	0.076
Did take and pass	2,514	0.498	0.158	1,795	0.154	0.076
Did not take	684	0.611	0.154	501	0.202	0.074
School did not offer driver training class	447	0.642	0.186	337	0.199	0.080
Status undetermined	233	0.601	0.185	153	0.183	0.059

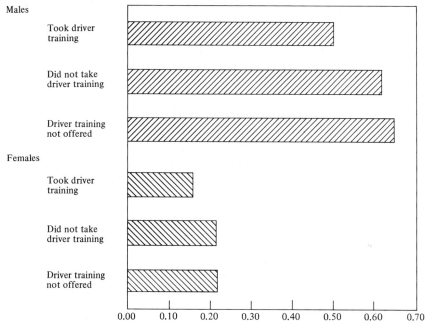

Figure 1. Average (mean) number of violations for trained and untrained drivers by sex (one-year record).

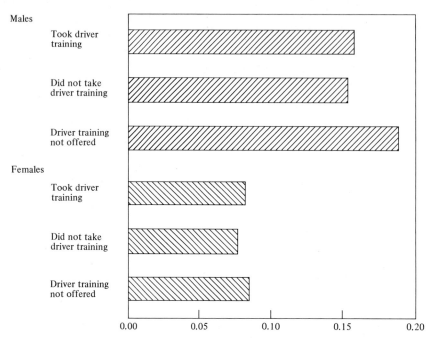

Figure 2.   Average (mean) number of accidents for trained and untrained drivers by sex (one-year record).

SOME POINTERS FOR WRITING STATISTICS CORRECTLY

1. Use numbers for percent
   18% or 18 percent
2. Use numbers for dates
   May 15, 1971
3. To show sums of money:
   a. If you need two words or fewer (*not* counting the word *cents* or *dollars*)
      write out the words for the numbers.
         three hundred dollars
         forty-two cents an hour
         eight billion
   b. If you need three or more words, use the numbers.
         $8.76 $8,487 $62,908,433
   c. For a series of numbers, use the figures, not the words.
4. Two-word fractions are written like this:
      seven-tenths of all drivers
      one-ninth of student drivers

Step 1. You Use Statistics.   Write down statistics or cases (appearing
on pp. 181–184) that could be used to support these topic and subtopic

sentences. You may also use reliable statistics you have found on your own.

1. Topic sentence: Road travel, still astonishingly high in numbers of miles, is essentially a pleasure activity.
   Subtopic sentence 1: Registered vehicles throughout the states ride, in total, long distances.

   _____

   _____

   Subtopic sentence 2: The facts show that passenger automobiles are basically in use for recreation.

   _____

   _____

2. Driver-training courses for young men and women are not so impressive after all.
   Subtopic sentence 1: There is some effect on the number of road violations when driver education is offered.

   _____

   _____

   Subtopic sentence 2: But little improvement in accident record stands out.

   _____

   _____

3. Topic sentence: Automobile construction is responsible in large degree for the safety of passengers.
   Subtopic sentence 1: The weight of the car is important.

   _____

   _____

   Subtopic sentence 2: The absence of safety features inside causes great damage in accidents.

   _____

   _____

   Subtopic sentence 3: Courtroom judges in increasing numbers willingly place blame on auto manufacturers.

   _____

   _____

QUOTATIONS AS DETAILS

Another source for supporting topic and subtopic sentences in your paragraph is quoted material from books, magazines, newspapers, radio, and television. You use someone else's words and ideas to support your own opinion on a given subject. Of course, if you read something or hear it on the radio, that thing is not necessarily true; however, by using reliable sources, you can impress your reader with the strength of your position.

If you want to show *exactly* what someone *wrote* or *said*, you need to use quotation marks.

If you want to *paraphrase* — that is, use your own words to give an idea of what someone else wrote or said — you don't need quotation marks. But mention your source in the paragraph nonetheless.

Hint:
1. Review the correct use of quotation marks on pp. 48–50 and p. 231.
2. Do not load up the paragraph with too many quotations or one quotation that is too long. Usually, no more than one-fourth of your paragraph should be made up of quoted material.
3. Use your own clear language in preference to dull or ordinary material you might want to quote.
4. Always mention your source: tell the date if you quote from a newspaper or a magazine. Underline titles of books, magazines, and newspapers. Use quotation marks for articles.

Examples:
1. Ralph Nader in <u>Unsafe at Any Speed</u> says, ". . .
2. A report on automobile safety in the <u>New York Times</u> of April 7, 1971 shows that . . .
3. C. Ogburn in "Motorcar vs. America" for <u>American Heritage</u> says, ". . .

Effective Quotations

Read the selection below (taken from a longer work) which uses quoted material. Answer the questions that appear after it.

SOME WORDS TO KNOW BEFORE YOU READ

invariably: unchangingly; constant
reconstructive: having to make over again
magnitude: size; extent
fortify: strengthen
laminated: made in thin layers
jocularly: humorously
fatigue-inducing: bringing about tiredness
eminent: well known; distinguished

Automobile Hazards

A great deal of improvement is also needed in windshields. Many industry spokesmen seem to overlook the fact that their proud wrap-around windshield can carve your wife's face to ribbons when her head goes through it — if, indeed, her entire body doesn't go through it. Troopers tell me a woman victim's first question when she comes to is, invariably, "Am I going to be scarred?" In an article on this subject in *Medical Tribune,* Dr. Paul W. Braunstein, clinical assistant professor of surgery, Cornell University Medical College, stated: "Soft tissue injuries, because they are not dangerous to life, frequently receive inadequate care . . . creating a reconstructive problem of great magnitude. The training of the young surgeon should include instruction in the fundamentals of plastic surgery. This is an admirable suggestion but a quicker solution would be to fortify the windshield glass so that it won't become a meat grinder for the features of the women who so often occupy the right front seat. Since about 1948 the makers of laminated safety glass — notably DuPont and Monsanto — have contended that increasing the thickness of the laminate from .015 inch to .03 inch would practically prevent penetration without incurring the risk of skull fracture. Yet it was not until mid-1965 that ten thousand Thunderbirds began to come off the assembly lines with this reinforced windshield which the entire industry had then adopted as standard equipment for all 1966 cars. This lag of almost twenty years is what is jocularly known in the trade as "the orderly development of the art!" The maddening reflection it produces is another condition of the windshield demanding intelligent attention by engineers rather than stylists. It is gratifying to hear an eminent safety engineer express himself on the subject: "One of the glaring examples, to me, of fatigue-inducing mechanism in an automobile is the absolutely impossible reflections and glare in the windshield of practically every present-day car," said William I. Stieglitz, chief of Design Safety and Reliability, Republic Aviation Corporation, at a joint conference on passenger car design and highway safety sponsored by the Association for the Aid of Crippled Children and Consumers Union in 1962. "It is a fundamental of the human being that the eye tends to focus on a near object rather than a distant object, and pulls to a bright object rather than to a dark object. This can be overcome only by conscious muscular effort and, therefore, it is a fatigue-inducing mechanism. I know cars that have beautiful steering wheels — I have one — a nice, bright, shiny chrome hub with two spokes that come out to the side. And when the sun's over here this reflects off the steering wheel to a nice, bright spot right on top of my windshield and visor. And every time I turn the wheel, this light flashes back and forth in front of my eyes. I have to fight to keep my eyes on the road. I know this creates fatigue — it diverts me — it cuts down my human capability. . . ."

— Paul W. Kearney,
Highway Homicide

1. Put a check next to the sentences that tell the source of the quotations used in the paragraph.
2. Why does the writer tell the professions of Braunstein and Stieglitz?

   _____

3. Put an X in the margin next to sentences that use numbers and statistics as details.

4. What is the topic of this paragraph? _____

   What is the writer's attitude toward his topic? _____

5. Circle the first word in each subtopic sentence.

Finding Facts on Your Own

Because the automobile has drawn so much criticism, individual and governmental groups have investigated many phases of automobile production, operation, and safety. Here are a few places you can turn to for statistics, cases, and quotations on several aspects of automotive use.

Reference Books
  Encyclopedia Brittanica
  Compton's Encyclopedia
  New York Times Encyclopedic Almanac
  The World Almanac
Books and Pamphlets
  American Automobile Association. *Teaching Driver and Traffic Safety Education.* New York, 1965.
  Cohn, David Lewis. *Combustion on Wheels, An Informal History of the Automobile Age.* Boston, 1944.
  Eighth Stapp Car Crash and Field Demonstration Conference. Lawrence M. Patrick, ed. Detroit, 1966.
  Engel, Lyle Kenyon. *The Complete Book of Fuel and Gas Dragsters.* New York, 1969.
  Flink, James J. *America Adopts the Automobile, 1895–1910.* Cambridge, Mass., 1970.
  Glenn, Harold T. *Youth at the Wheel.* Peoria, 1958.
  Kearney, Paul William. *Highway Homicide.* New York, 1966.
  McMillan, Robert K. *National Survey of Transportation Attitudes and Behavior.* Washington, 1968.
  Nader, Ralph. *Unsafe at Any Speed.* New York, 1965.
  National Research Council. Highway Research Board. *Urban Transportation Planning.* Washington, 1961.
  _____. *Traffic Safety and Accident Research.* Washington, 1968.
  _____. *Driver Characteristics.* Washington, 1967.
  _____. *Driver Personality and Behavior Characteristics.* Washington, 1961.
  _____. *Highway Safety; 6 Reports.* Washington, 1967.
  National Safety Council. *Accident Facts.* Chicago, 1970.
  Northrup, Herbert Roof. *The Negro in the Automobile Industry.* Philadelphia, 1968.
  O'Connell, Jeffrey. *Safety Last. An Indictment of the Automobile Industry.* New York, 1966.
Magazine Articles
  "Are Crowded Highways Getting Safer?" *U.S. News and World Report,* 68 (February 2, 1970), 50–52.
  "Drinking Drivers: Haddon Report," *Nation,* 207 (September 16, 1968), 229–30.
  "Drive to Make Autos Safer: What the Government Wants," *U.S. News and World Report,* 69 (August 31, 1970), 35–36.
  Fermi, L. "Cars and Air Pollution," *Bulletin of the Atomic Scientists,* 26 (May 1970), 43–44.
  Kasun, J. R. "Real Population Explosion," *America,* 123 (September 5, 1970), 112–14.
  Lear, J. "Green Light for Smogless Car," *Saturday Review,* 52 (December 6, 1969), 81–86.
  Macinko, J. "Tailpipe Problem," *Environment,* 12 (June 1970), 6–13.
  Morton, C. W. "Worst Drivers," *Atlantic,* 216 (July 1965), 125.
  "New Crusade to Make Your Driving Safer," *Changing Times,* 22 (February 1968), 7–10.
  Ogburn, C. "Motorcar vs. America," *American Heritage,* 21 (June 1970).
  "Safety: a Few New Requirements," *Consumer Report,* 35 (January 1970), 35.
  Scott, E. C. "What's Wrong With Driver Training," *Parents Magazine,* 43 (April 1968), 24–26ff.
  "Should You Teach Your Teenager to Drive?" *Better Homes and Gardens,* 48 (August 1970), 70ff.

"Who Knows Which Cars Are Safest? Massachusetts Study," *Consumer Report,* 33 (September 1968), 452–53.

"Women Are Safer Drivers," *Time,* 93 (June 13, 1969), 100.

Wright, J. W. "Sedan Racing: America's Hottest New Sports Thrill," *Popular Science,* 192 (June 1968), 68–71ff.

"Young and the Dead: Death from Motor Vehicle Accidents," *Scientific American,* 218 (March 1968), 58.

ENDING A PARAGRAPH

A paragraph must have some kind of closing, some indication that the ideas expressed are finished and that the writer has not just run out of things to say. In one-paragraph compositions of three hundred words, the closing may be made effectively in just one sentence. Often two or three sentences may conclude the paragraph. Here are a few pointers to help you write closing sentences.

SOME CLOSING-SENTENCE POINTERS

1. The closing sentence should leave no doubt in the reader's mind that you are finished with the paragraph.
2. The closing sentence should leave the reader with a feeling that you have done what you intended to do. It should clinch the main point of your theme for the reader by rounding off and making complete the entire paragraph.
3. The closing sentence should perform one of or a combination of these functions:
   a. Restate the main idea by referring back directly to the main idea stated in the topic sentence.

Hint: You do not have to use the same words that appear in the topic sentence. Find synonyms for the opinion word and the words that state the topic.

   b. Summarize one or more of the subtopics.
   c. Give the dominant impression of the experience being described.
4. Use transition words to help you conclude: *therefore, as a result, consequently,* and a number of others explained on pp. 132–133 are good for concluding, summarizing, and showing results.
5. Make the conclusion fit the tone of the paragraph. A funny, brief, clever conclusion might suit a humorous paragraph about automobile drivers. But a serious paragraph about dangerous drivers would require something more formal.
6. Remember: if the closing sentence briefly reminds the reader of your main point (it may hint at some of your subpoints too); if it lets the reader know absolutely what you were talking about; if it convinces him that you have done what you said you were going to do: you have written a satisfactory closing.

SOME SUGGESTIONS ON WHAT NOT TO DO IN CLOSING SENTENCES

1. Don't start a new topic.
2. Don't contradict the point you have tried to make. A one-paragraph composition that tries to prove that automobiles are dangerous in many ways should not end in this way that one student chose: "There are many uses for the automobile, however."
3. Don't make statements that are too obvious or overused. A paragraph dealing with the high costs of automobile maintenance would gain little by a conclusion like this: "Money is the root of all evil."
4. Don't say you are sorry for your lack of knowledge, lack of resources, or lack of interest. To say in your conclusion of a paragraph on sports-car safety "Although I do not know too much about sports cars, they seem very safe" is to make your reader wonder about your qualifications. If you are not qualified to write about the topic, select a topic for which you are qualified.
5. Don't end with a quick statement that indicates that your paragraph is over. Avoid endings like this:
   And that's all I have to say about the matter.
   The end.
   That's how it happened.
   I hope you have enjoyed my story.
   You see what I mean.
   That's all.
   It may sound unbelievable but it's really true.
   Therefore what I have said is true.
6. Don't take too many words to conclude. Be brief, to the point, and clear.
7. Don't make any sweeping statements that admit no possibilities of other ideas or actions. To conclude a paragraph in this way: "Therefore, all automobiles show no concern for the driver's safety"; or this, "This shows that there are no advantages in owning large, powerful cars," overstates your case by an *absolute* conclusion, that is, a conclusion that has no conditions or possible exceptions or limitations. Try to soften your point with words that permit other possibilities: *perhaps, it seems, we may conclude, I am in favor, a good suggestion is.*
8. Don't make your closing statement too obvious by saying things like: "As I have shown you in my paragraph . . . ," or "So my conclusion is . . ."

Step 1. Picking Good Endings.   Column I gives the topic sentence of a paragraph. Circle from Column II the closing sentence you think would best suit the paragraph. Explain your choice.

I

1. A father should share in the discipline of his child as his son grows up.

II

a. "Spare the rod, spoil the child!"
b. But the mother can do an excellent job in disciplining the child in the family.
c. So a boy needs a father who is a friend at times but who is a strong parent all the time.

2. The night a drunk driver hit our dog Blackie convinced me that alcohol and automobiles are deadly companions.

   a. Believe me, that's the way it happened.

   b. With that awful memory to haunt me, I will never drink so much as a beer if I know I have to drive soon after.

   c. Therefore, the night a drunk driver hit Blackie proved to me that alcohol and automobiles are deadly companions.

3. My uncle is the worst driver I know.

   a. It is therefore with great fear that I ever enter the car when my uncle is driving, because I always think back to this time when every one of us was so frightened and shaken that we were all literally trembling and thinking, "I'll never drive with him again! He shouldn't even have a license."

   b. Is your uncle a poor driver too?

   c. That is why I am in favor of yearly driver testing for license holders: men like my uncle could be noticed easily and removed from the road.

4. Highway authorities in New York State are taking important steps toward improving driving safety.

   a. Clearly marked roads, expanded highway lanes, and emergency repair areas at roadsides all show government involvement in safety.

   b. Also, automobile manufacturers have improved the cars themselves as a step toward safety.

   c. In spite of my limited information, I can conclude that governments are interested in driver safety.

Step 2. Rewriting Closing Sentences. Answer the following questions on closing sentences.

1. Reread "Jungle Boy" on pp. 59–60. How does the closing sentence give the *dominant impression of the experience* described in the paragraph? _____

_____

Write a different closing sentence which will *summarize* the main point of the paragraph. _____

_____

2. Reread "Horrors and High School Math" on p. 111. How does the closing sentence *form a judgment based upon the information in the*

paragraph? _____
_____

Write a different closing sentence which will *suggest some action that could be taken* based upon the ideas expressed in the paragraph. _____
_____

3. Reread "The House Didn't Catch Fire" on pp. 58–59. How does the closing sentence *restate the main idea* and *summarize the subtopics?*
_____
_____

Rewrite the closing sentence as a brief statement that gives the *dominant impression of the experience described.* _____
_____

4. Reread "Waking on a Monday Morning" on pp. 146–147. How does the closing sentence *restate the main idea* and *suggest some action that could be taken* based upon the information in the paragraph. _____
_____

Rewrite the closing sentence so that it *forms a judgment* based upon the information in the paragraph. _____
_____

5. Read "The Best Import Car" on p. 214. How does the closing sentence *summarize the subtopics?* _____
_____

Rewrite the closing sentence so that it *suggests some action that could be taken* based upon the ideas expressed in the paragraph. _____
_____

VERB-PART OPENERS FOR SENTENCE VARIETY

You can improve sentence variety by opening a sentence with a verb part or a group of words containing part of a verb. You have already dealt with two verb parts: the *infinitive* and the *-ing* word.

Using the *-ing* Opener

An *-ing* word used without a helping word (see p. 52) is not a verb, but it may be used effectively to open a sentence that contains a "legitimate" verb. Here is a complete sentence that contains a verb and subject:

An old Ford rattled down Marcy Street.

An *-ing* word may be added at the beginning.

Whining, an old Ford rattled down Marcy Street.
↙[comma here]

Hint: A comma must come after an introductory *-ing* word or an introductory group of words that contain an *-ing* word.

A single word that tells *how, when,* or *where* may be placed after the *-ing* word.

Whining annoyingly, an old Ford rattled down Marcy Street.
↙[how] ↙[comma here]

A group of words that tells *why* or *how* or *where* or *when* may now be added after the *-ly* word.

Whining annoyingly across the hot black road, an old Ford rattled down Marcy Street.
↙[comma here]
[These words tell *where.*]

Whining annoyingly through a broken muffler, an old Ford rattled down Marcy Street.
↙[comma here]

Sometimes a subordinator (see pp. 90–91) may appear as the first word in a verb-part opener:

After whining annoyingly through a broken muffler, an old Ford rattled down Marcy Street.
↖[subordinator] ↖[comma here]

Hint: Make sure that the first two or three words after the comma tell *who* or *what* is doing the action of the *-ing* word with which you have opened the sentence. See pp. 199–201 for some work with incorrect verb-part openers.

Step 1. Opening a Sentence Strongly. Add opening word groups to the complete sentences below by selecting an item first from Column I, then an item from Column II, then from Column III. You should have three new sentences for each statement below.

I	II	III
(-*ing* word)	(one word to tell *how, when, where*)	(a word group to tell *how, when, where, why*)
trembling	gracefully	in the sky at the lake
glowing	noisily	on the parkway below the hill
soaring	wildly	by the college near me
zooming	clumsily	through an open window
blasting	upward	in darkness with a whine
flying	there	on a warm summer night

speeding	yesterday	beyond the gray mountains
rumbling	brightly	along a lonely road
moaning	above	for his master at noon
creeping	fiercely	beneath a pale cloud
dancing	innocently	between the chairs
cheering	gloomily	across a stream
swimming	swiftly	in a dreary voice
speaking	today	at the campfire
drifting	slowly	beside an old oak

Example:

1. The boat returned home.

   a. *Speeding, the boat returned home.* _____

   b. *Rumbling noisily, the boat returned home.* _____

   c. *Drifting slowly across a stream, the boat returned home.*

2. A bird flew away.

   a. _____

   b. _____

   c. _____

3. The fire shone through the trees.

   a. _____

   b. _____

   c. _____

4. The youngsters giggled aloud.

   a. _____

   b. _____

   c. _____

5. One diver returned to the diving board.

   a. _____

   b. _____

   c. _____

6. A silver jet trailed above the house.

   a. _____

   b. _____

   c. _____

Step 2. Using New Words. Use the words given in the new *-ing* vocabulary (on pp. 176–177) to open sentences of your own. Use separate paper.

Step 3. Saying It Briefly.   The fewer words you take to express your ideas completely, the better your writing style becomes. *Compression* — tightening up ideas by stating them clearly and strongly in brief language — can be achieved through *-ing* constructions. For the first sentence in each group below, write an opening *-ing* word group and then attach it to the second sentence. Study the example given.

1. I stared out the window at an ugly gray cat in the street. I saw a German shepherd sneak around the corner. *Staring out the window at an ugly gray cat in the street, I saw a German shepherd sneak around the corner.*

2. The car shook from side to side. The car then died suddenly. _____

3. An automobile can use low-lead gasoline. The car works effectively and little pollution fills the atmosphere from the exhaust. _____

4. He stamped his feet. Then the old man shouted, "No, I won't move to the back of the bus!" _____

5. He knew we played an awful game of ball. The coach lectured us in a harsh voice about the need for teamwork. _____

6. Swede Savage drove in an old Ford against some of the best dirt-track drivers in the nation. He ran fourth fastest when his engine blew suddenly. _____

Step 4. *-ing* at the End.   The *-ing* construction works nicely at the end of sentences too. On a separate sheet of paper rewrite any five sentences you wrote from Step 1 or Step 2 above, this time placing the *-ing* word group at the end.

Sentence from Step 1: Drifting slowly across a stream, the boat returned.
Rewritten sentence: The boat returned, *drifting slowly across a stream.*

Step 5. Two *-ing* Words.   Two *-ing* words at the beginning produce an effective sentence. Complete each sentence below that begins with a double *-ing* construction by adding your own complete thought.

Example:
Running and skipping
Running and skipping, the three children hurried home.

Hint: The first ten words after the comma must tell who or what does the action of the *-ing* words.

1. Laughing and slapping his knee, _____

2. Working and studying, _____

3. Standing on the highway and thumbing a ride, _____

_____

4. Coughing and sneezing, _____

5. Wearing an old green cap and leaning against a streetlight, _____

_____

Infinitives as Openers

If you want to tell *why* the subject of a sentence performs some action, one effective way to do this is to open the sentence with a word group that starts with an infinitive. (An infinitive is made up of the word *to* and the present tense of the verb: *to hope, to sing, to laugh* are just three examples.)

[This tells *why* he had the tires checked.]

To ensure the safety of his car, he had the tires checked carefully.

[comma here]

Step 1. Using Infinitives as Openers. Use each of these infinitive word groups in front of your own complete sentence.

Hint: Use a comma after an infinitive word group when a complete sentence follows it.

Example:
1. To work in high places *To work in high places, a house painter needs a good sense of balance.*

2. To develop strong muscles _____

3. To learn the art of automobile racing _____

4. To listen to a rock concert _____

5. To travel across the country _____

6. To get a good job _____

Other Verb Parts as Openers

Word groups containing verb parts that end in *-ed*, *-n*, *-en*, or *t* may also be used to start sentences. Once again, a comma must come after the introductory word group; and the first words after the comma must tell who is doing the action of the verb part used in that introductory word group.

Spoken in a loud voice, the announcer's words reached the whole audience.
[verb part]   [comma here]   [This tells *what*
   [verb part]   were spoken.]

Disgusted with the papers and beer cans on the sidewalk, Mrs. Watson swept them into the street.   [comma]   [This tells *who* was disgusted.]

Step 1. Using Other Verb Parts as Openers. Begin a sentence of your own with the following verb-part openers. Be sure you study the examples given above.

1. Tested by leading authorities _____

2. Shattered in hundreds of pieces _____

3. Depressed and broken in spirits _____

4. Encouraged by our teacher _____

5. Annoyed with his speech _____

MAKING UP TITLES

The title is a helpful feature for the reader since titles give the first hint of what appears within the paragraph or essay.

HOW TO WRITE A GOOD TITLE	WHAT NOT TO DO IN A TITLE
1. Give the main idea of your paragraph in the title. 2. If you don't want to tell the topic in your title, pick out a word or word group from the paragraph that will hint at the kind of topic you are treating. Mr. Skibicki's title "A Few Minutes To Go" on p. 31 is one that does not reveal the full topic. 3. Arouse the reader's curiosity by the title. 4. Write the title last, after you have finished the paragraph. 5. If you can write an interesting, exciting title, good. If not, don't worry. It's better to be	1. *Do not* make the title the only statement of the topic. *A title is not a topic sentence.* If you tell the topic in the title as Miss Harris does on p. 58, repeat the topic in the topic sentence. 2. *Do not* try to be cute. If you want a funny title, be sure your paragraph deals with a humorous subject. 3. *Do not* use overworn expressions as your title: "A Stitch in Time Saves Nine" or "Love Makes the World Go Round" would be inappropriate titles for themes on prompt action and love because these titles are too familiar.

clear and to give a title that suits the paragraph than to be brilliant, clever, or original.
6. When you write your title, put it on top of page one. Capitalize all important words.

4. *Do not* write titles that are too long. A long full sentence is rarely used as a title.
5. *Do not* write a title that is too general.
6. *Do not* use quotation marks or underlining in your title when it appears on your composition.

Step 1. Topics and Titles. These titles could be effective, but the topic sentence that follows each is poor. Reread p. 7 on the topic sentence, and then rewrite the faulty topic sentence in the space provided.

Title
Example:
1. The Most Important Man

Poor Topic Sentence
This has to be the President of the United States

Rewritten Topic Sentence Based upon Title
The President of the United States, because of his many responsibilities, is the most important person in our country.

2. My Car, the Pest

I say this because it is always breaking down.

3. Stopping Car Thefts

It can certainly be done in a society with as many resources as ours.

4. Teen-age Drivers

It's good in one way but bad in another.

5. My Fear of Bridges

It all started when I was three years old.

Step 2. Understanding Effective Titles. Each statement in Column I is the topic sentence of a paragraph. Column II gives a title which is poor for one of the reasons explained in the charts on pp. 197–198. In Column III write why you think the title is poor; in Column IV try to write your own title.

I	II	III	IV
1. Many relatives have contributed to my happiness as a child.	Relatives	*too general*	*Relatives and Childhood Pleasure*
2. One frightening experience I recall is the awful time I was locked in a butcher's refrigerator for three hours.	Keeping Cool		
3. Minibike racing on the dirt roads near the Belt Parkway always meant fun and excitement for my brother and me.	My Brother and I Have Fun Minibike Racing near the Belt Parkway		
4. Police and student groups can learn to work together in harmony and cooperation.	Diggin' with the Fuzz		
5. I learned in several bitter lessons that telling the truth has more rewards than lying.	Honesty Is the Best Policy		

SOLVING PROBLEMS IN WRITING

Misused Verb Openers

One of the things you learned when you practiced with verb-part openers was to make sure that the first few words after the opening word group contained the subject of the verb part, the person or thing performing the action.

I Correct	II Incorrect
1. While dressed in a new overcoat,	1. While dressed in a new overcoat,

I *Correct*

1. While dressed in a new overcoat,
   [This tells who was dressed in an ✓ overcoat.]
   I brushed against a bus and dirtied my sleeve.
2. Feeling fine, the little old man
   [This tells that the man was feeling fine.]
   smiled at the trees and flowers.

II *Incorrect*

1. While dressed in a new overcoat,
   [This shows that the bus was dressed in ✓ an overcoat.]
   a bus brushed against me and dirtied my sleeve.
2. Feeling fine, the trees and flowers,
   [These words tell that the trees and flowers felt fine.]
   made the little old man smile.

It is obvious that the sentences in Column II do not say what the writer wants them to say (*trees* feeling fine? a *bus* dressed in an overcoat?). But the kinds of sentences you see in Column II appear frequently on freshman papers.

TO CORRECT THE ERROR MADE WITH VERB-PART OPENERS

1. Ask *who* or *what* is performing the action indicated by the verb part:
   Who is dressed in a new overcoat?
   Who is feeling fine?
   The words that answer that question must appear within the first few words after the verb-part opener.
2. Rewrite the sentence so that the subject is included in the opening word group. You will have to add a word to make a complete verb.

   Sentence 1 in Column II could be rewritten in this way:

   [added word to ✓ make a verb]
   While I was dressed in a new overcoat, a bus brushed against me and dirtied
   ↖[subject now included in opening word group]
   my sleeve.

   Sentence 2 in Column II could be written in this way:

   [added word to ✓ make a verb]
   Since the little old man was feeling fine, the trees and flowers made him smile.
   [subject now included in opening word group]

Step 1. Making Sense with -*ing* Words. For each item below, draw an arrow from the verb part to the person or thing that the *sentence says* is the subject. Then, rewrite the sentence so that it makes sense. One sentence is already correct.

Example:

1. Sailing through the air on graceful wings, my father pointed out the sea gull to me.

As the sea gull was sailing through the air on graceful wings, my father pointed it out to me. _____

2. After presenting the case to my mother, all my hopes were defeated.

_____

_____

3. Soaring into the nineties on this summer day, my mother escorted my sister and me to the local sprinklers located in the playground on Lefferts Avenue. _____

_____

4. While staring out my window, a fat gray squirrel rushed up the trunk of the tree. _____

_____

5. Smoking marijuana, a person's ambition is often decreased. _____

_____

6. While turning the ignition key, the battery suddenly died. _____

_____

COMMAS FOR CLARITY: QUICK REVIEW CHARTS

I. TO SEPARATE ITEMS IN A SERIES

A. We bought eggs, bread, and cereal.

B. My mother rushed to the garage, to the car, and then to the library.

C. Larry bought a Mustang, Gino bought an old Pontiac, but Andrew bought a sleek new motorcycle.

D. He was a tall, handsome, and hardworking man.

    Words 1, 2, and 3 describe "man." Since they are equally important, can be written in any order, and would make sense if the word *and* appeared between them (He was a tall *and* handsome *and* hardworking man), you need to use commas.

    However, in this sentence, *Steve ate four small chocolate candies,* commas are not needed. You could not reverse the order of the describing words, nor could you make sense if you used *and* between the words (Steve ate four *and* small *and* chocolate candies).

Hint: 1. Each item can be either one word (as in *A* above) or a group of words (as in *B* or *C* above).

> 2. There must be at least three items in the series.
> 3. The comma before *and* or *but* is *NOT* required.
> 4. To determine whether you need commas between describing words:
>   a. Try to reverse their order in the sentence;
>   b. Try to use *and* between the describing words.
> If you can do a and b, use commas.

Step 1. Commas and Series.   Put in the commas where they belong. One sentence needs no commas.

1. There were birds children and adults sunning themselves in the park.
2. A good novel presents an exciting march of scenes contains lively dialogue and arouses in the reader an interest in the characters.
3. Without a word without a cry of pain but with a look of determination in his pale blue eyes the old man pulled himself up from the bed.
4. One lively green frog leaped from the pond.
5. An attractive lively exciting cover often sells a book more than the printed words inside.

II. TO SET OFF A DIRECT QUOTATION (see pp. 48–50)

I said, "Sit down!"
"I'm not tired," she replied.
"But a person needs rest," I said, "even if she's not tired."

Hint: If you want to use a question mark or an exclamation mark after a quotation, do not use a comma, too.

"Where were you?" he asked.
   "Stand up!" she screamed.

Step 2. Commas for Quotations.   Put in the commas where they are needed.

1. I wanted to be an actress the young girl said but now I'd be happy with any good job.
2. Where could Carrie have run off to her sister asked.
3. One old man said I haven't seen her.
4. I know that girl someone shouted.
5. Everyone knows her she exclaimed.

III. TO SET OFF INTRODUCTORY SECTIONS

A. *Certain Transitions as Openers.* One word or several words.

[comma]

Nevertheless, try to speak in a loud voice.
In other words, be careful!
[comma]

B. *Certain Conversational Words.* To set off *yes, no, oh;* and *well, why,* and *now* used in conversation.

[comma]   [comma]

Yes, he will be there. *Why,* how did that happen? *Oh,* that is awful!
[comma]

C. *-ing Word or Other Verb-Part Openers* (see pp. 192–197).
-ing → *Sailing along the lake,* I felt peace and contentment.
opener   [comma]

verb-part → *To reach the top of the shelf,* the child stood on a chair.
opener
(infinitive)
verb-part → *Scribbled quickly,* the note was hard to read.
opener   [comma]

D. *Subordinated Word Groups as Openers.*

[subordinator]

Although the moon hung in the sky, the sun still shone.
[comma]

Because the vocabulary troubled us, we used a dictionary to check definitions.
[subordinator]   [comma]

Hint: Brief opening-word groups not covered in a, b, and c above usually do not have commas after them.

[no comma]
In a few months I will be twenty.

[no comma]
Beyond the trees stands a small house.

If the introductory subordinated word group is brief, you may omit the comma.
When he sang I left the room.
[no comma]

Step 3. Commas for Openers. Put in commas where they belong. One sentence needs no commas.

1. On the other hand drag racing is exciting.
2. Watching all the men on the corner I wondered if an accident occurred.
3. To run a car effectively a driver must have a good sense of judgment.
4. While I sat on the steps a sudden burst of rain drenched my shirt and black denim pants.
5. On that special day I stood on the stage with my diploma in my hands.
6. However hard work is not always unpleasant.

IV. TO HELP SEPARATE TWO COMPLETE THOUGHTS WHEN A COORDINATOR IS EXPRESSED (see pp. 85–86)

Hint 1: Coordinators are *and, but, for, or, nor.*

Memphis is considered by many as a large city, [comma] but it has few problems of traffic congestion.

Just turn the key, [comma] and you will see that this car is like no other you have ever driven.

Hint 2: The comma is usually left out when the two complete thoughts are very brief.

We ate [no comma] and they drank.
They flew, but we drove there. [no comma]

Step 4. Commas and Coordinators.   Select a sentence from Column I and coordinate it sensibly with a sentence in Column II using one of the five coordinators. Use a comma when necessary. Write your new sentences in the space provided.

I
1. I hate to drive in traffic.
2. Several people will march to Washington.
3. Road maps are complicated.
4. Safety devices now appear in automobiles.
5. A high mileage-per-gallon ratio is one way to judge a car.

II
They can go to Union Square in New York to demonstrate their support.
They are essential.
It is never pleasant stopping at every corner for a long wait.
Low maintenance is even more important.
They have decreased accident fatalities considerably.

1. _____

_____

2. _____

_____

3. _____

_____

4. _____

_____

5. _____

_____

V. TO SEPARATE WORDS OR WORD GROUPS THAT INTERRUPT THE MAIN IDEA OF THE SENTENCE

(Some of these types of words and word groups were used as sentence openers. See Chapter 3.)

A. *Transition Words to Interrupt.*

We felt, however, that whitewall tires were unnecessary.
[commas here]

But the kangaroo, to be sure, is an unusual animal.

B. *Subordinating Word Groups to Interrupt.*

That old truck, which has ignition trouble, is hard to start.
[commas here]

Mr. Davis, who drives to work, always complains about the traffic.
[commas]

Caroline, whose voice is soft, is really charming.

The subordinated word groups in B above do not give information to identify the subject, and they could be removed from the sentences without changing the meaning. We know which truck is hard to start (*that old one*) without the interrupter. We know who complains about traffic (*Mr. Davis*) without the interrupter. We know who is charming (*Caroline*) without the interrupter. Therefore, commas are needed to set off the added information. But if the subordinating word group is needed to identify the subject, commas are not needed.

[no comma]   [no comma]
A truck which has ignition trouble is hard to start.
[These words identify the truck. Without these words, we don't know which truck is hard to start.]

[no comma]   [no comma]
People who drive to work always complain about the traffic.
[Without these words it would seem that all people complain about the traffic.]

[no comma]   [no comma]
A girl whose voice is soft is charming.
[Without these words, we don't know which girl is charming.]

Hint: If *that* opens the subordinating word group, you usually do not need commas.

An idea that is clever is not always good.
[no commas]

Gasoline that contains lead pollutes the air.

C. *Interrupters That Describe*

1. *-ing* word groups to interrupt

A shaky station wagon, laboring up the hill, backfired in a crash.
[commas here]

The puppy, trembling, drew close to its mother.
[commas]

2. Interrupters starting with *-ed* words or other verb parts

[comma] [verb part] [comma]
Miss Kelly, *dressed* in red, ran for the bus.

[comma] [verb part (infinitive)]
The dog, *to get* his food, barked wildly.

[comma] [verb part] [comma]
A mirror, *broken* in small pieces, lay on the street.

Hint: The interrupting words in 1 and 2 above just add information about the subject. They could be left out of the sentence without disturbing the meaning. Therefore, commas are needed. However, when interrupting word groups like those above identify the subject, commas are not used.

[Not just any wagon backfires: this word group identifies the wagon and is essential to the meaning of the sentence.]

A wagon *laboring up a hill* can backfire.
—[no commas]—

[It is only a woman dressed in red who is attractive according to this sentence. This word group identifies the subject.]

A woman *dressed in red* is attractive.
[no commas]

3. Other describing words

[These words describe the driver. They could be left out of the sentence.]

The driver, a doctor, was not injured.
[commas]

The Mustang, a new white convertible, crashed into a pole.
[These words describe the car which has already been identified. The words could be left out of the sentence.]

Step 5. Commas for Interrupters. Select from Column II an interrupter that could be used sensibly within each complete thought in Column I. Decide whether or not commas are needed. Then, write each new sentence on the blank lines provided.

I

The automobile is Harriet's.
Tires are important.
Napoleon died unhappy.
A book is hard to put down.
An antenna is useless.

II

a science fiction writer
crossing a highway
that is exciting
twisted out of shape
standing in the driveway

Ray Bradbury is popular today.
A dog can get in trouble.

who wanted to conquer the world
which resist blowouts

Example:

1. *A dog crossing the highway can get in trouble.* _____

2. _____

3. _____

4. _____

5. _____

6. _____

7. _____

VI. SEVEN FAMILIAR PLACES FOR COMMAS

1. In dates, after everything but the month:

   On April 7, 1970, my life began.
         [commas]
   On Saturday, May 7, 1971, Alexander's Department Store had a sale on men's suits. [commas]

2. In an address:

            [comma]
   A riot occurred in Brooklyn, New York.
   Atlanta, Georgia, has many qualities of Northern big cities.
      [commas]

3. Before and after someone's title if the title comes after his name:

        [commas]
   Carl Berkson, Ph.D., practices psychology in Los Angeles.
      [no comma]
   Dr. Smithers has retired.

4. To set off someone's name, if that person is being spoken to in the sentence:

   Carol, why don't you do your assignment?
           [commas]
   I understand, Mr. Harrington, that you cannot pay this last installment.

5. In informal letters, after the opening words and the words before the signature:

   Dear Martin,
   Dearl Carl, ← [comma]
   Yours sincerely,
   Very truly yours,

   Hint: In a formal letter, use a colon after the salutation.
   Dear Mr. Porter:
   Dear Senator Byrd:

6. To indicate that words are left out:

> [Comma here shows that the words
> "man owns" are omitted.]
>
> The older man owns the sedan; the younger, the convertible.
>
> 7. To set off a variety of numbers:
>   [comma]
>   volume four, page eighteen
>   [comma]
>   six feet, three inches
>   19,385 students
>   [comma]

Step 6. Using Commas in Seven Ways. Fill in the commas where they are needed.

1. Robert Carswell M.D. lives at 541 Main Street Newburgh New York.
2. On Tuesday January 12 1970 the dog measured two feet eight inches.
3. David is nineteen; Barbara sixteen.
4. But Jerry the hero leaves the stage in Act IV Scene 3.
5. Harriet Walder climbed 5620 feet in Littleton New Hampshire on July 19 1953.

Step 7. Comma Review. Here are some sentences written by professional writers. All the commas have been left out. Put in the commas where you think they belong. In the blank space, write in the number of the review chart on pp. 201–208 that tells why the comma (or commas) is needed.

_____ 1. Life like every other blessing derives its value from its use alone.
—Samuel Johnson

_____ 2. God heals and the doctor takes the fee.
—Benjamin Franklin

_____ 3. To be sure in all ages people have been afraid of loneliness and have tried to escape it.
—Rollo May

_____ 4. Stopping in her tracks she first extended her arm bent her elbow and leaned forward from the hips—all to examine the watch strapped to her wrist; then she gave a loud double-rap on the door.
—Eudora Welty

_____ 5. We pray that peoples of all faiths all races all nations may have their great human needs satisfied.
—Dwight David Eisenhower

_____ 6. My eyes were naturally weak and I was subject to frequent headaches; which however could not chill the ardour of my curiosity or retard the progress of my improvement.
—John Milton

Step 8. New Words and Comma Rules. Each of these sentences contains one or more of the vocabulary you studied in this chapter. Use commas correctly in each sentence based upon the Comma Review Charts.

1. Alluding to sales of imported cars the manager graphically illustrated the failure of his salesmen.
2. Mrs. Russo who sustained complex injuries was lamenting her failure to use seat belts.
3. A definitive report on vehicular emissions will clear up the figures reported by private industry but statistically there are still many uncertain points.
4. The speaker brandishing the pages of his notes and sputtering his disapproval of government cooperation asserted "We need more help from federal agencies!"
5. Although chronic wheezing often indicates asthma few doctors will agree that no other disease causes similar breathing difficulties.

Step 9. More Review.   Follow directions. Use separate paper.

1. Write a sentence that you might speak to a friend. Use his name at the beginning of the sentence.
2. Write a complete sentence that tells your street address, your city, and your state.
3. Write a sentence that tells the name of some well-known singer. Use the words *a popular singer* after the person's name.
4. Write two *complete* sentences about the kinds of cars you like. Use the word *and* or *but* to separate the sentences.
5. Write a complete sentence that tells *three* television programs you like to watch. Use the word *and* only once.
6. Write a complete sentence about some sport you enjoy. Use the words *that I enjoy* somewhere in the sentence.
7. Write a quotation sentence about something you said at dinner to someone at home. Use the words *I said* somewhere in the sentence.
8. Write a sentence about two things you like to do during the summer. Use the word *although, when, if, while,* or *because* at the beginning of the sentence.
9. Write a sentence of advice to someone who has never crossed a busy city street before. Start your sentence with either of these word groups: *Crossing a very busy city street* or *To cross a very busy city street.*
10. Use the word *however, nevertheless, on the other hand,* or *besides* after the word *thought* in this sentence: *None of us thought that the robber was a professional.*

WORD OR SYMBOL? USING ABBREVIATIONS

When you take notes, it's often convenient to use some sign or shortened form of a word to save time. But in formal writing, you should avoid abbreviated forms of words.

What Not to Use	What to Use Instead
& or + or &c	and
Feb., Apr., Wed.	February, April, Wednesday Write out the word for the day or month.
bio, psych, eco	biology, psychology, economics Write out the word for all school subjects.
thru, tho, boro nite, lite, brite	through, though, borough night, light, bright Don't leave off the ends of words or make up short forms.
st., h'way, ave, blvd, rd, co	street, highway avenue, boulevard } Always write these out. road, company
ch., p., pp.	chapter page } Write these out, except in foot- pages } notes or bibliography.
lbs., oz., ft. in.	pounds, ounces } Measurements are spelled feet, inches } out.
L.A., Ill., Calif. Rocky Mts.	Los Angeles States, countries, Illinois cities, geographical California places are not Rocky Mountains abbreviated.
e.g	for example
no., #	number
{and etc.} {ect. }	etc. This is the abbreviation for *etcetera*. Do not use *ect.* or *and etc.*

Hint: Use *etc.* very infrequently.

WHEN YOU CAN USE SHORTENED FORMS	
1. +, &c, Co., Inc.	when part of an official name A & P, Tiffany & Co.
2. Mr., Mrs., Dr.	before someone's name is mentioned
3. Jr., Sr.,	after someone's name is mentioned
4. Ph.D., M.D., M.A.	after someone's name
5. FBI, NAACP, UN	Some organizations and government depart- ments are usually referred to by initials. No periods are necessary after the letters.

6. A.M., P.M. (or a.m., p.m.)	when numbers appear directly before 8:15 P.M. **Hint:** If you use the word *o'clock*, write out the number: ten o'clock *not* 10 o'clock.
7. $, No.	when numbers come after $5.00, Booth No. 6,

Hint 1: Abbreviations usually require periods.
     2: If you don't know what an abbreviation means consult any dictionary.
     3: It's better, in general, not to use abbreviations.

DO'S AND DON'TS ABOUT NUMBERS

DON'T use the number if you can write it out in one or two words.

Use	fifty	not	50
	three hundred	not	300
	eighty-eight	not	88
	nineteenth	not	19th
	eightieth	not	80th

DO use the number if it takes more than two words to write it out.

Use 654   not   six hundred and fifty-four

DO use the number for the year and day of a date.

February 2, 1971

Hint: Don't use -st, -th, -nd, -rd after any number in a date.

DO use numbers if you need to mention a series of numbers.

On the rack hung 50 red dresses, 340 skirts, and 15 vests.

DO use the number for percents and decimals.

Of the students 45% were boys.
The paper measures 8.73 inches in length.

DO use the number for items in street addresses:

480 Rockaway Parkway
1874 Ninth Avenue

Hint: If the street itself is named by a number, write the word out if the number is below ten. Otherwise, use the number, *without -st, -th, -nd, -rd* at the end:
251 East 91 Street
1880 18 Street
37 Fifth Avenue

> DON'T start a sentence with a number.
>
> Not *9 parents attended* but *Nine parents attended.*
> Not *350 seats were in the room* but *The room held 350 seats.*
>
> DO use the number for parts of a book.
>
> On page *18* the author presents a graph to illustrate his point.

Step 1. Down with Abbreviations.   To save printing costs, most want ads use a large number of abbreviations. In the space provided, rewrite this advertisement so that the unnecessary abbreviations are removed.

WANTED Jr. exec. psych.
or soc. major. Travel from N.Y.
thru western states, esp.
Nev. & Calif. for young
co. Manage 25
drug stores. Local sales
meetings every Wed P.M.
start Feb. 1972. Hi $$.
Write Weaver & Sons,
60 1st Av, Chi. Ill.

_____
_____
_____
_____
_____
_____
_____
_____
_____
_____

WRITING THE PARAGRAPH

Your assignment for this theme is to write a paragraph of at least fifteen sentences to discuss some aspect of the automobile. The topic you choose, of course, will determine whether you use concrete sensory detail (based upon your own experience) or statistical or quoted material from reliable sources. Read the paragraphs below written by freshmen about the automobile. When you finish, write the answers to the questions on topic sentences; statistical figures, cases, and quotations; closing sentences; and titles.

The Dangers of the Automobile

   Automobiles are dangerous because they pollute the air with harmful chemicals and because they are frequently unsafe to drive in. Polluting the air, the exhaust emissions of a car make people ill every day. Aside from its stress on heart ailments, carbon monoxide fumes cause nausea and dizziness. Writing in *Highway Homicide,* Paul W. Kearney reports that a faulty exhaust system that fed CO_2 into his car lulled him to sleep at the wheel, forcing him to drive clear across the four-lane divided Taconic State Parkway, and escape death by a miracle. Other hydrocarbons, nitrogen dioxide, and lead similarly make breathing hard to bear and may contribute to paralysis, blindness, insanity, and sterility. Poisonous car emissions also cause other fatal diseases. One is emphysema, a respiratory ailment; between 1950 and 1959, reports Gerald Leinwand in a study of air and water pollution, deaths from this disease rose from 1.5 in every 100,000 to 8 per 100,000. Bronchial asthma is another condition often aggravated by air pollution and after a person with asthma is disturbed for a long time by smog, he may die from lack of oxygen. Other diseases linked with air pollution are lung cancer and chronic bronchitis. But in addition to the danger of pollution, cars are often unsafe for the driver and his passengers because of bad design and construction. The Chevrolet Corvair was a perfect example of a car unsafe to the driver. Ralph Nader in *Unsafe at Any Speed* shows how one woman in 1961, Mrs. Rose Pierini, lost her left arm when her Corvair suddenly turned over on its top just beyond the San Marcos Overpass in Santa Barbara, California. Furthermore, the instrument panel can cause many dangers to the passenger. Nader says, "Dr. William Haddon of the New York Department of Health tells how one of his cases, a young girl, lost her eye by the instrument panel. When the car jerked forward, the girl's eye went into a protruding knob on the dash board." Announced in a Cornell study, total injuries from the instrument panel range from simple fractures of the pelvis to crushed chests. There is no doubt that in the areas of pollution and safety, automobiles are very dangerous; but with an educated public, well aware of these problems, important changes can be brought about.

— Barry Krakow

Step 1. Reviewing the Main Points. Answer the following questions about the preceding paragraph.

1. What two aspects of the topic does the topic sentence announce? _____

_____

2. What case does the writer use to prove the first part of his topic? _____

_____

3. What statistical information does the writer use to prove the first part

of the topic? _____
4. Check in the margin the case and the direct quotation that the writer uses to prove his second point.
5. What part of the closing sentence helps summarize the purpose of the paragraph? What part of the closing sentence brings in a new but re-

lated idea? _____

_____

The Best Import Car

Because the makers of the Porsche 914/4 give a better car for the money, I think that automobile is the best import car on the market. For $3,595 a driver owns a car that is a fun sports model with the economy of the reliable Volkswagen. The Porsche 914/4 is far from a racing car with only an eighty-five horsepower engine, but through controlled gear selection the car moves very well on the road. The acceleration of the Porsche is good also, going from 0 to 30 in 4.0 seconds and from 0 to 60 in 7.55. Looking at these acceleration figures and remembering that the automobile gets the same fuel economy as a Volkswagen with its 16.4 gallon tank, a potential owner knows he will get good speed and value. Handling is also excellent as a result of the placement of the engine in the middle of the car. The 96.5 inch wheel base and the quick steering response make the Porsche extremely maneuverable in traffic. A 36.1 turning radius and the 45/55 percent weight distribution also adds to handling ability. The rate of stopping is another good feature prospective car owners should consider carefully. *Motor Trend Magazine* in a recent issue stated, "Four wheel disc brakes combined with the 914/4's light weight (2,000 pounds) make braking fast, sure and straight." Although the ability to stop quickly is important for any sports-car driver, it is an essential feature, too, for the average car owner. As far as seating comfort is concerned, the Porsche 914/4 is exceptional for a car so small. Even a person six feet tall, *Motor Trend* shows, can assume an arms-out driving position and will be able to sit straight-legged without feeling cramped and uncomfortable. And the luggage capacity is remarkable! Since the engine is in the middle of the car, owners have a trunk in the front and a trunk in the back, adding a lot of room for a sports car. The Porsche 914/4 fulfills all the obligations it was built for; anyone can drive this car with comfort and safety and economy too.

—William Harvey

Step 2. Paragraph Review. Answer the following questions on the preceding paragraph.

1. What is the topic of this paragraph? Which word in the topic sentence

   tells the writer's opinion? _____

2. What figures does the writer use to prove

   a. good acceleration? _____

   b. good handling? _____

3. For what purpose is the quoted material from *Motor Trend* used? _____

   _____

4. Is the closing sentence effective? Why? _____

5. Is the title effective? _____ What other title might be good for

   this paragraph? _____

WRITING THE AUTOMOBILE PARAGRAPH: SOME PROGRESS REMINDERS

1. Write a topic sentence that tells the subject of your paragraph and your opinion of or your attitude toward the topic (see p. 7 for review).
2. If you intend to discuss several aspects of the topic, use subtopic sentences to introduce each new feature of the topic. Whatever details you use should back up the specific idea mentioned in the subtopic sentence.
3. Use statistics, cases, quotations, concrete sensory images, or a combination of these as details to support your ideas.
4. Study the chart on p. 184 and pp. 180–181 to review the correct writing of statistics.
5. Make sure your ideas flow smoothly and logically. Use transitions to smooth out the writing.
6. Use a variety of sentence types:
   Begin sentences with subordinators (pp. 90–92).
   Open at least one sentence with an *-ing* word (pp. 192–193).
   Open one sentence with an infinitive (p. 196).
   Open at least one sentence with a different verb part (p. 197).
   Open one sentence with one or two *-ly* words (p. 39).
   Use one coordinated sentence (pp. 85–87).
7. Write a title *after* you write the paragraph.
8. Check your paper for errors in agreement. Look out for run-on errors, sentence fragments, errors in capitalization, plurals, and careless errors that can be spotted easily through proofreading.
9. Strive for a paragraph of fifteen or twenty sentences, 350 to 400 words.
10. Study the student themes on pp. 212–214. Use clear and lively language in your own paragraph.

Some Topics for Automobile Themes

The suggested topics (they are not titles!) in Column I can be developed in paragraphs that use *statistics, cases,* or *quotations* as detail. Topics in Column II can be developed through narrative and description in paragraphs that use *concrete sensory detail* (see pp. 5–6). As your instructor suggests, use a subject from one column or the other if you cannot think of your own topic.

I	*II*
improvements in gasoline	your first driving lesson
training as a racing-car driver	a driving accident you had
drunk drivers in your city	your boyfriend's car
new safety devices for the automobile	a car you loved
citizens work for better cars	trouble with the car
teen-age drivers: killers of the road	your father (mother) and the family car
pollution and the automobile	a flat tire
the car as a necessity	talking a policeman out of giving you a ticket

good brakes and safety
the worst drivers
women drivers and safety
public transportation to the rescue
the benefits of driver education
automobile accidents and high speeds
night driving

a joy ride
a car theft
fixing up an old jalopy

THE PROFESSIONALS SPEAK

In the following selection notice how the use of sensory language allows
the reader to participate in the experience of an automobile accident. When
you finish reading, answer the questions.

SOME WORDS TO KNOW BEFORE YOU READ

sluggishness: slowness; lack of energy
terrain: area of land
traction: friction that allows a wheel to hold securely on to a surface
berate: scold
hover: hang suspended in the air
ineptitude: the quality of being unsuited to a task
allegations: statements made without any proof
convulsively: with a quick jerking action
serenity: peacefulness
unscathed: not harmed

Anatomy of an Accident

In a horrible way, it was almost symphonic—this continuing din of beaten metal
as our rented Volkswagen slammed over the rock-strewn shoulder of the rain-
slick Nova Scotia road. It was the prelude to a serious accident. And it was happening to us—to my wife and me. Many thoughts raced through my mind—some of
them very strange.

When it was all over, the 1971 Volks was a total wreck. Somehow we survived.
This is the way I remember every turn of the wheel, every brutal bump, every stray
thought—from the sudden beginning to the crumpling, metal-twisting, glass-
shattering end.

Our next-to-last day of a two-week vacation in Nova Scotia had begun badly.
Rain, pelting sheets of it, the kind that umbrellas and boots can't keep out, drowned
our plans to sightsee along the 100-mile drive from Liverpool to Halifax. As a result, we lingered over breakfast and delayed the start of our journey until about
11 A.M. Then, buckling our shoulder harnesses, we headed east along Trunk Highway 3.

It was a Sunday, and traffic was light. We passed a string of houses leading away from Liverpool and started to climb a long grade. Longing for the sports car I used to drive, I cursed the Volkswagen's sluggishness. Betsy tried to pick up something on the car radio, but, whether it was the rain, the terrain or our distance from large cities, she could raise nothing. Had we been able to hear the news, we would have known that Hurricane Beth was to blame for the downpour.

Instead, we diverted ourselves by trying to recall the high spots of our vacation. We remembered a wildlife park near Halifax, and Betsy said I reminded her of an elk while she pictured herself as a stork. Casting everyone we could think of as an animal, we were soon laughing as we drove through the rain.

Few buildings spoiled the expanse of trees on both sides of the roadway. In a clearing on the left, a sign announced that thousands of acres to the north had been set aside as a forestry project. As we approached the crest of the long grade, the road narrowed to two lanes divided by a faded white line. To either side of the road were gravel shoulders, overgrown with weeds and dotted with utility poles.

Although the rain had not dangerously decreased my visibility, curves now made it difficult for me to see very far ahead or behind. For all I knew, we were the only car on the road. I was traveling about 25 or 30 miles per hour, although the posted speed limit was 60.

How It All Began

It was just after 11:15 A.M. when I turned the steering wheel gently to the left. The road was level at this point, and the curve on which I had to turn was gradual. But the Volkswagen began to skid to the right. It did not seem to be a dangerous skid, but the unexpected movement of the car suddenly quickened my senses and I vividly recall noticing just then a 40-foot chain of rough gray rocks embedded in the right shoulder with a telephone pole at the end, and then a car 100 yards away coming toward me in the opposite lane.

I've skidded in an automobile before. A momentary loss of traction, I was thinking, that's all. Turn into the skid. Then, like all the other times, the car will snap forward as the tires once again grip the road. Betsy will berate me for going too fast, even though I was driving slowly. "That was a close one," I would hear myself admitting.

I turned the wheel to the right, and my hand fluttered toward the gearshift. Sometimes, I was thinking, the safest way to slow down is by shifting into a lower gear. But then, engaging the clutch will give me even less control over the car. My foot, meanwhile, hovered over the brake. Never brake in a skid, I advised myself. Braking may cause all of the wheels to lock and thereby throw the car into a spin.

My eyes flicked up to the rearview mirror. No one was behind me. All I could see was the road's shimmering, rain-spattered surface. But the oncoming car ahead was drawing closer. I was worried about that because I knew the skid, by ending suddenly, could swerve our car into the opposite lane or cause it to fishtail from lane to lane.

Perhaps two seconds had passed since we first began to skid. We were still moving forward and slightly to the right, toward the line of rocks with the telephone pole at the end. Thoughts began tumbling through my mind. I recalled an accident I had seen once in Quebec: A straight, endless superhighway. A car with a cracked windshield in the center. A portly woman leaning ponderously against the vehicle, blood streaming down her legs.

Even so, I was not yet imagining Betsy or myself injured. At worst, the car might be dented. I hoped the rental agency wouldn't notice. I found myself back at the Citadel Inn in Halifax.

"Of course you want full coverage," the man behind the counter was saying.

"How much is it?" I asked.

"One dollar a day."

"What's the alternative?"

"One hundred dollars deductible at no extra cost."

"I'll take that."

Well, the most it can cost is $100, I thought as we proceeded toward the threatening shoulder now less than a car's length away. One hundred dollars—the cost of four good meals. I suddenly remembered the lobster dinner we had enjoyed just two days earlier in Yarmouth.

Another instant passed. I turned the wheel slightly more to the right; that is, toward the shoulder of the road, in the direction of the skid, but saw with horror that I had accomplished nothing.

I began to appreciate for the first time that an accident, a big one, was about to occur. I felt humiliated. As a reporter I had typed "when the car went out of control" countless times, each time secretly scorning the driver's ineptitude. Betsy's allegations about my reckless driving notwithstanding, I pride myself on my ability. How could such a *stupid thing* be happening to me?

Onto the Shoulder

"Here it comes," I remember saying to Betsy, afraid to steal a look at her. And come it did. We skidded onto the shoulder, and the right front wheel sank into it, causing the car to dip sickeningly. The motion also tossed us forward against our seat belts. The sound of gravel drumming against the underside of the fender clattered in my ears. I forgot then about the oncoming car, knowing we would not be in its path now. To this day I don't know if that driver stopped when he saw us skidding off the road or continued on his way. My attention turned to the telephone pole rooted ominously at the end of the path strewn with low, stony obstacles. The first rock was inches away, so I spun the steering wheel hard to the left.

Nevertheless, with a booming jolt, rock and wheel collided. It was a low rock, and so we went over the top of it with a hellish sound of steel being bent, twisted and crumpled as the rock's sharp edges raked the underside of the car. Then we slammed over a second boulder, and again there were the tearing and ripping sounds beneath us. Perhaps seven or eight seconds had passed since we first lost traction.

Though now I shoved my foot hard against the brake, our Volks bounded convulsively over still more rocks on the shoulder. Gravel drilled our windshield, and brush tore at the doors. An unforgettable din of pounded metal swelled about us. Rattle followed rattle, crunch followed crunch.

I squeezed my eyes shut, while Betsy, she later told me, reacted in the opposite way, thinking I would not be hurt as long as she kept her eyes on me. I refused to think of bodily injury at all and so was more concerned about the fate of the Volks than of Betsy and myself. What I did realize was that the underside of the car was being bashed and ripped into shreds, and I was hoping that the rocks would stop us before we smashed into the telephone pole.

I now had no idea which way we were facing, but I felt that we had spun halfway around and were going backwards over the rocks. I recalled that a Volkswagen carried its engine in the rear and I hoped this would help absorb shock. At the same time, I saw my Great Aunt Lizzie in a hospital bed, telling me about the automobile accident that brought her so much pain in the last years of her life. A cake on the seat beside her had begun slipping to the floor. She grabbed for it, rammed into a telephone pole, and woke up in the hospital emergency room. She told me: "I heard someone say, 'We'll have to cut her clothes off.' Then I knew it was bad."

Heading toward a telephone pole of my own, I dreaded the possibility that we, too, might hear those words.

By now, I had stopped counting the number of bone-shaking bumps caused by the rocks. I knew only that there were more rocks and then that telephone pole.

Then suddenly we were sprayed with shards of glass from every window in the car. Simultaneously, stones from the seashore that we had been carrying in a paper bag scattered like confetti around the inside of the car. Shoes flew about, too. If this was the end, I was thinking, it's a hell of a stupid way to die. Cursing myself for putting Betsy in this situation, I began to wonder what her mother would say to me.

Perhaps 15 seconds had passed altogether. Our speed had slowed, but the Volks, battered and bent, struggled onward. I thought about the possibility of an explosion or a fire, and then, strangely, I was struck by the irony of all this violence happening to us in a setting of such serenity.

As unexpectedly as it began, our accident ended. With a final groan of metal, the Volkswagen tilted over on the driver's side and came to rest, rather gently as it turned out, against the telephone pole. The engine stopped, and all I could hear was the rustling of bits of glass every time one of us moved and the patter of the rain on the car. There were gnawing pains in my arm, hip and head.

"Are you all right?" Betsy screamed at me, and then repeated the question before I could answer. Her face was white. I urgently demanded the same information from her. Strapped though she was in her shoulder belt, her weight pressed against me. Beyond her, through the rain, I glimpsed the slate sky and the treetops.

As I squirmed against the door fixtures, Betsy asked again, "Are you all right?" I assured her that I was, and she said she was, too. I was astonished that my glasses still rested unbroken on my nose. I felt as if we were waiting for a carnival attendant to collect our tickets after a ride on the "whip."

I then remembered Kitty Genovese, the girl stabbed to death in Queens while neighbors ignored her shouts for help, and I wondered whether anyone would come to our aid. Before long I heard running feet and disembodied voices. "Better not move them," one voice suggested.

"Nonsense," I complained to the voice. "We're perfectly all right. We're perfectly all right." The rain refused to subside, and pieces of glass rattled whenever I moved. We managed to release our belts, and hands from unseen helpers were hoisting Betsy through her broken window.

Attempting to prove as much to myself as to our benefactors that I was able to get out unassisted, I stood up and, putting my hands where Betsy's window had been, heaved myself through the narrow opening. Betsy, trembling, stood on the road, her hand to her head. She said later that she feared the blood on her hand, which came from tiny glass cuts, had come from her head, where a lump the size of an egg had risen.

I looked from Betsy, who seemed more shocked than hurt, to the car. It lay steaming in the rain, its rear end against the telephone pole. We had apparently slowed down enough by the time of the final impact so that the pole had made only a small dent in the body. The overall damage, nonetheless, was total—some $1,246 worth, I learned later.

Nothing seemed unscathed, and virtually nothing was in its right place. The glove compartment had sprung open, spilling maps everywhere. The back seat had popped up. The Volkswagen's body was scarred and covered with dents. Its fenders and bumpers were crushed. The right front wheel was folded toward the underside. The left front wheel was twisted crazily. The frame was bent. The car, in short, was a complete wreck.

And we, miraculously, walked away from it.

Priest Stops to Help

A priest who stopped en route to deliver a sermon was the first person, besides Betsy, I remember talking to. He saw Betsy's pallor and urged me to get her to a hospital. She insisted she was not badly hurt and waited in a passerby's car while I and some others gathered our luggage. As I hauled the last item up to the car, I glanced back down the road in time to see a big Buick swerve perilously but not quite skid just where we had lost traction. The driver continued on his way, glancing in wonder at our wreckage.

Only after we started off to the hospital in the stranger's car did Betsy become aware of a piercing pain centered in a swelling on her left thigh as large as the one on her head. Neither of us said so, but we both were afraid her leg was broken. Betsy had apparently hit her head against the steering wheel and her leg against the gear shift. A doctor in the emergency room examined us both and prescribed a pain-killer for Betsy. He said her "broken" leg was just a bad bruise and her head injury was no more than a bump.

Peering into my eyes, the doctor asked what had hit me. I told him I didn't know but that the bruise on my temple may have occurred at one point when I was thrown against the door. His prescription for me was simply, "Good luck."

After his sermon, the priest returned to the hospital and drove us to a Mrs. Bashow's guest house in Liverpool. After helping us carry our belongings up the front steps, he stopped in the rain to offer his blessing. "You know," he said, "when I saw your car, I thought you were goners."

—Malcolm N. Carter

Step 1. Understanding the Selection.   On a separate paper, write the answers to these questions about "Anatomy of an Accident."

1. Where has Malcolm Carter used images of sound and color to make the scene particularly clear?
2. Copy out the one sentence you think most unforgettable because of its clear presentation of action.
3. Although this narrative uses chronological arrangement of details (see pages 45–47), the author uses *flashback* in several places. Where does he remind us of things that occurred in the past? Why do you think he uses such a device?

4. Do you think the accident could have been prevented? How? Does the author think so? Is it possible to lay any blame for this catastrophe?
5. Several difficult words may be figured out without a dictionary if you use your skills with prefixes and suffixes (see pages 414–419). What meanings can you give for these words: *divert, embedded, disembodied, perilously, benefactors.*

REACHING HIGHER

Here are several other areas in which statistical information might provide you with astonishing conclusions. Select one and write a well-written paragraph using the skills you have learned in this chapter.

poverty in your home state
ghetto health conditions
child beatings
dishonesty in politics
prison conditions in your city
hunger and the Southern black man
coal mines and working conditions
sex revolution on the campus
American Indian education
deserters in the Vietnam war
the makeup of the freshman class at your college

chapter 6
WORDS AS SNAPSHOTS:
IMAGES AND PARAGRAPH EXPERIMENTS

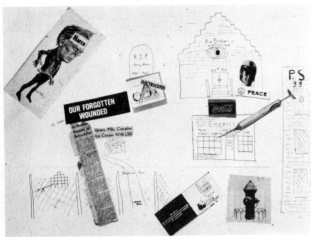

Len Basile

Annie Derkrikorian

Jacqueline Boston

INTRODUCTION

In their ability to paint pictures, words are often equal in strength to photographs or any other visual forms of communication. Words that make pictures we name *images;* and images themselves grow from the application of the senses to your written language. Quality writing relies heavily upon imagery: the more an author can get you to see, to hear, to smell, to touch exactly what he has seen, heard, smelled, or touched, the more outstanding and appealing his writing is.

How does a writer build imagery? It is no mystery, really, because each of us has the tools of response to the world we write about: hands, eyes, noses, and ears. We all hear and see and feel and smell the world around us. The hard part is training ourselves to become more aware of what we experience, to use the full power of our responses both to learn about a scene and to show it sharply through words to a reader.

This chapter asks you to employ in a variety of paragraph assignments your own sensory responses in clear pictures.

VOCABULARY

Step 1. Sharpening the Senses. These words help name sensations of touch and smell. Check their definitions in a good dictionary (or see Appendix A for assistance) and write them in the blank lines.

Smell   *Touch*

savory _____   supple _____

rancid _____   clammy _____

musty _____   gossamer _____

pungent _____   furrowed _____

medicinal _____   sinewy _____

Step 2. Applying New Words. From the vocabulary above, select a word that best describes the following:

1. a plant of soft wood _____

2. vinegar _____

3. ridges in a forehead _____

4. the arm of an athlete _____

5. rotten eggs _____

6. turkey roasting in an oven _____

7. perspiration on a cool day _____

8. a spider's web _____

9. an old trunk opened after many years _____

10. a hospital corridor _____

Step 3. Energetic Verbs.   Each of these verbs names an action that creates a specific picture. After referring in a dictionary to the ones you do not know (and to Appendix A to check yourself), write the definitions in the blank spaces.

1. totter _____

2. trudge _____

3. deplore _____

4. glare _____

5. grimace _____

6. sprint _____

7. saunter _____

8. swagger _____

9. clasp _____

10. spurn _____

Step 4. Setting the Action.   Write a sentence about each situation described below. Use one of the above words to name the specific action.

Example:
1. a man taking a slow, relaxed walk

   The clerk on his lunch hour sauntered slowly around the block.

2. an old lady crossing the street weakly

   _____

3. two teen-agers looking for a fight

   _____

4. two hands coming together for a firm shake

   _____

5. a child's face after he bites a raw, bitter onion

   _____

6. a girl's behavior towards a boy she dislikes very much

   _____

7. the way a girl might look at a boy she dislikes very much

_____

8. after breaking a window in a house down the block, a young boy running away from the scene

_____

9. a mother expressing her feelings about a son wounded in war

_____

10. a man walking home after a very hard day at work

_____

BUILDING COMPOSITION SKILLS

Exploring Imagery

Step 1. A Sensory Riddle. For some object with which you are familiar, speak aloud four or five sentences that describe the object. *Do not mention the name of the object.* Your description should be so complete that people in the class can identify easily what you describe. For the most complete descriptions, use a number of concrete details (see pp. 5–6) in your images. Here is one sensory riddle from a college freshman. Which pictures appeal to the sense of smell? Which picture gives the liveliest action?

White Rectangle

This smooth white rectangle sputters up Polo Road every evening with the clink of bells and squealing children down the street. One youngster steps up to the rectangular object, holds out a silver coin, and a man in a white hat swings open a door with a thump. Curls of smoke wind out and the odor of chocolate and strawberry and coldness fills the air.

—Marie Della Porta

Use the chart below to fill in details of the senses for the object before you speak. Miss Della Porta's chart is reproduced on the next page so you can see how to use your chart effectively.

SENSORY RIDDLE CHART

Images of Color and Action	Sounds Made by or Associated with Object	Smell	Sensations of Touch

SENSORY RIDDLE CHART

Images of Color and Action	Sounds Made by or Associated with Object	Smells	Sensations of Touch
white rectangle	sputters up Polo Road	chocolate	coldness
swinging door	squealing children	strawberry	smooth
curls of smoke	clink of bells		
child with a silver coin	door opens with a		
man in white hat	thump		

—Marie Della Porta

In case you have trouble finding something to describe, select one of these:

1. pencil
2. telephone
3. apple
4. school bus
5. razor

6. supermarket
7. bar
8. lecture hall
9. television set
10. swimming pool

Step 2. A Person in a Sentence.   Ask a volunteer to stand and speak about himself before the class for five or ten minutes. Write *one* sentence on the blank lines below which describes the volunteer in the midst of some action. See how many senses you can use in the one sentence: appeal to color, sound, touch, and smell. Use a lively word to show action. Study the student samples below. When you are finished, read your own sentence aloud.

[color]   [action] [touch] [color]
Staring through wire gold-framed glasses, Jean brushes a soft strand of brown

[sound]   [action]
hair off her forehead and then coughs nervously into a trembling hand.

—Beth Anna Winters

[touch]   [color]   [color]
His hairy arms stretching from black pants pockets, a yellow shirt hanging loosely

[touch]   [sound]
over a worn leather belt, Danny breathes deeply cold morning air and whispers,
"I don't know what to talk about."

—Albert Leone

_____

_____

_____

_____

Using Concrete Language

Step 1. Naming Specifically.   One way to create pictures is to use the exact word you want rather than a general term that needs descriptive words to make the picture specific. The word *elm* or *oak* is preferred to *tree* for that reason. The reader gets an added identification for the object through the exactness of the name. For each general term in Column I, write three different *specific* terms to replace it in Column II.

I   II

Example:

1. book   *dictionary, encyclopedia, notebook.* _____

2. bird   _____

3. game   _____

4. animal _____

5. dessert _____

6. tool   _____

7. workman _____

8. candy   _____

9. fruit   _____

10. flower _____

Step 2. Specific Actions.   A verb can give clarity to an image by naming an action that the reader can instantly visualize. Yet there are many verbs in the language that are poor in their ability to show actions; these verbs, in images, are inferior to verbs that name motions, sounds, and activities. Substitute for the word(s) in italics a verb that shows a specific action, that creates a picture. You may wish to select some form of the verbs listed in the box below. Check a dictionary for words you don't know.

slouch	weave	rumble
tremble	wiggle	zoom
zigzag	shoot	shift
shake	squirm	stroll
shuffle	coo	storm
chatter	screech	clutter

Hint: See Step 3 on p. 224 for other energetic verbs.

_____   1. The sun *was* in the sky.

_____   2. She *walked* happily into the room.

_____   3. He *walked* away angrily.

_____ 4. The train *arrived* at the station late.

_____ 5. The child *went* to his mother.

_____ 6. The old man *came* across the street.

_____ 7. Two birds *were* in the cherry tree.

_____ 8. He *sat* in his seat uncomfortably.

_____ 9. The car *came* around the corner.

_____ 10. A plane *was taking off* down the runway.

Step 3. Verbs in Your Sentences.   Write your own sentences for any five of the verbs listed in the box above.

1. _____

2. _____

3. _____

4. _____

5. _____

Step 4. Toward Completeness.   The more specific a picture is, the more completely does the reader see and understand it. To make a picture specific you need to use sensory language. For each item in Column I below, add a color and/or some word that shows a sensation of touch and write your word picture in Column II. Then, in Column III, write a sentence that shows the object in the midst of some action. Try to use a verb that indicates sound. Make your image as original as possible.

I	II	III
Example:	[touch] [color]	[sound]
1. tire	a soft black tire	A soft black tire hissed at the curb as air escaped from a loose patch.
2. bus		
3. trees		

4. umbrella

5. garbage can

6. basketball

7. toy

8. telephone

9. bee

10. apple

Step 5. Definitions in an Image.   Try to explain some hard-to-define emotion, idea, or concept like *hope, love, fear, power, hate, life, war, sorrow, joy, death* in an image rich in sensory detail. Study the student samples below. Use separate paper for your definition.

Life is a rosebush growing in my garden, full of thorns but fragrant and lovely.

—Alayne Finkelstein

Fear is sitting in a creaking dentist's chair seeing only the top of Dr. Rifkin's bald head as his trembling hand tries to zero in on a cavity.

—Janet Hutter

Hope is a blind beggar garbed in a tattered coat who hears a coin tinkle in his rusted cup.

—Rose Jachter

Life is an elusive, black fly buzzing through cool air, slipping past the blue-eyed youngster stalking him with a fly swatter.

—Terry Sanders

SOLVING PROBLEMS IN WRITING

MORE PUNCTUATION AIDS

The Period (.)
1. Use a period after a sentence that makes a statement.
   I watched a crow circle over a twisted oak.
   Everyone was tired.
2. Use a period after a sentence that makes a mild command.
   Take the subway into Queens.
   Buy United States Savings Bonds.
3. Use periods after initials.
   Robert E. Lee
   John F. Kennedy
4. Use periods after abbreviations.
   Ph.D. N.J. etc.

The Question Mark (?)
1. Use question marks at the end of sentences that clearly ask questions.
   Who wrote *A Farewell to Arms?* ← [Question mark: end of question]
   "Can't you hear me?" David shouted. ← [End of sentence: no question mark]
2. Some sentences, though they mention that a question is being asked, do not ask the question themselves. Such *indirect question* sentences are not followed by question marks.
   She wondered why he did not call. ← [Period]
   He asked who brought the station wagon. ← [Period]

The Exclamation Point (!)
1. Use the exclamation point at the end of a sentence that shows strong emotion, sharp surprise, a forceful command, or strong emphasis.
   I hate all men!
   I don't believe it!
   Call the police!
   I meant what I said!
2. Certain words and expressions like *what, oh, alas, hurray, bravo* often introduce exclamations.
   Oh! What am I going to do?
   What! You stole that car?
3. Only the individual writer can determine which sentences are spoken with strong emotion. *Do not overuse the exclamation point.*

Step 1. A Variety of Endings. Put in the correct end marks (a period, question or exclamation mark) below. Use capital letters to indicate the start of a new sentence.

Inauguration

Who can forget the exciting televised inauguration from Washington, DC, of John F Kennedy as President of the United States what a fine wintery day it was indeed all the congressmen and officials of state were dressed warmly in gray and black overcoats awaiting the inaugural address but President Kennedy wore no overcoat could that moment have been a hint of the unconventional, strong, and courageous path America would take under his leadership for the next few years in any case, he displayed the simple sense of challenge he represented as he stood before his audience without a coat with blazing eyes and a firm straight jaw he challenged every American with his famous statement, "Ask not what your country can do for you, but what you can do for your country"

QUOTATION MARKS
(See pp. 49–51.)

1. Use quotation marks to show someone's exact words.

   "Let the past be forgotten," she said unconvincingly.
   "I cannot believe," he said, "that she would do such an awful thing."
   He asked, "Where are all my friends?"

Hint: The exact words may be quoting what someone said in speaking, or the exact words may be a statement quoted from a book. In any case, quotation marks are needed.

2. Use quotation marks to set off the names of short stories, poems, chapters, articles, or essays that are parts of books, magazines, or newspapers.

   I read "Trade Winds" in *Saturday Review*.

   The anonymous poem "Frankie and Johnnie" appears in *Understanding Poetry* by Brooks and Warren.

UNDERLINING

Underlining is used in handwritten sentences to show when italics are needed.

1. Underline all titles of books, magazines, movies, TV shows, and newspapers to show that these titles should be in italics.

   Most people still enjoy Gone With the Wind.

   If the sentence were printed it would look like this:

   Most people still enjoy *Gone With the Wind*.

2. Underline names of ships, trains, and airplanes.

   Lindbergh's plane, The Spirit of St. Louis, landed amid cheers of congratulations.

Step 2. Quotes and Italics. Use quotation marks or underlining (to indicate italics) as required in the following sentences.

1. On such a beautiful day said my mother you should be outdoors in the sun.
2. Earl Wilson's column It Happened One Night appears in the New York Post and frequently reports of celebrities sailing for Europe on the Queen Elizabeth.
3. Frank Sinatra Jr., appearing on variety shows like the Dean Martin Show, has a number of middle-aged fans reports TV Guide.
4. The second chapter of D. H. Lawrence's Sons and Lovers is called The Birth of Paul, and Another Battle.

USING SEMICOLONS (;)

1. Use a semicolon to separate two complete sentences that are closely related (see p. 85).

   The landlord painted the fence; now he is painting the steps.

2. Use semicolons instead of commas to separate items in a series if some of the items contain commas themselves.

   [Comma]

   On our picnic Lynette brought a whole chicken which, because of deep fry-
   [End of first item in series.
   Use semicolon because commas
   [Comma]   already appear within the item.]
   ing, was a rich golden brown; two pounds of potato salad that her mother
   [End of second item in series.]
   prepared; and a basket of cold, delicious fruit.

HOW TO USE THE COLON (:)

1. A colon comes
   a. after the opening in a formal letter.

      Dear Mrs. Stevenson: Gentlemen:

      (Use a comma after informal openings.)

      Dear Steve,

   b. between the hour and the minute when you write the time in numbers.

      The plane left at 6:18 P.M.

   c. between the number of the chapter and verse in the Bible.

      Matthew 6:12 is inspiring.

   d. in a title, to separate the main name of the selection from a subtitle (see p. 222 for example).

> e. between act and scene in a play.
>   *Macbeth* II:iii
>
> 2. Use a colon when you introduce a long or detailed list of items.
>
>   √[colon]
>   Remember to bring to registration the following: two sharpened) [Commas
>   pencils with erasers, your admissions letter, your IBM registration } separate items in
>   card, and a check for $36.00 for student fees.) series.]
>
> **Hint:** Don't use the colon for a simple listing.
>
>   √[no colon]
>   We bought shoes, gloves, and dungarees.
>
> 3. Use a colon whenever you want to force the reader's attention to the state-
>   ment that comes after the colon; that statement usually explains or clarifies
>   the opening part of the sentence. [This part
>   of the sentence
>   [Colon pushes emphasis to   explains the
>   √what comes after.]   √first part.]
>   Of this I am sure: I do not want any more life insurance.
>
> 4. Use a colon before you introduce a formal quotation.
>
>   √[colon]
>   About greatness, Ralph Waldo Emerson said: "Every human being has a right
>   to it, and in the pursuit we do not stand in each other's way."

Step 3. Semicolons and Colons in Practice. Use the semicolon or colon correctly in each sentence below. Be prepared to explain your answer.

1. At 9 15 the bus arrived it was late as usual.
2. In Shakespeare's *King Lear* III ii the old king speaks these famous words "I am a man more sinned against than sinning."
3. These are the things all smart automobile drivers have handy a good flashlight, that is, one whose batteries have been recently tested a flare which may be used, if needed, in an emergency a spare tire and a jack that works easily.
4. One goal should guide every man in political office the wish to help the people who have elected him.

THE PARENTHESES ( )

Parentheses are used to set off words or word groups that are not as important as the rest of the sentence. *Parenthetical expressions* add information and/or make some side comment on or about the material in the sentence.

[The information in parentheses is a side comment that adds information.]

{ Abandoned automobiles (and there are thousands in New York State alone) line the roads and highways in ugly clumps.

[The information in parentheses is a side comment.] { If you have seen *Midnight Cowboy* (certainly you have), you know how unlikely friendships can develop through need.

[The information in parentheses adds information about the author's birth and death.] { Dylan Thomas (1914–1953) read his own poetry brilliantly.

Hint: 1. Although parentheses indicate less important information, do not ignore or fail to read what appears in parentheses.

2. Commas also set off parenthetical information, but commas give the material more importance.

 a. That old man (a carpenter) works hard.
 b. That old man, a carpenter, works hard.

 The words *a carpenter* are parenthetical in both sentences, but the commas in b make that parenthetical information more important than it is in a.
3. Don't use parentheses too often in your writing.

Step 4. Your Statements in Parentheses. Add your own parenthetical information to the blank spaces in the following sentences. Use parentheses (or commas) as explained above.

1. My old bike _____ still stands amid cobwebs in the garage.

2. Public-housing laws _____ have done little to integrate suburban middle-class communities.

3. If you want to earn a great deal of money _____ you will need the kind of training a community college can give.

THE DASH FOR INTERRUPTION AND SUMMARY

1. Use a pair of dashes to set off a sudden shift in thought or structure of the sentence.
[This question breaks into the complete thought expressed in the sentence.]
 That old maple—did you see it?—lost all its leaves in June.

Hint: Parentheses could be used here as well. But the dash makes the information more important and stresses its sudden break into the main idea of the sentence.

2. Use a single dash before a summary of details mentioned earlier in the sentence.

 Running a mile each day, exercising in a careful program, choosing food thoughtfully—these are the ways to keep weight down.
[This part of the sentence briefly summarizes the meaning of the details in the first part.]
3. Don't use the dash too often in your writing.

Step 5. Using the Dash. These four sentences all require dashes. Put them in where they belong.

1. I believe you are too how shall I say it? too lively to sit at a desk all day and type.
2. A torn wallet, two faded photographs, a small gold pin that was all that was left of the man who lay dead on the street.
3. I do not I repeat I do not believe that it is safe to skate on Mill Lake.
4. The lecturer yawned loudly a rude thing to do indeed before his audience.

THE HYPHEN AS DIVIDER

1. Use a hyphen to separate parts of certain compound words (words that are made by putting together other words).

teen-age	president-elect
thirty-one	well-bred
self-assurance	brother-in-law

2. Use a hyphen to divide a word when there is no room on the line to finish the word.

   After the union leaders approved the con-↙[hyphen]
   tract, the members voted it quickly into effect.

3. Use a hyphen to separate the years of birth and death of some important figure.

   Rudyard Kipling (1865–1936)

Do's and Don't's for Dividing Words
1. Don't separate the word if you can avoid it.
2. Do put the hyphen at the end of the first line, *never* at the beginning of the next line.

   approved the con-
   tract
       Not
   approved the con
   -tract

3. Do separate the word at the end of a syllable and nowhere else.

be-lieve	not	beli-eve
re-call	not	rec-all
per-mit-ting	not	pe-rmit-ting

Hint: Check the dictionary for proper syllables in words (see p. 461, "How to Read a Dictionary Entry").

4. Do divide the word, if pronunciation allows, so that a consonant starts the part of the word that appears on the next line.

writ-ten   stop-ping
            But
        leop-ard

5. Don't divide words of one syllable: *laugh, called, brought.*
6. Don't leave just one letter of a word at the end of the line. Write the entire word on the next line.

Not He tried to e-   *But*   He tried to
      rase his mistake.   erase his mistake.

7. Don't carry over to the next line brief word endings like *-ly* (happi*ly*), *-ed* (hint*ed*), or *-ing* (sing*ing*).
8. Don't divide people's names.

Harry, Barbara   *not*   Har-   Bar-
                          ry   bara

9. Do leave a space at the end of a line rather than fill it with part of a word that is incorrectly broken.
10. Do learn the difference between hyphen and dash.

In writing by hand	*In typing*
The hyphen is a short line (-). The dash is a longer line, about the length of three hyphens (—).	The hyphen is a short line (-). The dash is typed as two hyphens with no spaces before or after them (--).

Step 6. Breaking Up Words. In the blank spaces rewrite the words that appear below to show where you would use hyphens to break the word at the end of a line. Put an X for those words you would not divide.

1. confuse _____

2. presume _____

3. coughed _____

4. illustrate _____

5. persistent _____

6. broken _____

7. selective _____

8. fellow _____

9. David _____

10. guardian _____

THREE USES FOR APOSTROPHES (')

1. Possession (see pp. 323–329)
   A. If a word *does not* end in *s*, in order to show ownership, add an apostrophe *s* ('s).

      boy + 's = the boy's hat
      men + 's = the men's club

B. If a word *does* end in *s*, in order to show ownership, add only an apostrophe (').

ladies + '   The ladies' coats were soiled.
boys + '   The boys' bicycles all fell down.

Hint: If a person's name ends in *s* and the name is to indicate possession, add *either* apostrophe *s* or just an apostrophe.

Doris' book   or   Doris's book

2. Contractions
   To show where letters are omitted in words that are combined in contractions, use an apostrophe.

it's = it is   I'll = I will
doesn't = does not   you're = you are
hasn't = has not   I've = I have

Hint: Contractions are usually informal words and should be avoided in formal compositions. Write out the two words in your themes.

3. Special plurals
   To show the plurals of numbers, letters, and symbols, use an apostrophe *s* ('s).

There are two *t*'s in committee.
Our address has three 5's in it.
All &'s should be written as *and*.

Hint: Aside from these special cases, *do not* use apostrophes to show plurals.

Step 7. Correct Apostrophes.   For each word in parentheses, add an apostrophe or apostrophe *s* so that the sentence is correct and write the new word in the blank. If the word needs no apostrophe, put an X in the blank.

1. This is _____ book (Charles).

2. The radio did not work because _____ tubes were old (its).

3. Three _____ keys were found on the pavement (children).

4. I hope to get three _____ this semester (B).

5. A _____ dream is not always realized (man).

6. Those _____ telephone numbers _____ easy to get (girl, werent).

7. The voters approved of Senator _____ proposal (Javits).

8. Most _____ allowances are not enough to cover frequent dates (student).

9. _____ Mr. _____ daughter, _____ it? (Thats, Morris, isnt).

10. _____ moving his car to the other side of the street? (whos).

Step 8. A Punctuation Review. Use correct punctuation in the paragraph below. Although the ends of sentences are indicated by periods, sometimes you will have to change them to exclamation or question marks. The following list indicates what punctuation you will need. Do not add commas.

What to Add
Colons: 3
Quotation marks: 4 pairs
Exclamation marks: 1
Question marks: 1
Semicolons: 2
Periods: 4
Underlining (italics): 3
Hyphens: 2
Apostrophes: 3
Dashes: 1 pair
Parentheses: 2 pairs

Conrad's Photographic Eye

One of the real masters of vivid sensory images is Joseph Conrad 1857 1925. Pictures that are rich in color and sound, pictures that are set on the sea in all its beauty these fill the pages of Conrads works. Born in Poland, he settled in England in the 1890s at the age of thirty seven. Conrad came to love about the English language its musical qualities its sweet, yet harsh, sounds its rich, lively, fluid motion. Conrad knew no one can deny it the importance of the senses in creating word pictures. My task which I am trying to achieve is, he wrote, by the power of the written word to make you hear, to make you feel—it is, before all, to make you see.* How could that be more clearly expressed. It is Conrad's extraordinary power to make readers see that has led many MA and PhD students to study his novels like Lord Jim and Nostromo. What marvelous use he makes of the language. In the description of a railroad changing from the famous short story Heart of Darkness he says A slight clinking behind me made me turn my head. Six black men advanced in a file, toiling up the path. They walked erect and slow, balancing small baskets full of earth on their heads, and the clink kept time with their footsteps. Black rags were wound around their loins, and the short ends behind waggled to and fro like tails. I could see every rib, the joints of their limbs were like knots in a rope; each had an iron collar on his neck, and all were connected together with a chain whose bights swung between them, rhythmically clinking.* It must be a

* End of quote.

scene like this that John Galsworthy who, incidentally, was a writer and fellow traveler journeying on Conrad's ship the Torrens thought of when he wrote Conrads eyes never ceased snapshotting; and the millions of photographs they took were laid away by him to draw on.

CAPITAL LETTERS

Step 1. What Do You Remember?   Write a *full sentence* response to each question below.

1. What supermarket does your family do business with?

   _____

2. What river runs through your state?

   _____

3. What are three subjects you enjoy at college?

   _____

4. What season of the year do you find most enjoyable?

   _____

5. If you could board a plane and fly anywhere, in which direction would you go?

   _____

6. Which animal in the zoo do you think is funniest?

   _____

7. What high school did you attend (write the words *high school* as part of your answer)?

   _____

8. Which war do you think was the bloodiest?

   _____

9. What book have you read and enjoyed lately?

   _____

10. Write about the holiday you enjoy most; mention the month in which it occurs.

    _____

If you could not make up your mind about the spelling of some of these, study the reference charts on capital letters on the following pages.

QUICK REFERENCE CHART: WHEN AND WHEN NOT TO CAPITALIZE

Geography

Passaic River
Catskill Mountains
    not
a tall mountain

New York City
    not
our city

Yellowstone National Park
Market Street
    not
a noisy street

Historical Occurrences, Names, and Writings

Tonkin Resolution
Boston Tea Party
Seward's Folly
Fifth Amendment
The Constitution

School Things

LaGuardia Community College
    not
a new college

Mohawk High School
    not
our old high school

Coleman Junior High School
    not
a junior high school

English, Spanish, French
    not
American history
    not
economics, biology, business

Hint: Languages are always capitalized. Other subjects are not, except when specific courses (usually indicated by numbers) are meant:
Economics 13.2
History 64

a sophomore in college
the senior class

Buildings and Organizations

Dime Savings Bank
Sears Roebuck and Company
Brookdale Hospital
Pathmark Supermarket

Republican Party
San Francisco Giants
Girl Scouts

The Word "I"

Always capitalize the word I
  When *I* saw her, *I* was
  delighted.

Days, Months, Seasons, Celebrations

Monday
April
    not seasons
spring, summer, fall,
autumn, winter
Election Day
Festival of Lights
New Year's Eve

Religion, Race, Nationality

God, Lord
Bible, Genesis
New Testament
bless His Name
the Egyptian gods
Catholicism
the Jewish religion
Protestant beliefs
Negro, Indian
Dutch Reformed Church

Titles

Books, Stories, Shows, Poems

"Oh Captain, My Captain"
Love Story
A Tale of Two Cities
    not
a book by Dickens

The Washington Post
The Ed Sullivan Show
"The Legend of Sleepy
  Hollow"

People

President Nixon
Judge Black
Dr. Bracken
He is the president of the
  company.
Mr. Davis, President of the
  company
    or
Mr. Davis, president of the
  company

Harriet Parsons, Ph.D.
    not
a teacher, a lawyer, a
professor

Hint: If the title takes the place of a person's name, use a capital. The Mayor arrived late. The mayor's job is difficult.

Areas and Directions

Lower East Side
East-West relations
Far East
Midwest
lives in the West
    but not for
    directions
New York is six miles east of
here.
They drove north across the
bridge.

The Family

I get along with Mom.
    or
I get along with mom.
This is Aunt Celia.

No capitals to show relationship:
That is my sister.
Our uncle is generous.
My aunt is very helpful.

Writing Letters

Opening: Capitals for first
word and any names.
  Dear Mr. Stevenson:
  My dear Miss Trumball:
  Dear Jerry,
Closing: First word only:
  Sincerely yours,
  Yours truly,
  Very truly yours,

No Capitals for Plants, Animals, Games

daisies	a vicious lion
sycamore tree	baseball
an old oak	football
bananas	swimming
a bluebird	monkeys
six sparrows	apple

Step 2. Making Sense with Capitals. In each of these sentences, the first letter of several words is omitted. Decide whether or not you need a capital or small letter and then fill in the blank space.

1. Across the __otomac __iver in __ashington a number of tall __uildings shine in the morning sunlight, especially in the __astern region.

2. My __igh __chool even looks different from __orth __ounty __ommunity __ollege; __he college includes a __ampus of __rees and __lowers.

3. To study __ussian __istory, a student must be aware of the nature of the __remlin as well as the __ussian __evolution.

4. A __parrow fluttered from one __lm to another, occasionally dropping to the ground and playing with a __andelion in the __rass.

5. It is not true that science—__iology, __hemistry, __hysics, __sychology—attempts to deny the existence of __od; it is possible to believe, for example, in __reudian ideas and the __ible as well.

6. In the month of __une, my __other doesn't go to her job with the __ew __ork __elephone __ompany; __nstead she visits __incoln __ark and sits on a bench feeding the __igeons.

Step 3. Correcting Your Errors. Return to Step 1, p. 239. Make any corrections necessary based upon what you have learned from the reference chart.

Step 4. Review: Vocabulary and Capitals. Each sentence below contains vocabulary words introduced earlier in this chapter. Correct the sentences so that capital letters are used where they belong. The number in parentheses tells how many changes you need to make in the sentence.

(7) 1. in a musty chinese restaurant in new york's chinatown last summer i ate the most savory stew i ever tasted.
(5) 2. a sinewy youngster sprinted west on buffalo avenue; when he reached the junior high school he leaned against the gate and said, 'man, im tired!''
(4) 3. if your lover spurns you, valentine's day has no balmy february moment.
(5) 4. when aunt helen grimaces, her furrowed brow looks like the bark of the old maple that stands on merrick road.
(5) 5. in a gossamer dress of lace the young sophomore sauntered out of barrow auditorium, her arm clasped tightly to the president of the campus democratic party.

LEVELS OF LANGUAGE: FORMAL OR INFORMAL

A college professor of English, driving down a busy street, spots a large truck double-parked and blocking the roadway. He stops his car, sees a big hulk of a truck driver reading a magazine behind the wheel, and knows he must ask for the truck to be moved. The man wants to speak politely yet firmly: his sole purpose in talking is to get that truck from his path. Which of the two lines below should he speak?

A. I beseech you humbly, kind sir, to remove that vehicle from my pathway. It is obstructing my progress.

B. Would you mind moving that truck please? I can't seem to get through.

Even though he is a professor of English, statement A would certainly earn for the teacher a look of disgust and puzzlement; but what is more important, odds are that the truck driver would leave his truck right where it was. Statement B might, at least, result in a moved truck if the driver were co-operative, of course.

Statement A in the situation described would be the wrong level of usage. Special circumstances determine how we speak and what we say: how you talk to your brother or sister is probably quite different from how you talk to your mother—and both of these are different from the way you might speak to a dean at the college.

In writing, levels of usage operate too. Formal English is the language of newspapers, formal speeches, and most serious college writing. Informal English (the English you speak each day) is found in parts of novels, short stories, letters, books, and articles for general usage and advertisements. *Colloquialisms* (informal conversational expressions) and *slang* (vivid words or phrases used because they are brief, "loose," and colorful) mark informal language and are perfectly acceptable in informal situations. Although it is effective to use such informality for special effects in your writing or as part of the quoted words you show someone speaking, for the most part informal language should be avoided in your compositions.

But be careful! Do not substitute for an informal expression something stuffy and unnatural, something overdone like statement A above. Usually, however, students are guilty of too much *in*formality!

Here are some informal expressions used on freshman themes and some alternatives that could be used.

Informal	*Example*	*More Formal Expression*
cool, way out, super, swell, groovy	It was a cool movie.	excellent, effective, remarkable, superior, relaxed, provocative
sort of (a) kind of (a)	That policeman was *kind of* strange.	rather; somewhat

a couple of	Bring me *a couple of* books.	some; several; a few
dig on	My girlfriend and I were	enjoy; respond; appreciate;
groove on	*grooving on* a record by	love; listen
	Dylan.	
lousy, finky, stinko,	What a *lousy* time we had.	awful, terrible
enthused	The singer was *enthused*	enthusiastic about or over,
	about the piano player.	excited
a lot, lots of	I have *lots of* time.	much, a great deal
don't wasn't	They *weren't* planning to	Write out the contractions:
didn't weren't	vote for that candidate.	do not was not
aren't isn't		did not were not
couldn't I'm		are not is not
etc.		could not I am
a fix	What a *fix* I got into with	complication; troublesome
	this car!	time; awkward event
	I'll *fix* you!	punish

myself ⎤ used as	Mary and *myself* were late.	I
yourself ⎬ subjects		you
himself ⎦		he
real, mighty	He was *real* annoyed at me.	very, extremely, strongly
awfully, plenty		
faze	It didn't *faze* me in the least.	bother, disturb, annoy
sure	*Sure* I wanted to leave the	certainly, indeed, surely,
	house.	absolutely

Hint: If you want to use some informal word for special effect, put the word in quotation marks:

Because of so much construction and repairs, no one but the builders can "dig" New York any more.

See also "Biology Jailhouse," pp. 144–145, last sentence.

Step 1. Informal to Formal. Rewrite each of the sentence examples of informal usage above into more formal language. Be careful not to make your new sentences sound too high-flown. Use separate paper.

Step 2. More Informal Sentences. Here are several more sentences using informal language. Rewrite each one in the blanks so that it would be acceptable in a formal writing activity. Do not write anything too stiff.

1. They're a cool bunch to hang out with, but my old lady flipped when she caught me.

   _____

   _____

2. I don't dig any chicks who won't swing so I never called that square again.

_____

_____

3. Sure Pop gave the wheels plenty of juice but we couldn't talk those lousy couple of cops out of a ticket nohow.

_____

_____

4. I figure I should talk turkey if my old man hangs the accident on me. Otherwise he might think I was strung out or something, and then it's painsville for me.

_____

_____

5. Some groovy broad with a lot on the ball sure put some freak in his place. She cracked him one when he got fresh and like wow did he feel like a fink.

_____

_____

Step 3. A "Square" Dictionary. Write your own dictionary of several more informal expressions (slang, colloquialisms) that you define for someone who might not "dig" your language. Write a definition for each word; use each word in a colloquial sentence that you might speak or write; give one or two alternate words that could be used for the same effect; then, rewrite your original sentence in more formal English. You might want to define colloquial and slang expressions like *dough, kookie, wicked, uptight, with it, right-on, boss, bread, gig.* Use the chart below and the first sample to help you with this assignment.

A "SQUARE" DICTIONARY

Informal Expression	Definition	My Own Sentence	Alternate Words	More Formal English
up-tight	to be nervous	I was all up-tight about the driving test.	anxious, worried, troubled	I was troubled about the driving test.
_____	_____	_____	_____	_____
_____	_____	_____	_____	_____
_____	_____	_____	_____	_____
_____	_____	_____	_____	_____
_____	_____	_____	_____	_____

_____ _____ _____ _____ _____
_____ _____ _____ _____ _____
_____ _____ _____ _____ _____
_____ _____ _____ _____ _____
_____ _____ _____ _____ _____
_____ _____ _____ _____ _____
_____ _____ _____ _____ _____
_____ _____ _____ _____ _____

WRITING THE PARAGRAPH: DEFINITIONS THROUGH IMAGES

Webster defines *love* as "the attraction, desire, or affection felt for a person who arouses delight or admiration." Although this is surely an adequate definition, anyone who has experienced love knows how incomplete the dictionary meaning is. A great number of words in the language suggest through our own experiences a number of definitions that go beyond what the dictionary says. This is what is meant by the *connotation* of words: the ability to suggest or hint at meanings that are not part of what the word actually points out. The actual dictionary definition of a word (like the definition given above of the word *love*) is called *denotation*. In this paragraph experiment you are going to try to define any word you wish through a series of strong images based upon your own observations. Select a word that is rich in image responses for you, a word that calls up a string of pictures of happiness, tension, delight, or pain. Use sensory details to make each picture sharp and clear.

Step 1. Two Student Samples. Read the student samples below as examples of the definition in images. Answer the questions after the paragraphs.

Rain: A Still Puddle

Rain: thin strands of brown and blonde hair curling tightly and sticking to my forehead; my slumber disturbed by torrents beating a drum solo on the metal chairs in the backyard; drops splotched recklessly on my window, dribbling slowly to distort my sister Bethy's tricycle hiding from corrosion in the corner of the porch; skipping down Indian Trail to Neversink River and counting the hundreds of salamanders that wiggle near the bank; red and green lights shining wetly down long black avenues; windshield wipers whisking countless drops aside, all in vain; standing under the maple in front of the house with my hands stretched out and my mouth open, and blinking with delight as each trickle saturates my tongue; layers of streaming water blown by the wind like a gray bedsheet wavering on the clothes-line; trampling across soggy leaves in Lincoln Terrace Park as water oozes through my sandals; a single stone tossed into a puddle and breaking the rainbow into an explosion of color; worms wriggling from cracks between the squares of cement on the sidewalk on Avenue Z; pouncing on a still puddle in an April downpour.

—Carol Zubatkin

Green: Sparkling Eyes and Seaweed

Green: a row of unripened tomatoes sitting on the kitchen table; the dirty old blotter on my desk filled with doodles in pencil and red ink; wool velvet carpet in the living room; hundreds of pickles floating in the barrel at Mike's Delicatessen on our corner; the large, round, sparkling eyes of my cousin Elizabeth; ivy clinging to the side wall of the quaint old schoolhouse on Mill Road in Brooklyn; diced scallions peering out of a container of cream cheese, small clumps of lettuce, and a handful of olives all at Sunday breakfast; a slippery trail of seaweed stretching at the water line along Brighton Beach at low tide; a statue of a smiling Buddha sitting on the roof of the Ho Sai Kai Restaurant on sunny Pitkin Avenue.

—Leo Finkelstein

1. Which image in Miss Zubatkin's paragraph gives the most original

   picture of rain? _____

2. Which image in Mr. Finkelstein's paragraph is most vivid and easiest

   to visualize? _____

3. Why do both writers use a colon after the first word in the paragraph?

   _____

4. Why do both writers use semicolons to separate the series of images?

   _____

5. Put a check in the margin in either paragraph next to the image that gives the name of a place. Put an X next to the image that uses a comparison.

TIPS FOR THE PARAGRAPH DEFINITION IN IMAGES

1. Select a word that is rich in definitions for you, a word that calls a number of pictures into your mind. *Your success in the paragraph depends on the selection of a word that has important meanings to you.*
2. Write at least ten images that you associate with the word. Make your images rich in color, sound, smell, and touch.
3. Mention the names of specific places and people.
4. Vary the length of the images. Make some images long like Miss Zubatkin's picture of the rain hiding her sister's bicycle; write one or two brief images of strong visual quality like the first picture in Mr. Finkelstein's paragraph.

5. Use a colon after the word that you are attempting to define.
6. Use a semicolon after each image.

Hint: Each image is a fragment, not a complete sentence. Notice that the verb used in most of the images is an *-ing* or an *-ed* verb part. Some of the images, like "wool velvet carpet in the living room" and "the large, round sparkling eyes of my cousin Elizabeth" contain no verb part at all. But the *-ing* adds a certain liveliness to your picture, so try to use it often in the imagery.

7. Make up a title that uses both the word you are defining and a piece of your favorite image or two. What images do the words after the colon in Mr. Finkelstein's title come from?

Step 2. Words for Image Definitions. Here are several words that might suggest to you a series of sharp pictures. You can use one of these, if you wish, in your paragraph definition.

1. the beach
2. street corners
3. fear
4. basketball
5. Saturday mornings
6. school
7. fishing
8. July (any month)
9. winter (any season)
10. black (any color)
11. cars
12. church
13. wash day
14. loneliness
15. baby-sitting

WRITING THE PARAGRAPH: EXPANDING A POETIC MOMENT

One of the outstanding qualities of good poetry is its ability to suggest powerful and vivid scenes through a very economical use of language. Poets strive for *compression;* that is, they try to use as few and as carefully chosen words as possible to set scenes and create emotional reactions in readers. Since all of us have different emotional states and different kinds of imaginations, what one person sees or feels after reading a poem is often quite unlike another person's responses. The next paragraph you write will take advantage of your own special responses to brief moments in poetry.

As you read each of the following poems, think about the situation you see and its meaning to you. Then, by using sensory language, expand the poet's scene in a paragraph of your own. Try to suggest in the opening sentence or two what the most important meaning of the poem is. Describe the people as you see them, whether or not the poet has shown them. Through color, sound, action, and images of smell and touch, paint a scene rich in details that your own imagination creates. Use comparisons (simile, metaphor, personification: see pp. 127–131) for special vividness.

Step 1. A Poem and a Student Response. Read the following poem and then the paragraph written by a student. Write the answers to the questions on p. 249.

Lament

Listen, children:
Your father is dead.
From his old coats
I'll make you little jackets;
I'll make you little trousers
From his old pants.
There'll be in his pockets
Things he used to put there,
Keys and pennies
Covered with tobacco;
Dan shall have the pennies
To save in his bank;
Anne shall have the keys
To make a pretty noise with.
Life must go on,
And the dead be forgotten;
Life must go on,
Though good men die;
Anne, eat your breakfast;
Dan, take your medicine;
Life must go on;
I forget just why.
    —Edna St. Vincent Millay

The Meaning of Death

   In "Lament" I see a sad mother (who has lost her husband) unsuccessfully try-ing to explain the meaning of death to her children in a cold dark kitchen. Sitting at the breakfast table one December morning, the mother in a faded robe runs her hand up and down the yellow plastic tablecloth. There are the morning smells of instant coffee, cereal, and orange juice, but she does not notice them. Her sorrow-ful brown eyes are small like little stones. Tiny lines of age and worry fill her face and her hair, speckled with gray, falls sloppily onto her forehead. When she speaks to her ten-year-old son Dan, he stops tapping the table with his fork and listens. "Dan, even though your father is dead, I'll make you trousers from his old brown pants. You can keep the pennies in his pockets for your bank." Quickly, Dan looks away, staring at a vitamin pill and his cough medicine, a red syrup in a clear glass bottle. "Anne," the mother says, "I'll give you Daddy's keys to play with." But the three-year-old in a wooden high chair just frowns and plays with the oatmeal in her little dish. The mother cannot soothe the children, though, because she her-self is confused about the meaning of death. First she tries to comfort the children by keeping alive the father's memory. (That is why she talks of his keys with the pretty noise and his coins covered with tobacco.) But then she says just the oppo-site when she explains that the dead must be forgotten so life can go on. This con-tradiction is, I believe, the feeling many people experience in the loss of loved ones. We want to forget the person who died and to remember him as well. All the mother's sadness, bitterness, and confusion about death show in the last two lines: "Life must go on; I forget just why."
    —Sheila O'Connor

1. What is the main idea of the paragraph? What word in the topic sentence expresses the writer's opinion about the situation she sees in the poem "Lament"? _____

   _____

2. What detail best shows the mother to you? _____

   _____

3. Where has Miss O'Connor used images of setting to let us visualize the room in which the scene takes place? _____

   _____

4. How does Miss O'Connor *individualize* Dan and Anne? _____

   _____

5. What is your reaction to Miss O'Connor's simile about the mother's eyes: "small like little stones"? _____

   _____

6. How does the closing sentence summarize the paragraph: *Hint: reread the topic sentence.* _____

   _____

Step 2. More Poems for Expansion. Read to yourselves or listen as your teacher reads aloud the following poems, each one a description of a moment. Then, using Miss O'Connor's theme as an example, write your own paragraph that expands the scene from any one poem as you see it.

A Sight in Camp in the Daybreak Gray and Dim

A sight in camp in the daybreak gray and dim,
As from my tent I emerge so early sleepless,
As slow I walk in the cool fresh air the path near by the hospital tent,
Three forms I see on stretchers lying, brought out there untended lying,
Over each the blanket spread, ample brownish woolen blanket,
Gray and heavy blanket, folding, covering all.

Curious I halt and silent stand,
Then with light fingers I from the face of the nearest the first just lift the blanket;
Who are you elderly man so gaunt and grim, with well-gray'd hair, and flesh all
   sunken about the eyes?
Who are you my dear comrade?

Then to the second I step—and who are you my child and darling?
Who are you sweet boy with cheeks yet blooming?

Then to the third—a face nor child nor old, very calm, as of beautiful yellow-white
   ivory;
Young man I think I know you—I think this face is the face of the Christ himself,
Dead and divine and brother of all, and here again he lies.
                                        —Walt Whitman

Mag

I wish to God I never saw you, Mag.
I wish you never quit your job and came along with me.
I wish we never bought a license and a white dress
For you to get married in the day we ran off to a minister
And told him we would love each other and take care of each other
Always and always long as the sun and the rain lasts anywhere.
Yes, I'm wishing now you lived somewhere away from here
And I was a bum on the bumpers a thousand miles away dead broke.
 I wish the kids had never come
 And rent and coal and clothes to pay for
 And a grocery man calling for cash,
 Every day cash for beans and prunes.
 I wish to God I never saw you, Mag.
 I wish to God the kids had never come.

—Carl Sandburg

POINTERS FOR YOUR PARAGRAPH ON POEMS

1. Tell in the topic sentence just what you are going to try to show about the poem.
2. Set the reader in time and place: "a cold dark kitchen"; "one December morning."
3. Show people, their faces, and actions they perform.
4. Use a line or two from the poem somewhere in your paragraph.
5. Use several lively images of action, color, smell, and sound.

WRITING THE PARAGRAPH: THE WORLD OF YOUR DREAMS

One exciting source for a paragraph rich in imagery is a dream that seemed very real to you, a dream that you remember very clearly. Recalling the story of this dream, you need to fill in as many details as possible. Try as accurately as you can to name and describe the people in the dream and their actions. Set the scene in time and place so that the reader feels how real the moment was to you. Let your topic sentence state the main point of the dream, as Richard Fries' does below.

Step 1. A Student Sample. Read the following theme about a dream. Which details seem most real to you? What pictures do you see most clearly?

The Champ

 Ridiculous as it seems, I often dream that I am a finalist at the Golden Gloves bouts at Madison Square Garden. I am not at all a violent person, but in my dream

I see myself parade past the seats to the ring in my blue silk robe. Cigarette butts cover the linoleum aisle. There is a man in a gray moustache who removes his thick-rimmed glasses to look at me. Nudging his wife, he juts an index finger toward my cheek. She smiles showing awful yellow teeth. Climbing four cracked steps to the ring apron, I shut my eyes in sudden fear, the lids refusing to open. My feet flat on the floor, I finally remove my robe. Then, as I jog, my toes bouncing lightly on the surface, women in the first row applaud. White boots cover my calves; red trunks clash against my sunburned stomach. I feel beads of moisture dripping down my back and I swat them with tan boxing gloves. Suddenly, I glance at my opponent who looks at me coldly. He is tremendous: his chest muscles quiver as he sways in place; strong hairy legs bulge below black trunks; heavy arms with blue veins sweep through the air. He grunts, his upper lip moving angrily. With his glove he pushes back his hair, revealing a scarred forehead and pointed eyebrows. The referee struggles through the ropes, grasps the microphone and announces, "Ladies and gentlemen, the Golden Gloves Finals in the light heavyweight division, wearing black trunks, weighing one-hundred-seventy-seven and three-quarters from Bayside, Queens, Tony Vercelli. In this corner wearing red trunks at one-hundred-seventy-two-and-a-half pounds, from Canarsie, Spider Richards." The crowd screams and whistles and stamps. We stomp into the center of the ring; I imagine Vercelli (a name I never heard before) lying on the canvas panting, his face bloody. Then the bell rings, but I always wake up just before the opening round!

—Richard Fries

Step 2. Some Dream Ideas. Here are some "dream" titles that might suggest your own dream experiences.

1. Running Away
2. An Accident
3. Peace and Beauty
4. Attack!
5. Fear

6. A Strange Place
7. Something Unfamiliar
8. I Am a Hero
9. I Come to the Rescue
10. I Dream of Love

A Checklist for the Paragraph of Imagery

Submit this checklist to your instructor along with your theme.

_____ 1. Did I use several images of lively actions? Did I use a number of original verbs of motion and sound like those on p. 224? Here is one of my

images that show action: _____

_____ 2. Did I use a number of colors to help the reader see exactly what I wanted to describe?

_____ 3. Do I have at least three images that name sensations of touch? Have I used words like *soft, smooth, moist, rough, hard, cold, sticky?*

_____ 4. Have I identified in at least two images sensations of smell? Here is

one of them: _____

_____ 5. Have I mentioned time of day and season to make my imagery more specific?

_____ 6. Have I used comparisons like those explained on pp. 127–131 — similes, metaphors, or personification?

_____ 7. Have I used specific nouns (like those illustrated on pp. 226–227) wherever possible?

_____ 8. Have I used correctly some of the new methods of punctuation explained on pp. 230–239? Have I checked carefully for correct use of capital letters as illustrated on pp. 240–241?

_____ 9. Did I examine my Progress Sheet to check for my usual errors before I wrote the final copy of my paragraph? Did I look especially for run-on sentences, sentence fragments, and my usual spelling mistakes?

_____10. Did I try to write "formal English" wherever possible, avoiding slang and informal expressions like those explained on pp. 242–243?

_____11. Have I given my paragraph a lively title?

_____12. Did I read my paragraph aloud and eliminate any sentences that sound clumsy or confusing to the ear?

THE PROFESSIONALS SPEAK

Step 1. Images as Definition. Of all the twentieth-century writers, few can create strong moods through imagery as well as Thomas Wolfe. As you read this paragraph, look for the images that best convey a feeling of excitement and life. Write the answers to the questions.

SOME WORDS TO KNOW BEFORE YOU READ

remote: far off
interfused: blended; mixed with
livid: discolored bluish-gray appearance
illusive: unreal; deceptive
bleak: bare, deserted, cold
swarming: moving about in great numbers

Brooklyn Summer

Ah, yes, for in summer:

It is so cool and sweet tonight, a million feet are walking here across the jungle web of Brooklyn in the dark, and it's so hard now to remember that it ever was the month of March in Booklyn and that we couldn't find a door. There are so many million doors tonight. There's a door for everyone tonight, all's open to the air, all's interfused tonight: remote the thunder of the elevated trains on Fulton Street, the rattling of the cars along Atlantic Avenue, the glare of Coney Island seven miles away, the mob, the racket, and the barkers shouting, the cars swift-shuttling through the quiet streets, the people swarming in the web, lit here and there with livid blurs of light, the voices of the neighbors leaning at their windows, harsh, soft, all interfused. All's illusive in the liquid air tonight, all mixed in with the radios that blare from open windows. And there is something over all tonight, something fused, remote, and trembling, made of all of this, and yet not of it, upon the huge and weaving ocean of the night in Brooklyn—something that we had almost quite forgotten in the month of March. What's this?—a sash raised gently?—a window?—a near voice on the air?—something swift and passing, almost captured, there below?—there in the gulf of night the mournful and yet thrilling voices of the tugs?—the liner's blare? Here—there—some otherwhere—was it a whisper?—a woman's call?—a sound of people talking behind the screen and doors in Flatbush? It trembles in the air throughout the giant web tonight, as fleeting as a step—near—as soft and sudden as a woman's laugh. The liquid air is living with the very whisper of the thing that we are looking for tonight throughout America—the very thing that seemed so bleak, so vast, so cold, so hopeless, and so lost as we waited in our good clothes on ten thousand corners of the day in Brooklyn in the month of March.

> —Thomas Wolfe,
> *You Can't Go Home Again*

1. Put checks next to three images that use sounds. Which do you think

   is best? _____

2. Wolfe compares the magical quality of the night in two similes: "as fleeting as a step" and "as soft and sudden as a woman's laugh." Which

   do you think is better? Why? _____

3. What effect does Wolfe's use of dashes have upon the excitement he

   tries to create in the paragraph? _____

4. How does the closing sentence refer back to the topic sentence? _____

   _____

5. Wolfe's comparisons often have much more meaning than appear on the surface. Explain in your own words each of these expressions:

   a. "we couldn't find a door" _____

   _____

   b. "the people swarming in the web" _____

   _____

   c. "the huge and weaving ocean of the night" _____

   _____

REACHING HIGHER

Defining the Self in Images

There was a child went forth every day,
And the first object he look'd upon, that object he became,
And that object became part of him for the day or a certain part of the day,
Or for many years or stretching cycles of years.
The early lilacs became part of this child,

And grass and white and red morning glories, and white and
  red clover, and the song of the phoebe-bird.
                    —Walt Whitman, from "There Was a
                    Child Went Forth"

Whitman suggests that every experience a person meets in life becomes
a part of him. Some events play more important parts than others in contributing to our development. For the child in the poem it is lilacs, morning glories, clover, and a bird's song that became part of him. What experiences do you remember that became part of you? Can you capture them
in images?

Step 1. A Collage to Answer "What Am I?" Using old magazines, newspapers, paint, ink, pieces of advertisements, various other materials (foil,
string, macaroni, photographs), make a *collage* that you think will present
to the class a visual answer to the question "What Am I?" Select from the
sources you use things that you believe have become part of you. Look at
the "What Am I?" collage by Jaqueline Boston on p. 222 as one example.

After everyone has prepared collages, line them up in front of the room
so that nobody's name can be seen. One at a time, discuss the personality
of the person who made each project. What specific feature of the collage
tells you most about the person who made it? What kind of person is Miss
Boston? What one feature of her collage tells you most about her?

Step 2. A Paragraph to Answer "What Am I?" In order to answer the
question "What Am I?" you need to recall the memories that are the deepest
parts of *your* self, the most vivid events in your relations with people, parents, and the world that you feel have become part of you. What you have
seen and heard; what you have learned from others and seen in their faces;
what smells you recall at unforgettable moments; the books you have read
and the movies you watch: these all are the sources of defining your self.

Read the paragraph by Myra Weiser below as a model before you write.
As she does, use only images in your paragraph. Mention people and places
by name. Use color and sound.

What Am I?

"What Am I?" is a question which takes a lot of soul-searching for me to answer.
Sometimes I am the sound of an undertaker's voice reciting a eulogy for my father
who died of cancer when I was four years old. I am the muffled sobs of sorrow I
remember from my mother and the white lace handkerchief pushed against her
lips. But I am also the confusion of voices whispering and my Aunt Helen's arms
lifting me to hold me close and help me through something I didn't understand.
I am the mixture of apology and hope in my mother's gray eyes when I first met my
new father-to-be. I am the tension of my stepfather as he tries to read a book in
Brookdale Hospital, while my mother is inside having a baby. I am the rough kiss,

the whiskers and cigarette smells when my stepfather hears from Dr. Beck, "Congratulations. You have a little boy." I am Michael Barry's cries in the middle of the night, the egg yolk in his breakfast dish, his dirty diapers and the clean smell of baby lotion and powder after Mother bathes him. I am the noisy bustle of moving to Bayside, the clatter of dishes, the scrape of our old couch on squeaky new floors. I am the giggle of my friend Bobbi when I tell her about Saturday night's date. I am also the over-sized black and white poster of Bob Dylan that smiles at me from above my bed. I am the pink and white daisies on my bedroom wall, the torn white sneakers in the corner, my vocabulary-building book hidden in the closet. I am the quiet moments alone in my room when night comes and I can think.

—Myra Weiser

part II

THE LONGER COMPOSITION

chapter 7

A PLACE OF SPIRIT:
WRITING THE LONGER THEME

Howard Smithline

INTRODUCTION

There is a place that every one of us carries in his memories. Certain places have such a force that they live strongly in the mind and feelings long after the scene itself disappears from view. Sometimes you cannot forget a place you know closely because you see it and live in it and experience things there so often: the train station where you catch the local for school each day; the kitchen in the apartment in which you grew up; the empty lot on the corner where you set your first fire or played your first game of punchball; the doctor's office where weekly visits for allergy injections keep the smell of alcohol and iodine in your nose and the sounds of babies' cries in your ears. Perhaps it is a place you have not seen often, but one clear in your mind because of what happened to you there: the room of your first physical for the draft board; the hospital emergency room; the principal's office in high school.

Your first essay assignment—a longer composition of four paragraphs—asks that you select for exploration some place both important and unforgettable to you. (If it is a place you can visit again before you write, so much the better; then, you will be able to jot down on paper the sights, colors, sounds, smells, and actions that give the place its character.) You will be able again to use your skills at narration and description—in fact, any of the paragraphs you learned about in the first part of this book can be helpful in your essay. And you will learn how to plan an essay, that longer theme, so that the problems you might have had about organizing and finding enough to write in longer compositions no longer bother you. You will also find several suggestions about how to prepare this particular essay as you study some specific plans for writing that you might want to use to create your own composition. In its attempt to help you clear up problems in language, this chapter will look at some difficulties freshmen often have with pronouns.

VOCABULARY

The words in this activity will help you name sizes and shapes of things more specifically.

Step 1. Learning Words for Shape and Size. Check in the dictionary those words below that you do not know (Appendix A will help you too). Write definitions you understand in the blanks next to the word.

1. vast _____

2. minute _____

3. towering _____

4. corpulent _____

5. squat _____

6. oblong _____

7. illimitable _____

8. amorphous _____

9. rectangular _____

10. symmetrical _____

Step 2. Sizing It Up. From the vocabulary above, write a word that

1. means immense _____

2. indicates something that has no real shape _____

3. means heavy, fat _____

4. would describe a long square or circle _____

5. means very tall _____

6. means short and thick _____

7. means four-sided _____

8. shows proportion and balance _____

9. shows that something has no bounds or limits _____

10. means tiny _____

Precise Words for Shades of Meaning

The English language is so rich in vocabulary that it often has many words to express the same idea. Synonyms (two words that mean about the same thing) are abundant. Yet even among synonyms there are shades of meaning—small differences in force or tone or feeling of a word—that make one word more acceptable in a given situation.

Step 3. Exact Word, Exact Meaning. In Column I appear several words you might use to describe some place you remember. In Column II appear words whose meanings may be close to but not exactly like the words in Column I. For each word check your dictionary or Appendix A if you do not know the meaning and write a definition on the blank lines.

I	II	
1. dirty	obscene	_____
	fetid	_____
	squalid	_____
2. attractive	alluring	_____
	stunning	_____
	provocative	_____
3. unfriendly	impersonal	_____
	inimical	_____
	antagonistic	_____

4. roomy   uncluttered   _____

                      ample   _____

                      copious   _____

5. quiet   serene   _____

                      hushed   _____

                      muffled   _____

Step 4. Understanding Shades of Meaning. Write the answers to these questions on vocabulary.

1. Why might someone call a picture of a nude in a store right near an elementary school *provocative?* _____
_____

2. If you stood outside a house, would the sounds of a party you heard through tightly closed windows be *hushed* or *muffled?* Why? _____
_____

3. What would better describe a place so dirty that it smelled: *fetid, squalid,* or *obscene?* Why? _____
_____

4. Why might you use *inimical* rather than *antagonistic* to describe someone who showed a strong opposition to you? _____
_____

5. Would a two-story house built brick by brick by a man of eighty be best described as *alluring* or *stunning?* _____
_____

6. Why might *serene* better describe an absolutely calm and peaceful lake than the word *hushed?* _____
_____

7. Would the flow of money at an amusement park on a Saturday night in July be *ample* or *copious?* _____
_____

8. Would a movie house with enough seats for all its Saturday-night patrons be best considered *ample* or *uncluttered?* Why? _____
_____

9. Would the word *squalid* or the word *obscene* better describe a movie that many people thought was not decent but instead disgusting and

offensive? Why? _____

_____

10. Would someone who chose not to involve himself with people on any private level be better named *impersonal* or *antagonistic?* Why? _____

_____

Step 5. The Thesaurus for Synonyms. An important word book that groups words closely related in meaning is a thesaurus. There you can look up a word like *happy,* for example, and find well over a hundred words that suggest *happiness.* But you know from Step 4 above that even when words are considered synonyms their meanings are often quite different. Use the thesaurus (see p. 462) to look up the words in Column I. From all the words mentioned pick any three whose meanings you don't know and write the words in Column II. Using a dictionary, then write in Column III the definitions of those words. Study the example below.

I	II	III
1. happy	*opportune* *auspicious* *joyous*	*coming at the right time* *fortunate* *full of delight*
2. sad		
3. bad		
4. pretty		
5. to walk		
6. to enjoy		

7. to tell _____   _____

_____   _____

_____   _____

8. gentle _____   _____

_____   _____

_____   _____

9. good _____   _____

_____   _____

_____   _____

10. enjoyable _____   _____

_____   _____

_____   _____

BUILDING COMPOSITION SKILLS

Exploring the Topic

Step 1. Talking It Out.   Complete aloud one of these sentences about a place with one of your own endings. Then speak a few more sentences to expand what you said for the rest of the class. Mention some sound or smell that you remember about the place.

1. The noisiest place I know is . . .
2. Our campus is . . .
3. A summer place I remember most is . . .
4. If you saw our basement, you would . . .
5. A place that always scared me was . . .
6. My brother's (sister's) room is . . .
7. For me the hospital is . . .
8. Our street corner is . . .
9. One place I enjoy is . . .
10. When I want peace and quiet I go to . . .

Here are two freshman responses.

My sister's room is a pig sty! Silver hair curlers are piled in a heap on the dresser. Most of the drawers are opened and blouses and underwear hang out. A pile of dirty skirts sits in the corner and ten or twenty books lie all over the linoleum floor. But no one can reason with my thirteen-year-old sister Karen, the family know-it-all!
—Diane Carter

One place I enjoy is the Automat on Seventh Avenue early in the morning. Although some wierd characters sometimes sit around the tables playing with ketchup bottles and the mustard jars, I like to watch the steam come out of the oatmeal pot and the chef in his white hat spooning out scrambled eggs or piling a plate high with toasted corn muffins.

—Michael Bartlett

Step 2. Associations in Images. For each item listed below, write down two or three images under each column to indicate whatever smells, sights, touch sensations, actions, and sounds you associate with the place. Use your own paper. Make what you write specific through concrete pictures Study the example, for number 1, *schoolyard after classes.*

1. schoolyard after classes
2. college library before exams
3. gasoline station
4. pizza (hamburger) shop
5. movie house
6. rock concert
7. kitchen at breakfast
8. campus at early morning
9. supermarket
10. church or synagogue as services begin

Sights (colors and actions)	*Smells*	*Sounds*	*Touch Sensations*
tangles of arms reaching for an orange basketball; red, black, green bicycles leaning on the tree	sweet smell of lilacs from the school garden; cigarette smoke	clop of sneakers on pavement; screams of, "Get the ball!" from sixth graders; jingle of bicycles bells	warm June air; moist leather baseball glove

Step 3. Describing or Interpreting? Your reader should know how you feel about some object you have shown him based only upon the quality of the picture you write. Although you often need words that interpret or give opinions to set the frame of a moment, it is best to avoid telling the reader how to react when he reads one of your images. Instead use descriptive details that name colors, sounds, sizes, and qualities of feeling. Notice how the first two items in Column I use words that tell the reader how he should feel about the picture. In Column II words really describe the item so that the reader decides himself how to respond to the scene. For the other items in Column I write in Column II your own pictures that use words that really describe

I

1. an *ugly* smile

II

a cold toothless smile

2. a *lovely* morning   *warm, quiet sunny morning* _____

3. a *pretty* face   _____

4. *beautiful* evening   _____

5. a *swell* car   _____

6. *terrific* athlete   _____

7. *attractive* ring   _____

8. *horrible* tree   _____

9. *wonderful* beach   _____

10. *superb* turkey   _____

UNDERSTANDING ESSAY FORM

The basic difference between the theme of one long paragraph and the theme that is a four-paragraph essay is simply one of length and proportion. An essay of four paragraphs gives you more of a chance to develop your ideas, to use more details, to bring in other information you might have left out of a single-paragraph composition so it would not be too long.

For every part of the paragraph there is a similar part of the essay, so if you understand what makes up a paragraph, you will understand what makes up an essay.

In a one-paragraph theme you had to write a *topic sentence* which told readers the subject you would deal with and your opinion about that subject. In a four-paragraph essay you will need to write an *introductory paragraph* in which you have more space to build up to the topic you want to discuss. As the last sentence of this introductory paragraph, you will need to write one sentence—the *proposal sentence*—in which you announce to the reader just what the whole essay will be about. A proposal sentence is just like a *topic sentence,* except that the proposal sentence is usually more general because it must tell what the *whole essay* will deal with. The proposal sentence must permit you to discuss *two* aspects of your topic—one in each of the body paragraphs—so you need to give it a great deal of thought. The *topic sentence* of a paragraph, on the other hand, reveals only what one specific paragraph will discuss. The introductory paragraph merely tells the subject of the essay and does not usually try to support the topic at all.

In a one-paragraph theme, the first subtopic sentence introduced one aspect of the topic. In the four-paragraph essay, the first subtopic sentence becomes the topic sentence of its own paragraph. This topic sentence announces the specific purpose of the second paragraph of the essay. A transition is easily made by referring to an idea stated in the sentence directly before it, the *proposal sentence.* Again the topic sentence should be the first sentence in the paragraph. You develop the paragraph in the way you have learned by using details you remember from your own experience or from what you have read or heard. This second paragraph of your essay is the first *body* paragraph because it is the first paragraph that tries to support some aspect of the topic. And just like the one-paragraph theme, this first body paragraph needs some kind of closing sentence which simply lets the reader know that you have finished with one aspect of the topic.

In a one-paragraph theme your *second* subtopic sentence introduced another aspect of the topic. In the four-paragraph essay, the second subtopic sentence becomes the topic sentence of its own paragraph. This topic sentence announces the specific purpose of the third paragraph of the essay; again the topic sentence should be the first sentence in the paragraph. Furthermore, this topic sentence, aside from introducing the specific purpose of the paragraph, must make some brief reference to the *previous* paragraph: that helps tie all the ideas together and smooth out the transitions. You develop the paragraph in any of the ways you have learned and by using the kinds of details that best support your point. This paragraph also needs some kind of closing sentence to tell the reader that you have finished with another aspect of the topic.

In a one-paragraph theme, you needed a closing sentence to tell the reader that you had achieved whatever purpose you set for yourself in the paragraph. In the four-paragraph essay you need a conclusion, a whole new paragraph which allows you to summarize, or to give your dominant impression. But even more important, it permits you to show how the limited idea you have discussed in the essay has significance or importance in other areas. It lets you bring in a related idea, a larger and more meaningful issue in the world which may be understood through the points you have considered in your essay.

The following chart shows how the parts of the paragraph correspond to parts of the essay.

FROM PARAGRAPH TO ESSAY

The One-paragraph Theme   *The Essay*

Topic Sentence:

P	*Introduction: A Paragraph*
A	1. Give background to your topic.
R	2. Make the reader feel that what you are going to say will be of importance and interest to him.
A	
G	
R	3. Set the stage for the one sentence that will tell the reader what the whole essay will be about (*proposal sentence*).
A	
P	
H	4. Put the proposal sentence *last* in the introductory paragraph; make sure that the proposal sentence allows you to discuss *two* aspects of the topic.
1	
	5. Take as much time with the proposal sentence as you took with the topic sentence.

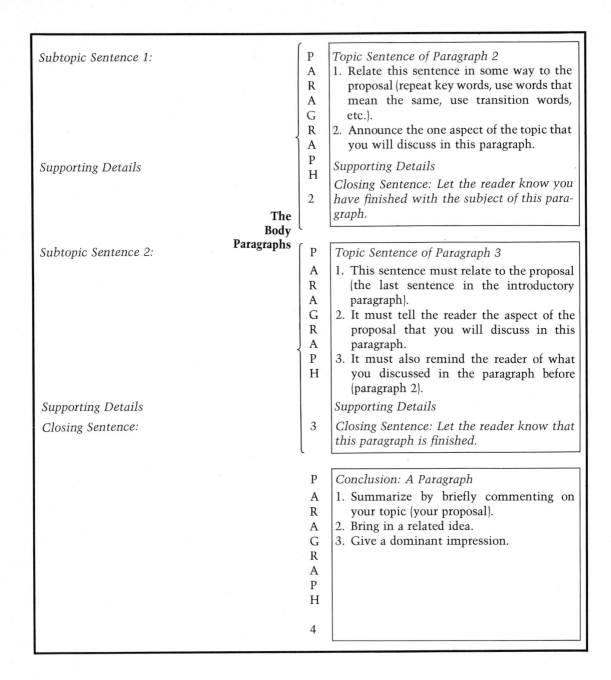

Step 1. The Essay: What Do You Remember? The following questions are based upon what you read about the parts of the essay and how they correspond to the one-paragraph theme. Use the table above for help, if necessary.

1. What is the basic difference between a one-paragraph theme and a longer

essay? _____

_____

_____

2. What is a *proposal sentence* (some people call it a *thesis statement* or *sentence*, a *proposition*, a *main-idea statement*, or a *topic statement*) and where does it appear in the essay? _____

_____

_____

_____

3. What features might an introductory paragraph include? _____

_____

_____

_____

4. What is the purpose of the topic sentence of paragraph 2 in an essay? How is it similar to the subtopic sentence in the one-paragraph theme?

_____

_____

_____

_____

5. What is the purpose of the topic sentence of paragraph 3 in an essay? How does this sentence help tie the ideas of the essay together? _____

_____

_____

_____

6. Why do paragraphs 2 and 3 need brief closing sentences? _____

_____

_____

_____

7. List several features of the concluding paragraph of an essay. _____

_____

_____

_____

BUILDING ESSAYS FROM ONE-PARAGRAPH THEMES

Step 1. Reviewing Paragraph Form. The first student sample you read in this book—"The Gloom Room" by Harry Golden—appears below for review. On the opposite page and the one after is Mr. Golden's four-paragraph essay on exactly the same topic. These pages should help you see clearly the basic differences between the one-paragraph theme and the four-paragraph essay. Reread Mr. Golden's paragraph below and write the answers to the review questions that appear beneath it.

The Gloom Room

On this dreary October afternoon in my writing class here on the second floor of Boylan Hall at Brooklyn College, a shadow of gloom hangs over the people and things that surround me. The atmosphere is depressing. There is an old brown chair beside the teacher's desk, a mahogany bookcase with a missing shelf, and this ugly desk of mine filled with holes and scratches. As I rub my hand across its surface, there is a feeling of coldness. Even the gray walls and the rumble of thunder outside reflect the atmosphere of seriousness as we write our first theme of the semester. When some air sails through an open window beside me, there is the annoying smell of coffee grounds from a garbage pail not far off. My classmates, too, show the mood of tension. Mary, a slim blonde at my right, chews frantically the inside of her lower lip. Only one or two words in blue ink stand upon her clean white page. David Harris, slouched in his seat in the third row, nibbles each finger of each hand. Then he plays inaudibly with a black collar button that stands open on the top of his red plaid shirt. There is a thump as he uncrosses his legs and his scuffed shoe hits the floor. A painful cough slices the air from behind me. I hear a woman's heels click from the hall beyond the closed door and a car engine whine annoyingly from Bedford Avenue. If a college classroom should be a place of delight and pleasure, that could never be proved by the tension in this room.

—Harry Golden

1. What is the topic sentence? _____

_____

_____

2. What is the first subtopic sentence? _____

_____

3. What is the second subtopic sentence? _____

_____

4. What is the closing sentence? _____

_____

_____

Step 2. "The Gloom Room" Paragraph as Essay. Study Mr. Golden's four-paragraph essay below, noting especially the explanations in the margin. Then, discuss the answers to the questions below. If your instructor asks you to write the answers, use separate paper.

The Gloom Room

October often looks and feels dreary because school is by then in full swing. Today, a rainy Thursday, is no different. What makes it worse is that I am forced to sit in my writing class on the second floor of Boylan Hall at Brooklyn College and write a theme. (It is no wonder that a shadow of gloom hangs over the people and things that surround me in this room.)

[The Proposal: It tells what the whole essay will be about.]

[The Topic Sentence: (Paragraph 2) It tells what this paragraph will be about.]

[As I look around, I see that the surroundings are old and depressing.] There is a broken brown chair beside the teacher's desk; no one will sit in it for fear of leaning back and toppling over onto the floor. There is also a mahogany bookcase with a missing shelf, and all the books are piled on the bottom in a stack of blue and yellowed covers, instead of standing in a straight row. This ugly desk of mine is filled with holes and scratches because other impatient students, no doubt, lost their tempers and took out their anger on the wooden surface. As I rub my hand across it, I feel coldness. Even the gray walls and the rumble of thunder outside reflect the atmosphere of seriousness as we write our first theme of the semester. When some air sails through an open window beside me, there is the annoying smell of coffee grounds from a garbage pail not far off. ⟨That smell is a perfect indication of our discomfort!⟩

[Details: Concrete sensory language, statistics, cases, quotations, paraphrase, or imagery to illustrate your point.]

[Closing Sentence: shows you are finished with this paragraph.]

[This part of the topic sentence reminds the reader about what you wrote in the last paragraph.] → [Aside from the unattractive surroundings,] ⟨the people around me show this mood of tension and displeasure.⟩ Mary, a slim blonde at my right, chews the inside of her lower lip. I can see by the way her forehead is wrinkled that she is having quite a bit of trouble. Because only one or two words in blue ink stand upon her clean white page, she looks around the room fearfully for some new ideas. Slouching

[This part of the topic sentence tells the reader what you will discuss in this paragraph.]

[Details: to illustrate the
point of the topic sentence.]

in his seat in the third row, David Harris nibbles each finger of each hand. Then he plays with a black collar button that stands open on the top of his red plaid shirt. The tension gets to him too; drops of perspiration run slowly down his cheeks. I hear a thump as he uncrosses his legs and his scuffed shoe hits the floor. A painful cough slices the air from behind me. I hear a woman's heels click from the hall beyond the closed door and a car engine whine annoyingly from Bedford Avenue. All these signs of gloom don't help my mood at all.

These last few painful moments make me wonder if what my friends told me about college was all true. Where are all the beautiful girls I'm supposed to be meeting and talking to in every room? Where are the freedom and relaxed atmosphere my friends bragged about? I'm supposed to be enjoying myself instead of suffering! Everybody seems to have forgotten that college is hard work too. My first days in writing class prove that delight and pleasure often disappear when assignments are due!

[Conclusion:
1. May summarize.
2. Makes transition by referring to an idea in the introduction.
3. May give a dominant impression.
4. May bring in a new—but related—idea.]

—Harry Golden

1. What is the difference between the opening sentence in Mr. Golden's one-paragraph theme and the opening paragraph in his essay?
2. How are the proposal sentence in the essay and the topic sentence in the one-paragraph theme alike?
3. How does subtopic sentence 1 in "The Gloom Room" paragraph compare to the topic sentence of paragraph 2 in "The Gloom Room" essay?
4. How do the details coming after subtopic sentence 1 in the one-paragraph composition compare with the details in paragraph 2 of the essay?
5. How does Mr. Golden's second subtopic sentence compare to the opening sentence of paragraph 3 in his essay?
6. How do the details after subtopic sentence 2 in his one-paragraph theme compare with the details in the third paragraph of Mr. Golden's essay?
7. Read the last sentence of paragraph 2 and of paragraph 3. Are these effective as closing sentences? Why?
8. What part of the first sentence of the conclusion in Mr. Golden's essay refers back to the main idea of the essay?
9. Where in the conclusion does Mr. Golden bring in a new but related idea?
10. How does the closing sentence of Mr. Golden's one-paragraph composition compare with the concluding paragraph of his four-paragraph essay?

WRITING PROPOSAL SENTENCES

The *proposal sentence* — the sentence in the essay that tells what you propose or intend to discuss in the remaining paragraphs — is the most important sentence in the essay. It controls and limits your entire composition. You can write only about what the proposal *says* you will write about.

GUIDELINES FOR GOOD PROPOSALS

1. Make sure your proposal sentence allows you to discuss what you want to. It should announce the topic clearly. It should express an opinion. If you find as you are writing that you no longer are discussing the topic you set for yourself, *go back and change the proposal sentence.*

2. The proposal should be so written as to allow you to discuss at least two specific aspects of the topic. Notice how Mr. Golden's proposal tells *specifically* the two parts of the topic: the gloom surrounding the people and the gloom surrounding the things in his classroom. Each body paragraph, then, can pick up *one* aspect of that topic. Paragraph 2 focuses on things. Paragraph 3 focuses on people.

   But it is not essential to mention in the proposal just what each paragraph will say. An alternate proposal for Mr. Golden's essay might be this:

   It is no wonder that gloominess is everywhere.

   Notice how in this proposal, the reader has no idea of exactly what kind of treatment Mr. Golden's essay will make of gloominess. But still, this alternate proposal permits the writer to discuss in one body paragraph the gloomy surroundings and in the other body paragraph the gloomy people.

3. Put your proposal *last* in the introduction. This makes it easier for you for several reasons:

   a. You can return to it often if you know exactly where it appears; by reading the proposal often while you write you can make sure that you are staying on the topic.

   b. You can make the transition between the proposal and the opening sentence of paragraph 2 very simple to write because the idea you must refer back to comes directly above your opening sentence. Mr. Golden's proposal mentions that he is in a room. The first words of paragraph 2 say "As I look around"; and because this looking around takes place in the room mentioned in the previous paragraph, the two paragraphs are thereby brought close together smoothly.

Step 1. Preparing Proposals. Column I suggests the subject of a student's essay. In Column II, write a proposal sentence that you think would serve to develop the student's ideas.

Hint: You do not need to state in the proposal exactly what each paragraph will illustrate. Just state the main purpose of your essay, the idea your whole essay will be about.

I

Example:

1. This essay intends to show that the writer prefers discussions held in cafeterias because they are free and friendly and lively, but that discussions in classrooms are often depressing because they are restricted and unenthusiastic.

2. This writer wants to show that the prison system in America needs reform in its conviction, treatment, and training of convicts; and if reforms are made, society will benefit by means of added workers and better-adjusted human beings.

3. This student wants to describe two different moods (brought about by the weather) created in the playground of his high school.

4. This essay intends to defend "open admissions" policies for colleges. Its first body paragraph will show that such a policy is long overdue. The next body paragraph will try to illustrate the advantages of open admissions to society and to the individual.

5. This writer wants to show in an essay that the emotion of love can be a force of great beauty when it involves men and women and their deep feelings for each other, but that love can be a force of destructiveness when men use love of country or God as a reason to fight other men.

6. This writer wants to prove that football is exciting for the player and for the spectator.

II

A meeting of minds at an active discussion in the cafeteria outweighs by far any interchange among students in the classrooms.

7. This essay will try to illustrate why the writer chose to come to college. His first body paragraph will try to illustrate the specific skills the writer expects to learn, skills that will help him on the job he hopes to get after he graduates. His second body paragraph will show how college is needed for status by showing one specific moment in which his lack of a college education hurt his pride.

8. This writer wants to show that he cannot confide in his mother because she always blames him whether or not he is at fault. He will tell about two specific incidents he told to his mother, one in which he was involved in an automobile accident and the other in which he attended a party which was later raided by police in search of marijuana. The boy was innocent in both instances but his mother blamed him.

9. This writer wants to show by giving several instances in each paragraph how she and her adopted sister get along much better than she and her "real" sister get along.

10. This essay will illustrate how the writer's bedroom is a place for escape when company comes and a place where the writer's most important personal problems are ironed out.

Step 2. Predicting Body Paragraphs from Proposals. These proposals all come from freshman papers. Based upon the topic stated in the proposal, tell briefly what you would discuss in each of the two body paragraphs.

Example:
1. I feel that college has two essential purposes.

Main point of paragraph 2: *how to think logically is what colleges should te*

Main point of paragraph 3: *to teach special skills for future*

2. Despite its many bad features, smoking cigarettes, cigars, or pipes has several good points to recommend it to large numbers of people.

Main point of paragraph 2:

_____

Main point of paragraph 3:

_____

3. In my life as an orphan there have been many troubled times and worries.

Main point of paragraph 2:

_____

Main point of paragraph 3:

_____

_____

4. Little did I realize then that in my eighteenth year I would learn the importance of clear thinking.

Main point of paragraph 2:

_____

Main point of paragraph 3:

_____

5. The railroad as a means of transportation is clearly dying out.

Main point of paragraph 2:

_____

Main point of paragraph 3:

_____

6. The new sense of "Afro" now being expressed by many American blacks will certainly harm the black man in this country.

Main point of paragraph 2:

_____

Main point of paragraph 3:

_____

7. The new sense of "Afro" now being expressed by many American blacks will certainly help the black man in this country.

Main point of paragraph 2:

_____

Main point of paragraph 3:

8. The town of Hunter in New York State, where we spend our summers in a shack, is a place I will always associate with adventure.

Main point of paragraph 2:

_____

Main point of paragraph 3:

_____

9. No one can deny that President Nixon's trip to China will have a number of important effects on today's world.

Main point of paragraph 2:

_____

Main point of paragraph 3:

_____

10. Love is not an emotion of passion but an emotion that grows with time and some pain.

Main point of paragraph 2:

_____

Main point of paragraph 3:

_____

INTRODUCTIONS: SPARKING READER INTEREST

Aside from its purpose as the paragraph that gets the essay started by stating the topic in the proposal sentence, the introductory paragraph must make the reader interested enough in what you have to say so that he wants to read on. Any one of the suggestions in the following list can help you write an effective introduction to lead up to the proposal statement. Each suggestion is followed by a sample.

Writing Top-notch Introductions: Ideas for Starting Essays

Hint: Always write the proposal sentence before you write the introductory paragraph.

1. Tell the reader why your topic is important.

   Sample: For fifteen years I lived on East 92nd Street in Brooklyn. I made friends there, earned bloody noses, broke Mrs. Segal's window playing stick-ball, and nursed back to health a small, frightened sparrow in a shoe box. That block was mother and father to me in a way, presenting a number of un-expected experiences that are so important in the life of someone growing up without "at-home" parents—my father ran away when I was six and my mother worked most of the day. So the block was my teacher, and in several ways the lessons I learned there taught me how to think fast to survive.

2. Give background information on your topic so that the reader knows, when he gets to your proposal, the background information which led you to consider the point you are treating in the essay.

Sample: For the sixteen years since the Supreme Court declared school segregation unconstitutional in 1954, many Americans have protested against the policy. We have seen governors and mayors blocking schoolhouse door-ways, hostile police, violent white mobs, and clever legal attempts. Black parents have rightly pointed to the horribly inferior conditions in the segre-gated schools their children attend, showing that even "legal integration" does not always mean a fair mixing of races and an improvement of conditions. And the federal government stays neutral, giving little more than money to those schools attempting integration. Because Americans have rejected important attempts to desegregate the nation's schools, and because the government has given little real support, integration has not succeeded at all thus far.

3. Show what many people believe is true if your proposal will attempt to suggest something else.

Sample: Education is the process by which the young people of today are trained to become functioning members of their society. This process is gen-erally accomplished in institutions known as schools where young people be-come acquainted with all phases of knowledge and, after a few years, are thought ready to accept responsibility as adults. In college the usual picture is a classroom filled with excited, bright-eyed youths soaking up important lessons for living. However, the American school system has failed miserably in trying to accomplish what it sets out to do; our system of higher education does not provide a person with the necessary training to take his rightful place in society.

4. State several points that may contradict, disagree with, or disprove the point you want the rest of the essay to make.

Sample: Working hard from his childhood on, my father has grown into a hard man. He is strict and overprotective and he screams when I tiptoe into the house at two in the morning on a Saturday. He threatens to disconnect my extension phone so he can get to make a call, but he will never give me the satisfaction of having my own number. I rarely sit down to chat with him because his opinions are so one-sided; besides, when I rush into my room and toss my books on the bed at seven o'clock after my last class, Dad's loud harsh snore already echoes through the house. Despite these difficult qualities, I am still Daddy's little girl and always will be. I am not ashamed of this either, because over the years I have grown to love my father very much and will always continue to share this unique type of love with him.

5. Ask questions to arouse the reader's interest.

   Sample: Can a large city ever encourage a feeling of friendliness and co-operation among its citizens? Can apartment-house dwellers who choose to race up the stairs to the isolation of their own dreary rooms ever learn to smile and whisper a neighborly "Good morning!" even to faces they never saw before? An unusual group of concerned citizens of Manhattan set an unusual experiment to seek the answers, and what they discovered is very interesting.

6. Use an interesting quotation that helps you build toward your proposal sentence (see pp. 49–51 and p. 231 for writing quotations correctly).

   Sample: Kahlil Gibran in *A Tear and a Smile* writes, "I looked toward nature . . . and found therein . . . a thing that endures and lives in the spring and comes to fruit in summer days. Therein I found love." This I believe to be true, because people do not "fall in love"; love that lasts is a feeling that must come gradually over a period of time and must develop only with emotional maturity.

Hint: Use quotations from your own reading of newspapers, magazines, books, or from television, radio, or the movies. Books like *Bartlett's Familiar Quotations* and the *Oxford Dictionary of Quotations* have many quotations arranged according to subjects; often you can find a meaningful quotation there to use in your introduction.

7. Tell a brief story—an incident that helps set the stage for your proposal. Make sure the story suits the purpose of your essay: don't be funny or "cute" unless you expect to deal with matters that are not too serious or unless you can work the humor into your point.

   Sample: A man with one shoe and a face filled with red sores wobbles down the summer morning street cursing to himself. From his back pocket he snatches a paper bag, uncaps the bottle inside, raises it to his lips, and takes a long gulp. Then, he drops down against a brick wall and, still cursing, closes his eyes. This is the Bowery, the place of the drunkard. Although the horrors on this street are everywhere, very little is done by police or other agencies to change the way of life of New York's fallen men.

8. Tell what the body paragraphs will deal with; in this way you tell the reader how you intend to treat the topic.

Sample: The automobile, plane, and railroad make an important contribution to the nation's economy. And these means of transportation also contribute to the leisure enjoyment of countless Americans. It is for these reasons that I believe that these machines are man's best friend.

Hint: Sentence 1 in the above introduction tells what the writer expects to develop in the first body paragraph (paragraph 2 of the essay). Sentence 2 above tells the purpose of the second body paragraph. The writer has divided the topic for the reader.

9. Use a series of images to build up to your proposal.

   Sample: Rocks tossed from behind trees; bottles broken on our blacktop driveway; whispering voices behind wrinkled hands at the A&P; taunts of "Kyke" and "There's a Jew" sailing at my back as I march to school alone: a Jew growing up in a small Midwestern town learns how to hate very early in life.

10. Show different aspects of the topic that you will not consider in the essay, as you lead up to the topic that you will consider.

    Sample: There are many different kinds of love. A mother loves her child. A man loves a woman. People love their countries or ideas or religions. But one kind of love that is frequently hard to find is the rare but important love a man has for a friend.

AVOIDING PITFALLS IN INTRODUCTIONS

1. Don't make your introduction too long. If each of your body paragraphs contains ten or fewer sentences, your introduction usually needs no more than four or five sentences. Longer body paragraphs may mean that longer introductions are acceptable.

2. Don't apologize for what you do not know or for your lack of experience or for your limited abilities. Even if any of this is true, to mention it in your paragraph is to make the reader feel that you do not know what you are talking about. Don't make any of these statements:

   a. "Although I am not qualified to discuss this . . . ."
   b. "My knowledge is limited so . . . ."
   c. "Many people who know more than I do would disagree, but . . . ."

3. Don't think of the reader as someone who is sitting next to you as you write. Don't say:

   "Now I will tell you . . . ."
   or
   "Now I am going to show you . . . ."

4. Don't talk about the parts of the essay in your composition. Don't say
   "In my next paragraph, I . . . ."
   or
   "My introduction and my conclusion will try to show . . . ."

---

5. Don't write an introduction that wastes words, one that you have just thrown on to your body paragraphs to fulfill the requirements of essay form. Your introduction should be an important part of the essay itself.
6. Don't use overworked expressions—trite sayings or quotations that have lost their meaning because of overuse. Don't use quotations or expressions that are too general, or that could be applied to hundreds of situations. To say "Too many cooks spoil the broth" in an essay about too many men at the top and giving orders in government would not really add anything of significance.
7. Don't say the same thing over and over again. If you don't have much to say by way of introduction, write only the proposal in a clear, well-planned sentence or two of some length.

Step 1. Writing Introductions to Proposals. Using any three of the proposal sentences from Step 2 on pp. 275–277, write three introductions. Put the proposal sentence last. Try to write a different kind of introduction for each proposal: check the Ideas for Starting Essays on pp. 277–280. And, make sure you avoid the errors explained in pp. 280–281. Use your own paper.

Step 2. Reading More Introductions. Discuss the introductory paragraphs for the essays in this book whose titles and page numbers are listed below. Are the introductions effective? Which of the items on pp. 277–280 does each introduction seem to follow? How might you improve each introduction?

1. "Practice in the High School Gym," pp. 299–300.
2. "Deprived Children," pp. 333–334.
3. "Women: Fragile Flowers? pp. 335–336.
4. "Hating a Job," pp. 403–404.
5. "Some Disappointments," pp. 364–366.

Step 3. Introductions: You Be the Judge. Decide whether or not the introductions below would be good first paragraphs for four-paragraph essays. Defend your opinions. Then, make any corrections that you feel will improve the introductory paragraphs. In some cases you may have to rewrite the paragraph completely. Use separate paper.

1. Good neighbors are very important. I know this because I have been a neighbor, have had neighbors, and will continue to have neighbors. Therefore I know how important good neighbors are. This essay will try to show how important it is to have good neighbors and that good neighbors are very important to have.

2. It is true that someone with my limited knowledge about poverty in big cities should not be writing about that important social issue. But I do have some opinions, and although people with more experience than I have could probably show my mistakes, I would like to show what I think poverty means.

3. Are you fed up with street riots and automobile fumes? Are you trying to escape

the summer heat of Newark and the noisy crowds that shove their way across Market Street? Well then pack a tent and a four-burner stove and head for the nearest camping grounds. Outdoor living for summer vacation is a relaxing and unusual way to spend some time with nature.

4. Working has its bad points but all people must work to earn enough money to survive. Work is hard, but if you expect to get anywhere you have to work hard. The people were nice but the job was miserable.

5. Now I will tell you all about a wonderful house on a hill. It was here I learned "Honor your mother and father."

Step 4. More Work on Introductions.   For any three of the proposals you wrote in Step 1, pp. 273–275, write three good introductions using any of the suggestions you studied. Use separate paper.

Then take any topic sentence you wrote for any theme assignment in Part I of this book, and assume that it is the proposal sentence of an essay. Write a good introduction following the advice you learned in this chapter. Use separate paper.

SOLVING PROBLEMS IN WRITING: PRONOUN PRACTICE

Pronouns as Subjects

PRONOUN CHART I: SUBJECT PRONOUNS		
Singular Pronoun Subjects		*Plural Pronoun Subjects*
I it		we you
he you		they
she who		

You remember from Chapter 4 that the pronouns that appear above may be used as subjects of verbs.

_____ *run(s).*

Any of the pronouns you see in the chart above could be used in the blank space in the sentence above.

Example: I run.
          He runs.
          They run.

Although you would never say or write *Me run* or *Him runs,* when you use two subjects (one of which is a pronoun) for the same verb you often forget to use the subject pronouns from the chart above. The following sentences from student papers fail to use pronouns correctly. Alongside the incorrect sentence you will see the sentence written with the right subject pronoun.

Incorrect

1. My father and *me* never got along.
2. *Him* and *me* watched fireworks from across the bay.

Correct

My father and *I* never got along.
He and *I* watched fireworks from across the bay.

HINTS FOR CORRECT PRONOUNS WHEN TWO SUBJECTS ARE USED FOR THE SAME VERB

1. Always pick a pronoun you want to use as a subject from Pronoun Chart I on p. 282.
2. Test each subject *alone* before you decide which pronoun to use. For example, suppose you do not know whether to use *her* or *she* in the blank space in this sentence:

   Her mother and _____ rushed into the house.

   First say:

   a. *Her mother* rushed into the house.

   Then say:

   b. *Her* rushed into the house.

   That would never sound right.
   Then say

   c. *She* rushed into the house.

   That is correct. Now combine the two subjects from a and c.

   Her mother and *she* rushed into the house.

Step 1. Speaking about Two Subjects. Combine any one of the subject pronouns (he, I, she, it, we, they, you, who) with the name of someone you know to tell a place recently visited. Speak your answers aloud.

Example: Jim and she saw The Rolling Stones at a concert.
My father and I drove into Brooklyn last night.

Step 2. Filling in Pronoun Subjects. Fill the blank space with any pronoun subject that makes sense to you. Use different pronouns in each sentence.

1. Matthew and _____ traveled to Colgate by car.

2. His father and _____ painted the house.

3. _____ and her sister never knew their father.

4. While _____ and their friends danced in the basement, the rooms upstairs were robbed.

5. When Margaret and _____ arrived, nobody welcomed them.

Pronouns after to Be   [part of *to be*]
   a. Everyone thought it was her.
   b. Everyone thought it was she.

   If you had to choose between a and b, you would probably select a as the sentence that you hear more frequently. However, sentence b is correct, and in writing you want to remember this suggestion:

After a form of the verb to be *use a subject pronoun.*

The verb *to be* has many forms, several of which appear below:

am	has been	should have been
is	have been	should be
are	had been	could be
was	will be	may be
were	must have been	
	could have been	

Hint: The expression "It's me" (It is me) is not correct formal English: "It is I" is what formal writing requires. However, "It's me" is used in conversation and is acceptable.

Step 3. Pronouns after *to Be*.   Complete each sentence below by writing a correct *pronoun* after the verb. Circle the pronoun you use. You may add any other information you like.

Example:

1. It was *he who lost his wallet.* _____ .

2. The latecomers were _____ .

3. The teacher knew that it had been _____ .

4. The leaders could have been _____ .

5. It will be _____ .

Step 4. Selecting the Right Pronoun.   Select *subject pronouns* to make each sentence below correct. Circle from parentheses the pronoun you would choose.

1. Steven and (he, him) drove to Los Angeles yesterday.
2. Although it was (me, I) who broke the vase, my mother blamed my sister.
3. The treasurer felt that it should have been (he, him) who gave out the checks.
4. Melissa and (she, her) did not want any dessert.
5. No one thought it was (he, him).
6. When (they, them) and their dogs left the house, everyone turned to watch.
7. (He, Him) and (me, I) bought an old car to race on Saturdays.

8. The whole neighborhood knew that the troublemakers must have been (they, them).
9. Her teacher and (her, she) both wore the same dress.
10. Both (him, he) and his father worked at the clothing factory.

Pronouns in Other Places

```
PRONOUN CHART II: NONSUBJECT PRONOUNS

Singular                    Plural
me                          us
him                         them
her                         whom
whom

Hint:  The words it and you may be used as subject or nonsubject pronouns.
```

The pronouns that appear above are not subject pronouns and do not appear as subjects in sentences. Yet the words above are usually found in two important sentence positions.

After verbs

   [verb]\   /[pronoun]
  Give **me** the book.

      [verb]\   /[pronoun]
  Jerome *selected* **her** as his partner.

          /[pronoun]
  You *told* **whom** about the riot?
  [verb]/

Although you would never write

  Give *I* the book
        or
  Jerome selected *she* as his partner

whenever you use *two* words after the verb (one of which is a pronoun), you probably have some difficulty selecting the correct pronoun. Look at these sentences; is *a* or *b* correct?

a
           /[verb]
The policeman <u>scolded</u> Harriet and <u>*I*</u> for jaywalking.

b
           /[verb]
  The policeman <u>scolded</u> Harriet and <u>*me*</u> for jaywalking.

You remember that *I* can be used only as a subject. In sentence *a*, the subject is *policeman* (for the verb *scolded*). Since the pronoun you need comes *after* the verb *scolded*, select the pronoun from the chart above. Since *me* appears in the chart, sentence *b* is correct.

HINTS FOR CORRECT PRONOUNS AFTER VERBS

1. Select the pronoun from Pronoun Chart II, p. 285.
2. If two words must come after the verb, test each word alone before you decide which pronoun to use. Suppose you do not know whether to use *he* or *him* in the blank in this sentence.
   The teacher praised his brother and _____ for their cooperation.
   First say
     a. The teacher praised *his brother.*
   Then say
     b. The teacher praised *he.* That wouldn't sound right. Then say
     c. The teacher praised *him.*
   That is correct. Now combine the words after the verb in a and c:
     The teacher praised *his brother* and *him* for their cooperation.

Step 1. Writing Pronouns after Verbs. Write sentences for any ten of the following verbs. Use *two* words after each verb, one a noun and the other a correct pronoun. Write about things that really happened and use as many different pronouns as possible. Look at the example beneath the list of verbs.

observed	invited	asked
hurried	begged	drove
told	pushed	required
allowed	annoyed	picked
questioned	brought	
chased	left	

Example:

1. *The movie left my sister and me with an unpleasant feeling.*
2. _____
3. _____
4. _____
5. _____
6. _____
7. _____
8. _____
9. _____
10. _____

Pronouns after Connecting Words That Show Relationship
Aside from their use after verbs, the pronouns in Chart II on p. 285 are

used after certain connecting words that relate one word or word group in the sentence to some other sentence part. First, look at some of the connecting words that show relationship.

  a. We read a *book* **about** *teen-agers.*

The word *about* relates the word *book* and *teen-agers* to each other by showing the kind of book.

  b. Charlene *ran* **toward** *David.*

The word *toward* relates *ran* and *David* by showing where the action was performed. Now, if you wanted to use a pronoun instead of *teen-agers* and instead of *David,* you would need a word from Pronoun Chart II (p. 285):

  We read a book **about** *them.*

  Charlene ran **toward** *him.*

There are many connecting words like *about* and *toward* that show relationships. Here is a list of several of the most important.

SOME CONNECTORS THAT SHOW RELATIONSHIP			
about; by; beneath; inside; above; for; over; outside; along; among; of	except; under; onto; at; across; on; over; into; after; to; with	within; beside; since; as to; toward; at; beyond; up; before; like; below	between; below; upon; by means of; through; along with; because of; by way of; on account of; in spite of; in front of

Step 2. Remembering Connectors. Study the connectors above. Then, after covering the chart, write from memory as many as you can in the blank space below.

  You probably would not have trouble writing *one* correct pronoun after the connector words mentioned above. No one would write

Give the book to *I*.

>   or

The boy ran toward *he*.

But as soon as *two* words are used after the connector, students have difficulties.

>   Give the book **to** Mary and (I, me).
>   The boy ran **toward** the child and (he, him).

Since the pronoun you need comes after a connecting word that shows relationship (*to* and *toward*), you must select a pronoun from Pronoun Chart II. The words *I* and *he* are not correct because they are subject pronouns (Pronoun Chart I) and must be used as subjects of verbs. Correctly written, the sentences above are:

>   Give the book to Mary and *me*.
>   The boy ran toward the child and *him*.

HINTS FOR PRONOUNS AFTER CONNECTORS THAT SHOW RELATIONSHIP

1. Select the pronoun from Pronoun Chart II, p. 285.
2. If *two* words come after the connector word that shows relationship, test the words one at a time before you decide which pronoun to use. If you don't know whether to use *I* or *me* in this sentence:

>   The coach spoke about Joe and _____.

First say

>   a. The coach spoke about *Joe*.

then say

>   b. The coach spoke about *I*.

That wouldn't sound right.
Then say

>   c. The coach spoke about *me*.

This is obviously correct.
Now combine the results in a and c above.

>   The coach spoke about *Joe* and *me*.

Step 3. Pronouns for You to Choose. Fill in both blanks in each item below. Use a pronoun in at least one of the blanks. You can use a noun *or* another pronoun in the other blank. Look at the two examples.

1. toward *him* and *me*

2. for *Carl* and *her*.

3. to _____ or _____

4. by _____ and _____

5. between _____ and _____

6. on account of _____ or _____

7. into _____ and _____

8. after _____ or _____

9. at _____ and _____

10. above _____ and _____

11. in spite of _____ and _____

12. below _____ and _____

13. instead of _____ or _____

14 except _____ and _____

15. with _____ and _____

Step 4. Writing Sentences with Connectors That Show Relationship. Use ten of the subject-verb combinations below in sentences of your own. After each subject-verb combination use correctly one of the completed word groups from Step 7 above.

Subject-Verb Combinations

the plane soared
you speak
he left
they drove
my mother shopped
the rock flew

a car rode
they sang
one man laughed
he watched
she cried
we smoked

Example:

1. *They sang only for Carl and her.* _____ .

2. _____ .

3. _____ .

4. _____ .

5. _____ .

6. _____ .

7. _____ .

8. _____ .

9. _____ .

10. _____ .

A Special Problem

Some of the words listed as connectors that show relationship also act as subordinators or coordinators. You remember that subordinators and coordinators (see pp. 85–92) introduce subject-verb word groups which are connected to complete sentences. So, it *is* possible to find a subject pronoun after one of the words listed as connectors that show relationship. But notice how differently the word is used in each of these sentences:

A	B
My brother ran <u>before</u> me.	<u>Before</u> I <u>ran</u> away, my brother left home.

In *A*, the word *before* is a connector that relates the word *ran* and *me* by showing where the action took place.

In *B*, the word *before* is a connector that subordinates the subject-verb word group *I ran away* to the complete thought *my brother left home*.

Step 5. Connectors in Two Ways. Fill in each blank correctly after the connector with a pronoun from either Pronoun Chart I or Pronoun Chart II.

Hint: 1. If the pronoun is the subject of a verb, use Pronoun Chart I.
2. Study the hints on pp. 283, 286, and 288.

1. They brought the hot sauce for my brother and _____.

2. We were very thirsty, for my brother and _____ ate hot sauce.

3. After Delores and _____ cooked the frankfurters, they raced to the lake.

4. One ferocious dog ran after Charles and _____.

How Pronouns Agree
a. The girl kissed <u>her</u> mother.
b. The boys brought <u>their</u> gloves.

In the two sentences above the underlined word is a pronoun that takes the place of the noun to which the arrow is drawn. In sentence *a*, the word *girl* is singular and the pronoun that refers back to it must be singular (*her*). In sentence *b*, the word *boys* is plural and the pronoun that refers back to it must be plural (*their*). It is easy to see that *boys* is plural and *girl* is singular.

c. She kissed <u>her</u> mother.
d. They brought <u>their</u> gloves.

In sentences c and d the underlined pronoun takes the place of another pronoun. *Her* takes the place of *she*; since *she* is singular, *her* must be singular. *Their* takes the place of *they*; since *they* is plural, *their* must be plural too. But with words like *boys*, *girl*, *they*, *she* it is easy to decide whether the word is singular or plural. Several pronouns—although they may look plural—are always singular. If another pronoun later on in the sentence refers back to one of these special singular pronouns, that pronoun must be singular too.

SPECIAL SINGULAR PRONOUNS

anyone	everyone	someone	one
anybody	everybody	somebody	neither
each	either	no one	none
			nobody

Hint: If a pronoun refers to one of these words, the pronoun must be singular.

Everyone	should bring	*his* own assignment.
Each	of them packed	*his* own bag.
Anybody	may raise	*his* own hand.
Either	of the boys can drive	*his* own car.
Anyone	can love	*his* own country.
One	of them sold	*his* own camera.
None	of them helped	*his* own country.

[This pronoun refers to one of the special singular pronouns.]

***HIS* OR *HER*?**

His is used as a pronoun even when the group contains men and women. *Her* is used when the group is clearly all women.

Everyone of them set *her* own hair.
Either of them can make *her* own clothes.

Step 6. Selecting the Right Pronoun. Write in the blank space the correct word from parentheses.

Example: Everyone sharpened ___*his*___ pencil (his, their).

1. Each of them should have eaten _____ lunch earlier (his, their).

2. Everybody likes to go back to _____ old high school for a visit (their, his).

3. All the players took off _____ helmets at the same time (their, his).

Step 7. Special Singulars in Your Sentences. Write sentences for ten of the special singular pronouns listed in the chart above. In every sentence use a different word group from those that appear below. Use separate paper.

Example: *No one walks his dog in the rain.*

his boat	his girl friend	his exam
his dog	her lipstick	his dinner
his driver's license	his radio	his matches
his draft card	his motorcycle	his parents

PRONOUNS THAT POINT OUT

This book is mine.
These papers ripped.
That girl fell.
Those cars sped along the highway.

Only *this, these, that, those* point out.

Don't Use Them *to Point Out*
Not   *Them* windows look dirty *but*
        Those windows look dirty.

Since *this* and *that* are singular, the words they point out must be singular.
Since *these* and *those* are plural, the words they point out must be plural.

[singular] [singular]
This kind of book is good.

not

[plural] [singular]
These kind of books is good.

or   [plural]   [plural]
     These kinds of cars save money on gasoline.

Step 8. Pointing Out with Pronouns. Fill in the blank with *this, that, these, those,* or *them.*

1. Never purchase _____ kind of furniture.

2. _____ types of people always complain.

3. If you are interested in _____ sort of television program, write to the network about your approval.

4. She told _____ all, "_____ kind of behavior doesn't belong here!"

5. _____ sorts of apples taste bad toward the end of September.

For Steps 10 and 11 use the review charts below. Make sure that you know the connectors listed on p. 287.

PRONOUN CHART I		PRONOUN CHART II	
Subjects		*After Verbs and after Connectors That Show Relationship*	
I	we	me	us
he		him	
she	they	her	them
it		it	
you	you	you	
who		whom	

> After "to be," use subject pronouns.
>
> Use *this, that, these, those* to point
>
> out. DON'T USE *them!*
>
>   *these* boys
>
> not *them* boys
>
> If you need a pronoun as one of two words, say one word at a time.
>
>   He asked Barry and (I, me).
> He asked *I.* [WRONG]
> He asked *me.* [RIGHT]
> Then: He asked Barry and me.
>
> **Hint:** Use a singular pronoun to refer back to a special singular pronoun like *anyone, everyone, anybody, someone, no one, neither, either, each.*

Step 9. Pronouns in Your Sentences. On separate paper, use ten of the following word groups correctly in sentences.

1. my brother and me
2. the girl and I
3. the teacher and us
4. you and them
5. him and her
6. the grocer and I
7. the grocer and me
8. this sort
9. Maria and who
10. the boy and me
11. him and me
12. he and I
13. those kinds
14. them and us

Step 10. Reviewing Pronoun Usage. Write on the blank line in the margin the correct pronouns you select from parentheses. Look at the example.

James Baldwin's Harlem

1. *him*
2. _____
3. _____
4. _____
5. _____
6. _____
7. _____
8. _____
9. _____
10. _____

    The picture that James Baldwin paints of Harlem is sad and ugly. For countless blacks and (he, him), Fifth Avenue in Manhattan is not the area you and (I, me) think of at the mention of that famous street. Baldwin's Fifth Avenue is the place of the project, the hideous housing developments in which many black youngsters grow to manhood. Their parents and (they, them) look down upon the filthy streets, streets Baldwin calls "cheerless as a prison." Although his brothers, sisters, and (he, him) grew up on 131st Street and Lenox Avenue, these blocks gave Baldwin and (they, them) few memories of pleasure and delight. The Negroes who have not moved out or died: it is (they, them) who still live in bitterness and confusion. Some are fanatical churchgoers, Holy-Roller members; the Moslems and (they, them) claim many young members of Harlem. But the Moslems, according to Baldwin, are united by one cause: hatred for white people. Against (they, them) and their world many militant blacks speak out. Other black people are not involved; their friends and (they, them) stay home and merely watch television, leaving the house only to go to a movie or the nearest bar. Or a man can do even worse, since an acquaintance and (he, him) can sit "stoned" on

11. _____
12. _____

the stoops of the houses waiting for another fix. Anyone who has (his, their) eye on city events knows that Harlem has destroyed the lives of thousands of men. (Them, Those) ruined lives is what Baldwin screams out against.

Step 11. New Vocabulary in Pronoun Practice. For each word in italics use a pronoun. Write the correct pronoun directly above the italicized word. The sentences all use some of the new vocabulary on pp. 260–262. Study the sample.

He   *they*
David and *his cousins* surprised Anthony with their inimical remarks.

1. It was *Beverly* who with muffled sobs told Alice and *her brothers* the stunning news.

2. The corpulent owner rushed at *the boy* and *his girl friend* because *the boy and his girl friend* broke a costly oblong window in his house.

3. I am not sure what you said. *Julio* brought that obscene book? It was *Julio!*

4. On account of *the dog* and the *little children,* the room would grow fetid if not cleaned daily.

5. Nancy said in an alluring voice. "It was *Nancy* who tried to phone you."

Step 12. Pronouns Do It. Circle the correct pronouns in the parentheses below.

1. It was (I, me) who came early.
2. Give the drinks to Harriet and (I, me).
3. Everybody found (his, their) own favorite book.
4. The girl and (I, me) finished before everyone.
5. Janet saw Ted and (they, them) at the movies.
6. Paul sent (them, those) flowers to Marie.
7. The porter and (he, him) discussed the weather.
8. (That, These) kind never succeeds.
9. Between you and (I, me), I don't like her.
10. You, David, and (I, me) need more money.
11. It could never have been (she, her).
12. He read the magazine to the old man and (them, they).
13. At the store Mrs. Wilde and (we, us) said hello.
14. With Carl and (I, me) close by, Tom ran upstairs.
15. None of the men brought (his, their) own car.

WRITING THE ESSAY

Think about some particular place that has some significance in your life: a room, an office, a schoolyard, a country cabin, or farm. Make sure that there are two specific aspects of this place that you can write about—one in each paragraph. Make sure you have a strong enough feeling about the place so that you can write an effective proposal sentence. And use your highest level of concrete sensory language for details: color, sound, touch, smell, images of action will be the essential source of support for the points you wish to make.

HOW TO PLAN THE ESSAY

You remember that the first six chapters of this book introduced some of the ways paragraphs may be organized. Essays, since they are composed of paragraphs, may be organized in similar ways, each paragraph following a pattern of organization that suits the topic. Since you now are aware of several different types of paragraphs and several different ways of presenting the illustrations of your point, you need to think through the method that will best suit your subject. Comparison, contrast, narration, several instances to support topic ideas, description, analogy, mood sketches, definitions through images: all these paragraph types may be extended to the essay itself. And, although statistics, cases, and quotations may be used effectively as details in entire essays as well as in paragraphs, this essay assignment in revealing an outstanding place will require your use of *concrete sensory detail.* The table below makes suggestions for ways in which you can develop and organize your essay and gives you some sample proposals other students have written for the various developments suggested. But feel free to use any method you think best suits the topic you are writing about. Whatever method you do choose, however, be sure that your language is filled with color and sound and images of action that make your reader excited by and interested in your writing.

Possible Plan for Body Paragraphs	*Paragraph Development*	*Sample Proposal*
1. Tell about two special moments you remember about the place, one in each paragraph.	Narration through chronology? Mood sketches? Analogy in one of the paragraphs?	1. In the schoolyard at the back of this public school in the Bronx I remember two important lessons in sportsmanship.
2. a. Compare and contrast the appearance of the place at two different times, or b. Compare and contrast the place you remember with some other place you remember.	Narration through chronology? Comparison-contrast? Definition in images?	2. a. The corner at Pitkin and Howard Avenues during July is two different places, one in the morning and another in the early evening. b. When I think back to the kitchen in our old apartment house, I realize how modern things are here in Springfield Gardens.

3. One paragraph to show *several* instances that support one aspect of the place you are discussing and
   a. the other paragraph to tell *one specific moment* that illustrates another aspect of the place

   or

   b. the other paragraph *also* to show several instances that support another aspect of the place you are discussing.
4. Describe the place fully in one paragraph.

   Tell in the next paragraph about a vivid moment that occurred at the place.

Three instances arranged through importance?
Three instances arranged through chronology?
Several instances?
Narration through chronology?
Mood sketch?
Instances arranged through importance?
Instances arranged through chronology?

Description using transitions by place?
Narration through chronology?
Mood sketch?

3. Not only did I learn in Kings County Hospital that nurses and doctors are really interested in patients, but that the patients themselves look after each other when pain or discomfort strikes.

4. The Electric Circus in Manhattan is an astonishing place and one experience I had there shows that the people there are equally unusual!

TOPIC TIPS FOR IMPACT

1. Select a place that is particularly clear to you. Perhaps you can even return there briefly before you begin writing.
2. *Use a sense chart* like the one described in Chapter 6, recording your impressions of the sounds you hear; the smells and sensations of touch you experience; the actions and colors you observe.
3. Don't pick some place that has little meaning to you: you will write best about a spot that is really important. Don't pick a place that you do not remember too well.

   The key to a successful essay on place is your ability to let the reader see with specific details what makes the place special to you.
4. Try to recall bits of dialogue, people's words as they participate in the place you are writing about.
5. Reread "Rush-Hour Lunch" on pp. 35–36 for its keen sense of detail, its colors, sounds, and images of action.
6. Keep in mind the proportion of your paragraphs. Generally, introduction and conclusion should be about the same length, and both of these should be shorter (or at least not longer!) than the two body paragraphs. A long introduction or conclusion should have very substantial body paragraphs as well. If you try *generally* for four to six sentences in your introduction and conclusion and ten to twelve sentences in each of the body paragraphs, you will have a reasonable and workable goal set for yourself.
7. If one of your paragraphs is straight description

   a. Describe the scene from one point of view: decide where you as reporter and observer are located and show all the details from that position.

> b. Name the place and the time and season in which your scene takes place.
>
> c. Build your description by moving from objects farthest away from you to objects that are closest by.
>
> d. Use strong and active verbs.
>
> e. Include a striking picture in your last sentence.

More Topics to Think About

If you have trouble thinking about a topic for your first essay on a place, try one of these as a starting point.

1. experiences at the train depot
2. hamburger stand versus a "fancy" restaurant
3. the park in your hometown
4. street-corner lessons
5. your sixth-grade classroom
6. the high school locker room
7. your "hangout" bar, candy store, soda shop, street-corner
8. study hall
9. your church on two occasions
10. the neighborhood pool
11. the supermarket: two experiences
12. a country resort: what you remember
13. your street at night
14. the football (baseball) stadium
15. the college lounge
16. a city rooftop
17. the town shopping center
18. the subway car: morning and evening rush hour
19. amusement-park memories
20. a hospital room you remember

LEARNING FROM OTHER STUDENTS

Step 1. An Essay on Place.   Read the sample below, an essay about a place a student remembered vividly. Write the answers to the questions that come afterwards.

Summer at Little Neck

During the summer months Little Neck Bay is both a place of peaceful tranquility and happy loud commotion. I have spent many beautiful times at this Garden of Eden and have found that others share my idea of beauty, too. Both my girl friend Irit and I have spent some memorable times there by day and night.

One summer night Irit and I joined an unexpected boat ride. Usually on hot July evenings we strolled near the bay. Our favorite stopover was the creaky boat dock where Irit and I would surprise the skipper, Doc, with our presence. It just so happened that this Tuesday evening Doc stood at the end of his small wooden boat racing the engine. "Wanna take a ride?" he shouted in his loudest voice. "I have to take some folks to their boats and pick up some others!" It was only a short trip (we were to go three quarters of the way to Douglaston and back), but were Irit and I excited! It was a clear night with the stars shining brightly and the sky dark blue, almost black. The water smelled salty; in the darkness streaks of many colors along the surface blended into a greenish-blue appearance. Cool breezes chilled us somewhat; Irit and I wished we had brought our wool sweaters, but I loved even that minor discomfort, for it helps me remember that night now as clearly as ever. It was a serene and memorable experience.

This is not the only time I can remember when Irit and I spent time together at Little Neck, for once we both rented a rowboat from the dock on the bay and took a not-so-serene trip halfway across the waters and back. Of all things, we rowed the boat that August afternoon further out than we had planned. Now we were courting danger because a few high school "smarties" in yellow sweat shirts and sailor hats zoomed back and forth close enough to drown us. I cannot swim, and although Irit and I knew how to row, splashes of white foamy water in our boat scared us. Usually, I watch my language, but when a person fears water the way I do, a few nasty words can slip out! Here we were trying to enjoy the lovely day around us and these characters ruined our fun! Finally, one of the workers from the dock rowed out toward us and helped corral the boys back to land. With peace once more on our side, we now could enjoy the clear sky and clouds, the gulls swooping low, the water calm and at one level, and the sun shining bright. The scene brought a welcome rest from our excitement.

I will never forget the beautiful times Irit and I shared together at the Bay. Even now I feel a new source of inspiration and hope setting within me. But I do wonder what it is like when I'm not at Little Neck. Does anything change? Do others enjoy the waters and sky as I did? As each new season comes my way, I long for summer that much harder as I plod through weary assignments and exams. Only in the summer do I come into full existence!

—Julie Penkova

1. Put a check next to the proposal in the introduction. Does it allow for *two* aspects of the topic to be explored, each in a paragraph of its own?
2. Is the introduction itself effective? Does the introduction tell a story, use an interesting quotation, give background information, or tell the different aspects of the topic that the essay will consider?

_____

_____

3. What is the topic sentence of paragraph 2? What word helps make the transition from the proposal to the topic sentence of the second paragraph?

_____

_____

4. The opening sentence of paragraph 3 refers to the previous paragraph *and* introduces another aspect of the topic. Underline once the part of that sentence that refers the reader back to paragraph 2. Underline twice the part of that sentence that introduces the topic paragraph 3 will discuss.

5. What details of color and action do you find easy to picture in your mind? Where does Miss Penkova use smell, touch, and sound effectively?

_____

_____

Why does she say "hot July evenings," and "that August afternoon" as she tells her moments on Little Neck Bay?

_____

Step 2. Another Student Sample. Write the answers to the questions after you read the following student's essay.

Practice in the High School Gym

All my life I have loved baseball. As a little boy I stood at the iron schoolyard gates and watched the ninth graders zip around the bases. I sit glued to the television and suffer with the Mets as Seaver or Koosman goes limp on the mound. It is easy to understand, then, why when March comes around I look forward to the start of baseball practice in my high school gym. What I liked most about senior practice was the thrill of all my friends around me in the locker room and the activity on the gym floor.

As I dressed in the locker room, I felt the warmth and enjoyment of all my friends who played on the team with me in the previous year. Bob on my left dressed hurriedly to rush out to the gym; as team captain, he rapped on the metal lockers and yelled, "Let's get the lead out! Cut the talk and let's move!" Richard on my right stuffed his red flannel shirt and his copy of *Hamlet* into the locker as he dressed, talking continuously about winning a school championship. As I looked around, I saw all the new fellows. Trying out for the team for the first time, they struggled with their uniforms. They were so nervous that they could not even put their bright yellow shirts on straight. Then I saw Coach O'Neill flying out of his office. Even he looked excited for the oncoming season which would last until June and the championship games. As he dashed out the door to the gym he looked at me and smiled as if to say, "Isn't it great to be back with the team again?"

Then, when all the fun in the locker room was over, we charged out onto the newly shellacked floor of the gym. As we stood in the shadow of a basketball backboard waiting for the coach to finish checking the new bats and uniforms, I could not help thinking how I felt like a father to all the new boys on the team. I looked at the brown painted stands halfway pushed out, but before we even got near to sit down, Coach O'Neill grabbed the silver whistle dangling from his neck and blew it hard. Sternly, he called us all together. His gray eyes looked mean as he barked out the drills we had to do. Then we started calisthenics because the coach said they would make us loose. As I did my push-ups to Coach O'Neill's crisp "One-two-three-four," I saw the yellow floor with its black stripes from the basketball court. Blood rushed up to my head, making me feel weak, but I still continued. Next we ran laps around the gym. As I ran I could see the huge panes of glass from the roof of the gym, the light of the sun blinding me every time I looked up. After a loud blast from a whistle, the coach told us to stop running and take a rest. Five minutes later we ended the workout with wind sprints in the hallway so as to make room in the gym for the football team on its workout session. These activities in the gym made me feel happy, and healthy.

Because I have so much fun in the gym, to me exercise is a wonderful part of living. I was surprised to read in the papers about "Flabby Americans" and of the poor physical condition so many people today are in because of little activity. Maybe some worthwhile exercises and exciting workouts in high school would start more people on physical fitness programs. My friends in public school say that gym teachers leave uninterested students pretty much alone to sit and talk on the sidelines as long as there is no trouble. But I think that this is wrong: physical education teachers should be convincing all those sideline talkers that partici-pating is the greatest part of sports.

—Thomas Albanese

1. Put a check next to the proposal sentence. Is it more or less specific than the proposal sentence in the previous essay "Summer at Little Neck"?

_____

2. Comment on the introductory paragraph. Is it effective? Does it contradict the part of the proposal, give a lively quotation, tell the importance of the topic, or outline the body paragraphs? _____

_____

_____

3. What action do you see most clearly in this essay? Where has the writer used color vividly? _____

_____

4. How does Mr. Albanese illustrate the topic he announces for the opening sentence of paragraph 2? _____

_____

5. How does the last sentence in paragraph 2 and in paragraph 3 serve each moment being described? _____

6. What part of the opening sentence of paragraph 3 tells the topic of that paragraph? _____

What part of the same sentence refers the reader back to paragraph 2?

_____

7. What is your opinion of the conclusion? _____

Your First Essay Checklist: A Questionnaire for Solid Results

Study this checklist carefully before you write your composition. Then, write *yes* or *no* in the blank line after each question about your essay and fill in any other information requested. Hand in this sheet with your theme.

Hint: If you have two or more *no's,* you had better do your essay over again before you submit it.

1. Do I have a four-paragraph essay, each body paragraph no fewer than ten sentences, the introduction and conclusion in proportion to the rest of the essay? _____

2. Am I sure that I understand the way an essay is put together, having studied the chart From Paragraph to Essay (pp. 267–268) and the sample essay written from a one-paragraph theme (pp. 270–272)? _____

3. Have I prepared carefully a proposal sentence that will let me discuss *two* aspects of my topic? Is the proposal sentence the last sentence in my introduction? _____

     This is my proposal sentence _____

   _____

4. Did I write an introduction *after* my proposal was clear to me? Did I follow any of the suggestions in the Ideas for Starting Essays on pp. 277–280? _____

5. Have I planned out the essay according to one of the suggestions on pp. 295–296 or used a logical plan of my own? _____

6. Have I introduced the topic of each body paragraph in the first sentence? Have I used transitions in those sentences? _____

7. Have I used lively colorful language rich in sound, smell, touch, and images that use color? Do I name people, places, and times of events specifically? _____

8. Have I used a variety of sentence patterns? _____
    a. Do I have several subordinated sentences? _____
    b. Do I have just a few coordinated sentences? _____
    c. Have I used a semicolon correctly? _____
    d. Have I opened some sentences with words that end in *-ing* or *-ly*? _____
    e. Do I have a quotation sentence using someone's exact words? _____
    f. Did I use correctly at least one of these punctuation marks: the colon, the dash, the parentheses? _____

9. Have I used correctly some of the new vocabulary introduced on pp. 260–264 of this chapter? _____

10. Have I proofread (see pp. 114–115) my essay very carefully, looking for the errors that appear most often on my Theme Progress Sheet? Did I check for run-on errors, sentence fragments, spelling mistakes, and especially for the kinds of pronoun errors explained in this chapter? _____

11. Have I written a strong title (see pp. 197–198)? _____

12. Have I written a concluding paragraph? _____

THE PROFESSIONALS SPEAK

In the selection below, the writer creates a mood in the place he describes by mixing his own thoughts with specific images of the room. How would you say the writer's inner feelings compare with the physical environment he describes? When you finish reading, write the answers to the questions below.

My Room at the Lilac Inn

As I look around this room in this third-rate boarding house, my eyes are greeted first by the entrance to its gloomy interior. The door is painted a dirty cream color. There is a crack in one panel. The ceiling is the same dingy color with pieces of adhesive tape holding some of the plaster in place. The walls are streaked and cracked here and there. Also on the walls are pieces of Scotch tape that once held, I presume, some sexy girls, pictures of *Esquire Magazine* origin. Across the room runs a line; upon it hang a shirt, a grimy towel, and washed stump socks belonging to my roommate, Jack Nager. By the door near the top sash juts a piece of wood on which is hung — it looks like an old spread. It is calico, dirty, and a sickly green color.

Behind that is a space which serves as our closet; next to that is the radiator, painted the same ghastly color. The landlady must have got the paint for nothing. On top is Jack's black suitcase, his green soap dish, and a brightly colored box containing his hair tonic. Over by the cracked window are a poorly made table and chair. On top of the table, a pencil, shaving talcum, a glass, a nail file; one of my socks hangs over the side. Above the table is our window, the curtains of cheese cloth held back by a string. There is also a black, fairly whole paper shade to dim such little sunlight as might enter.

This window is my only promise of a better future. Through it, I can see the well-lit and nicely furnished living room of a modern apartment house across the street. Someday I'll live like that.

There, next to the window, leaning against an aged bureau, as if resting, are my faithful crutches. On the oilcloth covering the top of the bureau lie some seventeen odd books. These I used at the ——— University here in Washington, D.C. I am attending a six-month course, getting the fundamentals needed to be a Service Officer for veterans. There are enough books on that bureau to take at least a year's reading for absorption. Beard's *American Government and Policy, Anatomy, How to Interview, Soldier to Civilian,* government laws, manuals, textbooks, a public speaking guide and what-have-you are all reflected in the cloudy mirror. On the bureau stands a picture of my love, my faithful wife. I think of her. I wish I were with her tonight.

Standing alongside this bureau is this *thing*. A leather cup, straps and buckles dropping from it. Below this cup, the flesh-colored *thing* and calf, and on its foot a brown sock and oxblood shoe. This is a prosthesis. I've called this wooden leg a lot of other things. This is the replacement for the real one that was shot off in France. O, what the hell! A leg isn't everything. You've got to keep living. There are a lot worse things in this world to reckon with than an arfificial leg.

On the parlor chair, here probably because there's no other place for it, my brown pants are thrown, together with my old khaki shirt. On the floor my recently painted foot locker that was in many an army camp with me is still doing service.

Jack Nager grunts alongside me in the double bed as he turns over; he is getting a good sleep tonight. His below-the-knee stump quivers as he touches some close-to-the-skin nerve on the bed. His foot was also a donation for democracy. I reach to turn out the twenty-five watt bulb on the shadeless lamp; I find the light switch. The room is in darkness. From the street three stories below comes the sound of a motor car; it fades away. Occasionally a click, click of heels hitting the pavement as someone passes by. Within the house the sound of muffled voices, the flushing of a toilet, someone blowing his nose.

I forget everything and concentrate on sleep.

—John J. Regan in *The Purple Testament*

1. What key word or words in the first sentence show the writer's attitude toward the place he is describing? In the first paragraph and a half there are several words that repeat this attitude. Write down three of them; if their meanings are unclear to you, look them up.

_____

_____

_____

2. Which image best appeals to your sense of sight? _____

_____

3. Copy out three images in which the writer has best used the sense of

sound. _____

_____

4. Put a check in the margin in two places where the writer's thoughts take over from the actual description of the place.

5. What is a prosthesis? _____ Notice how John Regan gives you the definition of the word in the sentence after he uses it.

6. Although you do not learn before paragraph 4 that the writer is a veteran and before paragraph 5 that he is wounded, the writer gives hints in paragraph 1 and 2 as to his identity and condition. What hints do you find in the first two paragraphs that suggest who and what the writer is?

_____

_____

7. How does the physical setting of the room compare with the writer's

inner thoughts and feelings? _____

_____

REACHING HIGHER

Step 1. Study the picture on p. 259, and using what you observe, write an essay that explores the meaning you find in the photograph. Use your best sensory language to portray the scene as you see it: use color, sound, smell, and action.

Step 2. With your own camera prepare an essay in snapshots about some place near your home that you can observe often and at different times. Take at least fifteen to twenty pictures and, selecting five or six of the best, arrange them in some order. Mount them one on a page. For each photograph write first a title (see pp. 197–198), and then one sentence that you see as the major point of the picture: try to use in that sentence concrete images to create a scene that matches the photograph itself.

Step 3. The following essay contains thirteen sentence fragments and nine run-on sentences. Correct all the errors directly on this page. Study the run-on and fragment review charts on p. 25 and 56.

The Key to Comfort

Rooms often portray a person's character and personality your character is displayed in the way you keep your room in order. Whether it's neat or disorganized. To me my room is the most important room in the house the way it's kept shows the kind of atmosphere I want it helps me seclude myself when the going gets too rough at home.

The atmosphere I try to have in my room is one of solitude. I think that comes because of the way my room is decorated. Soft walls in an off-white color. Nothing but my mirror hanging on the walls. A high dark brown dresser. The desk in the far corner is walnut on the top books stand in piles. Which I keep very neat and orderly. The stereo set and my collection of albums and tapes are in the far corner. Next to my amorphous black leather reclining chair. My room is the only room in the house that is so relaxing.

Because the surroundings are so restful. I found that it served as an important place one February evening last year. When my house was filled with guests from a card party my mother was having. I had my final examination in history the next day I knew if I did not find a quiet place to study I would fail. I excused myself from the incessant noise of my mother's guests and determined to get peace and quiet. Marched upstairs to my room. Upon opening the door to my room. I had almost given up hope. There was still so much noise. Loud roars of laughter. People chattering. Dimes and nickels clinking on the table. I quickly slammed the door with me inside the room suddenly the noise was outside, I was trapped in a welcome silence. Because of the solitude in my room I was able to study, I passed the final examination.

Rooms help people relax and find quiet. And the appearance of a room sets the scene for relaxation. If more people would set aside a certain amount of time each day to solve their problems in a serene room of their choice. The mental pressures that many Americans suffer might disappear. Most people try to relax in an atmosphere that is more distracting than peaceful, to me, the quiet well-decorated, well-kept room is the key to comfort.

Step 4. A Collage on a Place. Using the technique of collage, try to characterize some important feeling or impression that you have about some place you know well. Look at the collage by Jaqueline Boston on p. 222 for an example. What impression does Len Basile try to convey? What visual feature best shows you this impression? What kinds of materials has he used in making his collage? For your own collage, see if the people in your class can determine (without knowing in advance) what place you are portraying and what your impression of the place is.

chapter 8

WOMEN IN THE WORLD OF MEN: WRITING A STRONG ARGUMENT

INTRODUCTION

Since Susan B. Anthony led the fight for reform in women's rights in the late 1800s, the position of the female in American society has changed sharply. The usual picture of the sweet and innocent young thing at home mending socks or baking an apple pie on Saturdays has, for the most part, vanished. The twentieth-century woman is moving—for some, too quickly, for others, not quickly enough—into a world once thought exclusively for men. Although smoking on the streets or drinking alcohol might in earlier times have destroyed the reputation of any female, today these activities draw not even a second glance. A cigarette commercial boasts to its female audience, "You've come a long way, baby!" Betty Friedan and Karen Horney —spokeswomen for Women's Lib—think women have not come a long way at all. Yet women doctors step through hospital corridors in greater numbers than ever before. The idea of a woman as a top business executive or college president is now accepted, even approved, by large numbers of people. And females make up over 30% of America's job force.

Some modern women have fought very hard to change the world's view of them. They have marched up major streets waving banners and chanting noisily. They have argued strongly on television and radio. They have urged wider sexual freedom for women, complaining against the "double standard" where men are permitted free sexual activity while women are condemned for it. They have raised and lowered their hemlines; they have burned their brassieres; they have met in conventions and conferences in large numbers to set forth the new constitution for Women's Liberation.

Where do you stand on the issue of women's rights? Do you think that men and women are exactly alike and deserve complete equality? Do you think women are different from men and as a result require special treatment? Do you think women are pretty much ignored for the top jobs in our society? Do you think women *should* be ignored for top positions in business and government? This theme assignment asks you to look at your own attitudes toward women in society and their changing position in the twentieth century.

But you will have to be able to support your attitudes in some way as you write your essays. Everybody has opinions on Women's Liberation, from the local grocery clerk to the man who represents you in Congress— and sometimes the opinions are forced out with anger and annoyance. The true test of an opinion, however, is the way in which it is made convincing and believable. Anyone can scream angrily his point of view, and although some people can be frightened into believing things just on the basis of loud shouts, most educated people require some reasons before they are convinced to accept opinions. You can convince someone reasonably about why you have certain impressions by illustrating those impressions through dramatic experiences in your own personal life. Or you can try to prove that the opinion you hold is true by using information that you gather from other sources. If you choose that path, you will have to learn how to avoid the faults in reasoning many freshmen show when they write essays in which they try to persuade people to change their beliefs.

In this chapter you will also learn more about tying together more closely the parts of the essay. You will examine some of the vocabulary of liberation, and you will practice with a problem in writing that causes a number of difficulties: the idea of ownership.

VOCABULARY

Step 1. Familiar Words in the Women's Struggle.   Much of the language of Women's Liberation includes words like these. Write definitions for the words you know.

_____ feminist	[These words identify people in
_____ suffragette	Women's Lib, both for and
_____ chauvinist	against it.]
_____ hormonal	[These words name biological
_____ puberty	ideas related to discussions on
_____ mortality	women's equality.]
_____ inferiority	
_____ stereotype	[Women active in the battle for
_____ degradation	equality try to fight these conditions.]
_____ discrimination	

Step 2. Finding the Clues.   Each of the above words is used below in a sentence that also gives the definition of the word. For the words you do not know above, pick out the part of the sentence that gives the definition and then in your own words write the meaning in the blank spaces above. If you need help, see Appendix A.

1. *Degradation*—a condition in which someone or something is made lower in dignity or quality—is said by many women to originate in man's anger at females.
2. To a *chauvinist,* that is, a person who has blind enthusiasm for a cause or idea, even logical discussions cannot change his mind.
3. Although the word *suffragette* was really meant to describe those women who fought for the right to vote in the early 1900s, the word is sometimes used today for any woman involved in rights of females.
4. Since health education has taught many women how to prevent the death of babies through proper care, *mortality* rates have decreased.
5. *Hormonal* differences (differences based upon substances given off by the glands of the body) between men and women do not show that abilities of men are better than those of women.

6. *Inferiority*, which indicates something poor in quality, is a feeling women of today fight strongly.

7. When women or men reach the point in their development where they are sexually mature and can bear children, that stage is called *puberty*.

8. *Feminists*, believing that women's activities in social and political life should be greatly extended, often try to advance their goals by speeches, television appearances, and newspaper articles.

9. Fixed ideas held about people or races and based upon oversimplified opinions (*stereotypes*) are responsible for many incorrect impressions.

10. Women must continue to fight against *discrimination*: the favoring of one person over another because of certain qualities (like sex or race) that should not really enter into the act of selection.

Step 3. More Words in the Struggle for Equality. Write definitions for the following words that you know.

Conditions of Inequality

enslavement _____

repression _____

oppression _____

downtrodden _____

prejudice _____

exploitation _____

Conditions of Equality

emancipation _____

enfranchisement _____

People Who Fight for Ideas

activist _____

revolutionary _____

Step 4. The Dictionary for Clear Meanings. Use your dictionary to look up any words above you do not know; then, in your own words, write clear meanings on the blank lines above. If you think you know what a word means, write in your own definition and check it in a dictionary.

Step 5. Using Words in Freedom's Fight. From the vocabulary above, write a word that

1. means the state of freedom. _____

2. describes someone who works hard for a cause. _____

3. names the act of using power over someone in a cruel and unfair way.

_____

4. tells the state of being free especially with the right to vote. _____

5. describes people who are kept from advancing and who are ruled over severely, people who are "trampled upon." _____

6. names the condition of being a slave. _____

7. names someone who works to overthrow established ideas or systems.

_____

8. indicates an unfavorable opinion or feeling made before any knowledge

   is available. _____

9. shows the selfish use of people or resources for private profit or gain.

   _____

10. names the act of keeping something under control. _____

BUILDING COMPOSITION SKILLS

Exploring the Topic

Step 1. A Questionnaire on Women.   The statements below examine your attitudes on women in our society.

If you agree with the statement completely, put the number 1 in the blank space.

If you agree with the statement in some degree, put the number 2 in the blank space.

If you completely disagree with the statement, put the number 3 in the blank space.

If you have no idea or feeling at all about the statement, put the number 4 in the blank space.

_____   1. Women should not hold positions of great responsibilities because they are much more emotional than men.

_____   2. Unmarried women can never be truly happy.

_____   3. A woman's place is in the home raising her family.

_____   4. Women make better bosses than men.

_____   5. Housework does not have to be as dull as Women's Liberation claims it is; a woman can find her job in the house creative and rewarding.

_____   6. The right of abortion is one that all women should be able to use if they want to.

_____   7. Women are "catty": they always talk about each other and find faults easily.

_____   8. Women enjoy being treated like little girls and being taken care of by the men who love them.

_____   9. Women's Liberation will never achieve anything by marching and demonstrating. All that will happen is that men will be even more against women's achieving any rights.

_____   10. Women often make the best schoolteachers.

Step 2. Illustrating Opinions.   Select any statement from the above questionnaire for which you have written a 1 or a 3 in the margin. Discuss the reasons you have for believing what you do by giving an illustration from your own personal experience.

Step 3. Woman Talk. These famous statements on women come from people in our time and in the past. Discuss with the class the one that you think most appropriate in today's world.

1. "The female of the species is more deadly than the male."
   — Rudyard Kipling

2. "Women are wiser than men because they know less and understand more."
   — James Stephens

3. ". . . the Black movement is primarily concerned with the liberation of Blacks as a class and does not promote women's liberation as a priority. . . . The feminist movement, on the other hand, is concerned with the oppression of women as a class, but is almost totally composed of white females. Thus the Black woman finds herself on the outside of both political entities, in spite of the fact that she is the object of both forms of oppression."
   — Kay Lindsey

4. "While little boys are learning about groups and organizations, as well as the nature of the world outside their homes, little girls are at home, keeping quiet, playing with dolls and dreaming, or helping mother."
   — Germaine Greer

5. "Women tend to make their emotions perform the functions they exist to serve, and hence remain mentally much healthier than men."
   — Ashley Montagu

6. "The great question that has never been answered, and which I have not yet been able to answer despite my thirty years of research into the feminine soul, is: What does a woman want?"
   — Sigmund Freud

7. "A girl should not be too intelligent or too good or too highly differentiated in any direction. Like a ready-made garment she should be designed to fit the average man."
   — Emily James Putnam

8. "Every single woman I ever knew is a puzzle to me, as, I have no doubt, she is to herself."
   — William Makepeace Thackery

CLEAR REASONING AND EVIDENCE

When you relate from your personal experience some moment about a given topic or subject, you are not attempting to *prove* your idea. You merely *illustrate* a point by using a specific instance from your life—and you have seen how dramatic and effective your own personal experiences can be in illustrating your feelings or impressions about some topic. When you seek to argue a point by giving *proofs,* however, you often need more than just a single instance from your life. To try to prove that women are incompetent as doctors based upon one experience you had with a bad woman doctor would be foolish and really unconvincing. For a reader to be convinced that what you are offering is indeed *proof,* you need material that is solid and plentiful, evidence that is believable, reasoning that is not faulty. The fifteen types of poor reasoning below show some of the more familiar kinds of incorrect evidence freshmen frequently use in essays that attempt to convince readers of the truth of their ideas. Each logic trap is followed by an example.

FIFTEEN FAULTS TO FAIL THE ARGUMENT

1. *Don't* give too few instances to prove a point.

   Example: Women cannot be trusted to make decisions when the pressure gets rough. My mother cries as soon as some high-pressure situation arises.

   How could one instance support the point?

2. *Don't* use famous people's names as the sole proof of your point.

   Example: Humphrey Bogart, Mama Cass Eliot, and Chet Huntley—a varied group certainly—all smoke cigarettes. What could be wrong with smoking?

   How does the mentioning of the names prove that there is nothing wrong with smoking?

3. *Don't* praise or blame the *people* who state a proof you think is good and ignore the idea.

   Example: If William Buckley, a brilliant magazine editor and a clever and amusing man, thinks that a visit by the President to China is wrong he certainly must know what he is talking about.

   Praising Buckley's intelligence and cleverness does not prove that a trip to China is bad.

   William Buckley is a do-nothing conservative who hates progress. Therefore his idea about a trip to China being bad is stupid and worthless.

   Attacking Buckley's politics does not prove his idea is stupid and worthless.

4. *Don't* try to prove something by showing that people always believed in a certain thing.

   Example: Ever since the question of China's entry into the United Nations came up, America has opposed it. Therefore, there is no reason to accept China now.

   People may have believed one thing a long time ago. But they can change their minds.

5. *Don't* try to prove something by showing that everyone is doing it.

   Example: Young people all over the world are using marijuana without harm. And many middle-aged people too are joining in on "pot parties" of the drug culture. Marijuana cannot be so harmful, then.

   So what if everyone does it? How does that prove it is not harmful?

6. *Don't* try to prove something by saying the point over and over again.

Example: Women ought to have the same rights as men. Women's rights are just as important as men's rights, so I think it only fair that women get whatever treatment men get. After all, women have rights, too.

There is no proof here at all, just the same point made again and again.

7. *Don't* use a source to back up an idea unless the source is reliable and an authority.

Example: My brother Jerry says politicians are liars and cheats, and I have always trusted his judgment.

What makes Jerry an authority on politicians?

   The president of Apco, a leading oil company, shows that lead in automobile gasoline is really not a polluting agent.

An oil company that had to remove lead from its fuel might have to spend large sums of money. It might be expected to try to disprove lead as a polluter.

8. *Don't* make a comparison that is weak or not true.

Example: I know I can drive a motorcycle. I can ride a bicycle, can't I?

The writer failed to realize that there are many differences between bicycles and motorcycles.

9. *Don't* appeal to a person's prejudices or unreasonable emotions.

Example: Minority group people should not be allowed to work at all kinds of jobs. After all, other Americans will be squeezed out of work and then what will happen? You and I will be out of jobs.

This writer tries to arouse the reader by appealing to personal involvement. Where is his proof that the reader will lose his job to others?

   Anyone who opposes Governor Badley's reelection is anti-American, antiprogress, and antiworking class.

This writer uses words intended to fire up emotions unreasonably. Instead of real proof, he uses names that are designed to arouse feelings without solid proofs.

10. *Don't* draw conclusions that do not follow from previous information.

Example: When Astor was president of the union we really made progress. Now that Alterman took over, men are losing jobs and getting less and less overtime.

The writer doesn't take into account other factors. He has not proved that the loss of jobs has anything to do with the new president.

   When I went to college I got all A's and B's. Anyone who wants to can get good grades.

The second sentence doesn't follow from the first because the writer does not take into account individual learning problems, emotional difficulties, intellectual abilities.

11. *Don't* prove that someone or something is good or bad only because he or it associates with other "good" or "bad" things.

Example: How could he be a gangster? He goes to work in the morning, has dinner out with his family on Sundays, and he is best friends with the mayor and the principal of our high school.

This proof of innocence is built by trying to associate a person with good and solid qualities of citizenship. But it does not prove the man is no gangster. If he dealt in drugs, what would his friendship with the mayor prove?

Since the college president's right-hand man was found guilty of robbing city funds, surely the president himself must have some illegal dealings too.

This is "guilt by association": The president is not guilty of crimes because one of his associates is guilty.

12. *Don't* generalize—that is, don't make one true fact the source of a broad conclusion. *Don't* state the proof so strongly as to admit no possibilities of exceptions.

Example: Women drivers are the worst drivers on the road.

It may be true that some women—like some men—are poor drivers, but this is certainly not true of all of them.

13. *Don't* try to show that if something happened *after* an event, that thing is necessarily a *result* of the event. Just because an incident comes after another incident, it doesn't mean that the second event was caused by the first.

Example: Five convicted killers said that when they were younger they enjoyed watching programs of violence on television. This proves that watching violent actions on the screen can lead to murder.

Did the killers murder *because* they watched violence on television? This might be a contributing factor, but as a proof alone, it is not very solid.

14. *Don't* state you proof in *either-or* terms.

Example: It is no wonder that he failed so many courses. A college student goes to school or he works; he certainly cannot do both.

What about the people who work only an hour a day, or those who work weekends or summers? This writer suggests that there are only two alternatives, when there are many.

15. *Don't* ignore information that contradicts the point you wish to make.

Example: A large number of investigations suggest that legalizing heroin would be a positive step toward controlling drug abuse.

On such a controversial issue, the writer should make sure to mention those investigations that disagree with the statement. Much material is available on the failure of parts of the British system in which drugs have been legalized.

Step 1. Finding Foggy Thinking. Each statement below contains some error in argument such as the ones described above. In the blank lines tell what kind of error the writer makes. Then tell how you would correct the statement.

1. Samuel Taylor Coleridge and Edgar Allan Poe both used drugs and still created great works of art. Writers should use some drug if they need stimulation for their work. _____

_____

2. So many people liked *Love Story*. You don't know what is good if you did not like that book. _____

_____

3. Man got along for so many years without needing to go to the moon. I don't see any reason why he should change now. _____

_____

4. If those dirty foreigners do not like the conditions in their neighborhood, let them work or go back where they came from. America is built on muscle and hard work, not complaints. _____

_____

5. How can you take any of his ideas seriously? Anyone who keeps his hair so long and who wears dungarees and sandals all the time: what could he know about liberty? _____

6. There is nothing wrong with the quality of cereals made for the public. The American Association of Breakfast Food Producers makes that point very clear in its latest report. _____

_____

7. That family does not go to church on Sundays. They must all believe that God does not exist. _____

_____

8. Anyone who is a communist has no love for his country, America.

_____

_____

9. Those boys left the party right after the diamond ring was stolen. They must have taken it! _____

_____

10. How could Burkee's chicken soup be bad? Their tomato sauce, mushroom soup, and baked beans are delicious. _____

_____

Step 2. Straight Thinking, Strong Proofs. How would you go about proving or disproving each statement below? Discuss your answers aloud, making sure to avoid the faults in argument you just learned.

1. Women's rights have improved in the 1970s.
2. Women drivers are awful!
3. The struggle for women's liberties is not only a modern battle.
4. Mothers who work bring about great harm to the development of their children.
5. Women executives in business are more efficient than men.

6. The attitude of modern single girls toward sex has changed in the last ten years.

7. A woman competing with a man in a man's sport would never stand a chance of success.

8. Women enjoy staying home and taking care of their families.

9. Even in art, women take a back seat: no women writers, for example, have achieved the same degree of excellence as men.

10. Women all over the world are gaining new freedoms in the wave of Women's Liberation.

11. Women are, in general, less intelligent than men.

12. Wife beating is a thing of the past.

Step 3. Proof for Attitudes in Women. Return to the questionnaire in Step 1, p. 310. Select any item for which you have written the number 1 or 3, and in the blank lines below show how *you would attempt to prove* your opinion.

Hint: This time do not use personal experience as proof. Plan on using other kinds of details. See crucial questions 2 to 4 on p. 329.

_____

_____

_____

_____

MEETING THE OPPOSITION

If you are trying to defend a point that you know not everybody agrees on, you know that your main purpose in seeking moments of personal experience, in finding statistics or quotations, is to present effective support through details for your own point of view. But you should not always ignore the issues raised on the other side of the argument. What the opposition (those who disagree with you) believes can give you the content of a good solid paragraph.

WHY TO MENTION OPPOSITE OPINIONS

1. It shows that you know what others are saying.
2. It shows that you are not purposely overlooking the points other educated people suggest in order to make your own ideas look stronger.

> 3. It shows that you are fair and that you do not see things in black and white only, that you are willing to consider ideas and points that do not agree with your own.
> 4. It gives you more to write about: you can go on to attack the ideas others have, if you wish.
>
> **Hint:** The introduction is a very good place in any essay to mention the points of view that oppose yours: as you discuss those ideas that do not go along with your own, you build up to your own proposal which states what you believe and what you will try to prove.

Step 1. Seeking the Opposition. Assume that the proposal in Column I is one that you would try to support in an essay. Write in Column II three *opposing* arguments that others might raise against your point of view.

I

Example:

A. A woman's place is at home with her family.

II

1. *Women are efficient workers.*
2. *Women are creative on the job.*
3. *Some women are psychologically unfit for the dullness of housework.*

B. Modern styles for women are ridiculous.

1. _____
2. _____
3. _____

C. There are little differences between the way men and women behave in executive positions.

1. _____
2. _____
3. _____

D. Women should never have received the right to vote.

1. _____
2. _____
3. _____

E. Women are much better cooks than men.

1. _____
2. _____
3. _____

Step 2. Paragraph Practice: The Opposition in Introductions. Select any proposal and opposing ideas from Step 1 above. Write a brief introduction below which mentions the opposition's points as it builds to the proposal statement. You may change the proposal somewhat.

Hint: Transitional expressions like *however, but, on the other hand* will help you introduce the proposal.

_____

_____

_____

_____

_____

_____

_____

THE OPPOSITION IN THE BODY PARAGRAPHS

If you know sound arguments that are raised in opposition to your proposal, you can build one body paragraph around those opposing arguments. Paragraph 2 of your essay can mention a few of the points made by people who disagree with you, and you might show with solid details the evidence these people give for believing what they do. Another possibility, if there is a large number of arguments on the opposition's side, is to state in the second paragraph of your essay as many of the most effective arguments against your position as you possibly can. Then you can write paragraph 3 in one of two ways.

1. Try to disprove the arguments of the opposition. Give details to convince your reader that you are right and that "they" are wrong.
2. Say that the points the opposition raises are good, but that you believe differently. Give details to convince the reader that your points are just as good as the points made by those who oppose you.

Step 1. Paragraph Practice: The Opposition in a Body Paragraph. Select any proposal from Step 1 on p. 317 as the proposal of an essay and write a brief first body paragraph in which you show what arguments could be used against your proposal. Develop just a few arguments with specific details, or mention a number of arguments that are frequently used against the proposal. Use your own paper.

Hint: In this paragraph do not try to prove that the opposition is wrong.

TRANSITIONS IN THE ESSAY

When you learned about paragraph development, you learned a number of words that helped you move smoothly from one idea to the other. These *transitions*, even in the essay, play important parts as you write each paragraph, and you will need them still as you write. But because the essay is developed with certain paragraph shifts, there are key additional places where transitions of some kind must appear so that the reader feels that the paragraphs have a close relationship to one another. Before you study the transition signboards below, make sure you understand the parts of the essay explained on pp. 266–268.

Review Hints:
Remembering the Proposal Sentence
1. It is the last sentence of the introduction.
2. It must tell the reader the purpose of the essay.
3. It should allow you to discuss two aspects of your topic. It can state both aspects quite specifically, or it can merely suggest what these aspects are.

Hint: See pp. 273–277 for more about proposal sentences.

ESSAY TRANSITION SIGNBOARD I: FIRST SENTENCE OF PARAGRAPH 2

What to Do	*Why*
1. Tell what part of the proposal you want to discuss in paragraph 2 by *a.* repeating one of the two aspects if you have mentioned them clearly in your proposal or *b.* stating (for the first time) the aspect you want to discuss based upon the suggestion made in the proposal.	These steps help show your reader that you are moving logically from your proposal sentence to the first part of your topic.
2. Use transition words (pp. 14–15, pp. 81–83, pp. 131–134) to help you connect the opening sentence of this paragraph with the proposal.	This makes the move from the proposal to the next paragraph smooth and not too quick.

Step 1. Analyzing Transitions in Paragraph 2.   Column I states a proposal. Decide whether or not you think the sentence in Column II would be effective as the opening sentence of the second paragraph and tell why in Column III. Base your ideas on Essay Transition Signboard I.

I	*II*	*III*
1. I cannot say that Southwest College is a bad school, but there are a few reasons why I am disappointed.	One of my greatest disappointments is the registration procedure.	_____ _____ _____ _____

2. An important feeling I
   often experience but always try to overcome is
   loneliness.

   Graduation day, June 20,
   1970, proved to be a lonely
   but memorable experience.

   _____
   _____
   _____
   _____

3. So I believe that a
   woman's place *is* in the
   home.

   And it is essentially to help
   her children grow that she
   needs to be there.

   _____
   _____
   _____
   _____

4. Peace is a goal that I believe cannot be realized in
   our lifetime.

   President Kennedy said,
   "Ask not what your country
   can do for you but what you
   can do for your country."

   _____
   _____
   _____
   _____

5. My father has always
   been a complete stranger
   to me.

   As a boy my main love was
   for sports, especially baseball, but my father ignored
   completely my activities.

   _____
   _____
   _____
   _____

Step 2. More on Paragraph 2 Transitions. Comment on the opening sentence of paragraph 2 in each of the following essays.

1. "Summer at Little Neck," pp. 297–298
2. "Practice in the High School Gym," pp. 299–300
3. "Women: Fragile Flowers?" pp. 335–336

Step 3. Your Own Opener for Paragraph 2. For the proposal in Column I write in Column II your own opening sentence for the second paragraph of an essay.

I

Example:
Proposal: Women drivers are better than
men drivers.

II

Opening sentence of paragraph 2:

*They are certainly more familiar with
safety regulations.*

1. I have never been able to enjoy games and
   hobbies because I have always had an impossible drive to win.

   _____

2. Women can perform adequately any job
   men can perform.

   _____
   _____

3. In situations of great danger and at times when patience and understanding are required, women are much more competent than men.

_____

_____

ESSAY TRANSITION SIGNBOARD II: FIRST SENTENCE OF PARAGRAPH 3

What to Do	*Why*
1. Refer back to the main idea of the previous paragraph (paragraph 2)	to show that paragraph 3 grows logically from paragraph 2.
or	
refer back to the last event, instance, or proof you discussed in paragraph 2.	to tie together the two body paragraphs, both of which develop your proposal.
2. Tell what part of the proposal you intend to discuss in the paragraph by	to remind the reader of the whole topic of the essay.
a. repeating the second aspect if you have mentioned it in the proposal, or	to let the reader know exactly what paragraph 3 will contain.
b. stating for the first time—based upon the suggestion you made in the proposal—the aspect of the topic you want to discuss in paragraph 3.	to remind you, the writer, to stick to the topic that you stated in the proposal.

Hint: 1. Coordination (pp. 85–88) and subordination (pp. 89–97) are especially effective in opening sentences of paragraph 3.
2. Use transitional expressions (pp. 14–15, pp. 81–83, and pp. 131–134) as needed.

Step 4. Writing Openers for Third Paragraphs.   Column I states a proposal. Column II describes the content of the second paragraph of an essay. In Column III, write an opening sentence for paragraph 3 based upon what you understand from Essay Transition Signboard II.

I (Proposal)

Example: Higher education does not provide people with the training they need in our society.

1. Women have led the fight against two major modern problems: day care for children and pollution of the environment.

II (Content of Paragraph 2)

This paragraph shows a number of instances in which college graduates are not able to deal with social problems like poverty and drug addiction.

Paragraph 2 shows how women have approached and to some degree solved the problem of children's day care.

III (Your Opener for Paragraph 3)

Not only are college students poorly trained in social problems, but they also do not receive good instruction in the technical skills they need on the job.

_____

_____

_____

_____

2. On my trip across Amer- Paragraph 2 describes a time   _____
   ica I learned the real   in which the writer had no   _____
   meaning of friendship.   money for food but was
   helped by a friendly group of   _____
   strangers he met on the road.
   _____

   _____

3. Open-admissions pro- Paragraph 2 shows why the   _____
   grams in colleges, having   writer feels the programs
   taken long enough to de- took so long to develop.   _____
   velop, are a must for a
   more productive Ameri- _____
   can society.
   _____

Step 5. Paragraph-3 Openers in Essays. Read the opening sentence of paragraph 3 in each of the following essays. Which part of the sentence refers back to the previous paragraph? Which part announces the topic of the paragraph to follow?

1. "Some Disappointments," pp. 364–366
2. "Practice in the High School Gym," pp. 299–300
3. "Summer at Little Neck," pp. 297–298

ESSAY TRANSITION SIGNBOARD III: FIRST SENTENCE OF THE CONCLUSION

What to Do

1. Make some reference to the main idea of the previous paragraph (paragraph 3).

         or

   Refer back to the last event, instance, or proof you discussed in paragraph 3.

2. Refer to something you wrote in the intro-duction:
   a. Pick up the idea of the proposal.
   b. Pick up a point from the background material you may have given.
   c. Repeat why you felt your subject was important.
   d. Refer to any questions you may have asked.
   e. Refer to any quotation you may have used.
   f. Pick up the idea of the story you may have told in the introduction.

Why

to show that paragraph 4 grows logically from paragraph 3.

to tie paragraph 3 more closely to the conclu-sion you will start to develop.

to remind the reader about how your whole idea started.

to help you begin writing the conclusion which may be based upon one of the suggestions you made in the introduction.

to help you make sure that the introduction is an important part of your essay, not just a bunch of sentences you threw together to waste words.

SOLVING PROBLEMS IN WRITING

Showing Possession with Nouns

a. It is the *car of the man.*
b. It is the *car belonging to the man.*
c. It is the *man's car.*

In sentence *a*, the car belongs to the man. Ownership is shown with the words *of the man.* The car is owned. The man owns it.

In sentence *b*, the car belongs to the man. Ownership is shown with the words *belonging to the man.* The car is owned. The man owns it.

In sentence *c*, the car belongs to the man. Ownership is shown by using an apostrophe s ('s) after the word that tells who owns the thing. The car is still being owned. The man still owns it. But in this sentence the owner is named *before* the thing that he owns. And the only way we know the owner is through the apostrophe *s*.

It is the man's car.
[owner]
[thing owned]

Sentence *a* sounds clumsy and unnatural. You would rarely say or write such a sentence. Sentence *b* is natural but takes too many words to say something very simple.

Sentence *c* is the most convenient and most usual way of indicating ownership. When we speak of *possession* it is usually this form of showing ownership that we mean. And, because of the misunderstood apostrophe, this method causes students many difficulties.

As you practice with possession, keep in mind that ownership involves two separate ideas:

1. Somebody or something is the owner. That word will contain an apostrophe.
2. Somebody or something is being owned. That word usually comes soon after the word with the apostrophe.

Step 1. Owner and Owned: Seeing Possession Parts. In each sentence below, circle the word that indicates who or what owns or possesses something. Put an X over the word that shows what (or who) is being owned.

Example: The (child's) toy fell into his mother's waiting arms.

1. George's former girl friend just married Alexander's best friend.

2. The dog's soft brown coat gleamed in the light of the evening fire.

3. The history professor's students stayed after class to ask about Jefferson's ideas on slavery.

HOW NOT TO USE APOSTROPHES

Don't use apostrophes to show plurals. There is one minor exception to this rule (you will see it on p. 237), but it is more important for you to remember that apostrophes do *not* usually indicate plurals. Plurals are formed by adding -*s*, *es*, or by any one of the special methods explained on pp. 108–109. But apostrophes play no part in showing that there is more than one thing being discussed.

For example, a familiar student error is one like this:

The store sells *turkey's* and *chicken's.*

If an apostrophe *s* is used at the end of a word, it means that the word owns something. What, according to the sentence, do the turkey and the chicken possess? Nothing belongs to either of the two words written with apostrophes. The student who wrote the sentence above wants only to indicate more than one turkey and more than one chicken, so his sentence should be:

The store sells *turkeys* and *chickens.*

Step 2. Spotting Wrong Possession. Correct any incorrect use of possession in each of these sentences by changing the word to its proper plural form.

1. His sister's laughed when they looked at the boy's face.
2. Use these pencils' at your desk's.
3. Three robberies' took place on our street within two days' of each other which shows the increase of crime's in New York City.

HOW TO FORM POSSESSIVES: TWO SIMPLE REMINDERS

Reminder I for Possession:

If the word that shows the owner *does not* end in *s*, add an apostrophe *s* (*'s*)

girl   The girl's dress ripped.
        [apostrophe *s*   [This is owned by the *girl.*]
        added to
        girl]

senator   The senator's campaign failed.
        [apostrophe *s*   [This is owned by the senator.]
        added to *senator*]

Hint for Reminder I: It does not matter if the word is plural or singular. If the word does not end in *s*, add an apostrophe *s.*

This word is plural, ⟶ *men* The men's cars crashed.
even though it does   [apostrophe *s*   [These are owned
not end in *s*:   added to men]   by the men.]

Step 3. Possession Reminder I in Sentences. Change the words below so that they indicate ownership. Then write your own brief sentence to use the word correctly.

Example: city *city's*

The city's roads are crowded on weekday mornings.

1. William _____   _____

2. children _____   _____

3. woman _____   _____

4. friend _____   _____

5. women _____   _____

Reminder II for Possession:

If the word that names the owner *does* end in -s, add only an apostrophe (').

boys   The boys' bicycles broke.
    [an apostrophe   These are owned
    added to *boys*]   by the boys.]

governors   The governors' meeting ended when the chairman fainted.
    [an apostrophe   This is owned by
    added to   the *governors*.]
    governors]

Hint for Reminder II: It does not matter if the word is plural or singular. If the word ends in *s*, add only an apostrophe.

This word is singular: → *Doris*   Doris' trip was canceled.
it ends in *s*.   [apostrophe   This is owned
    added to   by Doris.]
    Doris]

Step 4. Possession Reminder II in Sentences. Add apostrophes to the words below so that they indicate ownership. Then write your own brief sentence to use the word correctly.

Example: nurses *nurses'* *The nurses' caps flew away.*

1. students _____   _____

2. Mr. Jones _____   _____

3. operators _____   _____

4. cities _____   _____

5. monkeys _____   _____

FOUR SPECIAL CASES WITH POSSESSION

I. *Compound Words or Word Combinations:* Only the last word shows possession.

compound word: editor in chief   The editor in chief's staff works hard.
[apostrophe *s* to show possession]

combination of words that names one thing: secretary of state   A secretary of state's position is important.
[apostrophe *s* to show possession]

II. *Time and Money Words:* Words that indicate time values, in certain uses, are said to show ownership.

hour   One hour's rest is too much.
[apostrophe *s* added to *hour* (Reminder I)]
[This word is thought of as "possessing" the rest.]

minutes   Five minutes' rest is all you need.
[apostrophe added to *minutes* (Reminder II)]

Words that indicate money value, in certain uses, are said to show ownership.
[apostrophe *s* added to *quarter* (Reminder I)]

quarter   A quarter's worth of gasoline will not take you far.
[This word is thought of as "possessing" the worth.]

dollars   He bought three dollars' worth of chocolate.
[apostrophe added to *dollars* (Reminder II)]

III. *Two People as Owners:* When both people are thought to be equal owners of the same thing, only the last word shows possession.

McGraw-Hill's textbooks
Standard and Poor's Index

If two people own things individually, show possession for both words.

Harry's and Jerome's cars crashed.

IV. *Pronouns and Ownership:* Pronouns never have apostrophes to show possession.

his book	NOT	his' book
That is *hers.*	NOT	hers' or her's
The pen is *yours.*	NOT	yours' or your's
Those are *ours.*	NOT	ours' or our's
Is it *theirs?*	NOT	theirs' or their's
The cat hurt *its* paw.	NOT	it's or its'

Step 5. Practice with Special Possession.   Select from parentheses the correct word and write it in the blank space in the margin.

_____ 1. My (brother's-in-law, brother-in-law's) company closed last month.

_____ 2. The (attorney general's, attorney's general) case was argued strongly in court.

_____ 3. The (commander's in chief, commander in chief's) instructions failed to reach the soldiers.

_____ 4. "Two (dollar's, dollars', dollars) worth of candy, please," a small voice asked.

_____ 5. An (hours, hour's, hours') work in the garden may improve things.

_____ 6. In five (second's, seconds', seconds) the space craft will lift off for the moon.

_____ 7. (Abbot's and Costello's, Abbot and Costello's) movies are still popular.

_____ 8. Both (Carl and Mary's, Carl's and Mary's) assignments were not done.

_____ 9. We have our tickets, but (its, it's) not a bad idea to buy (yours, your's, yours') at the gate.

_____ 10. I think the paper is (mine's, mine, mines) but if it is (theirs, their's, theirs') I will return it.

REVIEW: IF YOU THINK A WORD NEEDS AN APOSTROPHE BECAUSE IT SHOWS POSSESSION:

1. See if you can figure out what is being owned.
2. See if the word in which you want to use an apostrophe is the owner of something. Usually, the thing owned appears in the sentence soon after the owner.

   Exceptions: It is David's.
                   We ate at Carl's.

   Here the thing owned is not specifically mentioned, but understood.

   David's (book)
   Carl's (house)

3. Sometimes the owner is more than one. Make sure the word shows plural with the right ending.
   a. If the word does not end in *s*, add an apostrophe *s*.
   b. If the word does end in *s*, add an apostrophe.

   Example: a. You want to show that a boy owns books. The word *boy* does not end in *s*. The possessive is shown this way:

   the *boy's* books
        \[Add apostrophe *s*.]

   b. You want to show that many boys are the owners of books. The word *boys* ends in *s*. The possessive is shown this way:

   the boys' books
        \[Add apostrophe after *s*.]

Step 6. Possessives in the Right Places.   Underline the correct word in parentheses. Sometimes you will need a word that shows possession. Other times, you will need a word that shows plural.

1. That (bird's, birds') feathers floated to the ground.
2. On (Thursday's, Thursdays) and (Sunday's, Sundays) the (director's, directors) work load is light.
3. The (lady's, ladies', ladies) fur coats were stolen from the restaurant.
4. If Carl (Harris, Harris') house (burns, burn's) down, his insurance (company's, companies', companys) agent will bring a check for the mortgage.
5. Many (woman's, women's, womens) jobs are more difficult than (mens', men's, mens).
6. I received my tax return yesterday; when you get (yours', your's, yours), check to see if (it's, its) correct.
7. Five (minute's, minutes, minutes') time is not enough for a short quiz; but Mr. (Jones, Jones') feels (its, it's) enough!
8. My (mothers-in-law, mother-in-law's, mother's-in-law) house, because of (it's, its) large backyard, is a (childs, child's) dream.
9. Five million (dollars', dollar's) worth of heroin was uncovered in a recent raid.
10. The (citizen's, citizens') committee voted that all (student's, students') tuition fees should be partially refunded.

Step 7. Adding Possessive Endings. In the blanks at the ends of the words below, add s, 's, s' or just ' so that the sentence is correct. For some words you need to add nothing.

1. Michelle_____ and Gladys_____ houses burned in the fire.

2. We bought apple_____, pear_____, and banana_____ at a very high price;

   but our_____ are not as sweet as your_____.

3. That pocketbook is mine_____; those student_____ took it.

4. The ladies_____ card game ended early because the ladies_____ had to leave.

5. My neighbor_____ houses all look older than mine_____.

Step 8. More Possession Review. Change the word in parentheses so that it can be correctly used in the sentence. Then write the word in the blank space.

Hint: You may have to make the word plural before you use possession.

(lady)   1. Many _____ handkerchiefs were on sale at the department store.

(man)   3. Several _____ stores closed when a strike by employees broke out.

(month)   2. Three _____ salary came to $850.

(baby)   4. Many _____ parents ignore them when they cry.

(women) 5. Those _____ organizations often fight for liberty.

(Anyone) 8. _____ opinion is
needed because no one
knows much about the new
program.

(Child) 6. _____ games often
are very intelligent.

(Phyllis) 9. Carol and _____
friendship faded after an
argument over boyfriends.

(monkey) 7. A _____ tricks in the
zoo attract crowds of laughing people.

(teachers) 10. Five _____ examination papers were stolen
from their desks.

WRITING THE ESSAY

Think about some feature of woman's place in a man's world, some point
of view you hold about the trends in Women's Liberation—perhaps something suggested in the early pages of this chapter or in the list of suggested
topics on pp. 338–339. Make sure that you have a strong enough opinion
about the topic you select so that you can convince your reader that what
you say has merit. Once you think you know what topic you want to write
about, and you can prepare a proposal that states what it is that your essay
will discuss, you need to consider the reasons you have for believing what
you do about your topic. Then your concern is with details: how can you
illustrate or prove your point to the reader? If you ask yourself these questions before you begin the essay, you will know before you write just what
source of supporting details you will use.

ON THE HUNT FOR DETAILS: FOUR CRUCIAL QUESTIONS TO ASK YOURSELF

1. What moments have I experienced in my own life that can help me illustrate
   my reasons for believing what I do about the topic?
2. What have I read recently in books, newspapers, or magazines—or what can
   I read quickly and easily before I write—that can help me support my reasons
   for believing what I do about the topic?
3. What have I learned from the television, the movies, or the radio that can
   help me support my reasons for believing what I do about the topic?
4. What have I learned from reliable friends, parents, relatives, teachers that can
   help me support my reasons for believing what I do about the topic?

Suppose you believe that as drivers of automobiles, women are really
very competent. And you can remember two specific moments in your life
which will illustrate to the reader why you feel the way you do, moments
which might even persuade him to believe what you believe. After you
write an introduction (see pp. 277–282), you might show in each body

paragraph one of those moments expanded with concrete sensory details. Maybe you sat alongside your mother in the family Ford when her skillful driving prevented a near-fatal accident. Perhaps at another time your girl friend's quick thinking on the road prevented you from getting lost on the way to a party. Or maybe you want to compare a moment you sat in a car driven by a woman with a moment you experienced in a car driven by a man. You will not have *proved* that women are excellent drivers or that they are better drivers than men; but you will have *illustrated* to the reader how your own experiences explain the opinion you hold. That is a very effective way to build an essay. And because you answered question 1 before you started to write, the preparation of your essay will not be difficult.

But you may want to use a number of reasons to back up your opinion that women are very competent drivers. Make a list of the reasons you have. Eliminate any you think would be hard to illustrate or prove. Then perhaps your list will look something like this:

1. Women think very quickly in times of danger.
2. Women are very cautious on the road.
3. Women are courteous drivers.
4. Women are particularly familiar with safety regulations.
5. Women do not drink before they drive so they have fewer fatal accidents than men.
6. Women have fewer accidents, in general, than men.

If you can support any of these reasons, you can use them effectively in your essay. Consult now the Four Crucial Questions on p. 329. Did you live through incidents which could illustrate any of these reasons? Did you, on the other hand, see a study by the National Highway Safety Board in which there appear important statistics about women drivers and their safety record? Did you read an article in *The Ladies Home Journal* or *Seventeen* or *Motor Trend* where a traffic commissioner of a large city commended women drivers for their courtesy (and could you quote or paraphrase accurately from this article)? Did you hear on one of the radio or television talk shows an interview with the president of Mutual State Insurance Company where you learned about the driving patterns of women and the effects of these patterns on insurance rates? Did a driving instructor you once had tell you that over the last twenty years on the job, he found that the women he teaches always remember the driving regulations much better than the men do?

Whatever points you decide to develop in your essay should have some kind of support. If you feel that you have a great deal of support to offer for *two* of the reasons above, fine. Forget about the other four. Discuss one of the two points in the first body paragraph (paragraph 2 of the essay), using support you think convincing from books, television, radio, newspapers, magazines, friends, your own experience. Discuss the other point in the next paragraph. There too, you need to use as many details as you think will convince the reader that you are right.

But perhaps you want to discuss in your essay *all* the reasons listed above. Fine. First try to pick out the reason that is *most* important to you, the one you can defend with the most solid and convincing support. Save that one until later! In the paragraph that comes after the introduction, discuss all the *other* reasons that make you believe as you do, giving brief support for each reason that you mention. In the third paragraph of the essay, discuss the one most important reason you have. You can illustrate it by relating an experience from your own life; or you can use any of the other kinds of details to convince the reader of your point of view. By saving the most important reason for last and for treatment in its own paragraph, you hit the reader hard with your most striking evidence. Your most important point stays with the reader as he comes to the end of your essay.

Perhaps you want to show in the paragraph after the introduction the arguments many people give when they say women are *not* good drivers (see pp. 316–318). In paragraph 3, then, you can go about trying to show why all those reasons are, in your opinion, wrong. You would support the points you made with some strong details. Or you can say at the beginning of paragraph 3 that you think there is some truth in what others say; and then go on to develop your own reasons for believing what you do about women drivers.

The pages you have just read offer only suggestions: you can decide what you want to put in each paragraph, how many points you want to discuss, whether you want to stress certain ideas more than others. You will need to think about the various ways of developing paragraphs so you can figure out which method will be best for your essay. The earlier chapters in this book illustrate paragraphs that narrate, describe, give several instances, use statistics and quotations, define, create moods, compare and contrast, present analogies: these approaches to paragraphs you can use to develop the paragraphs within your essay.

But you must have answers to one or more of those crucial questions on p. 329 before you start writing. In that way you will know just what details to use before you write, and you will not run out of things to say during the preparation of your essay. Everyone has opinions (you have hundreds of your own about the status of women in a man's world), but the details that illustrate your opinions are what convince the reader that you know what you are talking about.

HAND PAGES FOR REVIEWING DETAILS

1. Imagery and Sensory Language   pp. 6, 58, 127–131, 223–230
2. Using Statistics and Cases   pp. 178–181, 184
3. How to Paraphrase   pp. 186–187
4. How to Use Quotations   pp. 186–187, 231–232

Step 1. Practice Planning for the Essay. Read the proposal sentences below. Consult the list of Four Crucial Questions. Then tell briefly what you would discuss in each body paragraph and the kinds of details you would use. Study the example.

	Body Paragraph 1	*Body Paragraph 2*
1. Even in the field of hard physical labor, women should not be overlooked.	*Discussion of women laborers in Russia. Statistics from New York Times Almanac.*	*American women overlooked for jobs of hard physical labor. Paraphrase of TV interview with Women's Liberation leader. More statistics from Labor Department.*
2. To say that women and men are the same is ridiculous.		
3. Because of unfair discrimination against them, many women are forced into horrible lives.		
4. I believe that women teachers who have their own personal problems often do a poor job in the classroom.		

5. Any woman who works and cannot care for her children herself must be prepared for a number of problems.

_____   _____

_____   _____

_____   _____

_____   _____

_____   _____

_____   _____

6. So much attention has gone to the problems of the black man; but it is the black woman who has the real difficulties in American society.

_____   _____

_____   _____

_____   _____

_____   _____

_____   _____

_____   _____

LEARNING FROM OTHER STUDENTS

Step 1. Arguing from Personal Experience. Although the theme below offers no *proof* for its main arguments, dramatic illustrations serve to explain to the reader just why the writer holds the opinions she does. Read "Deprived Children" below and write the answers to the questions after the essay.

Deprived Children

An untrained observer watching a group of children at play may see no real difference between them. The child sitting in the sand pile looks similar to the one squealing happily down the sliding pond. Yet a closer look might reveal many differences. Each child has his own physical appearance; each has his own mental abilities; each has a home life that may not resemble the others'. A few people do notice, however, that some children appear insecure and unhappy; I believe that these are frequently the children of working mothers.

Children of working mothers are deprived of the security of a healthy and loving environment. As a young child with a working mother, I felt her absence deeply. On my first day in third grade, for example, a violent storm shook the streets of Brooklyn. Happy at the idea of a new teacher and new friends, the class grew even more excited by the trees whipping back and forth across from our first floor windows and the sound of September rain pounding against the glass. However, this happiness soon wore off when streets flooded and winds of sixty miles an hour soaked the sidewalks. All the classes moved to the basement, and the principal, Mr. Greenwalder, announced that only children whose parents came for them could go home. Nervously hugging my new notebook to my thin jacket, I prayed somehow my mother would get to me. A slow line of mothers holding yellow rain-coats and black umbrellas and boots trudged in to pick up their nervous children while I stared at a speck on the floor. The hours unfolded gradually, and soon I stood in the midst of the huge gray basement, alone except for my faithful teacher, Mrs. Timmins. The fear of a trip home in the hurricane disappeared in the pain and shame I felt that day by not having a mother at home like everyone else. As a child of a working mother I often felt that sense of loss and shame.

The results of such feelings in the children of a working mother can be very serious as the example of my brother Richie clearly illustrates. My older brother, younger sister, and I grew up in the care of indifferent housekeepers. At eleven years old, Richie often left the house for hours at a time with no excuses or expla-nations of his absences. No one really knew his friends, and my mother's own daily battle with tiredness after work kept her from questioning Richie's activities. As we grew older, Mother's continued absence became an accepted part of our family life, and neither my sister nor I could detect the gradual change in our brother. Richie grew into a sullen, moody, overweight teen-ager. He failed miserably in school, finally dropping out. He rarely spoke to anyone in the house. Although these signs all pointed to tragedy, I was too busy with my own problems to pay any attention—and Mother just was not around. One night a call from a far off hospital told us that Richie's condition was fair after a drug overdose. My mother's eyes looked confused as if to say "How did it happen?" when we sped to the hos-pital, but through the shock I *knew* the cause. Richie survived and is now in the midst of costly psychiatric care. But in my opinion, this whole tragedy might have been avoided through the presence and guidance of a mother. My mother was never there.

In many cases, then, the child of a working mother is under great stress. He must become independent early in life and learn to accept the loss of a parent. He can easily fall under bad influences and must be strong enough to resist if he wants to stay out of trouble. At a very young age he must learn the difference between right and wrong and must often face the difficult chore of choosing alone. These tasks present a challenge to the child of a working mother, and one can only hope that he will succeed in mastering them.

—Phyllis Gold

1. What does the essay, based upon the proposal sentence, attempt to illus-trate? _____

_____

2. How does the purpose of paragraph 2 differ from the purpose of para-graph 3? (**Hint:** Read the topic sentences carefully.) _____

_____

3. Has the writer convinced you that what she believes is true? How has she achieved this? _____

_____

4. Which images do you find most appealing? _____

_____

5. Do you find any examples of the kinds of poor reasoning pointed out on

   pp. 312–314? Where? _____

_____

Step 2. Two Themes That Meet the Opposition.   Both of the student samples below use in body paragraphs arguments made against their own proposals. Read the essays and write the answers to the questions that appear below.

Women: Fragile Flowers?

   Whenever people discuss the idea of women in the world of men, a male voice always cries out that women are biologically different from men, even in the animal kingdom. Such was the case last Tuesday when a hot discussion on "women's lib" filled our freshman English class. With an air of authority George Kerman rattled off biological "facts" to back up his statements on how women are "different." Although I felt that I wanted to contradict him, I knew better. I had no biological statistics to back up my beliefs, just a bit of pride that hurt when he compared women to female peacocks. But now I can stand my own ground well assured of my resources. Women are not the weaker sex.

   Many like George would paint a pretty picture of womankind as a fragile flower easily bent. The argument that women are biologically different from men always hints that women are *inferior* to men, inferior in terms of stamina, stability, and thinking. A number of scientists argue that males are sturdier and able to withstand stress more admirably than females. Dr. Edgar Berman, a former surgeon and one-time State Department consultant on Latin American health problems, agrees with George. "Women should be excluded," Dr. Berman says "from high executive positions because of their monthly raging hormonal imbalances." People like Dr. Berman point out that women cry while men keep a stiff upper lip, meaning that women have poor responses to life's problems. There are also statements on record that women usually have lower I.Q.'s than men do, and that this accounts for the low percentage of women in professional jobs. All these remarks certainly do seem to point a finger at women as delicate butterflies, needing protection and care and not needing positions of responsibility in the world today.

   But the finger is pointing in the wrong direction because *men* lack all the important biological features. The term "biologically different" used against women tries to be impartial but it still is an expression of a male's prejudice. In fact, men are the weaker sex. The female of almost any species is sturdier than the male. Dr. James Hamilton, an endocrinologist, shows that from worms to humans the male is less able to tolerate life's everyday stresses. "There can be little doubt that the male has a higher mortality rate in almost all forms of animal life studied." Even during the first week of life, the death rate for infant males is 32% greater than that of females. Later on in life the society puts strain on the man to compete, produce, and succeed; this also affects the survival rate. Another part of the problem of male mortality is the male hormone testosterone which brings about a higher metabolic rate in most tissues, wearing them out faster. But there is no proof that the woman's monthly "hormonal imbalance" is a sign of inferiority. True, many women do experience some discomfort each month; some even are quite ill for a day or two. But most women do not suffer with any reactions. Federal surveys in every job category show that women take off the same amount of time from work as men. Although crying is often another "proof" of a woman's difference from men, United States Public Health data show that females have a much lower suicide rate—less than half that of males (isn't it better to cry?). And there are no sex differences in regard to I.Q. On all forms of intelligence tests the female I.Q. is not significantly different from the male's. Women are, in my opinion, biologically superior to men.

Woman has not been able to prove she is not the weaker sex because the society has assigned her to an inferior position. Few brilliant women have tried to develop their talents simply because there has been a small market for brilliant women in this country. The few who have bothered to develop their creative talents find that the world views them as "odd balls." The stereotype of a brilliant woman is that of a horsefaced, flat-chested female in support shoes, one who has hidden all her sexual instincts in her search for a career. It may be fun being treated like a fragile flower by a boyfriend or a date, but there's a time and place for everything. It is time society stopped giving out positions based on stereotypes. We women must develop and make use of our wasted female brain power.

—Stella Tesoriero

Call Them What You Like

During one of the early Women's Liberation demonstrations in New York City a few years ago, Roger Grimsby, television reporter for ABC, interviewed the leader of the protest. Mr. Grimsby asked one shapely, bra-less figure, "What do you girls . . ." when her sudden interruption cut him off. "We're not girls. We're women." She turned angrily away from him and staring into the camera with bulging eyes and trembling lips, said "Remember that, men! Don't call us girls anymore!" To me that idea is ridiculous. I will still use the word *girl* in my vocabulary, for I believe it does not in any way degrade females.

On the radio, too, I have heard representatives of Women's Lib state specifically and hostilely that females over the age of twelve should be addressed as women instead of girls. They say that when a male passes puberty he is considered a man, but when a female passes puberty she is still considered a girl and not a woman. This, according to women activists, means that women are inferior because a female is spoken of as an adolescent at the same age that a male is considered an adult. A male of thirteen finds himself struggling with a man's responsibilities: his parents urge him to go to work at least part time; high school guidance counselors insist that he decide on a career; he competes on high school teams and in high school classrooms just the way his father competes on the job. But female teen-agers are frequently babied by the society. Fathers who cannot afford it love giving their "little girls" all the money they need so that work is not essential. Teenage females do not have to suffer to find a career because, as their parents say, a girl will get married and be supported by a husband. And there is very little competition for the kind of status men need to face the world. Since many women live and operate in a man's world, it is felt that they cannot live decently if they are made inferior to the problems that will arise later in their lives. One major step, women activists say, towards sexual equality would be to have the men stop referring to mature females as girls.

I disagree because I do not believe that the word *girl* means as much as Women's Lib says it does. A word is simply a vocal sound; it has no meaning except what the mind attaches to it. Therefore, the word *girl* is relative to the person who says it. For instance, I watched a construction worker on Sixth Avenue eyeing a female in tight black pants as she swung her hips down the street. First he let out a shrill wolf whistle. Then he turned to his friend and in a low hungry voice said, "How do you like that *girl*?" What he means by *girl* is very different from what old Professor Campbell means when he turns away from his neatly typed pages of philosophy notes and says gently to two latecomers, "Girls, take your seats." Both the teacher and the laborer use the same word, but in their minds the word has different meanings; the construction worker sees the girl as a sex object while the professor sees the girls just as other students. And although some females feel degraded at being sex objects, others are delighted at the meanings that go along with a construction worker's use of the word *girl*. Professor Campbell, on the other hand, can lead no one to believe that he suggests something inferior when he says *girls*. For him the word is just a simple means of identifying students of one sex. Therefore, the solution does not lie in changing the word *girl,* but in changing the way men view females. If women activists feel that the word *girl* to mean sex object is wrong, it is the attitude they should be fighting, not the word itself.

I do not plan to change my vocabulary for the sake of Women's Liberation because, as I mentioned before, the meaning of words is relative to the mind of the speaker. This is true of almost any word. Negroes in past years have objected to the word *Negro* because it was often used as a way of indicating inferiority. What they suggested was the word *Black* as a replacement. But the word *Black* is used with as much scorn as the word *Negro* by people who, no matter what the word to describe it is, have no tolerance for other races. Censorship of words does not solve anything. Simple *words* do not make problems. The feelings behind the use of the words do, however.

—Joseph DiLisi

1. The second paragraph in Mr. DiLisi's essay shows what people who disagree with his proposal believe. What arguments does he use to show that the word *girl* does make females inferior? _____

_____

2. What details does Miss Tesoriero use to show why people think women *are* the weaker sex? _____

_____

3. Where in Mr. DiLisi's essay do you find examples of concrete sensory language? _____

_____

4. Do you find any examples of the types of poor reasoning explained on

pp. 312–314 in either of the essays? Where? _____

_____

5. Which essay did you enjoy better? Why? (If you say one was more interesting, say *why* it was more interesting.) _____

_____

Your Views on the Woman's Place: A Checklist of Requirements

Examine this checklist before you write. After you finish your theme, fill
it out and submit it with your essay.

1. Is my proposal clearly stated in the last sentence of paragraph 1? _____
2. Did I use smooth transitions as explained in the Essay Transition
   Signboards 1, 2, and 3 on pp. 319, 321, and 322? _____
3. Did I avoid the traps in logic and clear reasoning by studying the Fifteen Faults to Fail the Argument on pp. 312–314? _____
4. Did I consider carefully the types of details I want to use in my essay
   by asking myself the Four Crucial Questions explained on p. 329?
   Do I know the difference between *illustrating* my opinion and *proving*
   my opinion is correct? _____
5. Did I use a variety of sentence patterns: coordination and subordination; sentences with verb-part openers? _____
6. Did I try to use strong verbs, clear expressions, and images that appeal
   to the senses? _____
7. If I used statistics, cases, or opinions expressed by others, have I mentioned the source of my information? Have I used reliable sources? _____
8. Did I reread my essay, looking for errors, especially in the use of possession and in the kinds of mistakes I usually make? Did I examine my
   own Progress Sheet? _____
9. Did I try to use some of the new vocabulary words introduced in this
   chapter? Here is a sentence from my theme that uses one of those

   words: _____

   _____ _____

10. Did I read carefully the three student themes on pp. 333–337 to help
    me see how other students presented their ideas on women's rights? _____

Some Topics to Think about

In case you have trouble finding a topic, here are some possibilities:

1. equal sex standards for everyone
2. a woman belongs at home
3. the Russian woman versus the American woman
4. I don't want to be liberated.
5. my experience with a woman doctor (lawyer, salesman, dean, insurance agent)

6. two women teachers I know
7. a memorable woman in a good book
8. woman executives are deadly
9. woman executives are excellent
10. children of working mothers
11. prejudice I experienced as a woman
12. women football players? men go-go girls? how far will it go?
13. the worst (best) part of being a woman
14. where women (men) don't belong
15. a woman president

You may wish to challenge one of the statements in Step 3 on p. 311. You may wish to write about a topic suggested in the questionnaire on p. 310.

THE PROFESSIONALS SPEAK

This selection from *The Female Eunuch,* one of the most important books in the modern woman's movement for liberation, uses statistical details to prove women's difficulties in the job market. Write the answers to the questions that appear beneath it.

The Woman as Worker

In England women form thirty-eight percent of the workforce; in the U.S.A. the proportion is only slightly smaller, around thirty-five percent. This means that in both countries half the women between the ages of sixteen and sixty-four work out-side their homes. Of the seventeen million married women in the U.S. who go out to work, ten million have children under the age of seventeen. The average wage of an Englishwoman doing administrative, technical or clerical work is less than £12 ($28.80) a week, while men in the same industries earn an average wage of £28 a week. Male manual workers earn an average wage of £20 a week; women, £10. The same disparity between the earnings of the sexes is visible right across the board in the United States, where male professionals and technicians can ex-pect to earn $9,370 annually and females, $5,210. Male clerical workers can ex-pect to earn $6,380, women $3,844. While a sales*man* can live on a respectable $6,814, his female counterpart must do with $2,116. The skilled operator, who is nearly always a man, nets about $7,224 annually; skilled women may expect $3,826. Men in the service industries get paid an average wage of $4,532 annu-ally for more important work than the women waitressing, cleaning and answering the telephone for the starvation wage of $2,076. The average male employee in the United States earns $6,610 a year; his sister $3,157, less than half.

— Germaine Greer

1. What conclusion does Miss Greer want the reader to draw about the way

women are treated in occupations? _____

_____

2. What statistics are used to compare English women and English men?

_____

_____

3. What details illustrate the disparity between the earnings of the sexes

in America? _____

_____

Here are two letters by black women to the editor of the *New York Times*.
What is the point of view of each toward liberation for females? With whom
do you most agree? Why?

Gloria Steinem is a key figure in the Women's Liberation movement of
today.

An Open Letter to Gloria Steinem

Dear Miss Steinem:

How are you? I am asking your help. You see, I am in something of a dilemma.
I have learned that it is your view that we blacks have a great deal in common
with women's liberationists and, you see, Miss Steinem, I am both black and a
woman, excuse me, female, and I am having trouble identifying, uh, relating to
your group.

I mean, Miss Steinem, there are some difficulties there. Now you take food, Miss
Steinem; that presents a difficult problem. It seems that women libbers don't
want to cook it. But, Miss Steinem, I'm a good cook (I come from a race, oops, ethnic
group, of good cooks, a heretical position, I know) and our problem is to find someone to buy the food. You know, feed us. We black women gripe, Miss Steinem, because we have to buy it ourselves. We have a saying, Miss Steinem. We say that if
he buys the bacon, we'll cook it. We mean that, too, Miss S. We'll get up at two
o'clock in the morning and cook it if he's hungry and we won't ask him where he's
been. Of course, we'd appreciate it if he said he had a flat tire or, better still, was
by the bedside of a sick friend, but *c'est la vie* Miss Steinem, you can't have everything. About such matters, we are philosophical. As one of our earthy philosophers
observed, "He didn't take away anything that he didn't bring back."

We are for equal pay for equal work, Miss Steinem, especially for spinsters, but
we think it would be so much nicer if the man made enough money to support us.

I even see a few misguided soul sisters in the Women's Liberation Movement.
Come now, ladies. We've been more than equal for nearly four hundred years, ever
since we stood in some Southern sun and chopped cotton from morning till night.
Now you are complaining because some man believes that your place is in the
home where you can stay all day and watch the stories and look after the children,
rather than work over somebody's steaming stove and farm the children out to
their grandmother or a neighbor and then come home and do your work. And you
don't want to do that. You've got to be kidding.

As for the dramatic charge of sexual exploitation, Miss Steinem, if the man has
reached puberty plus ten years, such a charge is charitable; if he has been around

long enough to acquire position or possessions or a steady job, such a charge is sheer fantasy, Miss Steinem, sheer fantasy.

Would you believe that there are women meeting the clock every day in factories, offices, stores, lunch rooms and school rooms who don't think that the life of a housewife is so bad? Think it over, Miss Steinem.

—Mary E. Mebane (Liza)
From *New York Times,* October 29, 1971

What We Should Be Doing, Sister

Dear Liza,

After reading your open letter to Gloria Steinem (Mary Mebane [Liza], Oct. 29, 1971) I felt I had to reply for a couple of reasons—because I am a black woman and because I am a personal friend of Gloria's.

Not believing that I am one of the "few misguided soul sisters in the women's liberation movement" but someone who feels a dual oppression as a black woman, I thought maybe we could establish some rapport. Your letter indicates you have an interpretation of the women's movement as something other than it is, i.e., "that women-libbers don't want to cook," or that they want to get us all out of the house, and into poorly paid factory jobs.

As a black woman who has been actively involved and still is in the black movement, part of my frustration has been that—after risking my life in sit-ins, pickets, marches; you name it—I was allowed to make coffee, not decisions. And so from there came the realization that I was going to help the brothers realize that as black women we cannot allow black men to do us what white men have been doing to their women all these years. I decided to point out, as Bobby Seale said in "Seize the Time," that real manhood doesn't depend on the subjugation of anyone; to remind him that the racist Patrick Moynihan lied when he said that the problem with black men is black women.

Because we know that the problem with black men is white racism and no amount of going back to the kitchen is going to give a black man a job. It is an insult to black men to say that black women must be behind them pushing them into their manhood. Sister, I want to make sure that, come the revolution, I will be able to use all my talents and creativity and energies, which has nothing to do with cooking grits for the revolutionaries.

Black women do work. In fact, most women in this country work, and yet a black female with a bachelor's degree earns slightly less than a high-school educated black male. It is incorrect to assume that all black women are living at home with a man and depending on a man's income. The reality is that a large percentage of the black work force is women. We are often heads of household, and supporting children as well. That's why black women are concerned about equal pay for equal work, and decent day care for their children.

As many women die each year from botched, illegal abortions as American men die in Vietnam—and a disproportionate number of these are black and brown women. That is why we want repeal of all abortion laws. It is a fact that black women are having abortions, and if the brothers are concerned about genocide, then they will fight with us to establish community-controlled health clinics. We know that once the black warrior has planted his revolutionary seed in our black (or white) womb, we're the ones who often face the reality of raising, clothing, feeding that child by ourselves, while he is sowing oats in other fields. If we can't get equal pay for equal work, how can we survive? How can the children survive? To assume that black women are not concerned about themselves as women is really a putdown. Because we do get raped, we do get sterilized against our will, we do get left with unwanted pregnancies, we do get worse treatment in jails, the courts, the schools, in fact in every institution in this country, than men. We are on the welfare rolls in infinitely greater numbers than men, for sexist reasons. We do, in fact, suffer from a dual stigma in this racist and sexist society.

Gloria Steinem happens to be one woman involved in the Women's Movement and the broader struggle for the liberation of all people. She fights her oppression where she feels it, not as a white—liberally saving black people, but working for all women. She talks about sexism and racism whenever she speaks. She almost always speaks with Dorothy Pittman Hughes, Flo Kennedy or myself because we are black women who have lived that dual oppression all our lives, and the parallel that is "the deepest truth in American life."

Sister, what we should be doing is coming down on the white male press together instead of writing letters against each other for the delectation of white male editors. You might not agree with the things I have said, but I have only attempted to offer you a different viewpoint, which is not as much in the minority as you might think.

—Margaret Sloan, *New York Times*, December 8, 1971

REACHING HIGHER

Step 1. Analyzing Photographs.   Look at the picture on p. 306 and write a paragraph in which you compare and contrast (using any of the methods explained in Chapter 4) the situation in the picture with modern attitudes toward women in your city.

Step 2. An Essay in Pictures and Words.   Using a camera you can easily operate, take a number of pictures (on or near the college campus) which show either the advances made by women in a man's world or the way in which women are kept down in a man's world. Take pictures of women (a relative, a friend, a stranger) at work, women at leisure, women on their way to their jobs or at the supermarket or in their homes. Select the ten best pictures, and for each write one sentence which summarizes the main point of the snapshot.

Step 3. More Topics on Liberation.   The struggle for freedom and equality over the centuries knows no sex or nationality. Using any effective kinds of details, develop any one of these liberation ideas in a four-paragraph essay:

the black man's struggle in South Africa today
the Jew and equality in large cities
one slave revolt in the South
the Italians' charge of prejudice today
one ancient struggle for freedom

segregated schools mean inequality.
the American Indian and equal opportunity
the Irish immigrant in New York of 1900
unfair treatment for Mexican-Americans
what Hungarians fought for in 1964

Step 4. Reviewing Paragraph Details. The topic sentence of every paragraph controls the content of that paragraph by telling the reader what the subject is and what the writer's response to that subject is. Every detail in a paragraph must relate to the idea stated in the topic sentence. Beneath each topic sentence below is a group of details that might or might not be expanded to develop the paragraph. Draw a line through any details you think should not be used because they do not support the topic sentence.

1. *The hundredth-anniversary parade for Women's Liberation in New York was a success.*
   thousands of women represented
   peaceful march through the city
   cheers of support from onlookers
   march in Los Angeles successful too
   too many parades in New York

2. *Many women throughout the world do not want to be liberated from their homes and families in order to work.*
   Women in small European villages cherish their positions as homemakers.
   American women in cities like to get out of the house to go to jobs.
   easier for American women to work because of available modern conveniences
   Some educated women believe that mothers must be available at home to their children all day long.
   Some women view working in the house as creative and fulfilling.

3. *Susan B. Anthony worked hard for women's rights.*
   founded Daughters of Temperance, nineteenth-century Women's Liberation group
   born in 1820
   voted for President Lincoln
   helped pass first laws in New York giving women right over children and property
   organized with Elizabeth Cady Stanton the National Women's Suffrage Association

4. *Compared with women of a hundred years ago, women of today enjoy a number of "freedoms."*
   smoking in streets no longer considered unladylike
   women driving cars nowadays a familiar sight
   government should not allow so many women drivers
   women not unusual in men's jobs

Step 5. A Letter to the Editor.   Write a one-paragraph letter to the editor of your college publication or of your local newspaper in which you discuss your view of *one* feature of the liberation movement for women today.

Step 6. Two Views in Comparison.   Write a paragraph in which you compare and contrast the views of Mary E. Mebane and Margaret Sloan as they appear in the letters on pp. 340–342.

chapter 9

THAT VITAL SOMEONE:
A PERSON IN YOUR LIFE

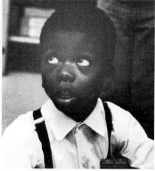

INTRODUCTION

Hundreds of people brush past our lives every day: crowds on the buses; long lines at restaurants and movie houses; bodies on campus running, strolling, laughing, pushing, drifting between classes; men and women and children in the family, on the block, in the homes of friends. With most of these people nothing more develops than a meeting of the eyes, then a quick glance away and a rapid forgetting. With others, relationships build, some with our delight and thanks, others against our own wills. Yet for every one of us there is just a handful of important people in our lives — perhaps even just one human being who has greatly influenced our personalities, our emotions, the ways in which we think.

What person has had a major influence on your life? Is it a mother who urges you on, who talks out problems with you, who sacrifices her own goals and needs so that you can advance? Is it a father who ignores you, who by his absence has made you feel angry or unsure of yourself? Was it a teacher who changed the way you think or who helped you build excellence in some special skill or talent or creative act? Was it—is it—a boyfriend or girlfriend who added a glow of love to your life or who brought you misery, tension, and pain?

In this theme assignment you will illustrate the effect of one significant person on your life. Using a combination of paragraph types that best serve your purpose, you will explore your own feelings in relation to that special someone. You want your essay to reflect some deep meaning for you so you may have to write about things that are painful or embarrassing. But those moments will make for successful compositions.

In terms of specific writing skills, you will learn about new ways to achieve sentence variety, about confusing verbs, and about the correct formation of tenses.

VOCABULARY

Step 1. Words to Name Relationships among People.

In the blank spaces below write definitions for the words. Check a dictionary for any word you do not know: Appendix A gives added help.

peer _____   crony _____

contemporary _____   fraternal _____

familial _____   conjugal _____

sibling _____   paternal _____

cohort _____   maternal _____

Step 2. Naming Relationships. Each item in Column I names or describes a relationship. In Column II write from the vocabulary above the word that you think best expresses the relationship. Each word is used only once.

I	II
1. a person who acts like a mother to other people	_____
2. a brother or sister	_____
3. someone of the same rank as someone else	_____
4. a member of a group	_____
5. a marriage relationship	_____
6. fatherly	_____
7. living at the same time	_____
8. a family relationship	_____
9. a close friend	_____
10. brotherly	_____

Step 3. Your Own Sentence. For any five words that are new to you from the list above, write your own sentences.

1. _____

2. _____

3. _____

4. _____

5. _____

Familiar Words, New Uses

The describing words below are familiar to you in the way they are usually employed. But these words when used in an unusual way create original pictures. A word like *icy* to describe a lake or a street is not unusual; but to say *an icy smile* lets the reader see a different and expressive picture.

Step 4. Writing Original Pictures. Each word in Column I appears in Column II in its most usual use. Check in a dictionary for any meanings you are not sure of. (See Appendix A for further help.) In Column III use the word in an unusual way to describe some aspect of appearance or personality. Study the two examples below.

I	II	III
1. foggy	*foggy* afternoon	*a foggy thought*
2. hollow	a *hollow* tube	*a hollow laugh*

I	II	III
3. shining	a *shining* light	_____
4. pasty	a *pasty* liquid	_____
5. metallic	*metallic* jewelry	_____
6. athletic	an *athletic* walk	_____
7. murky	a *murky* lake	_____
8. fiery	a *fiery* blaze	_____
9. leather	*leather* suitcase	_____
10. acrid	an *acrid* odor	_____
11. velvet	*velvet* dress	_____
12. tinkling	a *tinkling* bell	_____

Step 5. Writing Sentences.   For any five word groups you wrote in Column III above, write complete sentences. Make sure not to use the words in a usual way.

1. _____

2. _____

3. _____

4. _____

5. _____

BUILDING COMPOSITION SKILLS

Exploring the Topic

Step 1. People You Have Known.   Below are listed several personality traits. Select any one of these traits that you have observed in a person you know well. Speak aloud briefly to the class an incident that, in showing the person in action, will illustrate what you mean.

1. friendliness
2. selfishness
3. anger
4. unhappiness
5. kindness

6. meanness
7. devotion
8. laziness
9. ambition
10. pride

Step 2. Faces with Meaning: A One-minute Talk.   A person's face is a miracle of expressions and feelings and often tells the personality that lies beneath. Many times people say, "He looks mean" or "She's really beautiful." Right or wrong, the faces of people in our lives do reveal impressions of their character. Look at the pictures of faces on p. 345. Select one which gives you a certain feeling or impression, a face which expresses something you understand, feel, appreciate, or hate: is it *pain, delight, shame, peacefulness, anger, pride?* Once you can name the impression, decide what features of the face give the impression you have. Are the eyes fierce or soft? Are the lips heavy, or thin and pale? Do the eyebrows or the slant of the chin create important impressions? Once you have thought this out, discuss your conclusions with the class in a talk of no more than a minute.

Step 3. A Face in Your Own Life.   Think of someone you know whose face expresses a strong feeling or impression. Then describe three or four features that contribute to the impression. Use a number of varied images —color, sound, touch. You may want to use a comparison for a lively picture. Using the blanks below, write as a title on the first line the person's name, then a colon, then a few words to indicate the expression of the face in a special setting. Describe the features below the title. Study Miss Livinsky's sample below.

My Father: Peacefulness During a Nap on the Couch

1. softly fluttering eyelids
2. quiet breathing and whistling through closed lips
3. unwrinkled brow, still as a lake
4. square chin dropping gently with each breath

—Judith Livinsky

_____

_____

_____

_____

_____

Step 4. Describing a Fellow Student: One Paragraph.   Ask one of the people in the class to stand up in front of the room as a model. Take notes on what you see so that you will be able to write a short paragraph. As you watch the person up front, decide on one single impression that he creates: is he *handsome, nervous, playful, cheerful, serious, strange, relaxed, confident in himself?* After you state the impression in the topic sentence, describe the details that you feel contribute to that impression. Use images (see p. 6) to discuss the person's face, his clothing, the way he stands, how he uses his hands, the way he speaks to the class. Read your brief paragraphs aloud, as your instructor directs. But before you write, study the following sample and the chart of hints.

Richard

Richie Fries sits confidently atop the brown desk before us on this English theme day in late November. He speaks immediately, brown eyes sparkling at his audience of fellow classmates. His pressed blue shirt stresses his tall straight posture as his hand motions express words. He scratches his neat black hair as if in thought. "Next question!" he says. "Gotta wake you up. Ya look like you're falling asleep." The class watches his every expression, but there is no sign of nervousness in Richard, not a drop of sweat falling from his brow. "Look at me," his apple cheeks shout. "Look at me," his smile says. "Look," his position at the edge of the table screams. "Look at me. This is my moment of glory." His actual words race by at record pace. "My father tells me I should think in seventy-eight and talk in thirty-three," Rich speedily adds. Susan asks him to smile and change his position. Propping himself upon his elbow, he leans back on the desk. "Hey, why isn't this guy in Hollywood?" I think to myself. His eyes dance. They illuminate when he talks and glow softly when he is silent. His exciting brown eyes hold the class in a strong grip. They are only brown, same as so many other eyes, but they twinkle and they bubble and they look squarely at their audience without so much as a nervous blink. His eyes smile even when his lips fall. The girls like him: he is lively, has a good physique—I suppose it is understandable. Michelle asks where he goes to meet girls and the class giggles squeamishly. After a long, funny answer, Richie leans back, the edges of his lips pushing his cheeks up. His brown eyes now stare at no one. Everybody is writing. He takes a deep breath. Then, in a sudden leap from the table, Richie returns to his seat like a conqueror.

—Debbie Osher

HINTS FOR SUCCESSFUL PARAGRAPHS ABOUT A CLASSMATE

1. Mention time, place, and the single impression you have of the student in the first sentence.
2. Use some details of setting. Miss Osher says "brown desk."
3. Use only those details in the rest of the paragraph that contribute to the single impression. *Leave out any details that do not help create the impression.*
4. Mention the person's size, the color of his hair and eyes, his clothing. Use images of sound, color, and touch.
5. Write a sentence that tells what the model says. Miss Osher shows Richard saying "My father tells me I should think in seventy-eight and talk in thirty-three."
6. Toward the end of the paragraph, describe the one feature of the person's face that gives you the impression you have. Notice how Miss Osher concentrates on the eyes of her subject.

Sentence Variety

WORD GROUPS THAT SHOW WHERE, WHEN, AND HOW

about	except	within	between
by	under	beside	below
beneath	onto	since	upon

inside	at	as to	by means of
above	across	toward	through
for	on	at	along with
over	over	beyond	because of
outside	into	up	by way of
along	after	before	on account of
among	to	like	in spite of
of	with	below	in front of

The words in the chart above all help show relationships in sentences (you examined them in an earlier chapter on p. 287 when you learned about pronoun problems). They introduce word groups that tell where, when, or how things happen.

An old man hobbled away *down the street.*

The words *down the street* show where the old man hobbled.

An old man hobbled away *in tiny steps.*

The words *in tiny steps* tell how he hobbled.

An old man hobbled away *on a cold afternoon.*

The words *on a cold afternoon* tell when he hobbled.

Using word groups that tell where, when, or how at the *beginning* of sentences helps improve sentence variety.

Step 1. New Sentence Openings. Rewrite any *five* sentences below so that they open with a word group that starts with one of the words in the box above. Make your opening word group tell where, when, or how. Study the example.

Example: Through thick courtroom smoke, the lawyer laughed.

A man ran quickly.	We ate hungrily.
A child sang.	She stamped her feet.
A cat meowed.	The lawyer laughed.
The teacher shouted.	The policeman fired a shot.

1. _____

2. _____

3. _____

4. _____

5. _____

Step 2. Reversing Verb and Subject. Sometimes for effect you can put the verb *before* the subject when a sentence opens with a word group that tells *when, where,* or *how.*

Subject first: Down the street an old man hobbled.
[subject] [verb]

Verb first: Down the street hobbled an old man.
[verb] [subject]

Rewrite each sentence below so that the verb comes before the subject.

1. Across the sky a red and white kite sailed. _____

_____

2. Beyond the window two young children quietly played. _____

_____

3. Down a broken road the large truck rumbled. _____

_____

Step 3. Three Word Groups to Open. Another effective way to write a sentence is to use three word groups (each beginning with one of the words in the box on p. 351) that tell where, when, or how right at the beginning.

[1]   [2]   [3]

Down the street, across the corner, into an old house, the frightened little girl ran quickly.

Start each sentence below with three word groups that tell where, when, or how. Use words from the box on p. 351 to begin each group. You may want to use the same word to open each group. Study the examples.

Example: He finally finished the job.

In the coldest weather, with strong determination, through endless hours, he finally finished the job.

Example: A wave of heat spread uncomfortably over Long Island City.

In the streets, in the doorways, in the houses, a wave of heat spread uncomfortably over Long Island City.

Hint: Use a comma after each word group you add.

1. He looked for his friend. _____

_____

2. The President spoke seriously. _____

_____

3. The policeman held the robber tightly. _____

_____

SOLVING PROBLEMS IN WRITING

Verbs as Time Tellers

Using Tense Correctly. Every verb has three main forms, and from these all the different tenses are made. The present tense, the past tense, and the future tense you have little trouble using; but other tenses in the language are not so simple. Look for a moment at the word *to speak* and its three main parts. Underneath you will find an explanation of the tense that is made from each part.

TO SPEAK

I	**II**	**III**
speak	spoke	spoken
The Present Tense	*The Past Tense*	*Tenses That Show Continuing Action*
They *speak* too loudly.	I *spoke* to him.	He *has spoken* to them.
She *speaks* softly.	They *spoke* aloud.	I *have spoken*. (*These actions began in the past, but may go on into the present.*)
The Future Tense		She *had spoken* before they arrived. (*This action began in the past but was over before another action in the past.*)
They *will speak* tomorrow.		Before next week, she *will have spoken* at nine different colleges. (*This action will be finished before some definite time in the future.*)
I *shall speak* too.		

Hint: How to Form Tenses That Show Continuing Action:

1. Always use the third main part of the verb. (You will see later the main parts of many other verbs. These parts are always arranged in the same order as those above.)
2. Always use a helping verb.

has   had   will have
have   shall have

For *most* verbs, the principal parts are easy. All you need to know is the infinitive. If you take away the word *to*, you have the first main part of the verb (and you can form the present and future tense). If you add *-d* or *-ed* to the first main part, you have *both* the second and third main parts (and you can form the past tense and all the tenses that show actions that continue). Here are two examples:

	I	II (add *-ed*)	III (add *-ed*)
to talk	talk	talked	talked
	They talk. She talks. We will talk. I shall talk.	I talked. They talked.	She has talked. They have talked. She had spoken. They will have spoken.
		(add *-d*)	(add *-d*)
to dance	dance	danced	danced
	They dance. She dances. We will dance. I shall dance.	I danced. They danced.	She has danced. They have danced. She had danced. They will have danced.

Step 1. Writing Main Parts of Verbs. From each infinitive below make the three main parts in the same way as you see above in the examples *to talk* and *to dance.* Write them in the columns listed.

	I	II	III
to laugh	_____	_____	_____
to move	_____	_____	_____
to whisper	_____	_____	_____
to help	_____	_____	_____
to demonstrate	_____	_____	_____

Step 2. Using Tenses. Follow directions.

1. Use *will* and the correct form of *to laugh* in your own sentence. _____

_____

2. Use the past tense of *to move* in a sentence of your own. _____

_____

3. Write a sentence which uses *have* and the correct form of *to whisper.*

_____

_____

4. Fill in the blank with the correct form of *to help.*

She had _____ before the police arrived.

5. Fill in the blank with the correct form of *to demonstrate.*

By early next week, they will have _____ their skill as painters.

Troublesome Verb Parts

Unfortunately, a number of verbs do not form their parts as easily as the ones above. Like the verb *to speak,* all the main parts of these special verbs are different. These verbs—called *irregular* because they are different from the usual—also happen to be among those we use most often, so it is not surprising to hear and see a number of mistakes in spoken and written English. Although the list below does not include *all* the irregular verbs, it tries to indicate those most frequently used incorrectly. The starred verb is not irregular, but it still confuses many students.

Thirty-two Headaches: Irregular Verb Parts You Need to Know

I	II	III
am	was	been
begin	began	begun
break	broke	broken
bring	brought	brought
burst	burst	burst
choose	chose	chosen
come	came	come
do	did	done
drink	drank	drunk
* drown	drowned	drowned
eat	ate	eaten
fly	flew	flown
freeze	froze	frozen
give	gave	given
go	went	gone
know	knew	known
lend	lent	lent
ring	rang	rung
rise	rose	risen
run	ran	run
see	saw	seen
sing	sang	sung
sit	sat	sat
steal	stole	stolen
swim	swam	swum
take	took	taken
teach	taught	taught
tear	tore	torn
think	thought	thought
throw	threw	thrown
wear	wore	worn
write	wrote	written

SOME ADVICE IN MAKING TENSES

1. If you can say *now, today, at present* before the verb, select the form from Column I.

   Example: Now I *take* French.
   Now they will *write* a letter.
   At present she *swims* well.

2. If you can say *yesterday* before the verb, select the form from Column II.

   Example: Yesterday I *wore* a black tie.
   Yesterday they *swam* at sea.

3. If you can say *frequently* or *often* and one of the helpers (has, have, had, shall have, will have) before the verb, select the form from Column III.

   Example: Often I *have done* good work.
   Frequently they *have stolen* bicycles.

Step 1. Saying Aloud Correct Verb Parts. Many of us do not use the right verb parts because the correct forms sound incorrect to us. That happens simply because we are so used to using the incorrect verb form. Speak aloud each sentence below so that you learn the sound of the correct verb— no matter how strange it sounds to you.

1. We *had drunk* two quarts of beer when the girls arrived.
2. I *rang* the doorbell at three.
3. She *did* her work carefully.
4. They *have* already *begun* their art projects.
5. After the boy *had swum* across the lake, he rested.

Step 2. Correcting Students' Errors. Cross out any incorrect verb part in the sentences below which have been spoken or written by college freshmen. Put the correct verb part in the blank space in the margin.

saw _____ 1. I ~~seen~~ him running away.

_____ 2. They nearly drownded in that huge wave.

_____ 3. Anyone who has drank too much wine knows how I felt that day.

_____ 4. All of us seen them steal the car.

_____ 5. The instructor has gave the assignment very carefully.

_____ 6. My father teached me right from wrong.

_____ 7. He has wore that same coat for a long time.

_____ 8. I thought they brung their own car.

_____ 9. I flown to Washington, D.C., before President Kennedy's assassination.

_____ 10. The balloon bursted with a loud smack.

Step 3. Using *Has* or *Have* with Verbs. You use *has* or *have* with a verb form from Column III if you want to show an action that started sometime in the past but is still continuing.

She *has spoken* for five minutes.

[She began in the past but
is still speaking now.]

If the action began in the past and ended in the past, use the past tense (Column II verb form).

She *spoke* for five minutes.

[She began in the past,
but ended before now.]

For each infinitive in parentheses, write the correct form of the verb in the blank space in the margin.

Hint: If *has, have, had, will have* or *shall have* appears before the verb, pick the form from Column III on p. 355.

drowned   1. One child had (*to drown*) before the lifeguard arrived.

_____   2. Before the next month, the chairman will have (*to choose*) his assistants.

_____   3. I (*to see*) him in front of the movie house.

_____   4. They (*to know*) each other from college days.

_____   5. She (*to bring*) her lunch to work every Tuesday.

_____   6. They had (*to come*) to the meeting before the speaker arrived.

_____   7. The policeman will have (*to give*) twenty parking tickets by tomorrow.

_____   8. All of us (*to give*) at the office.

_____   9. Barbara and Melissa have (*to take*) a long walk to the shopping center.

_____ 10. One thin buzzard (*to fly*) off a dying tree.

Step 4. More Practice. Change the infinitive in parentheses so that the verb is correct. Write the correct verb in the blank space in each sentence.

Hint: You will need *have* or *has* as a helper in four sentences.

(to fly)   1. The 707 _*flew*_ to New York.

(to fly)   2. Every day this week the 707 _____ to New York.

(to be)   3. Steven _____ very late each day.

(to freeze)   4. Every Christmas Eve for six years now the lake _____ .

(to swim)   5. For the past thirty minutes Kathy _____ back and forth across the lake.

(to break)   6. At that second the tiny birch tree _____ in the wind.

Step 5. Using *Had* as Helper.   If a sentence expresses two actions in the past and one of the actions came before the other, the verb that names the earlier action needs *had* as a helper.

The man thought that he *had seen* a ghost.
    [This is one ↗   ↖[This past action came
    past action.]   before the man had the
                              thought.]

   Complete each sentence below by using *had* with the correct form of the verb in parentheses and any other words you need to complete the thought. Study the example.

(to come)   1. Yesterday we heard that you *had come late to class* .

(to bring)   2. We ate the peaches you _____ .

(to begin)   3. Steven rang the doorbell just after the party _____

_____ .

(to see)   4. We saw Harriet after we _____

_____ .

(to ring)   5. Before the priest arrived, the old church bell _____

_____ .

Step 6. *Will Have, Shall Have* with Verbs.   Use *will have* or *shall have* with a verb part if you want to show that an action will be finished before some definite time in the future.

By tonight, I *will have made* twelve telephone calls.

Hint: In formal writing *shall* is used only with *I* and *we*. *Will* is used with any subject.

Use each of these word groups in a sentence of your own.

I shall have seen   I will have done
We will have taken   They will have sat

1. _____

2. _____

3. _____

4. _____

Shifting Tenses

When you write, be careful not to switch back and forth from present to past tense. If you are telling about an event that occurred in the past, use the past tense. Look at this sentence:

I saw my friend Thomas and he asks me, "Where are you going?"

Saw is a past-tense verb.

Asks is a present-tense verb and should be replaced by *asked,* a past-tense verb.

Are is not incorrect, even though it is in the present tense, because the writer is quoting someone's exact words. The correct sentence would be:

I saw my friend Thomas and he asked (not asks!) me, "Where are you going?"

Step 1. Tense Shifts. Correct the tense shifts in each sentence below. Write the verbs correctly in the spaces in the margin. Only one sentence is correct.

_____ 1. When I waved to him over there he turns his back and

_____   goes into the house.

_____ 2. I asked for a Coke so he brings me one with too much

_____   ice. But I drink it anyway.

_____ 3. I told him the bench was wet, but he sits down without

_____   listening and then gives a loud yell of anger.

_____ 4. Every Sunday she eats an ice-cream cone and then weighs
                 herself.

Step 2. Using the Past Tense. In every blank space below, write the past tense correctly. The verb you need is in the parentheses.

1. The professor (see) _____ that his students (write) _____ answers poorly.

2. When Mr. Jones (give) _____ a party, his daughter (sing) _____ several songs.

3. The crops (freeze) _____, and the farmers (bring) _____ a special adviser in from Washington.

Some Confusing Verbs

Lie, Lay

The words *lie* and *lay* are two different verbs.

To lie means *to rest or recline.*
To lay means *to put or place something.*

Here are the three main parts of *to lie* and the tenses that are made from them.

lie	lay	lain

lie	lay	lain
I lie in bed.	He lay down for a nap.	The car has lain in the driveway.
The book lies there un- noticed.	She lay there quietly.	She had lain in bed for hours before the doc- tor arrived.
Tomorrow we will lie in the grass.		

Hint: The past tense of *to lie* is the same as the present tense of *to lay.* That is where much of the confusion comes from.

The *-ing* form of *to lie* is *lying.*

The flowers *are lying* on the table.

A cat *is lying* in the yard.

Here are the three main parts of *to lay* and the tenses that are made from them.

lay	laid	laid
I lay the pencil on the desk.	The cowboy laid his gun on the bar.	She should have laid the carpet on the hallway floor.
The child usually lays his head on a small pillow.		After Lynn had laid out the map, directions were easier to follow.

Hint: There must always appear after the word *lay* or any of its forms the thing that is being put somewhere.

The *-ing* form of *to lay* is *laying.*

He *was laying* out his clothes on the bed.

Step 1. Using *Lie* and *Lay*.   Follow directions.

1. Write a sentence using the words *he lies* to mean *he rests.* _____

   _____

2. Write a sentence in which you use *lay* to mean *put* or *place.* _____

   _____

3. Use *has lain* correctly in a sentence. _____

   _____

4. Use in a sentence the word *lay* so it means *rested* or *reclined.* ————

———————————————————————————————————

5. Use the word *laid* in a sentence so that it means *put* or *placed.* ——————

———————————————————————————————————

6. Use the words *has laid* correctly in a sentence. ——————————————

———————————————————————————————————

7. Use *lying* to mean *resting* in a sentence. ————————————————

———————————————————————————————————

8. Write a sentence in which you use the word *laying* correctly. ————

———————————————————————————————————

Rise and *Raise*

Rise means *get up or go up.*
Raise means *lift up.*

Hint: There must always appear after the word *raise* or any of its forms the thing that is actually being raised.

Here are the main parts and the tenses of *to raise.*

raise	raised	raised
[thing being raised]		
He raises his hand.	She raised our scores.	He has raised enough
I raise the flag at dawn.	[thing being raised]	money to start a
	[thing being raised]	business.

-ing form: raising

   The farmer was raising beans.

Here are the main parts and some of the tenses of *to rise.*

rise	rose	risen
Everyone rises when the judge enters.	He rose to shake our hands.	The sun has risen earlier than usual.
I will rise when he speaks.		

-ing form: rising

   We were just *rising* to leave.

Step 2. *Raise* and *Rise:* Which Is Right?   Pick out the correct word from parentheses and write it in the blank space.

_____ 1. The smoke (rose, raised) through the chimney.

_____ 2. No one had (risen, raised) his hand to ask a question.

_____ 3. Six young girls had (risen, raised) before the important
writer rushed into the room.

_____ 4. By next month, Mr. Crawford will have (raised, risen)
two acres of corn.

_____ 5. The boy (raises, rises) these kinds of questions each
morning.

Sit and *Set*

Sit means *to take a seat.*

sit	sat	sat
I sit in the last row. She sits quietly.	They sat in the office.	The dog has sat there without moving. She had sat down before they asked her to.

Set means *to place* or *to put.*

Hint: There must always appear after the word *set* the thing that is being put somewhere.

set	set	set
[thing being put somewhere] I set my dictionary where I can reach it easily.	Yesterday she set her coat in the closet. [thing being put somewhere]	By the time she had set the pot on the stove, [thing being put somewhere] we were not hungry anymore.

Step 3. Completing Sentences with *Sit* or *Set*. Write the correct form of *sit* or *set* in the blank space below.

1. Just as you had _____ down, the president arrived.

2. Just as you had _____ the book down, someone else asked for it.

3. Why will they not just _____ quietly for a while?

4. If she _____ the flowers so near the edge of the garden, where

   will we _____ in the afternoons?

Leave and *Let*

To let means *to allow.*
To leave means *to go away from.*

Let me speak to you.   We want *to leave* early.
                    not
Leave me speak to you.

Stay or *Stand*

To *stay* means *to remain.*
To *stand* means *to be in a straight up-and-down position.*

I *stayed* in bed with a cold.
                not
I *stood* in bed with a cold.
I should have *stayed* home.
                not
I should have *stood* home.

Can or *May*

Can asks whether or not you are able to do something.
May asks whether or not you will get permission to do something.

Can I drive the car? (This question means: Do I have the ability to drive the car?)
May I drive the car? (This question means: Will you give me permission to drive the car?)

Step 4. *Leave, Let; Stay, Stand; Can, May.* Circle the correct word in parentheses:

1. If you (leave, let) me go early I will visit my aunt in the hospital.
2. I (stood, stayed) in the house waiting for your call.
3. "(Can, May) I (leave, let) my car on this side of the street?"
4. She (stood, stayed) in bed with a cold for a week.

WRITING THE ESSAY

From all your associations with people, select one individual who has had a deep and important effect on your life—a relative, a friend, an acquaintance—and write a four-paragraph essay in which you explore this effect. Make your proposal sentence state clearly just what you will attempt to illustrate about the person: pp. 277–280 will refresh your mind about writing good introductions.

Although you may choose any suitable method of development for each of the *body* paragraphs (paragraphs 2 and 3, that is) the most forceful presentation will probably be one dramatic, full, expanded moment in each paragraph. For example, if you are trying to show the kindness of someone close to you, tell in each body paragraph one specific instance which illustrates this kindness. If you want to show the hate or the love you have for someone, show in each paragraph a concrete event which will make the reader love or hate the person you are writing about. Perhaps, you will want to show how your feelings toward someone you know changed, or how someone you know can show opposite qualities: in that case, compare and contrast two specific moments which show the reader these opposite qualities.

But if you do not want to use narration—the story-telling device—you have a number of other possibilities for developing paragraphs. Perhaps, you will want to define with concrete word pictures some abstract word (pp. 245–247); or you might want to use several instances to explore one specific aspect of the personality of someone close to you (pp. 110–111). You might want to use one of many devices of comparison and contrast within one paragraph: one of the four patterns explained on pp. 134–144; the analogy (pp. 144–148); or the mood sketch.

In any case, make sure that each paragraph expands through clear details one aspect of your topic (if you use narration, of course, each *moment* represents another aspect of your topic). The four crucial questions you ask yourself before you write (see p. 329) will help you pinpoint the kinds of details you will need to use. You might repeat your favorite author's exact words; you might say in your own words what you remember some psychologist said on television; you might even use numbers, percentages, or case studies to illustrate your idea on the subject you have chosen. Several topics for you to consider appear after the student sample.

Learning from Other Students

Before you begin to write your essay on character, read the selection below. Notice how Miss Pomerantz successfully uses two specific moments to illustrate her proposal. After you finish reading "Some Disappointments," write briefly the answers to questions that appear below it.

Some Disappointments

My girl friends always envied the fact that I had an older brother, and until about two years ago, their envy was understandable. Gary taught me everything about life until I was old enough to learn for myself. Having a brother three years older had its little advantages. I not only knew all about baseball, but I could also name every single New York Yankee on the team and every team in both leagues. Gary forced me to watch "boy" TV programs like *Combat* and *Battleground*, but now I switch on such shows myself without a second thought. It was Gary who tried to stop me from reading girlish romance magazines so that I could read more important literature. And he tried to get me to like classical music, although I stuck with the Beatles. As I grew older I followed in the path he laid for me, but Gary suddenly changed. I can remember two distinct moments when my faith in my brother was shattered—when I discovered that he was not the very special person I thought him to be, but instead, someone quite ordinary.

I realized the change in Gary one winter Saturday when I rushed excitedly into his room to talk about *The Red Badge of Courage,* a book I had just read and loved. "Let me read you this part," I shouted. "You'll just love it." Gary lay on the wrinkled sheets of his bed, eyes shut, dreamily humming along with the Laura Nyro song drifting from the radio. "I'm not interested," he replied, returning to his dreamy thoughts about the lyrics. Those three words stung me deeply and I felt an angry reply jump to my lips. Instead I tried to look away from Gary, to seek comfort in the familiar surroundings of his room. But this depressed me. Musty old newspapers sat scattered on the bare floor. One dim bulb threw shadows on the pale walls and in the dark corners. Rows and rows of books lay forgotten on the scratched mahogany shelves, gathering dust. A white shirt with rolled-up sleeves hung on the closet doorknob; one black sock stretched from under the bed. A poster of Uncle Sam stared down from the wall, pointing his finger and telling me he wanted me for the United States Army. When I saw Gary's spotless radio and his beloved collection of "soul" records, I exploded. "You're never interested in good books anymore. You're all wrapped up in yourself. You listen to that creepy jazz all the time and if you read the back of a cereal box, that's your reading for the day. What's wrong, Gary?" With his eyes still closed and a sly smile crossing his face, he said, "I've seen the light." I fled from the room, wondering if I had dreamed what had just occurred. Was that stranger in there my brother?

That moment in Gary's room was mild, though, when compared to the changes I saw in his temper. I will never forget the way he looked one weekend evening as he stalked to the front door on his way out. He wore a blue-denim shirt unbuttoned halfway down his chest, revealing a clump of black hair; faded bell-bottomed jeans clinging tightly to his hips; a green army jacket, worn out at the elbows. Gary's blonde hair was uncombed and his moustache pointed downwards, giving him the look of the bad guy in an old western. Those warm gray eyes that once encouraged and helped me now looked confused and distant and cold. "Where are you going so late?" my mother called from the kitchen above the clatter of dishes. "Get off my back!" he snapped. "I'm twenty years old, and if I want to stay out all night, I will." I stood rooted to the floor, shocked at his outbreak. Through the door, out of the house, down the front porch steps Gary stormed. The sharp smell of after shave lotion still hung about the room. As the door slammed, my mother rushed into the living room. We looked helplessly at each other. "What's happened to him?" she moaned. "It wasn't easy raising two children all alone after your father died. Gary should have become the head of the family and look what's become of him! Is it my fault?" Wishing desperately to relieve her, I could only remain silent. There have been many times since when my mother and I have stood shocked at one of Gary's outbursts, unable to say a word and wondering why this was happening.

I often wonder why Gary had to change so drastically; I was very fond of him the way he was. As a child I had a brother unlike any others, but now he is just like anyone else who thinks that bad language and sloppiness will cure the ills of society. Gary has also announced to my mother—who turned sick and cried when she heard it—that he no longer believes in God. I have tried to tell him during these past few years that his way will not work, but as usual, he does not listen. Strangely enough, however, even with my brother's awful new behavior, he is still helping me. Gary has shown me that his course in life is wrong and that mine is better and more effective. He sees all the ugliness in life, but I look for and find beauty. In his denial of God, I strengthen my own faith. I see his restlessness and I seek a purpose.

—Barbara Pomerantz

1. Based upon the proposal sentence, what does Miss Pomerantz set out to illustrate? _____

_____

2. What two moments does she use to support her proposal? _____

_____

3. Which picture of Gary do you find easiest to see? _____

_____

4. Which quotation sentence is most realistic? _____

_____

5. What key words in the first sentence of paragraph 2 repeat the main idea of the proposal? _____

_____

6. Circle the part of the first sentence of paragraph 3 that refers back to the idea of paragraph 2. Underline the part of the first sentence of paragraph 3 that introduces the new idea of the paragraph.

REVEALING CHARACTER IN YOUR ESSAY: WHAT TO SHOOT FOR

1. Select a person who means a great deal to you in your life, someone who has affected you strongly. If your material is very private, ask your teacher not to mention your name if he reads your theme to the class.
2. Write a proposal sentence that permits you to explore two aspects of this person you wish to write about. Then, write an introduction to go before the proposal. Study pp. 277–282 for ideas on introductions.
3. If you choose to expand one moment in each paragraph, make sure that you mention time and place and that you fill in some details of the setting. Notice how Miss Pomerantz describes Gary's room.
4. Use details that are based in sensory language. Give the reader the sights, the colors, the sounds, and the smells of the moment. Make sure that your essay includes a description of your subject in action.
5. Check your transitions carefully, especially at the opening of paragraphs 2 and 3.
6. Use a line or two of spoken details. Miss Pomerantz writes: "With his eyes still closed and a sly smile crossing his face, he said, 'I've seen the light.'" See pp. 49–51 for hints on expressive quotation sentences.

> 7. Use a variety of sentence openers. Try to write a sentence like one of those explained in this chapter on pp. 350–352.
> 8. Use some of the new vocabulary explained on pp. 346–348.
> 9. Check your Theme Progress Sheet for the errors you have made in your last few papers. Revise your essay to eliminate errors including those you may have made in using verbs.
> 10. Write a conclusion. Look ahead to pp. 423–427 if you have trouble.

Some Essay Titles for You to Consider

Here are some titles which may suggest essay topics for you.

1. Love Means Trouble
2. My Sister's Illness
3. Learning about Friendship
4. My Mother's Sacrifice
5. Why I Hate My Cousin
6. A Younger Brother
7. My Father's Return
8. We Don't Get Along
9. A Friend Who Turned against Me
10. Grandmother: A Burden
11. My Mother's Shame
12. A Remarkable Neighbor

Moments and People from the Printed Page: an Essay on a Book

The pages of novels, biographies, and other forms of nonfiction are rich in unforgettable characters who make exciting topics for essay reports. As you read a book of your own choosing (some suggestions appear in Step 1 below and your instructor will offer some others), keep alert for *two* dramatic moments that illustrate something significant about some memorable character in your book. Each moment can be effectively expanded in a body paragraph as you try to illustrate your proposal. Study the guidelines below and the student model on pp. 368–369 before you write.

ESSAY GUIDELINES FOR BOOK CHARACTERS

1. Decide on some important personality trait of the hero in your book. Is he *brave, mean, thoughtless, loving, pitiful?* Write a proposal sentence which indicates that personality trait.
2. Let each body paragraph relate one specific moment which illustrates from the book the impression you stated in the proposal sentence.
3. Select moments that are important in the growth and development of the hero. A moment which focuses on the hero in the midst of a crisis or a turning point (especially where some important decision must be made and acted upon) is especially emphatic for the reader.

---

4. Make the sounds and colors and smells of each moment alive. Show the actions of the character. What is he doing? What is he thinking about? What is he saying?
5. Follow the suggestions on pp. 277–282 for writing good introductions: be sure also to include the author's name and the title of the book in your first paragraph.
6. Make sure that you use in your essay a quotation right from the book. This may be a sentence or two that describes an action or something said by one of the characters.

Step 1. Reading an Essay Sample. In the student essay below, notice how the two body paragraphs effectively support the proposal sentence. After you finish reading Miss Dubin's theme on *My Antonia,* write the answers to the questions.

Antonia's Strength

History books are filled with words of praise for the pioneers who settled the West. But the struggle with personal hardships by the courageous families who cleared Nebraska and Kansas come to life in Willa Cather's *My Antonia.* In the novel the heroine, Antonia Shimerda, faces familial hardships with unusual strength.

She shows it first after her father's suicide. A girl in her early teens, Antonia loved her father deeply. When Jim Burden, the narrator of the novel, arrives at the house for the burial, Antonia rushes out to him and sobs, her heart almost breaking. But at the funeral she is much more controlled. Her dead father lies in the coffin with his knees drawn up. "His body was draped in a black shawl," writes Cather, "and his head was bandaged in white muslin, like a mummy's; one of his long, shapely hands lay out on the black cloth; that was all one could see of him." Yet Antonia, in spite of that awful figure, follows her mother up to the coffin and makes the sign of the cross on the bandaged head of her dead father. When Antonia's mother, a woman with little maternal softness, pushes her youngest daughter Yulka up to the body, the child cries wildly. After a neighbor insists that the child not touch the body, it is Antonia who puts her arms around the younger girl and holds her close. I'll never forget the warmth of that scene: Antonia, herself so sad, comforting her little sister as a fine, icy Nebraska snow falls outside.

That quiet moment of courage Antonia matches later on with physical strength. On an April afternoon after Mr. Shimerda's death, Jim Burden rides out to the house; he has not seen Antonia for three months. When he spots her as the sun drops low, he watches her drive a team of horses up to the windmill. She wears her father's boots, his old fur cap, and an outgrown cotton dress with sleeves rolled up. Antonia has taken upon herself to work the fields in her father's absence. Although she cries briefly at not being able to attend the sod schoolhouse, she states in her broken English, "I ain't got time to learn. I can work like mans now. . . . School is all right for little boys. I help make this land one good farm." Jim is disappointed at her mannish ways: she yawns at the table, eats noisily like a man, and boasts often of her strength and the chores she can perform. But this is just an outgrowth of what is really strength of character. To accept the challenge of the soil as a man in her father's place is certainly an act of courage.

Antonia's courage should be a lesson for women of today. Living the soft life, I and many of my contemporaries complain about the slightest trouble. We complain when the washing machine is broken or when we have to walk to the bus. We complain if we have to wash dishes by hand or if the garbage barrels need pushing out to the street. Antonia Shimerda would look these minor inconveniences in the eye and say, "I can work like mans now."

—Phyllis Dubin

1. What does the proposal sentence announce as the purpose of the essay?

   _____

   _____

2. What images of action does Miss Dubin show? _____

   _____

3. What moments do the body paragraphs illustrate? _____

   _____

4. Which selection from the book itself do you find most impressive?

   _____

   _____

OTHER APPROACHES TO YOUR BOOK ESSAY ON CHARACTER

Compare and contrast two characters with different traits, showing a dramatic moment to illustrate each personality.

Show how the hero changes by relating two different instances, one from an early part of the book and one from a later part.

Show how the hero responds to a moment of crisis and then show how a moment in your own life was similar to or different from the hero's. Or, show how you would have behaved in the hero's place.

Show how a moment in a book compared with the same moment in a movie about the book.

Suggested Books about Unforgettable People

The books below offer exciting portraits of people. Select one of these for your essay; or, choose a book of your own.

The 42nd Parallel. John Dos Passos. People caught in the strain of an America approaching World War I. The unusual style of this book makes it a landmark.

Giants in the Earth. O. E. Rölvaag. A Scandinavian family pioneers the old West: a wife who hates the land and a husband who glories in it.

The Old Man and the Sea. Ernest Hemingway. An old fisherman and a young boy build a relationship.

The Red Badge of Courage. Stephen Crane. The Civil War and a young volunteer meet head on.

The Grapes of Wrath. John Steinbeck. An Oklahoma family pushes to California for a better life but finds only bitterness.

Not Without Laughter. Langston Hughes. A black boy grows to manhood in the South.

Maggie, A Girl of the Streets. Stephen Crane. What effects poverty has on the human spirit.

Fire Sermon. Wright Morris. A young orphan learns to live with his overpowering grandfather.

The Mayor of Casterbridge. Thomas Hardy. A young man in a drunken moment sells his wife. She returns to him twenty years after.

Of Human Bondage. Somerset Maugham. Philip Carey and his growth through a bitter boyhood; he is always aware of his club foot.

Lord Jim. Joseph Conrad. A man who thinks of himself as a hero saves his own life at sea at the cost of others' lives under him.

Death Comes for the Archbishop. Willa Cather. A novel about a bishop and a priest in pioneer America.

All Quiet on the Western Front. Erich Remarque. A painful book about a young German during World War I.

THE PROFESSIONALS SPEAK

The story below develops through details of one specific moment the character of both the narrator and someone he meets in the park. Write the answers to the questions that appear after the story.

SOME WORDS TO KNOW BEFORE YOU READ

togs: clothing
Perstando Et Praestando Utilitati: Latin for Persevering and Excelling in Practicality

The Stick Up

I felt good. I think the park had something to do with it. Trees, grass, bushes—everything in brand-new togs of shining green. The warm yellow sunlight sifting down through the trees, making my face feel alive and healthy and casting shadows on the paved walks and the unpaved walks and the wooden benches. Slight breezes tickling my nostrils, caressing my face, bringing with them a good clean odor of things new and live and dripping with greenness. Such a good feeling made me uneasy.

The park breathing with people, old and young. Playing checkers and chess, listening to portable radios—the Dodgers leading the Giants. I walked to the end of the park and stood near the wading pool where the water spurted skyward.

Little children in their underpants, splashing the water and pretending to swim, and throwing water at each other and yelling and shouting in wild childish happiness. One Negro child with a soft dark face and big brown eyes pretended to enjoy herself, but her big black eyes gave her away—anxious and uneasy. As if she were not sure that all of a sudden the other children would not turn on her and bite her like a bunch of mad dogs. I knew that feeling—even now. Barefoot women sat round the pool watching the children, reading books, trying to get brown without the expense of a Florida vacation. A little blonde-headed girl got smacked in the face and ran bawling to her black-haired mother. A double-decker Fifth Avenue bus passed to the east, with curious passengers looking from the top deck. The tall buildings of New York University looked over and down upon a noisy humanity playing in the park. *Perstando Et Praestando Utilitati—*

The kids were having loads of fun and it made me think back. I substituted a country woods for the beautiful city park. I made believe the wading pool was the swimming hole on old man Gibson's forbidden grounds. And something turned over and over in my stomach and ran like a chill through the length of my body, leaving a funny taste in my mouth. I took a sudden trip into the past. Meeting kids I had known many years ago, as if they had remained kids and had never grown up. My face tight and full now as I swallowed a mouthful of cool green air. It was the first time I had been homesick in many years. Standing there trying to recall names, faces and incidents. After a moment I shrugged it off. I could never really be homesick for the country woods and the swimming holes of Georgia. Give me the city— the up-north city.

I turned and started walking back through the park, passing women, young and old, blond and brunette, and black and brown and light brown in white uniforms, pushing various types of baby carriages. I had almost reached the other end of the park, when a big lumbering giant of a white man came toward me. I tried to walk out of his way, but he maneuvered into my path and grabbed me by the shoulders. He was unshaven, his clothes were filthy and he reeked of rot-gut whiskey and days and nights without soap and water. He towered over me and coughed in my face and said in a deep rasping voice—"This is a stick up!"

I must have looked silly and startled. What was he up to, in broad open daylight? Oh—no—he must be kidding. And yet, crazier things happen every day in this crazy world of New York City. Especially in the Village.

He jabbed his big forefinger into my side, causing me to wince. Then he nudged me playfully and said, "I'm only kidding, buddy. But cheesuz christmas, I do need just four more cents for the price of a drink. How about it, professor? It's just four lousy cents. Didn't hardly take me no time at all to hustle up the rest of it this morning, but seems to me I just can't get this last four cents don't care how hard I try. It's a goddamn shame!"

I made a show of feeling in my pockets. I had no loose change and knew it. I wanted to say, Well, you sure won't get it from me, but I said instead, "Gosh, I don't have it. I'm sorry."

I started to walk away from him. He put his big arms around me, surrounding me with his foul odor. His shirt was dirty and greasy, smelled like sour food and whiskey vomit. A deep gash started near his right eye and beat a trail down into his mouth. An awful cloud came between me and the springtime, blotting out the breeze, the sunshine, the freshness that had been everywhere.

"Look, buddy, I ain't no ordinary bum you meet on the street. I want you to know that. I'm just down on my luck—see?"

I wanted to shrug my shoulders, wanted to say, I don't give a damn what you are! Through the years I had built up a resistance against people like him, and I thought I was foolproof. He rambled on, "I know—you—you think I'm just one of them everyday bums, but it isn't so. I'm just as educated as the next feller. But I know what you think though. I—"

My nostrils quivered, my neck gathered sweat. I wanted to be away from him. "You don't know what I think!"

He leaned heavily on my shoulder. My body sagged under his enormous weight. My knees buckled. "You don't have to be that way, mate. Just because a feller is down on his luck. Can't never tell when you'll need a favor yourself. Listen, I'm an educated man. Look, I used to be a business man too."

I kept thinking angrily to myself, of all the people in the park, most of them white, why did he single me out? It wasn't the first time a thing like this had happened. Just a week before I was on the subway and a white drunk got on at Thirty-fourth Street. He looked around for a seat and there were plenty available next to other people. But he finally spied me, the only Negro in the half-empty car, and he came and sat down beside me, choosing me to be the benefactor of his infinite wisdom and his great liberal philosophy and his bad-liquored breath.

I tried to pull away from this one in the park but his huge hand held me by the shoulder. With his other hand he fumbled in his shirt pocket, then in the back pocket of his trousers. He fished out a dirty ragged snapshot. "Look," he said, "that's me and my family. I used to be a business man out west. Had a good business too. Yes indeed."

It would have been comical had it not been so tragic, the way pride gleamed in his eyes as he gazed at the picture. I suppose it was he, although you had to stare at it hard and stretch your imagination. He looked like a million dollars, posing with a wife and two fine-looking children. I began to wonder what had happened to him along the way—what had become of his family—then caught myself going soft. Oh—no—none of that sentimental stuff. I glanced at my watch deliberately. "Look, my friend," I said, "I've got—"

His eyes were like red flint marbles. He coughed like he would strangle to death and directly into my face. My entire being came up in revolt against everything about him, but still he was a human being, and he might have gotten his four cents, maybe more, if he hadn't made his next pitch the way he did.

"Look, professor, I don't think I'm any better than you or anybody else. I want you to know that. We're all fighting together against them goddamn gooks in Viet Nam, ain't we? You look like an intelligent young man. I'm an educa—How about it, professor? Just four little old lousy cents—"

All of my inner resentment pushed outward as I squirmed and wrested myself angrily from his hold. "I've got to go! Goddamnit—I don't have any four cents for you!"

I started walking away from him toward the street corner trembling with anger, but uplifted by the fresh air rushing into my entire body. I stood at the intersection waiting for the light to change. Something made me turn and look for the big man. I saw him lumbering toward me again. My body became tense. A flock of cars were passing. Why in the hell didn't the light change to green? But then he stopped and sat down heavily on the last bench in the park. Amid a fit of coughing I heard him mumble—"Damn. This is getting to be a helluva country, when you can't chisel four lousy pennies offa prosperous-looking nigger!"

    My hands clenched unconsciously. I smiled with a bitter taste in my mouth. The light changed to green. I started across the street.

—John Oliver Killens

1. Why does the narrator say he feels "uneasy" in the first paragraph?

   _____

2. What does his reaction to the Negro child (paragraph 3) tell you about his own personality? _____

   _____

3. What details give you the best picture of the "big lumbering giant of a white man"? _____

   _____

4. What does the man want? How does he try to work on the narrator's sympathies? _____

   _____

5. How do the narrator and the man he meets differ in their position in society? _____

   _____

6. Why do you think the narrator does not want to give what the drunkard asks for? _____

   _____

7. What other important difference is there between the two men? Did you realize this difference before the very obvious statement of it by the drunk at the end of the story? Where? _____

   _____

8. The narrator, early in the story, says "Give me the city—the up-north city." After the incident do you think he would still choose the city over his early life in Georgia? Why? _____

   _____

9. Write one sentence in which you tell what you think is the main idea of this short story. _____

_____

REACHING HIGHER

Step 1. Pictures of Expressive Features. Decide which feature of the human body you think best expresses emotion or personality — the eyes, the hands, the head, the nose, the lips. Then, from pictures in newspapers and magazines, cut out and mount a number of these features in different aspects of expression. When you show your mounted selections to the class, ask students to identify the particular emotion or personality each picture presents. Look at the sample "Eyes," at the start of Chapter 6.

Step 2. Putting Voices on Record. The human voice is a clue to a person's background and character. Using a tape recorder, ask five different people to speak the same sentence into the microphone. (You can use any sentence you like — make up one or take it from a book.) Play the tape back to your class to see how other students describe the quality of the voices and the nature of the people who speak.

Or, pick some controversial topic (legalizing marijuana, welfare, government controls in business, busing for balanced integration) and let five different people speak out for two or three minutes each. Then see what students in the class can determine about the speakers.

Step 3. Remembering Earlier Skills. This paragraph contains a number of errors in capitalization and commas. Make all changes necessary.

A Portrait

All eyes focusing upon her as she rose from her seat Beth Ann cautiously stepped up to the brown desk in front of the Classroom to serve as subject for our theme in Freshman Composition in our room in ingersoll hall. A nervous smile passed across her whte teeth. Immediately she released a quiet crack of laughter. The teacher who sat at a desk in the back of the room prompted Beth Ann to speak. When she finally managed to blurt out several words i noticed the active movements of her hands. Someone asked "do you like chinese food?" In answering Beth Ann acted out a story of her chinese friend and a memorable tale about almost eating a Turtle last Summer. Her hands floated up and down and waved back and forth as she related this experience with eastern food. Long slender fingers capped by white nails glittered in the february sun; and as she spoke of her boyfriend these fingers wound around each other hinting at the closeness between her and Greg an engineering student at pace college in new york. When she spoke of her great love for dancing Beth Ann's eyes widened. "In dancing you must use your body as a paintbrush" She said. But in speaking Beth uses her hands and fingers as paintbrushes. These hands show everyone her confidence in herself.

chapter 10
SPOTLIGHT ON THE JOB WORLD

INTRODUCTION

Brass Spittoons

Clean the spittoons, boy.
    Detroit,
    Chicago,
    Atlantic City,
    Palm Beach.
Clean the spittoons.
The steam in hotel kitchens,
And the smoke in hotel lobbies,
And the slime in hotel spittoons:
Part of my life.
    Hey, boy!
    A nickel,
    A dime,
    A dollar,
Two dollars a day.
    Hey, boy!
    A nickel,
    A dime,
    A dollar,
    Two dollars
Buys shoes for the baby.
House rent to pay.
Church on Sunday.
    My God!

Babies and church
and women and Sunday
all mixed up with dimes and
dollars and clean spittoons
and house rent to pay.
    Hey, boy!

A bright bowl of brass is beautiful to the Lord.
Bright polished brass like the cymbals
Of King David's dancers,
Like the wine cups of Solomon.
    Hey, boy!
A clean spittoon on the altar of the Lord.
A clean bright spittoon all newly polished,—
At least I can offer that.
    Com'mere, boy!
              —Langston Hughes

Like the black workman in "Brass Spittoons," a good part of your life—for better or for worse—will go to your job. Many of you are well aware of the importance, therefore, of choosing your work carefully so that your life is meaningful and you have more than nickels and dimes and "Hey, boy!"

to face up to. Your college years may provide a significant job-training experience, offering you the courses that teach you specific skills you can effectively use (in one way or another) on your job. How well your school actually does this, of course, depends upon the college you attend and the kind of curriculum you choose.

However, few people disagree that an even more valuable experience comes from the jobs with which you can experiment now before you make some permanent commitment to a career. Pumping gasoline, part-time typing at an insurance office, sales work in a department store—although you may never want these jobs again, what you learn there about "business sense," about people and how to relate to them, about employers and their ways will all serve you well as you take up your life's work, whatever that may be. Many colleges, realizing that on-the-job experience makes up an important part of learning, now offer work-study programs so students add to their intellectual growth under the supervision of the college. And the need and desire for part-time jobs on and around the campus still place a great demand on the college placement office.

This theme assignment asks you to explore your views of and experience with the job market. You will have a chance to share some experiences you have already had as a worker and to learn what other people feel about working and its place in a freshman's life. You will study an effective means of applying for a job and a method of presenting directions that is clear and interesting.

VOCABULARY

Some Words for the Business Scene

Step 1. Meanings from Context.   Try to use clues in the sentence to determine the meanings of the words that appear in italics. Write your definition in the space provided; then check Appendix A to see if you are correct.

1. When a business is sold, some of the purchase money is held in *escrow* by a third party; in that way the seller does not get all his money until the buyer has a chance to see that all terms of the agreement are fulfilled.

   escrow means _____

2. The letters from Mr. Green and several other *correspondents* proved the success of the new product.

   correspondent means _____

3. So many *liabilities* meant one thing to the president of the company: he would have to take money from his own personal account in order to pay what he owed.

   liabilities means _____

4. It is not the slow-moving and lazy man who achieves in business, but rather the *dynamo.*

   dynamo means _____

5. Neither a policy of very active government control in business nor a policy of *laissez-faire* will end the depression; probably a path somewhere in the middle will best succeed.

   laissez-faire means _____

6. The modern day *entrepreneur*—anyone who boldly undertakes a business venture—must often make enemies on his way to success.

   entrepreneur means _____

7. Several thousand dollars worth of bonds, a large holding of land in Arizona, a million-dollar building in Trenton: these *assets* give the Marion family a leading voice in the business community.

   assets means _____

8. If credit companies ask for *collateral* before granting a loan, it means they want something to confirm payment.

   collateral means _____

9. Just what an employee brings forth on the job, his *productivity*, is what often determines his future with the company.

   productivity means _____

10. The company's *insolvency* shocked everyone; but the notice of bankruptcy in the papers did not lie.

    insolvency means _____

Words for the Job Situation

Step 2. Checking Definitions. Write in the blank spaces definitions for the words listed below. Use your dictionary for those you do not know; then look at Appendix A to see if you are correct.

What Employers Look For in Workers:

initiative _____

probity _____

promptitude _____

compliance _____

assiduity _____

What Workers Look For in Employers:

indulgence _____

amity _____

generosity _____

inspiration _____

compassion _____

Step 3. A Dialogue with New Vocabulary. Read the sentences below that employer or employee might speak and from the new vocabulary select the word you think describes the missing character trait each complains about.

1. *Employer:* Whatever I ask him to do, he refuses. He never acts in accordance with my wishes, showing no _____.
Employee: Perhaps if you gave him a raise or a bonus every now and then, showed more _____, he might find it easier to follow directions.

2. *Employer:* That fellow in Department C is not to be trusted. I catch him in a lie very often. He lacks _____.
Employee: Well, if you gave in more to his shortcomings or to the little things he did wrong—showed more _____—then he would not have to lie.

3. *Employer:* I like a worker who sets his own tasks for himself, someone who takes the lead on his own. This is a man with _____.
Employee: It might be easier for your workers to do that if you stimulated them by your own excitement for the work, if you could arouse a strong, positive feeling in them. You ought to be an _____ to your workers.

4. *Employee:* You never understand that I have my problems: my father's grandmother has pneumonia, my wife just left me, my apartment burned last night. When someone has such a hard life, you should show more _____ for him.
Employer: But this is the fifth time you've told me this story as an excuse for coming to work three hours late. How can I show pity if you never show _____.

5. *Employee:* I'll never understand why you display such a feeling of _____ for Smith. If you are not equally friendly to all your workers, don't you think they will be jealous?
Employer: I am naturally friendly to hard workers. Smith's _____ makes me particularly friendly!

Step 4. Job Vocabulary in Different Forms. The word in italics in each sentence is another form of the word from the above vocabulary. Write on the lines what you think the word means in this form; then check your dictionary or Appendix A.

1. A *compassionate* supervisor is rare. _____

2. A woman who works *assiduously* should be denied no promotions.

    _____

3. Mr. Prager is *indulgent* of our need for five minutes longer on our coffee

    breaks. _____

4. The possibility of Christmas bonuses is *inspiring* to employees. _____

    _____

5. When he forces us to *comply* with his new rules, he is bound to arouse

    discontent. _____

BUILDING COMPOSITION SKILLS

Exploring the Topic

Step 1. The Meaning of a Poem. Read "Brass Spittoons" at the start of this chapter. Then in the blank lines provided, write *one sentence* to tell the main point of the poem. Study the two student samples. After you write your own sentence, read it aloud in class and discuss it.

Examples: In "Brass Spittoons," Langston Hughes shows the filth and slime of a black man's job world where only the lowest forms of labor stand open to him.

—Frank Hope

"Brass Spittoons" shows that a workman can feel pride in his achievement even if his job and life have little happiness.

—Roseanne Koenig

Your sentence _____

_____

_____

Step 2. A Short Talk about a Job. Talk for about a minute on a job you had some time in your life or some job you would like to try. Be specific about the nature of the work and your reactions to it. You may want to complete one of the following sentences as a start:

1. One job I always hated was . . .
2. To earn extra money in high school I . . .
3. A job I liked was . . .
4. A boss should never . . .
5. My boss was fair when he . . .
6. Don't ever work as a . . .
7. My job taught me . . .

8. A job that was more fun than work was . . .
9. The worst thing about working is . . .
10. My dream job would be . . .

Step 3. What Makes a Good Job.   Below are listed several qualities people look for in jobs. Number them in their order of importance to you. In the blank lines write a sentence that tells the reason for your number-one choice.

_____ good pay

_____ peace of mind

_____ chance for advancement

_____ good vacations and other benefits

_____ meeting interesting people

_____ personal happiness and satisfaction

_____ responsibility to society

_____ family encouragement

_____ easy work

_____ challenging work

_____ dangerous work

_____

_____

_____

Step 4. Sounds of Work: On Paper and Tape.   Think of some job you have observed often and write on the lines below at least ten sounds you hear on such a job. (Use your own paper if you need more space.) Then, if you can get a tape recorder, take it to your job and record the sounds for ten or fifteen minutes. Read your written list to the class before you play back the sounds you recorded. Which is more complete, your written record or the one that the tape recorder makes? Study Donna Longi's list of sounds on the next page.

_____

_____

_____

_____

Sounds While Baby-sitting

1. hum of the refrigerator
2. creak of footsteps from the apartment upstairs
3. low wail of a Dylan song on the radio
4. scratch as I light a match
5. flip of pages as I read my biology book
6. little Herbert's sneeze in the next room where he sleeps
7. tiny crash of metal as the canary bounces from side to side in his cage
8. faraway ringing of a telephone
9. the whoosh of water from the faucet and the gurgle down the drain when I take a drink
10. Snoops, the dog, snoring quietly beneath the kitchen table

—Donna Longi

The Interview: Gathering Your Own Statistics

Select some aspect of employment that interests you and conduct at least five interviews with people in your community to find out how they feel about this area of work. Your instructor might want the class to break into interview groups where you can ask fellow students some questions. Some general areas you might wish to investigate are:

1. Should freshmen work and go to school at the same time?
2. Should men on welfare be forced to work for the city or state?
3. Are college students good workers?
4. What qualities do people look for in jobs?
5. What jobs do college students like best as they go to school?

THE INTERVIEW: TIPS FOR GOOD TECHNIQUES

1. Write down beforehand several questions relating to the general idea you are investigating. If you chose to interview people about number 1 above, for example, some questions you might have prepared are:
   a. Should freshmen work and go to school at the same time?
   b. What should a college student who needs money do to support himself?
   c. Do you think working interferes with studying?
   d. Aside from financial aid, how else can a job help someone who goes to college?
   e. Are college students too young and inexperienced to take on important work while they are going to school?
2. Good questioning is a real skill. Try to make your questions draw out the answers you want to know.
3. Listen carefully to what people say. Take notes as they speak, eliminating any information that is not important. Be careful to get as much important material as you can as accurately as you can. If someone says "sometimes" or "maybe" make sure that you do not change those remarks into "always" or "definitely."

---

4. Ask everyone the same questions. That gives you a basis for comparing any differences of opinion.

5. Identify some of the people who agree to give information to you. Be specific, especially if you want to quote somebody's exact words. Say "Charles Davidson, a freshman at Fairleigh Dickinson, said . . ." If you want to present your interviewing results in statistical form, you do not need to identify every person you interview. You can say, "Seven out of the ten people I spoke to agreed that . . ."

6. Write down exact quotations where you can. This requires very careful listening and some quick writing on your behalf. But often the interviewee says something so unusual or so important that you want it down exactly as it is said; then when you write up your findings in an essay, you can add liveliness and interest to your own work.

7. If the person you are interviewing is himself important, take down some details of his character and appearance to spark your own presentation of his ideas.

APPLYING FOR A JOB YOU WANT: PREPARING A RÉSUMÉ

When an advertisement for some good job appears in a local paper, the employer often receives hundreds of responses. If you are one of those interested in such a position, you will want to make sure that your response attracts the employer's interest. Your answer should be brief but to the point; and your qualifications should be clearly stated. A convenient method of presenting your qualifications is through a résumé (RĔZ-you-may), which is a statement of your particular accomplishments in summary form. In a résumé, a prospective employer can see at a glance just why you feel he should select you for the job he is offering.

Notice in Darrel Farnsworth's résumé below how information is grouped together for easy reference and how his qualifications as an accountant's assistant are made clear.

RÉSUMÉ

Darrel M. Farnsworth
108 East 93rd Street
Brooklyn, New York 11212
Telephone: DI 8-4859

EDUCATIONAL BACKGROUND: Jefferson High School 1967-1971.
        Diploma 1971. LaGuardia Community College 1971-Present.

HONORS AND AWARDS: Math Department medal.

JOB EXPERIENCE:
    1970-1971   Manager of High School G.O. Store
    1968-1970   Stock boy at Martin's Department Store

EXTRACURRICULAR ACTIVITIES: Junior Basketball Team.
    Senior Class Treasurer.

SPECIAL TRAINING: One-term accounting course in high
    school. Enrolled in accounting program at LaGuardia
    Community College.

REFERENCES:
    Mr. Ronald Durrell
    Instructor of Accounting
    LaGuardia Community College
    Long Island City, N.Y.   11101

    Mr. Martin Cohen
    Chairman, Math Department
    Jefferson High School
    Brooklyn, New York   11207

    Mr. Harvey Wheeler
    Stock Manager
    M and G Department Store
    1830 Broadway
    Brooklyn, New York   11284

HOW TO WRITE YOUR RÉSUMÉ

1. Include your name, address, and telephone number.
2. Sometimes an office will advertise several available positions, so make sure to indicate the job for which you are applying.
3. If you have a specific salary in mind, include it in the résumé.
4. Include honors or awards that show your qualifications for the job you want. Otherwise leave out this part.
5. Include all your job experience. Any job can give you skills which may be helpful in the position you are seeking.
6. Extracurricular activities show your interest in voluntary service and often reflect skills that might be handy on the job. Mr. Farnsworth's work as treasurer of his senior class would help him qualify as an accountant's assistant.
7. Show whatever specific training you have had that makes you eligible for the job.
8. List three references—their names and addresses—so that information about your character and abilities is easy to obtain. Make sure you include people who know you well enough to give a fair evaluation of your character. It is a good idea to ask someone's permission before putting him down as a reference.

Step 1. Writing Your Résumé. Prepare a résumé about yourself on the blank page below. Assume that you want to apply for a job for which you feel well qualified.

RÉSUMÉ

EDUCATIONAL BACKGROUND:

HONORS AND AWARDS:

JOB EXPERIENCE:

EXTRACURRICULAR ACTIVITIES:

SPECIAL TRAINING:

REFERENCES:

APPLYING FOR A JOB YOU WANT: A LETTER OF APPLICATION

The letter that you send along with your résumé should be a brief and sincere attempt to arouse the employer's interest in you. Paragraphs in a business letter are often just three or four sentences long, making the letter easier to read quickly. The first paragraph usually includes a statement about how the job came to your attention and expresses your interest in the position.

The second paragraph mentions briefly the highlights of the résumé which you send along with the letter: if you are not planning to send a résumé, the second paragraph (and the third as well, if you need more space) should indicate all your special qualifications for the job.

Another paragraph can indicate any special conditions you may have to present. If you are not sending a résumé, mention the three references in this paragraph. Another brief paragraph should show your willingness to come for an interview — suggesting a convenient time and a day. Examine Mr. Farnsworth's letter that will accompany his résumé.

```
                                        108 East 93rd Street
                                        Brooklyn, New York  11212
                                        March 3, 1971



Mr. Harry Koster
Chief of Division of Receipts
Comptroller's Office of the City of New York
New York, New York  10007


Dear Mr. Koster:

     I read in the New York Chief yesterday that you
need a part-time accountant's assistant to help in the
processing of city income tax forms.  Because of my
interest in accounting and city government, I think I may
be well qualified to take on the job you are advertising.

     You can tell from my résumé that I have had both
training and experience in the field of accounting.  My
course of study at college is designed to qualify me as
an accountant after graduation.  My interest and skill in
mathematics contribute to my qualifications for this job.
```

My schedule at college now requires me to attend classes late in the afternoon, so for this semester I am available for work from 9 a.m. to 11:30a.m. every day but Wednesday when I can work from 9 a.m. to 11:00 a.m.

I would be happy to come up for an interview any morning during the week. I think you will find me an eager and cooperative worker.

Very truly yours,

Darrel M. Farnsworth

Darrel M. Farnsworth

Step 1. A Letter with Your Résumé. Write a letter of application to accompany the résumé you wrote in Step 1 above. Use separate paper. See pp. 467–468 for the correct form of the business letter.

Step 2. Answering an Ad. Write a letter of application for one of the following advertisements that appeared in an issue of the *New York Times*. If none of these jobs interest you, answer an ad in your own local newspaper.

Hint: If the address gives a box number and nothing else, address your letter this way:

Y 6188
New York Times
New York, New York 10036

THE MASTER SPEAKS: A PARAGRAPH ON A PROCESS

The chores around the house, the small-paying jobs you had as a child, the part-time employment (or the full-time work) you now experience—all these give you skill in how to perform some process. You know how to clean the garage quickly, how to make sandwiches at a crowded lunch counter, how to run a busy gas station when the boss leaves early. Even if you have never worked in your life, you still have some special knack that someone else could learn from you. Or maybe you would like to *learn* so well how something works that you can show someone else how to do it. But writing down in a paragraph some directions that seem clear to you often creates problems, so examine the pointers below before you write.

You As Expert: Making the Process Clear

1. Make sure that you try to explain something you yourself understand very well.
2. Decide in what way your explanation will develop:

   Will you show how to do something? Here you will give a clear picture of beginning, middle, and end. When your reader finishes, he should know that if he follows your directions he can, if he likes, do exactly what you have shown him. You will have to mention the tools needed and the materials; you will have to use words he understands and to define any technical words he may have trouble with.

   Will you show two or three different ways of doing the same thing? Here you need to make sure to keep your directions especially clear so that the reader does not mix up instructions.

   Will you show how something works? If you know quite well how a car engine operates or how a rexograph machine works, you can teach the reader about these processes. But in many cases, showing how something works may mean that you will have to do some reading on your subject to find out some more details. Often you yourself have to learn through reading how something was done before you can explain it well. If you wanted to show how a transistor or a firecracker or a hand grenade works, the library is the best place to begin.

   Will you show how something was achieved? How a ghetto formed, how George Washington crossed the Delaware, how a prison revolt was ended: these topics may also require some research work in the library.

   Will you show how to go somewhere from someplace else? Your directions must be easy to understand; your language must be simple; your steps must follow logically one after the other.

3. Tell in your topic sentence exactly what you intend showing the reader how to do. Your topic sentence should also do one of these:

Tell how you feel about this process: is it *easy, difficult, dull, exciting?*

or

Tell why you think it is important to know how to do this thing,

or

State some important thing the reader should know or do or own if he wants to succeed at performing this process himself.

4. Before you write the paragraph, make a list of the steps in the process. Make sure you have not left anything important out.
5. Once you have the steps listed, decide on how you will arrange them. You can select an order which:

mentions the stages chronologically (see pp. 45–47); tells the details in their order of importance (see p. 80);

tells the details in the order of location—that is from one place to the next;

gives the easiest material first and builds up to the stages that are more difficult to understand.

6. Make sure that your paragraph is not just a simple listing of one step after the other. Make some comment on each of the steps, using clear language that helps the reader visualize the process.
7. To avoid dullness, make your paragraph rich through lively verbs and actions, through colors and sounds, through images of touch and smell.
8. Subtopic sentences will help you unify the parts of the paragraph as you repeat a key idea each time you introduce a new stage.
9. The transition words you learned on pp. 14–15, 81–84, and 131–134 will help you move clearly and simply from one part of the process to the other. Be careful not to use too many transitions. And you certainly want to avoid saying over and over, "Then . . . And then . . . And then . . ." or "After that . . . after that . . . after that."
10. Give your paragraph a title.

Step 1. Making a List. For any one of the processes listed below, list on the blank lines the steps that could be developed in a paragraph. Name the process in the space provided.

how to deliver newspapers　　　　how to enjoy television
how to set long hair　　　　　　　how to eat pizza
how to change a tire　　　　　　　how to get into college
how registration works at college　how to make fudge
　　　　　　　　　　　　　　　　 how to play soccer

how I failed my _____ test

Process: _____

_____

_____

_____

_____

_____

_____

Step 2. Deciding on an Order. What method of arrangement would you use to explain the processes listed below? Tell in a brief sentence the reasons for your choice. See item 5 on p. 389 before you begin.

1. how to get from the outside of your school building to the cafeteria

_____

_____

2. how to become a good rock singer _____

_____

3. how to form your own band _____

_____

4. how the pollution problem grew out of hand in your town _____

_____

5. how to avoid being caught for not having an assignment _____

_____

6. how a doorbell works _____

_____

7. how to bake a cheesecake _____

_____

8. how it was possible to eat for a whole day on $1 _____

_____

Step 3. Checking a Process through Research. For the topics listed below, and with the help of card catalogs, the Reader's Guide (see p. 465), and your librarian, write down the names of three books or magazines you could use in order to check the steps in the process indicated.

1. how a cloud chamber works

    a. _____

    b. _____

    c. _____

2. how to grow orchids in your house

    a. _____

    b. _____

    c. _____

3. how Freud used hypnosis

    a. _____

    b. _____

    c. _____

4. how the United States involved itself in the Vietnam war

    a. _____

    b. _____

    c. _____

5. how to improve your reading speed

    a. _____

    b. _____

    c. _____

Step 4. A Student's Directions. Read the following paragraph before you write your own process theme. Answer the questions beneath it.

An Egg Cream Delight

Anyone who has worked as a soda jerk in a New York fountain shop knows that making and drinking an egg cream take special skill. To begin select a tall, clear glass; let no colors or fancy designs hide the delicious drink that will soon fill the container. Press down three or four times on the silver squirter marked *chocolate* so that dark, sticky syrup slips down the sides of the glass to the bottom. This leaves a layer of brown about an inch and a half thick (about two heaping teaspoonfuls for the egg-cream maker at home). Be careful not to do anything else until any chocolate clinging to the sides of the glass oozes its way down. Once that happens, carefully add an amount of cold milk that is twice as much as the chocolate. Now the heavy band of brown sits comfortably under a layer of white, and by taking a breath at this point, the person awaiting the drink knows how close joy really is! After this comes the most difficult stage: adding the carbonated water. Only a tiny trickle of soda water should fizz into the glass at a time so that just a small, quiet hiss sounds at the counter. (You people at home, unless you have seltzer water in dark green bottles with siphons, will have to suffer with a second-rate egg cream; popular brands of club sodas do not do the job right.) Now stir the three liquids very gently with a metal spoon that has a long handle. As the stirring continues slowly, a foamy white layer rises to the top with the thickness of cream or beaten egg whites. That is probably the reason for the name *egg cream,* even though no eggs or cream make up the drink. Beneath this snowy top sits a well-mixed liquid of the color of cocoa. Now remove the silver spoon and lick it to see if the drink is too sweet: a bit more soda water always fits in the glass. But do not add any more syrup or milk or the whole soda is ruined. The last step is to raise the glass to the lips and drink so that an equal amount of foam and liquid fills the mouth at the same time. Too much foam at the bottom after the drink disappears means the drinker has failed. But what a wonderful failure. Who will stop him from trying another time?

—Martin Berglund

1. What process does this paragraph describe? _____

_____

2. What opinion does the writer express in the topic sentence? _____

_____

3. How are the details arranged? _____

_____

4. What details of sound, color, and touch does Mr. Berglund use to add

liveliness and clarity to his paragraph? _____

_____

Step 5. Writing Your "How to . . ." Paragraph. Select something you can do well, or wish to learn how to do (by checking through library sources) and write a paragraph of twelve to fifteen sentences in which you explain the process in a clear and logical way. Study the pointers on pp. 380–389. Here are some suggested topics just in case you need some help.

1. how to baby-sit
2. how to drive a truck
3. how to shovel a walk
4. how to roast a turkey
5. how to take notes in Professor _____'s class
6. how to make ice cream
7. how the Mets won the World Series
8. how Lincoln was shot
9. how a steam engine works
10. how to get a Saturday night date

11. how drug addiction works in the body
12. how an army physical works
13. how to play tennis
14. how to sell clothing
15. how to learn typing
16. how to wait on tables
17. how to play stick ball
18. how pollution causes death
19. how to stop poverty
20. how burglar alarms work

SOLVING PROBLEMS IN WRITING

Words That Compare: Which Form to Use

When we use describing words in our language, we can often compare one thing with another merely by changing the ending of a word. For example:

One boy is tall. Another boy is taller.
Parker is the tallest boy at the party.

You have to be careful, however, to use the correct ending.

Use -er at the end of a word if you want to compare only two items.
Use -est at the end of a word if you want to compare three or more items.

Examples:

One person or thing is	Of two people or things, one is	Among three or more people or things, one is
short	shorter	shortest
quick	quicker	quickest
silly.	sillier.	silliest.

If the word you are using to compare has *three or more* syllables:

Use *more* in front of the word if you want to compare only two items.
Use *most* in front of the word if you want to compare three or more items.

Hint: If you are not sure how to make the correct form of the word, use your dictionary.

One person or thing is	Of two people or things, one is	Among three or more people or things, one is
attractive	more attractive	most attractive
enormous	more enormous	most enormous
done quickly.	done more quickly.	done most quickly.

Some words do not form comparisons in the usual way; these you have to memorize because they are irregular.

One person or thing is	Of two people or things, one is	Among three or more people or things, one is
bad	worse	worst
done badly	done worse	done worst
good	better	best
done well	done better	done best
little	less	least
many	more	most
much.	more.	most.

Step 1. Correct Comparisons. Fill in the spaces in the three columns below. The word you write must make sense in the blank line that appears in the sentence on top of the column. Look at the example.

Hint: For some words you have the choice of either adding an ending (-er or -est) or using more or most. But remember, use one or the other—not both.
Wrong: She is more thriftier than her friend.
Right: She is more thrifty than her friend.
                           or
              She is thriftier than her friend.

The teacher is _____ . Between Professor Merryl and Professor Grace, Professor Grace is _____ . Of all the teachers I have had, Professor Grace is _____ .

1. attractive *more attractive* *most attractive*

2. kind _____ _____

3. good _____ _____

4. dull _____ _____

5. lively _____ _____

Hint: Check spelling rule 2 on p. 455.

Step 2. Changing Wrong Comparisons.   Each sentence below uses a comparison incorrectly. Draw a line through the wrong word and write in the blank space at the right the word or words that you would use to make the sentence correct.

Example: He runs the ~~most~~ fastest on the
          team.   *fastest* _____

1. Flip Wilson is more funnier than Jerry
   Lewis.   _____

2. Between Mary and Ramonita, Ramonita
   is prettiest.   _____

3. I felt worser than my father about the
   crash.   _____

4. It was the most stupidest assignment I
   ever had to do.   _____

5. The importantest man on the block is
   Dr. Hawkins.   _____

Step 3. Your Own Comparisons. Use correctly in a sentence of your own
each of the following forms. Study the example.

1. ugliest

   Of all man's problems, war is ugliest. _____

2. worst

   _____

3. better

   _____

4. more slowly

   _____

5. worse

   _____

SOME WORDS NOT TO CONFUSE

Often our speech patterns cause us to confuse certain words or to use incorrectly
several others. The brief explanations below will help you understand which
words to use in your written works.

I. Already or all ready
   Already means *by this time* or *before
   the specified time.*
   When you arrived I had *already* eaten.
   All ready means *fully prepared.*
   The soldiers stood *all ready* for action.

II. Between or among
   Use *between* when you talk only about
   two people or things.

Between you and me that book is really
dull.
   Use *among* when three or more things
are involved.
Among the students only Carol answered
correctly.

III. Different from or different than?

Although *different than* is sometimes used when a subject and verb follow it, *different from* is usually preferred.

Smoking marijuana is *different from* using hard drugs.

IV. Fewer or less

Use *fewer* if what you are talking about can actually be counted.

He has *fewer* books than I do.

Use *less* to show worth, quantity, or degree.

That car costs *less.*

What New York needs is *less* pollution.

V. Somewheres or somewhere?

Do not use an *-s* at the end of any of the compound direction or time words.

Use somewhere   NOT   somewheres
    anywhere   NOT   anywheres
    nowhere   NOT   nowheres.

VI. Hardly, scarcely, or barely with verbs

If you use *hardly, scarcely,* or *barely* do not use NOT or the contraction *-nt.*

I *could hardly* breathe.
            NOT
I couldn't hardly breathe.

VII. Myself

Avoid using *myself* as a substitute for *I* or *me.*

She took Larry and *me* to the dean.
            NOT
She took Larry and myself to the dean.

My brother, sister, and *I* watched television.
            NOT
My brother, sister, and myself watched television.

Use *myself* to stress the word *I* in a sentence or to show that the subject and object are the same.

I *myself* will judge.

I shaved *myself* this morning.

VIII. Could have or could of

Use *could have* when what you want to say is *could've. Could of* (though it sounds like *could've*) is never correct.

Also use should have NOT should of
would have NOT would of
might have NOT might of
I *would have* driven if I had my glasses.
            NOT
I would of driven if I had my glasses.

IX. Learn or teach

Learn means *gain information or knowledge.*

Teach means *give information so that someone else learns.*

He *taught* me right from wrong.
            NOT
He learned me right from wrong.

X. Good or well, bad or badly

Good or *bad* describe people or things.

A *good* child is rare.

What a *bad* movie that was!

Use *well* or *badly* to describe verbs.

She reads *well.*

She dances *badly.*
            NOT
She reads good.

Hint: After one of these verbs, use *good* or *bad: is, am, are, were, have been, look, remain, appear, taste, smell, feel.*

She looks *bad.*

The soup tastes *good.*

The news was *bad* this morning.

If you want to indicate someone's health, use *well* with one of the above verbs.

I feel *well* today.

Step 1. The Right Words in Your Sentences. In the blank lines write a brief sentence of your own that uses correctly each word or word group.

1. different from _____

2. already _____

3. could hardly _____

4. fewer _____

5. among _____

6. myself _____

7. learn _____

8. less _____

9. well _____

10. all ready _____

Step 2. Correcting Sentences. Several sentences below contain errors. Underline each mistake based upon what you learned from the explanations above, and write a correct word or word group to replace it in the blank space in the margin. If the sentence is correct, mark it C.

Example: The waitress <u>should of</u> brought more bread and butter.

should have _____

1. For a child she plays the piano very good.

   _____

2. Johnny Cash's last record is much different than his earlier ones.

   _____

3. He taught us fractions but I never learned them well.

   _____

4. Supposedly, there are less people in this college than in my high school, but I myself do not see how that can be true.

   _____

5. Norman apologized for not coming to our party, but he could of called earlier.

   _____

6. If I had to choose between roses, carnations, and daisies, I would have picked daisies.

   _____

7. The attendant had all ready parked the other cars when we drove up.

_____

8. At the park concert the musicians played loudly enough, but I couldn't barely hear.

_____

9. Although I looked up and down the street, my dog was nowheres in sight.

_____

10. That suit looks well on you.

_____

WRITING FORCEFUL SENTENCES

The Active Voice for Verbs

Many verbs can express the same thought in two different ways. Which of these sentences do you find more satisfactory?

1. The tired employee locked the office door.
2. The office door was locked by the tired employee.

If you selected sentence 1 you probably realized, correctly, that the extra words needed to make sentence 2 really added nothing of importance to the sentence. Why take more words to say exactly what you could say with fewer words?

Notice further that in sentence 1 the subject (*the tired employee*) performs the action of the verb. (It is he who *locked the office door*.)

But in sentence 2 the subject (*the office door*) does not do anything. In fact, something happens to *it* (it was locked by the tired employee).

Because the subject of sentence 1 actively performs the action of the verb, we say the verb is in the *active voice*.

Because the subject of sentence 2 is acted upon by the verb, we say the verb is in the *passive voice*.

Hint: In most cases, the active voice is preferred to the passive.

It is easy to change passive-voice sentences to active. Just remember these pointers.

1. Passive-voice sentences always use some form of *to be* in combination with the verb. Look for word groups like *is seen, will be observed, can be cleaned, was done, should have been bought, would have been eaten.* You will have to remove the *to be* part to write an active-voice sentence.
2. Decide who performs the action of the verb. Usually the performer appears after the word *by*. Make that word the subject.

Passive:

The pencil was sharpened *by* Harriet.
             [This is a clue   [This is who
             to who performs   performs the
             the action.]   action of the
                                      verb *sharpen*.]

Active: [*Was* is removed.]

Harriet sharpened the pencil.
    [The person who performs the
    action is now the subject
    of the verb.]

Step 1. Passive into Active. In the space provided, change the passive-voice sentence into active voice.

Hint: Sometimes the person who performs the action is not mentioned in the passive-voice sentence. You will have to determine the performer of the action before you write the active-voice sentence. Study the example.

Example: The two employees were quickly brought before the manager.

(Here we do not know who actually brought them to the manager. Decide who you think performs the action and then rewrite.)

The guards quickly brought the two employees before the manager.

1. The latecomers were fired by the department supervisor.

   _____

2. Our egg-salad sandwiches were spoiled by the hot summer sun. _____

   _____

3. The *Long Island Press* is sold by our neighbor Billy. _____

   _____

4. This basement apartment was painted in vivid red. _____

   _____

5. The old woman's eyes were filled with tears of sorrow. _____

   _____

Avoiding *to Be* as Sentence Verbs

Very often you combine part of the verb *to be* (*is, am, are, was, were, has been, have been, will be*) with a verb in a sentence. In many cases the verb has more impact without the help of *to be*. Just write the sentence in the simple present or past tense.

The girl was speaking

is just as clear as, means the same thing as, and uses fewer words this way:

The girl spoke.

Step 2. Removing the Unwanted *to Be*.   Rewrite each sentence below so that the forms of *to be* are eliminated. Study the example above.

1. Three children were singing just below the window. _____

   _____

2. Strange white clouds were sailing across the sky while a flock of sparrows was flying southward. _____

   _____

3. Dick Gregory will be speaking at the campus tomorrow afternoon. _____

   _____

4. Crowds of visitors are looking at the Statue of Liberty from the rear of the Staten Island Ferry. _____

   _____

5. The quarterback was darting across the field; he was holding the football tightly under his arm. _____

   _____

WRITING THE ESSAY

Your Views on Employment

Write a four-paragraph essay of about four hundred words in which you discuss your views about employment. You may want to use as the basis of your composition some idea suggested in the section of this chapter called Exploring the Topic. You may want to work out one of your own ideas or you may want to look ahead to some possible titles offered on p. 405. In any case, write your proposal before you do anything else, making sure it is written so that you can discuss *two* aspects of the topic. In that way you can develop in each body paragraph one of the two features of the subject you have chosen. Before you write, decide upon the kinds of details you will need to support your proposal. Toward that goal, ask yourself these key questions:

IN SEARCH OF DETAIL: SOME CRUCIAL QUESTIONS

1. What have I experienced in my own life that will provide me with enough details to support each aspect of the topic?
2. What have I read recently—or can read easily—that will provide me with enough details to support each aspect of the topic?
3. What have I seen or heard on television, on the radio, in the movies, or from my friends or teachers that can provide me with enough details to support each aspect of the topic?

If You Choose in a Body Paragraph
to use your own personal experience to support your proposal:

to use materials from books or periodicals in order to support your proposal:

to use statistics or cases to support your proposal:

to use materials you have learned from TV, the radio, movies, friends, teachers:

Remember to
use concrete sensory details: colors, sounds, smells, touch sensations, and images of action should fill each body paragraph.
1. identify your sources
2. make sure your sources are reliable
3. paraphrase some of your material
4. use exact quotations in some places
5. follow logical arguments
6. select supporting material that is clear and convincing
1. prepare your own statistics based upon the interviews you conducted as part of an earlier activity in this chapter (pp. 382–383)
2. check government bulletins, encyclopedias, yearbooks, almanacs, or other reliable sources of studies relating to the topic you have chosen
1. identify your sources
2. use only reliable sources
3. make sure you remember correctly whatever details you are using; if you cannot be accurate you should not be using the source
4. make sure that the reader sees *why* you have chosen to rely upon the source you are mentioning

Once you have your proposal and have determined the kinds of details you feel will best support your topic, you can begin thinking about the various patterns of essay organization and paragraph development that you have learned so far. Any one or combination of these pointers may serve you well in your essay:

Develop the body paragraphs by expanding in each a specific moment to illustrate each aspect of the topic (see pp. 58–61).

Compare and contrast two moments from your life (each in a body paragraph) which support the two aspects of your topic.

Develop a paragraph by using three instances to support some aspect of the topic (see pp. 72–77).

Develop a paragraph through a number of instances (see p. 79).

Write a definition, expanded through a series of vivid word pictures, to build a body paragraph (see pp. 245–247).

Expand a moment from a poem that relates to your topic in order to build a body paragraph (see pp. 247–249 and the poem on p. 376).

Use one of the techniques of comparison-contrast within a body paragraph (see Chapter 4).

If you are arguing a point, show in a body paragraph what those who *dis*-agree believe (pp. 316–318).

Expand your "How to . . ." paragraph (see pp. 388–393) into a four-paragraph essay.

Develop your introduction in any of the suggested ways (see pp. 277–282).

Write a closing paragraph that clearly serves as a conclusion for your essay (look ahead to pp. 423–427).

Step 1. Helping Plan an Essay. For the proposal sentences below, show how the writer might develop each of the two body paragraphs in his essay. State briefly in the appropriate columns below what might make effectively developed paragraphs.

Proposal Sentence	Your Idea for Developing Paragraph 2	Your Idea for Developing Paragraph 3
1. Students should be encouraged to work while they go to school.		
2. To me it is very clear just what an employer should and should not be like.		

3. A salesman's job is filled
   with unpleasant experiences.

Step 2. Reading a Student's Theme.   A student in a freshman composition class wrote the essay below. After you read it, write the answers to
the questions.

Hating a Job

Everyone wants a job he can enjoy. Besides good wages, people have to like
the working conditions and the general atmosphere surrounding them. But because these things were lacking for me, the one job I ever held brought me very
little pleasure. A Christmas assistant at the United States Post Office has little
enjoyment.

Basically, the dullness of the job is responsible for that. As soon as I heard my
orders in the first day of work one dreary November afternoon, I knew a boring
month lay ahead. My supervisor, a small, bald-headed fellow with a gruff voice,
sat me in an aisle where I sorted mail going into cities of Germany. "You read the
front of the letter," Mr. Warren explained quickly, "and then you shove the letter
in the right box." As he rushed away, I stared at the twenty steel boxes before me.
Sitting on a stiff metal chair, I reached for the first letter. In a tiny black scrawl the
words raced across a blue airmail envelope. I squinted my eyes. I turned the letter
sideways and upside down. I held it up to the light. Finally, I made out on the fourth
line the word *Munich,* and after ten minutes, had slipped the note into the right
box. From five in the afternoon until two o'clock in the morning, surrounded by the
musty smell of paper and burlap bags, I sat on that awful chair straining to read
handwriting. Since I saw German cities all day, I felt as if I sat in a European geog-
raphy class. But although cities like Hamburg and Munich stand out easily on
maps, nothing looked clear on a hand-written letter. What dullness! Letter after
letter, card after card moved slowly into their proper places. Sometimes to break
the monotony, my supervisor allowed me to tie up the bundles of mail accumulated
in the boxes with pale yellow string. A half-hour dinner break and a fifteen minute
time off for coffee did not do much to stimulate my initiative or to raise my level
of productivity. I cannot imagine a duller job.

But what made the job even more tedious was the contrast of endless activity
around me. Though I sat still with my little idiot boxes, everything else sped by in
a sense of panic about the mail moving on time. Large boxes on wheels like over-
sized laundry carts squeaked along the floor. Either I watched a cart like this rush
by or groups of jovial mailmen laughing noisily and carrying large white bags on
their shoulders. Into every door of this room fled bag after bag of mail. The mail
reached us much faster than we could send it out; therefore, unruly piles of mail
sat at the end of every aisle. A radio blared endlessly the news on WCBS. Assiduous
hands flew up and down lifting and tossing, raising and pushing, sorting and

packing. So much mail fell in wrong boxes that I still do not know how people received their Christmas cards. And when each shift ended, employees just stood up, grabbed their coats and sped out the door leaving an unbelievable mess wherever they stood. Outside, mail trucks rumbled by every few minutes; voices around me talked and laughed and hummed. This constant activity just added to my own dislike for the work.

Some dullness on every job cannot be avoided, but when an employee sees action all around him, his own dissatisfaction increases. I cannot understand how people work at the same dull job in a factory, for example, when the person at the next table does something more active or interesting. And good wages is not the only way to make a worker happy. Employers should take into consideration the employee's need for variety and see to it that every worker is trained to do several different kinds of work. In that way boredom might decrease, productivity might rise, and everyone, including the boss, would benefit.   —Joseph Rafferty

1. What does the proposal sentence state as the topic of the essay? Does Mr. Rafferty state clearly what two aspects of the topic he will develop in the body paragraphs, or does he merely suggest possibilities? _____

_____

_____

2. What is the topic of paragraph 2? _____

_____

3. What is the topic of paragraph 3? _____

_____

4. Circle the transitions in the first sentence of paragraph 2 and the first sentence of paragraph 3. _____

_____

5. From Mr. Rafferty's essay copy out:

   a. two images that use color _____

   _____

   b. a sentence that portrays a lively action _____

   _____

   c. an image that names a specific sound _____

   _____

   d. an image that states a sensation of touch _____

   _____

Some Topics to Think About.   If you need some more suggestions for a topic, perhaps one of these titles may help.

1. Two Bosses I Have Had
2. A Job I Loved (Hated)
3. Don't Ever Work as a . . .
4. A College Education and Job Success
5. Will Forced Labor End Welfare?
6. What Makes a Good Job
7. How to Be a Salesman
8. How to Be Elected
9. Working in a _____ Shop
10. Washing a Car
11. How Plastic Surgery Is Performed
12. When to Make Your Job Choice: Early or Later in Life
13. Farming in the Open Fields
14. The First Time I Earned Money
15. Getting Fired
16. My First Day on a New Job
17. A Factory Worker's Day
18. My Father as My Boss
19. Working After (Before) School
20. Why Freshmen Should (Should Not) Hold Jobs

Measuring Your Own Skill: Making the Job Essay Pay

Read this self-evaluation before you write the final draft of your theme. After you revise your composition, submit this page with the final copy of your essay. Grade yourself *Good, Fair,* or *Poor* based upon how well you fulfilled each of the items on the list.

Grade

1. My proposal clearly introduces the subject of my theme and allows me to discuss two aspects of the topic, each in a body paragraph (pp. 273–277).   _____
2. The details in each paragraph illustrate the ideas I wish to discuss.   _____
3. The language I have used is clear and vivid, filled with lively verbs and actions wherever possible. I have tried to use sensory language in appropriate parts of my theme (pp. 5–6, 223–230).   _____
4. The transitions in my composition are smooth and easy to follow.   _____
5. I have written an introduction that plays a meaningful part in my essay (pp. 277–282).   _____
6. I have used a variety of sentence structures to avoid dull paragraphs. _____
7. I have written an effective title (pp. 197–198).   _____
8. I have studied my Theme Progress Sheet so that I could avoid my usual errors. I have checked especially for run-ons and fragments and for errors in making comparisons or in using words often confused.   _____

9. I have tried to avoid the words *was, were, is, am, are, seems*. I have tried to write active sentences, not passive ones. I have used at least two new vocabulary words from this chapter.   _____

10. My last paragraph serves as a conclusion to the idea I am advancing (pp. 423–426).   _____

THE PROFESSIONALS SPEAK

Read the following selections and write answers to the questions.

SOME WORDS TO KNOW BEFORE YOU READ

weld: put together pieces of metal by hammering, heat, or other means
gaudy: showy without taste; flashy
futile: useless

Six O'Clock

It is six o'clock in the morning. Another night of work is over. How strange the silence is to my ears, after listening to the roar of machines and the crash of steel for eight hours. The *snap, bang, bang* of the shears still resound dully within my aching head. Slowly we stumble out through the steel shop into the welding room. Our footsteps echo hollowly amid the now quiet machines. Those electric welders, whose iron tongues were spitting out flaming sparks a short ten minutes ago, are now cold and silent. Overhead the pale dawn shines dimly through the grimy sky-lights. My feet feel like leaden weights, my eyes burn, my head bobs wearily up and down, my shoulders ache. Slowly we trudge down the long sloping hall by the office. Those posters on the wall. How gaudy, how futile they look now! They read, "Taxes on your bread," "Safety-First Week." Who the hell cares about taxes and safety at six in the morning? The door swings open on creaking hinges. A breath of cool sweet air brushes against my hot cheek. It feels like the refreshing touch of spring water upon a dusty throat. I'm tired, so tired. Bed will feel like heaven today. The door bangs shut after me, bringing a feeling of quiet relief. We hasten across the drive, our feet making crunching sounds amid the black ashes. Into the time office we pour. Where's my card? Four fifty-nine, four five nine. Ah, there it is. Bong, bong, bong. There goes the hurried ring of the time clock. It swallows our cards, punches them, and vomits them out in a split second. It's my turn now: *bong*. One minute after six. I shove it quickly into the box on the night shift board. I say, "Mornin', Dutch," to the watchman, and hustle out the gate. Free at last! It feels good, climbing the long ash hill toward home and rest. Five minutes after six, and the sun shoving his flaming head over the foggy hills. Another weary night is over.

—William Leigh, Jr.

1. How does the writer feel about the job moment he describes? _____

_____

2. What sounds most faithfully reproduce the scene of work in a steel shop? _____

_____

3. What sentences show the writer's thoughts about the things he observes? Underline them in the paragraph.

4. Copy out an image that, because it uses color and action, gives you an especially clear picture. _____

_____

5. Pick out:
   a. an image that appeals to the sense of touch _____

   _____

   b. an example of personification (see p. 128). _____

   _____

Read the speech below delivered by John Fitzgerald Kennedy at a Chicago luncheon in 1963. What problems did President Kennedy foresee for the job market? How does he propose to solve these problems? Where does he use statistics most dramatically to support his ideas?

SOME WORDS TO KNOW BEFORE YOU READ

inordinately: excessively
platitudes: words or expressions that are dull or lifeless
comprise: include; contain
phenomenon: occurrence
fervent: showing great warmth and sincerity of feeling

How Shall We Keep Our Manpower Employed?

I am glad to be in Chicago because I am struck every time I come by the strong public spirit which runs through this city in the determination to make Chicago second to none . . . and also by the happy spirit of community effort which joins business, labor, the civic groups and all the rest, in selling Chicago to the people of Chicago, to the country and the world. . . . I don't think that there is any doubt that if this country continues to grow, if we can maintain a rate of economic vitality and prosperity, Chicago will be among the leaders.

There is, I think, the central thesis, however, that we face serious problems in this country in the decade ahead if we are going to maintain that growth, and I want to mention one of those problems because I think it concerns us all, in government, in the city, the national government, the state, labor, management, all of us as citizens. I think the number-one domestic concern of the United States is going to be in the 1960's the question of jobs—jobs for a tidal wave of men and women who are going to be hitting our labor market in the next five years. It is a concern which requires the united effort of all of us. Some people may think it strange that jobs, which were the great issue of the thirties, when we were in a depression, should also be the great concern of the sixties, when we enjoy a relative period of economic prosperity. The difficulty in the thirties was that there was an inordinately low supply of jobs for the men and women who wished to find work.

The difficulty now is the tremendously high demand for work, which exceeds the supply of jobs. But now, as then, every effort must be made by all of us to strengthen the economy so that we can find work for the people who want it. This involves not only Chicago in this country, but it involves our position of leadership in the world. Mr. Khrushchev has said that the hinge of history would move when he was able to demonstrate that his system could outproduce ours. The hinge of history will move if we are not able to find jobs for our people, not only during recessions but also during periods of prosperity. I regard this as the number-one problem we are going to face in this country in the coming years. It is serious enough to warrant a careful examination by all of us to realize that it cannot be reduced by platitudes and hopes, and the effect of this problem is being felt and will be felt here in Chicago, Illinois, and across the country. There are three reasons for it: First is the labor released by the revolution in farm technology. Agriculture has been this nation's largest employer, engaging more people than steel, automobiles and public utilities, and the transportation industries combined.

But now one farmer can produce the food and fiber needed for twenty-five Americans, compared to only seven at the turn of the century. New fertilizers, insecticides, research and all the rest have made this one of the great productive miracles of all time—one of the great stories for the United States around the world in contrast to the failure of our adversaries—but it is a fact that since 1947 our farms have increased their output 30 percent at the very time that the man-hours worked on those farms were cut in half. Farm employment during that period declined by three million, an average of 200,000 a year; comparable to the population of the city of Akron, Ohio, being thrown out of work every twelve months. In the last two years alone, farm employment dropped by a half million, while farm production and farm income were both rising. It is estimated that, disturbing as it may sound, only one out of every ten boys growing up on the farms of the United States will find a living in agriculture.

This leads us to the second growing tide of manpower: our nation's youth.

The crest of the postwar baby flood has swept through our elementary and secondary schools and is now about to engulf the labor force. Last year, for example, 2.8 million young Americans reached the age of 16. This year, 3.8 million will be coming into the labor market at that age. Altogether, in the 1960's, 26 million new young workers will enter the labor market, an increase of 40 percent over the 1950's and a far greater number than this country has ever had to absorb and train in our history.

Already workers under the age of 25, although they comprise less than one-fifth of our labor force, constitute more than one-third of our unemployed. Last year, the unemployment rate for men age 25 and over was 4.4 percent. But for those age 20 to 24 it was 9 percent, and for those 14 to 19 it was a shocking 13 percent. Although young people are staying in school longer than their fathers, the rate of school drop-outs—four out of every ten—is too high, for job openings for the untrained are declining, in factories, mines, farms and railroads, in the construction and service industries.

Moreover, the jobless rate is always highest among the unskilled. In our modern society, even high school graduates find that their skills are inadequate. But Labor Department surveys show that their rate of unemployment is at least far below that of school drop-outs, not only in the year of leaving school but in the later years.

The latest surveys also show that unemployment rates among college graduates are much lower than among those graduated from high school. But unfortunately, only one out of every ten finish college. In short, as challenging as it will be to provide, first, jobs for the 26 million new young workers entering the labor market in the 1960's, far more difficult will be the problem of absorbing the 7.5 million who will not finish high school, including nearly 2.5 million who will not even finish the eighth grade.

I ask you to mark these figures well, for youth unemployment poses one of the most expensive and explosive social and economic problems now facing this country and this city. In the last decade, for example, arrests of youths increased 86 percent. What will the figure be for the next decade, when the net increase of potential young workers in the labor force rises fifteen times as fast as it did in the 1950's?

Finally, underlying all of these trends is the third phenomenon, both cursed and praised, and that is technological advance, known loosely by the name of automation. During the last six years, the nation increased its manufacturing output by nearly 20 percent, but it did so with 800,000 fewer production workers, and the gain in white-collar jobs did not offset this loss. Since the Second World War, the real output of the private economy has risen 67 percent, with only a 3 percent rise in man-hours.

I do not wish to be misunderstood. Increasing productivity and advancing technological skills are essential to our ability to compete and to progress. But we also have an obligation to find the nearly two million jobs which are displaced by these advances.

This city is no stranger to any of these problems. You have seen your railroads laying off machinists and boilermakers, as the proportion of diesel locomotives rose from less than 15 percent of all locomotives in 1947 to 97 percent today. You have seen your downstate coal mines laying off workers as new machinery makes it possible for forty-six men to dig the coal that one hundred men dug in 1947. And you have seen your steel mills employ seventy-nine men to produce the steel products which required a hundred men only ten years ago. Chicago, I might add parenthetically, also proves the exception to this pattern, since it now takes ten men to manage the Cubs instead of one.

This is not a blue-collar problem alone. Office and clerical workers are increasingly being displaced by automatic computers and processes. The Farmers Home Administration of the United States Government processes 35 percent more loans per employee than it did only two years ago.

This administration intends to press ahead with government economy, but we also have to find in the private economy jobs for those people who are willing.

All these trends you have seen in this city and state—workers displaced by automation, school drop-outs roaming the streets, men looking for work who have left the farm, the mine, the factory, the railroad or the distressed area. You have your share of jobless Negroes and women and older workers and all the rest, even though under Mayor Daley's hard-driving leadership this city is creating new jobs faster than almost any city in the country. The same is true on a larger scale of the nation as a whole. Our civilian labor force grew by nearly 12 million during the last fifteen years, but the number of jobs grew by only 10 million. In the last five years we saw an annual increase of only 175,000 private jobs, outside of agriculture, compared to 700,000 in each of the previous ten years. Our total Gross National Product output grew at a rate of only 3 percent, while unemployment remained continuously above 5 percent. And last year's loss of man-hours, in terms of those willing but unable to find full-time work, was a staggering one billion work days, equivalent to shutting down the entire country with no production, no services, and no pay for over three weeks.

Some fourteen million Americans had some unemployment in 1962, and 28 percent of last year's unemployed were out of work fifteen weeks or longer. Fifteen percent were out of work a full six months or longer.

This nation must do better than that. . . .

Tax reduction alone will not employ the unskilled or bring business to a distressed area, and tax reduction alone is not, therefore, the only program we must put forward. To mention but a few, we urgently need to improve our schools and colleges, to reduce the number of drop-outs, to reduce the number of unskilled workers, to keep young people out of the labor market until they are ready for the jobs which automation creates, instead of those it is sure to replace.

We urgently need a youth-employment-opportunities program to give young people training and job experience instead of hanging around the streets, out of work and out of hope. We need to step up our efforts for aid to distressed areas, for the retraining of the unemployed, particularly in those areas where it has been chronic, for more security for our aged, for improving our housing and our transportation industries, and for ending race discrimination in education and employment, which helps increase, of course, the chronic unemployment of minority groups. . . .

Twenty-five hundred years ago the Greek poet Alcaeus laid down the principle which best sums up the greatness of Chicago: "Not houses firmly roofed," he wrote, "or the stones of walls well builded, nay, nor canals and dockyards make the City—but men able to use their opportunities."

Chicago is blessed to have such men at their head, and my fervent hope is that the United States of America in meeting the needs of this decade will also be peopled by "men able to use their opportunities."

—John Fitzgerald Kennedy

1. What serious problem did President Kennedy make the central focus of his speech? _____

_____

2. What three reasons does he develop as causes for the extent of the problem? _____

_____

3. Put a check next to each paragraph that uses statistics as supporting detail. Underline what you think are the most impressive statistics.

Step 1. Job Jargon.   Every job situation has a peculiar language of its own, words which only fellow workers really understand; the language peculiar to a trade, a group, or a profession is called *jargon.* Students use words like *cut, crib sheet, frat;* editors say *blue pencil;* restaurant workers shout *"Stretch one!"* or *"Hand me a monkey dish!"* Choose any job category that interests you (professional baseball, designing, auto racing, for example) and investigate it through interviews or library resources; then on your own paper prepare a list of ten or fifteen jargon words, words that are used with special meanings on that particular job. Also write definitions for the jargon words. Look at the sample below taken from a student's list.

Jargon for Luncheonette Countermen

Jargon	*Definition*
1. Adam and Eve on a raft	poached eggs on toast
2. Stretch one.	Coca-Cola
3. Draw one.	cup of coffee
4. GAC	grilled American cheese
5. Down	on toast

—Carl Dixon

Step 2. A Moment at an Unpleasant Job.   Reread "Brass Spittoons" by Langston Hughes. Then think back to a time you had to work at a job as unpleasant as the speaker's job in the poem. In a one-paragraph composition, expand the details of that job with sensory language; be sure to illustrate whether or not you found some moment of pride or glory or pleasure in this unattractive task.

Step 3. Remembering Earlier Skills.   Read the brief essay below and correct all run-on errors and sentence fragments (there are six of each). Then answer the questions about essay form.

Factory Work Is Horrible

   The worst job which I ever held was working part time in a sweater factory. I disliked two particular tasks the most. Unloading trucks and steaming sweater material.
   Unloading trucks was a horrible experience. Every Wednesday a truck would come to the factory I was assigned the miserable job of unloading. Each truck would have one hundred cases of material. Weighing fifty pounds each. Carrying these cartons up two flights of stairs. I despised that work. After I unloaded the cartons and they all stood on the floor upstairs, it was then time to put them into stock the stock room was very small and if the cases were not piled properly they would not fit. Piling the stock in the right order was also important. If things were messed up when I had to locate something, it would be impossible to find. No one should ever choose to work in a stock department.
   When I first started the job. I thought stock work was bad steaming sweater material was worse. In the back rooms of the factory stood huge steaming machines. Which made sounds like gasoline trucks exploding it was at least ninety-five de-

grees at all times back there. Each time I placed material on the steam boards, I burned two or three fingers. After the steaming process I took the material off the steamers as I lifted it it would stretch down to the floor. Like melted chewing gum. I hated steaming so much that I finally quit the job.

Working in a factory, I realized that it must be the worst type of job anywhere.

1. Check pp. 277–282; write a better introduction to this composition on the lines below. _____

_____

_____

_____

_____

2. What details could you add to paragraphs 2 and 3 in order to make the scenes more vivid? _____

_____

_____

3. What is your opinion of the conclusion? What could you do to make it more appropriate? _____

_____

_____

_____

chapter 11

DEFINITIONS FROM THE HEART:
LIFE'S MOMENTS FOR MEANINGS

"El Amor y la Muerte" ("Love and Death") from *The Complete Etchings of Goya* with a foreword by
Aldous Huxley. © 1943 by Crown Publishers, Inc. Used by permission of Crown Publishers, Inc.

INTRODUCTION

The dictionary is a valuable tool for defining words whose meanings we do not know. Yet, when it attempts to explain certain words, it is often inadequate. If you have ever looked up *hate* or *patriotism, fear* or *loneliness,* for example, you know that your own ideas of those words are not really the same as the definitions the dictionary gives. Your own definitions are much more specific. You might not define fear as "a painful feeling of coming danger or trouble," but if you ever slink down a dark city street on a winter evening and hear the gasp of the wind in alleys, in hallways, through ghostly trees—you have a personal and very real sense of the meaning of fear.

As a human being—moving, learning, confronting—you constantly redefine vocabulary based upon the experiences you meet. When Carl Sandburg said

Hope is a tattered flag and a dream out of time . . .
The shimmer of northern lights across a bitter winter night,
The blue hills beyond the smoke of the steel works

he built his definition of hope from the moments in his daily life.

For this theme assignment, you will write a definition from your life by selecting a word whose meaning you learned or understood in two clear moments that live in your memory. You will learn about word parts to help you determine definitions of new words; you will learn how to write conclusions in essays; and you will learn about some confusing words and the proper placement of words in sentences.

VOCABULARY: WORD PARTS AS CLUES TO MEANINGS

Important Prefixes and Suffixes

A prefix is a letter or group of letters that is placed at the *beginning* of a word to contribute to its meaning.

A suffix is a letter or group of letters placed at the *end* of a word to contribute to its meaning.

If you know some of the prefixes and suffixes used most frequently, it is often possible to determine the definition of a word, or at least to get an idea of the kind of word being used, without using the dictionary.

For example, if you saw the word

asocial

and you knew that the letter *a* placed at the beginning of a word meant *not,* you could figure out easily that *asocial* meant *not social.* If you saw the word

heroism

and you knew that *-ism* added to a word meant *the quality of,* you could conclude easily that heroism meant *the quality of being a hero.* And if in your reading you saw a sentence like

The doctor prescribed an *antirheumatic* medicine.

and you knew that the prefix *anti-* meant *against,* you could figure out that *antirheumatic* meant *against* some rheumatic disease.

Here are some of the most common prefixes:

PREFIXES THAT SAY NO

a-: not (asocial)
an-: not (anarchy)
un-: not (unattractive)
im-: not (impossible)
in-: not (insecure)
non-: not (nonviolent)
mis-: wrongly (mistreated)
ir-: without, not (irresponsible)
il-: not (illiberal)
mal-: bad or wrongful (maladjustment)
anti-: against (antimissile)
contra-: against (contradict)

PREFIXES THAT SHOW PLACEMENT

ab-: from or away from (abstain)
circum-: around (circumference)
com-: with, together (commission)
trans-: across (transport)
dis-: away (displace)
sub-: under (submarine)
inter-: among or between (interlocking)
intra-: within, inwardly (intramurals, introvert)
in-: in or on (invest)
de-: down from (deflect)

PREFIXES THAT TELL TIME

ante-: before (antedate)
pre-: before (predict)
post-: after (postdate)
ex-: former or out of (exconvict)
re-: again, back (repeat)

PREFIXES THAT TELL DEGREE

hyper-: too much (hypertension)
super-: above or highest (superman)
poly-: many (polyangular)
pro-: in favor (proponent)
semi-: half (semicircle)
extra-: beyond, outside (extracurricular)

PREFIXES THAT MEAN ONE

uni-: single, one (uniform)
homo-: same (homogenize)
self-: one's own person (self-propelled)
mono-: one (monologue)
auto-: self, same (autograph)

Step 1. Making Words with Prefixes. Select the correct prefix that has the meaning described and use it before the word or word part that appears. Write the new word in Column I and a sensible definition in Column II. Check your dictionary to make sure that the word you have written is correct.

		I	II
1. (bad or wrongful)	+ practice	=	
2. (under)	+ way	=	
3. (not)	+ legitimate	=	
4. (again)	+ examine	=	
5. (against)	+ aircraft	=	
6. (one)	+ lateral	=	
7. (within)	+ state	=	
8. (among)	+ state	=	
9. (the same)	+ -nym	=	
10. (before)	+ establish	=	
11. (out of)	+ -hale	=	
12. (across)	+ Atlantic	=	
13. (together, with)	+ mingle	=	
14. (one)	+ cycle	=	
15. (not)	+ mature	=	

SUFFIXES TO SIGNAL MEANINGS

Relating to or Pertaining to	*Someone Who*
-al (formal)	-er (speaker)
-ic (tonic)	-or (debtor)

```
-ance (performance)                    -ist (florist)
-ence (permanence)

Able to Be                             Filled with
-ible (terrible)                       -ous (joyous)
-able (capable)                        -y (juicy)
                                       -ful (sorrowful)

State or Quality of                    Without
-ship (statesmanship)                  -less (mindless)
-ment (management)
-ion (tension)
-ness (happiness)
-ism (terrorism)
-hood (manhood)
-tude (aptitude)
```

Step 2. Suffixes for Correct Words.   Change the words in italics in the sentences below to the proper form by adding a correct suffix. You may have to change the final letters of the starting word before you add an ending. Write in *a* the new words and in *b* the meanings of the suffixes you added. Check the dictionary for spelling. Study the example.

Example:
1. On *chill* days we run home quickly.

    a. *chilly* _____
    b. *filled with* _____

2. The *illustrate* showed his prizewinning drawings.

    a. _____
    b. _____

3. His writing was so *poet* that his teachers expressed surprise.

    a. _____
    b. _____

4. The *anesthetize* carefully prepared the bottles of blood and plasma for the operation.

    a. _____
    b. _____

5. With such a *fault* record of public service, it is no wonder that the voters see him as a man of great *competent.*

    a. _____
    b. _____

6. Modern attempts to stop *pollute* are much more *rely* now than they were when science was in its *infant.*

    a. _____
    b. _____

7. A *pacify* is a person who believes that world *tense* should be solved with *statesman* rather with *military.*

    a. _____
    b. _____

Ten Roots to Rescue Meanings

Roots—or stems—are those parts of words to which pieces may be added at the beginning or end. For example, in the word *reclassification,* the root is *classify.* Several roots, coming from Greek, Latin, or other languages, appear frequently in English words; therefore, to know a select number of roots is to improve your skill with word recognition. The ten roots below play an important part in our vocabulary.

			Example
Roots of the Senses	spect, spic	means "look"	spectator
	loqu, locut	means "speak"	eloquent
	tang, tact	means "touch"	tangent
	vid, vis	means "see"	vision
	voc, vok	means "call"	vocal
Roots of Action	vers, vert	means "turn"	divert
	pos	means "place"	position
	port	means "carry"	porter
	mor, mort	means "die"	moratorium
	mit, mis	means "send" or "put"	admit

Step 3. Roots for Definitions. Underline the root in each word in italics below. In *a* write a meaning of the word based upon your knowledge of the root. In *b* write the definition given by the dictionary. How close do the two come in meaning?

1. There sounded a *moribund* howl, then silence.

   a. *dying*

   b. *on the verge of death*

2. We need a *tangible* suggestion to make the plan work.

   a. _____

   b. _____

3. She is so *loquacious* that it is often hard to stay in her company for long.

   a. _____

   b. _____

4. The sight of a child at play *evokes* memories of one's own youth.

   a. _____

   b. _____

5. Please *remit* your payment.

   a. _____

   b. _____

Step 4. Prefix, Root, and Suffix in Combination. Each word below is made from a prefix, root, and suffix. Write below the word the meaning of each part and then a suitable definition of the entire word in Column I. Use a dictionary if you need to. Look at the example.

Example:
1. submitter *under put one who* *I someone who gives in to someone else.*

2. circumlocution

3. inversion

4. subversion

5. comportment

6. intangible

7. exposable

8. invisible

9. disposal

10. introspection

BUILDING COMPOSITION SKILLS

Exploring the Topic

A Strong One-Sentence Definition.   In order to write a logical definition that is clear and easy to understand, write a sentence of four parts:

1. Name the term to be defined.
2. Use the word *is.*
3. Name the general group of things to which the term belongs.
4. Name some specific characteristic that identifies the term from the rest of the group.

You will have to use your dictionary or encyclopedia as a starting point in the preparation of accurate and precise meanings.

Examples:

[term] ["is"] [general group to which term belongs] [specific characteristic: shows the special use of the plot of ground]

A garden is a plot of ground for cultivating plants.

[term] ["is"] [general group to which term belongs] [specific characteristic: shows how this pardon is different from any other kind]

Amnesty is a pardon for offenses against a government.

[term] ["is"] [general group to which term belongs]

A church is a building for public Christian worship.

[specific characteristic: shows the special nature of the building]

> **TOWARD ACCURATE DEFINITIONS**
>
> Don't use *where* or *when* after *is*.
> *Wrong:* A closet is *where* you store clothing, food, or tools.
> *Right:* A closet is an enclosure for storing clothing, food, or tools.
>
> Don't use in your definition the word (or one of its forms) you are attempting to define.
> *Wrong:* Anger is the act of being angry.
> *Right:* Anger is a feeling directed at someone who performs a real or imagined wrong action.
>
> Don't use negatives in your definition.
> *Wrong:* Sadness is *not* being happy.
> *Right:* Sadness is a feeling characterized by sorrow or depression.
>
> *Exception:* Sometimes negative qualities are the specific characteristics of words. In those cases, negatives are acceptable parts of definitions.
>
> *Example:* A widow is a woman *without* a husband.
>   ⌐[negative]

Step 1. A Definition in a Sentence. Fill in the blanks below to create logical one-sentence definitions. Use your dictionary. Study the examples above and below.

The Term	*Is*	*General Group*	*Specific Characteristic*
1. A silkworm	*is*	*a caterpillar*	*which spins a fine thread to make a cocoon.*
2. Summer	_____	_____	_____
3. Prejudice	_____	_____	_____
4. Courage	_____	_____	_____
5. A computer	_____	_____	_____

6. A stamen   _____   _____   _____

_____

_____

8- Buddhism   _____   _____   _____

_____

_____

8. An isobar   _____   _____   _____

_____

_____

9. A wrench   _____   _____   _____

_____

_____

10. A bill of lading   _____   _____   _____

_____

_____

11. A guild   _____   _____   _____

_____

Step 2. A Brief Paragraph as Definition. Often you need to expand a one-sentence definition into a paragraph so that the reader can visualize important details he needs to help him identify clearly the thing you are defining. Your paragraph should begin with a one-sentence definition as you have already learned, adding significant features in five or six more sentences. After you read the sample, write on a separate sheet of paper a one-paragraph definition of any of the suggested words on the next page. You will certainly need a dictionary; an encyclopedia or reference text can give any other information you need.

MAKING THE CONCRETE DEFINITION GROW

Some questions you should try to answer as you expand your definition are:
1. What are the physical features of the object: size, shape, color?
2. What may the object remind readers of? Does the object look like any other object?
3. What materials contribute to the object?
4. What is the object used for?

What Is Rayon?

Rayon is a man-made fiber produced from cellulose and used to weave fabrics. Chemicals dissolve the cellulose (wood pulp or short cotton fibers) which machines then force through tiny holes. The dissolved material, hardened in warm air or liquid, forms filaments which may be either twisted into threads or cut and spun. Spun filaments of rayon may look like wool, linen, or cotton. Because yarns with new features are developed all the time, rayon now has a variety of uses: it appears in automobile tires, in grease-proof cellophane sheets, in sponge rubber as a substitute for cellulose, and in special glass that cannot be shattered.

—Caroline Narby

1. test tube
2. bookkeeping
3. osmosis
4. vector
5. feudalism

6. pony express
7. abacus
8. tuberculosis
9. oceanography
10. allegory

Step 3. Judging the Dictionary.   Although the dictionary is your main line of defense in finding definitions, very often the meanings given for abstract words—words that stand for ideas more than for physical things—are not adequate. Frequently a word appears so much that people who use it have different ideas of its meaning. With such words it is important for you to add to the dictionary definition exactly what you mean when you use the word.

Look up the words below and write in the blank lines a definition based upon what the dictionary says. Then, check *yes* or *no* to show whether or not you think the dictionary meaning is complete, effective, and accurate. Tell the class the reason for your choice by adding information to the definition in order to make it reflect what you mean when you use the word.

	Adequate: Yes?	No?
1. democracy _____	_____	_____
2. ghetto _____	_____	_____
3. maturity _____	_____	_____
4. religion _____	_____	_____
5. happiness _____	_____	_____
6. truth _____	_____	_____
7. pride _____	_____	_____
8. beauty _____	_____	_____

Step 4. Talking about Meanings from Life.   Think of some specific moment in your life in which the meaning of an abstract word (like those in Step 3 above) became clear to you because of some experience you had.

Then, in a talk of a minute or two with the class, explain this experience. You may wish to write your response briefly. Read what Mr. Stearns said in one freshman group before you select a word to define. More words to choose from appear after his talk.

Ghetto

I learned what *ghetto* meant after my first drive down Washington Street in Brooklyn one December morning. A dozen empty buildings in one side of the street had broken windows and large black smears from a fire. I saw boarded-up doors, overturned garbage pails, and clumps of newspapers along the sidewalk. Three black children without coats played with the stuffing of an abandoned couch on an empty lot. A scraggly mutt stretched out on the corner. Everything looked so old and depressing and worn out. No dictionary ever gives that idea in its definition.

—Carl Stearns

1. fear
2. joy
3. tiredness
4. violence
5. teacher

6. friend
7. unselfishness
8. old age
9. success
10. courage

HOW TO WRITE CONCLUSIONS

The concluding paragraph of an essay is very much like the closing sentence of a paragraph. It should do all the things you learned in Chapter 5. A good conclusion should therefore

tell the reader that your essay is coming to a close;

give the reader a feeling that you have accomplished what you set out to do.

But a closing paragraph permits the writer to develop some larger application for his topic. A good conclusion takes the topic out of its specific importance in your life or out of its limited truth to a small area of information and applies it to a broader issue. What you do therefore is to illustrate that what you have written about has importance beyond the ideas developed in your body paragraphs. You show that you have used what you have written to help you think about other ideas. This is not an easy chore. You run the risk of sounding too "important," too philosophical, too much like a show-off. As a result, the concluding paragraph needs especially careful thought and must often progress through several rewritings. But the product pays off strong dividends: it helps the reader see that the narrow topic you developed has relevance in other critical areas. It gives you an opportunity to develop an idea that has an important relationship to your topic, but is new in the frame of the essay itself.

Let us examine the conclusion of an essay you read earlier and the relationship of the conclusion to the rest of the theme. Stella Tesoriero wrote in "Women: Fragile Flowers?" (pp. 335–336) this proposal sentence:

Women are not the weaker sex.

In her second paragraph Miss Tesoriero tried to show how others would argue against her proposal. (She brings up the arguments of women's inferiority in stamina, stability, and thinking). The third paragraph answers these arguments by presenting proof that they are incorrect and that women have a biological superiority to men. Here is Miss Tesoriero's conclusion; as you read, try to determine how she has worked upon her previous paragraphs to develop a broader issue:

Woman has not been able to prove she is not the weaker sex because the society has assigned her to an inferior position. Few brilliant women have tried to develop their talents simply because there has been a small market for brilliant women in this country. The few who have bothered to develop their creative talents find that the world views them as "odd balls." The stereotype of a brilliant woman is that of a horsefaced, flat-chested female in support shoes, one who has hidden all her sexual instincts in her search for a career. It may be fun being treated like a fragile flower by a boyfriend or a date, but there is a time and place for everything. It is time society stopped giving out positions based on stereotypes. We women must develop and make use of our wasted female brain powers.

This conclusion shows why women have not advanced in society. That is *not* an idea that is clearly part of Miss Tesoriero's proposal sentence:

Women are not the weaker sex.

Yet by bringing in the related idea of stereotyping and the reasons for woman's inferior position in today's world, the writer offers a new significance for the topic. From the topic idea of woman's superiority to man, Miss Tesoriero moves into a larger application: the reason why women have for so long been kept down in society. She is showing the reader how the ideas she developed in paragraphs 2 and 3 (the superiority of man or woman) suggest a broader, more general application for the topic (the reasons why women do not show their superiority).

Her new application works effectively in the essay, but it is not the only possibility she could have chosen. The conclusion—based upon the proposal and the supporting body paragraphs—might have treated any one of these broader issues:

women in the future replacing men in high-pressure jobs

women as top political leaders

the failure of male scientists to treat women fairly in experimental data

a world in which men stay home to raise children and do housework.

This list is not complete, but any point above developed with sufficient supporting details might nicely suggest a wider and more general truth for the ideas proposed in the rest of the essay.

Notice, furthermore, that the first sentence of Miss Tesoriero's conclusion refers back to the ideas developed in previous paragraphs by mentioning the topic that the writer set out to develop. Look at the two sentences side by side:

Proposal	*First Sentence of Conclusion*
Women are not the weaker sex.	*Woman* has not been able to prove she *is not the weaker sex* because the society has assigned her to an inferior position.

The italicized words in the first sentence of the conclusion act as a transition because they bridge the conclusion to the topic as stated in the proposal. In addition, these words help summarize the topic for the reader who has read two full paragraphs since he last saw the proposal. This device of summary is excellent early in the conclusion because it reminds the reader of what the essay set out to do, and permits the reader to evaluate the writer's success in developing the proposal.

TIPS AND REMINDERS FOR DRAMATIC CONCLUSIONS

(See pp. 189–190, Some Closing Sentence Pointers.)
1. Remind the reader that you have achieved what you set out to do and that your essay is drawing to an end.
2. Strive to establish a new, a larger, a more general application for your topic.
3. Summarize briefly the main point of your essay.
4. Make the conclusion an important part of the essay, not something you glued on to add more words.
5. Do not:
    start a whole new topic;
    contradict your entire point;
    make obvious or overused statements;
    apologize for your lack of knowledge;
    end suddenly with a one-sentence conclusion like,
       "That's all I have to say."
    draw conclusions that are absolute (make sure that you allow for possibilities of exceptions);
    talk about your own essay by mentioning words like "my introduction," "so my conclusion is," "my proposal sentence said."

Step 1. Essay Conclusions. Reread the following essays, paying special attention to the concluding paragraph. Write in the blank lines below the title the writer's proposal (you may have to restate it in your own words so it is clear when you remove it from the essay). Then, in the blank space alongside, write the broader issue that the writer tries to develop in the conclusion. Study the example.

	Larger Application (Broader Issue) in Conclusion

1. "Deprived Children," pp. 333–334. *Proposal:* *Children of working mothers are frequently insecure and unhappy.*

   what children left on their own must learn.

2. "Practice in the High School Gym," pp. 299–300. *Proposal:* _____

3. "Call Them What You Like," pp. 336–337. *Proposal:* _____

4. "Antonia's Strength," pp. 368–369. *Proposal:* _____

5. "Some Disappointments," pp. 364–366. *Proposal:* _____

6. "Hating a Job," pp. 403–404. *Proposal:*

Step 2. Finding New Areas of Relevance. For each essay you have reread in connection with Step 1 above, suggest some *other* area of importance the writer could have developed in his conclusion. Base your suggestions on the proposal sentence and the two body paragraphs. Study the example.

1. "Deprived Children," pp. 333–334.

Possible New Area of Relevance for Conclusion

what the responsibilities of motherhood involve.

_____

2. "Practice in the High School Gym," pp. 299–300.

_____

_____

_____

3. "Call Them What You Like," pp. 336–337.

_____

_____

_____

4. "Antonia's Strength," pp. 368–369.

_____

_____

_____

5. "Some Disappointments," pp. 364–366.

_____

_____

_____

6. "Hating a Job," pp. 403–404.

_____

_____

_____

SOLVING PROBLEMS IN WRITING

Some Words Not to Mistake

accept: This word means *to receive, to welcome, to say yes to.*

We *accepted* their offer to help.

except: This word means *leaving out, excluding.*

Everyone *except* Joe Namath reported for practice.

amount: This word refers to things in large masses, things that cannot be counted.

A large *amount* of water filled the tub.

number: This word refers to countable things.

He received a large *number* of parking tickets.

hanged: Use this to indicate that someone's life was taken by execution.

The angry mob *hanged* the nervous criminal without a trial.

hung: Use this to refer to things, not to people.

Two workmen hung the mirror in fifteen minutes.

being that: Avoid this expression in formal written English. Instead use *since* or *because.*

Since (*not* being that) I felt sleepy, I returned to the lounge.

former: Between two objects, *former* refers to the first thing named.
latter: Between two objects, *latter* refers to the second of two things.

Neither the car nor the motorcycle would start; the *former* because of a bad carburetor and the *latter* because of a faulty ignition system.

Hint: If three objects are involved, do not use former and latter. Say first, second (or next), last.

A dog, a cat, and a horse appeared in the cartoon; the first did a tap dance while the last played a guitar.

into: means a movement from one place to a position within.

He ran *into* the room (means he was outside the room when the action began).

in: means movement within one place.

He ran *in* the room (means he was already within the room when the action began).

regardless: Use this word, not *irregardless.*

Regardless of our suggestions, he voted in his own way.

affect: a. means *to assume* or *pretend.*

He *affected* a smile of agreement.

b. means *to influence.*

Good study habits *affect* learning speed.

effect: a. means *to bring about.*

His disposition *effected* a change in our mood.

b. means a *result* or *outcome.*

The *effect* of his speech cannot be measured.

Hint: If *the* or *an* is used before the word, you *must* choose *effect.*

Name _____ Class _____ 429

Step 1. Making the Words Work. Follow instructions.

1. Tell in a sentence what happens to your own personality when you get very little sleep at night. Use the words *the effect* in your sentence.

   _____

   _____

2. Tell in a sentence which vegetables you dislike. Use *accept* or *except* correctly. _____

   _____

   _____

3. Use *regardless* in your own sentence. _____

   _____

4. Use *hang* or *hung* in a sentence about a man's conviction in a murder case. _____

   _____

   _____

5. Write a sentence about a diver and the ocean or a lake. Use *in* or *into* correctly. _____

   _____

   _____

6. Use *affected* to mean *pretended* in a sentence. _____

   _____

   _____

   _____

7. Write a sentence about nailing a picture to a wall. Use *hanged* or *hung*, whichever you think is correct. _____

   _____

   _____

8. Write two sentences about two friends you have. In the first sentence mention both by name. In the second sentence use *former* and *latter* correctly. _____

   _____

   _____

9. Correct this sentence: He had to return his tickets for the high school reunion game being that his mother was sick. _____

_____

_____

10. Write a sentence about the long-range effects of chocolate on the teeth. Use *amount* or *number* correctly in your sentence. _____

_____

_____

FOR CLEAR EXPRESSION: RIGHT FORM, RIGHT PLACE

Balancing Connected Parts: Keeping the Same Form

Words or word groups in a series must match in form.

Hint: You can recognize a series by commas and the words *and, but, or, nor.*

The housewife liked to bake, to sew, and to cook.
—[all infinitives]—

not

liked to bake, to sew, and *cooking.*

We prefer dancing and singing.
[both -*ing* words]

not

dancing and *to sing.*

We heard that the President spoke to his advisers, contacted newsmen,
[verb]   [verb]
and then made his announcement to the public.
[verb]

not

We heard that the President spoke to his advisers, contacted newsmen
and *of his announcement to the public.*

Step 1. Making the Parts Fit. Add a word group that completes the series with a balanced part.

1. She chose not to speak or _____ .

2. David called to his wife, asked her for the time, and _____

_____ .

3. Many people do not enjoy joking, laughing, or _____ as much as he does.

4. He told us that he liked books, television programs, and _____

_____ .

Balancing Connected Parts: Repeating the Series Opener

By using the same form for words in a series you balance the parts of the sentence for clearer expression. But often you need to repeat for each part of the series the first word in the opening item of the series. The sentences on the right are clearer because they repeat the opening word.

Not

They approved his plan because it was logical and it promised to succeed.

He spoke out for the party, for its leaders, but not its principles.

But

They approved his plan *because* it was logical and *because* it promised to succeed.

He spoke out *for* the party, *for* its leaders, but not *for* its principles.

SOME SERIES OPENERS THAT OFTEN NEED REPEATING

because, for, of, by, to, at   that, so that, a (an), who, which, could.

Step 2. Balance through Repetition. Rewrite the incorrect underlined portion in these sentences so that it balances with the rest of the series.

1. The coach announced that athletes need special diets, that sweets add needless fat and calories, and <u>we should avoid chocolates at all costs.</u>

   that we should avoid chocolates at all costs.
   _____

2. For breakfast every morning I eat a grapefruit, <u>egg, and glass of milk.</u>

   _____

3. Our guidance counselor is a man <u>of special training</u> and who knows students' problems. _____

4. He spoke up forcefully to his parents, to his teachers, <u>and even his closest friends.</u> _____

5. People should register for their national elections and <u>vote every time.</u>

   _____

   _____

Balancing Connected Parts: Paired Words and Matching Forms

A special effect of balance in sentences comes about through certain connectors that work in pairs. These paired connectors must be followed by words that have the same form. In the sentences below, connectors are in boldface. X's appear over words that do not match in form. Underlined words show matching forms.

The registrar is **either** <u>working</u> at his desk **or** <u>visiting</u> the dean.
NOT

xxxxxxxxxxxxxxxxxxxxx
The registrar is **either** working at his desk **or** on a visit with the dean.

I wondered **whether** <u>to make</u> the telephone call **or** <u>to see</u> her in person.
NOT

xxxxxxxxxxxx
I wondered **whether** I should make the telephone call **or** to see her in person.

Words That Work in Pairs:

either . . . or	whether . . . or
neither . . . nor	not only . . . but also
both . . . and	if . . . or

Step 3. Paired Words and Forms That Match.   Add a word group to each sentence below, making sure what you add matches the underlined segment.

Example:

1. We saw not only <u>all the movies he directed,</u>

   but also the television commercials he wrote. _____

2. You should either <u>go to the ballpark</u> for the game or _____

   _____ .

3. Barbara is both <u>setting her hair</u> and _____ .

Step 4. Balanced Sentence Ideas: More Practice.   Each sentence below contains an error in sentence balance like those you have examined in the previous pages. Underline the incorrect part and rewrite it in the blank spaces.

1. Dr. Hathaway is a surgeon of great fame and who performs extraordinary operations. _____

   _____

2. A good politician studies carefully the speeches of his opponents and how they raise money for their campaigns. _____

   _____

3. He did not know if he should report to the police or to go to his priest for some advice. _____

   _____

4. I need a job with convenient hours and which pays a good salary.

_____

_____

5. She not only is writing letters to local officials but also calls congress-

men each week on the telephone. _____

_____

6. He knew either to change his plane reservations or that he would leave

in the next few hours. _____

_____

7. Everyone likes eating hot dogs and to buy custard at the neighborhood

carnival. _____

_____

8. Our instructor told us both to underline words in the book and writing

notes in the margin are good aids for studying later on. _____

_____

9. At the Central Park Zoo we laughed at an ostrich, monkey, and tired

old hippopotamus sunning himself on his back. _____

_____

10. At the beach we enjoy skimming the waves, running along the shore-

line, and to play in the sand. _____

_____

DESCRIPTIVE WORDS IN THE PROPER PLACE

Words or word groups that describe must stand as close as possible to whatever is being described. Words like *only, just, even, almost, hardly* — depending upon where they are placed in the sentence — affect the meaning
that the writer wishes. Look at the word in five different places in the same
sentence below and examine the explanation of the meanings.

1. *Just* he suggested that we leave early.
   (This means he was the only one who spoke.)
2. He *just* suggested that we leave early.
   (This means that he merely told of one idea.)
3. He suggested *just* that we leave early.
   (This means that he made no other suggestion.)
4. He suggested that *just* we leave early.
   (This means that he meant nobody else should leave early.)

5. He suggested that we *just* leave early.
   (This means that he felt we should do nothing else but leave early.)

Step 1. Explaining Placement.   In the spaces provided, explain the meaning created by the italicized word in each sentence below.

1. The lawyer told us *only* that we should remain silent. _____

   _____

2. The lawyer told us that *only* we should remain silent. _____

   _____

3. *Only* the lawyer told us that we should remain silent. _____

   _____

4. The lawyer *only* told us that we should remain silent. _____

   _____

DESCRIPTIVE WORD GROUPS: PUTTING THEM IN THEIR PLACE

Word groups placed too far from the words they describe often create confusing sentences.

1. Our neighbor sold dresses to my sister without buttons.
   (The *sister* has no buttons?)
2. At the age of five, the doctor administered a smallpox vaccination to me.
   (The *doctor* was five years old?)
3. I watched as an old car pulled down the street that had a flat tire.
   (The *street* had a flat tire?)

Here are the sentences with the describing words in the proper places.

[This word group describes *dresses:* put
it close to what it describes.]

1. Our neighbor sold dresses *without buttons* to my sister.

[This word group describes *me:* put
it close to what it describes.]

2. The doctor administered a smallpox vaccination to me *at the age of five.*
3. I watched as an old car *that had a flat tire* pulled down the street.

[This word group describes *car:* put
it close to what it describes.]

Step 1. In the Right Places.   Add the italicized word group in the right place in the sentence so that it expresses a logical and clear idea. Rewrite the sentences in the space provided. You may want to rearrange words.

1. *with sneakers on*

   The man quickly reached the door of the plane. _____

   _____

2. *that played at the bottom of the cage*

   The monkeys screamed wildly at the spectators. _____

   _____

3. *in a tuxedo*

   I felt strange riding on a bus to my sister's wedding. _____

   _____

4. *last month*

   In history class I could not understand why the Civil War took so long

   in starting. _____

   _____

5. *in an old but reliable pot*

   Betty cooked spaghetti for her guests. _____

   _____

Step 2. Changing Faulty Placement. In the sentences below, words or word groups do not appear close enough to the words they describe. Rewrite each sentence by putting the words in the proper places. Mark any correct sentence C.

1. He only eats too much on Sundays. _____

   _____

2. Mr. Jones is a handsome man; he has thick eyebrows, a straight nose,

   and long hair with glasses. _____

   _____

3. We spotted an old television in a New England barn without knobs or

   a channel selector. _____

   _____

4. She fled down the block swiftly. _____

   _____

5. The little child ran to his mother from across the room that had lost a

   favorite toy. _____

   _____

WRITING THE ESSAY

For this theme, select some abstract word and in a four-paragraph essay write a definition of that word. Write a proposal sentence which makes very clear the word you have singled out for definition and the approach you will take with that word. The proposal must allow you to discuss two aspects of your definition—one in each body paragraph. Write an introduction following any of the suggestions on pp. 277–282.

In the body paragraphs you have to choose as usual from several kinds of illustrative details. You can use sensory details, statistics, statements from books, comments made on television or radio, actual cases which you know: any of these will add lively support to your paragraph topics. The methods of paragraph development which appear in Part I of this book can suggest the ways in which your details may be put together successfully.

But the most fruitful definition is one that starts in your own experience. For that reason you are urged to relate in each body paragraph one specific moment in your life, a moment when you learned an important feature of the definition of the word you have chosen. What you will produce in your essay, therefore, is a personalized definition, one which gives the reader a background of your experience through which to understand your application of language. The student theme you will later examine develops a definition in this manner, illustrating two moments (expanded with concrete sensory language) in which the writer learned the meaning of some abstract term in his vocabulary.

Your conclusion requires special attention in this essay. As you learned on pp. 423–427 of this chapter, your concluding paragraph will attempt to develop a broader issue which is related to your proposal, an issue which illustrates the importance of your topic beyond the limited application you have made in your essay.

Step 1. Examining a Student Theme. Read Miss Fogel's theme, looking especially for the two specific moments she uses to illustrate her definition and the sensory details that allow you to visualize the scenes she describes. Write the answers to the questions after the selection.

Excitement

Whenever one attempts to define an emotion, one encounters a rather obvious problem. An abstract term simply cannot be defined so that everyone who uses the word instantly understands it. A *test-tube*, an *apple, a bus:* these words bring to mind some specific object which—except for minor variations—most of us see in the same way. But an emotion is felt by each individual in a different way and may even be felt differently by the *same* individual under varying circumstances.

Excitement, for example, means one thing to a five-year-old and something quite different to the same girl late in her teens.

The day that my entire third grade class would visit my house stands out as an early memory of excitement. On a spring morning I leaped out of bed, pulled on my clothes and rushed excitedly into the kitchen for breakfast. I gulped down my juice in such haste that I stained my starched blouse. Grandma told me that I had better change into a different blouse, but I insisted that I had no time to waste. I simply *couldn't* come late to school! Not today! Not when my whole class would be coming over to the house to see our cherry tree in full bloom with small pink flowers that smelled like perfume. I grabbed a sweater and ran to say goodbye to Grandpa, his whiskers tickling my nose when I kissed him. Now Grandma took my small hand in hers, and we started to school. As soon as I reached the old brick building, I dashed to the big double doors, then up two flights of stairs, and straight to the kindergarten room, my feet clop-clopping in the empty hallways. I tried the cold doorknob, but to my great disappointment it did not move. Where *was* everyone? Why were they all so late? I looked at the clock that ticked noisily above the stairway. The big black hand pointed to the nine, but the little one somehow disappeared. Where was that silly thing? Didn't the clock know that I was only a little girl and needed *both* hands to tell time? Finally the big hand slid towards the ten, revealing the little one that hid beneath it. Let's see now. That means it's ten to nine. Only ten minutes to go! But when ten minutes passed and a stream of classmates poured into the room, Miss Esmond reminded me that we would still have to wait until recess. "Now, Sarah," she smiled, her nose wrinkling, "don't be impatient. That tree won't leave your backyard no matter what time we get there!" We still had an hour and a half of spelling, reading and arithmetic, but all that while my mind thought only of the tall cherry tree that stood in my back yard, its thick brown bark and fragrant blossoms soon to be surrounded by an entire class of squealing boys and girls, all my friends.

Some thirteen years after this immature though very real involvement with an emotion, I experienced excitement of a different sort. I stood in Manhattan among thousands of people who showed their support for Soviet Jewry. During the last hundred hours of 1970 we marched continuously at 67th Street and Lexington Avenue in front of the Soviet Embassy, chattering noisily and singing old songs as our excited breathing formed white patches of smoke in the December air. But what started out as an orderly march ended up as a scene of chaos and excitement. As the people in the back of the crowd inched their way up front, angered policemen in blue uniforms shoved the crowd back with wooden barricades. Those up front snapped angrily at the police, harsh words jumping back and forth between the policemen and the crowd. I stood among those brave ones up front, and as a "reward" for my bravery, I found myself at the bottom of a giant heap of people trampled on from all sides. When I first touched the hard cement, I shrieked in fright, but, when I regained my senses, I struggled to separate myself from the mass of tangled bodies. A middle-aged man in a black hat must have seen my outstretched arm poking through a web of assorted legs; he pulled me to my feet. Panic-stricken, I watched as a boy — no older than I — received a smack on the head from a flying billy-club that smashed down like a hammer into a stone wall. Someone bellowed out over a megaphone, "Move back! Move back!" but didn't the idiot realize that he was ordering the crowd to do the impossible? There was no place to move! I shrank back in terror as a policeman charged at my brother. Tarnished buttons glinted in the sun as a large form pressed towards us through the angry crowd. I shut my eyes tightly and recited a short prayer. "Please, G-d! Don't let the cop hurt Yudie!" And G-d answered my prayer. My eyes popped open and I heard the snapping of Yudie's knee when his powerful kick knocked the policeman's club from his hand. I grabbed the sleeve of Yudie's jacket and together we weaved our way out of the infuriated mob.

In both instances I experienced excitement, one moment simple and innocent, and the other complex and explosive. Since such different situations aroused the same kind of emotion, I wonder if our emotions are reliable at all until we have a full chance to test them with time and experience. I have to laugh when I hear my thirteen-year-old neighbor say she loves her high school boyfriend. Does she have an idea of what the word means? How does she know it will mean the same for her next week? Love is an emotion and to rely upon an early or untested experience for the definition is to me ridiculous. Still, many young people marry at seventeen or eighteen, claiming deep love for their partners. Then, of course, the divorce courts leap into action just a short time after! It seems to me that decisions based upon emotions must be very carefully made so that we understand the full range of meaning we attach to any special feeling.

—Sarah Fogel

1. Put a check next to the proposal sentence. What two aspects of the topic does Miss Fogel announce? _____

   _____

2. Name the two specific moments treated in the body paragraphs.

   a. _____

   b. _____

3. Circle the words that make transitions in the first sentence of paragraph 2.

4. Underline that part of the opening sentence of paragraph 3 that reminds the reader of the previous paragraph. Circle that part of the sentence that announces the content of paragraph 3 itself.

5. Copy out an image that

   a. uses sound _____

   b. shows color and/or action _____

   c. names a sensation of touch _____

6. What general comment does Miss Fogel make in her conclusion? How is this general comment related to her topic? _____

   _____

   _____

Some Titles for the Definition Essay

Here are some suggestions for titles of your essay on the definition of a word you have learned through personal experience:

1. My Definition of Fear
2. When I Learned the Meaning of Love
3. Two Moments of Anger
4. How I Learned What Prejudice Means
5. My Experience With Loneliness
6. What Is Hope?
7. What Is Pain?
8. What Is Joy?
9. What Is Sadness?
10. Learning the Meaning of Injustice
11. I Learn to Hate
12. Brotherhood in Action: Two Moments in Definition
13. The Meaning of Pride
14. The Meaning of Poverty
15. My Definition of City
16. Excitement: Two Moments in Definition
17. My Meaning of Unselfishness
18. My Definition of Education
19. Teacher: Two Moments in Definition
20. My Definition of Fun

A Definition Checklist: Evaluating Your Own Essay

After you write the first copy of your essay and *before* you write the final copy, study this checklist, making any changes you may need to improve the quality of your paper. If you cannot check excellent or good for most of the questions, you need to revise your essay carefully. Then, after you are satisfied with your final copy, fill out the checklist by putting an X on the blanks that best describe (in your opinion) the way you followed the directions. Submit the checklist with your essay.

EVALUATION

	Excellent	*Good*	*Fair*	*Does not appear*
1. My proposal sentence explains the intention of my essay and allows me to discuss *two* aspects of my topic, one in each body paragraph. My proposal comes as the last sentence of paragraph 1.	_____	_____	_____	_____

2. My first sentence of para- _____ _____ _____ _____
   graph 2 tells what aspect of
   the topic I will discuss and
   makes a transition to the
   proposal sentence.

3. My first sentence of para- _____ _____ _____ _____
   graph 3 refers back to para-
   graph 2 *and* states the topic
   that will appear in paragraph 3.

4. Each of my body paragraphs _____ _____ _____ _____
   expands one single mo-
   ment in my life as an illustration of the word I am
   defining.

5. There are several exam- _____ _____ _____ _____
   ples of concrete sensory
   images in my paper. My essay contains several words
   that show colors and actions, name sounds and
   smells, state sensations of
   touch. I have used simile,
   metaphor, and personification (pp. 127–131) to improve the visual qualities
   of my paper.

6. Before I prepared my final _____ _____ _____ _____
   copy, I studied my own list
   of misspelled words and
   my own Theme Progress
   Sheet. I was careful to look
   over my paper for my usual
   errors. I proofread my essay
   very slowly according to
   directions on pp. 114–115.

7. I have chosen for my topic _____ _____ _____ _____
   some word which has deep
   and important meanings
   for me.

8. I have used a number of _____ _____ _____ _____
   sentence types in order to
   achieve variety in writing.
   I have employed:
   subordination (pp. 89–
      97)

coordination (pp. 85–
89)

-ing openers (pp. 192–
196)

-ed openers (p. 197)

a semicolon (p. 232)

openers with word
groups that show
relationship (pp. 350–
352).

9. I have checked over my   _____   _____   _____   _____
paper for describing words
that are misplaced and for
errors in confused words
described in this chapter.

10. I have written a conclusion   _____   _____   _____   _____
that applies my topic to
some other issue or idea
that may be viewed in the
light of the subject I have
developed (see pp. 423–
427).

THE PROFESSIONALS SPEAK

In the following selection Eugene N. Doherty illustrates the meaning of
proud words through an expanded moment. Look for the concrete sensory
details that you find most clear and visual. Discuss the answers to the questions aloud or write your responses on separate paper, according to your
instructor's directions.

SOME WORDS TO KNOW BEFORE YOU READ

candid: honest
reminiscing: thinking back to days past
reluctant: unwilling, hesitant
infuriated: made angry
futility: hopelessness
appalled: shocked
elation: high spirits

Proud Words

Jeff was taller than I, but only half as broad, and not nearly so strong. He loved
to whistle and he chattered endlessly, even when no one was near to listen. His

lustrous brown eyes were soft, yet boldly candid, and his face was quick to wrinkle in a smile, which infected everyone he knew. All through high school and my two years of college he almost worshiped me. He kept a scrapbook of my basketball career, my football jersey and varsity letters decorated his wall, and it was he who cried the night I was eliminated from the Diamond Gloves competition. Sometimes I would complain to my father, "He follows me around like a puppy dog. Everywhere I go I expect to find him there, smiling at me and wagging his tail." Secretly I enjoyed his admiration and I was intensely fond of him. But I used proud words to him the last day of my furlough.

The night had been particularly well planned. I meant to leave a crimson stain on our little hamlet that would warm me through the long months overseas. I had showered and shaved with care; and, as I contemplated abandoning the forest greens in favor of a natty civilian suit, my brother dashed into my room. He was so excited the words gushed out, "I promised Mary and her mother that I'd take them to a shower, but let's meet somewhere and have a few drinks." As he spoke, he retrieved one of my shoes from under the bed.

I had plans for the evening that didn't include reminiscing about the good old days with my seventeen-year-old brother. "Not tonight, Jeff. Wait up for me and we'll have a few when I get home."

A concerned look swept across his face and he seemed reluctant to talk. Finally he stammered, "When are you leaving?"

"As soon as I finish dressing."

"Gee, Euge, I promised Mary that I'd take them. They'll have fits if I don't show up!"

"Well, call 'em and tell 'em you can't."

"I can't do that. They're depending on me. I've got to have the car."

"You better call 'em. I'm using the car tonight."

I was more than a little surprised to hear him give up so easily, but he merely spun on his heel and retreated to his room, where I heard him making hasty preparations to go out. Happy that this incident didn't explode into unpleasantness and contented with the image surveying me from the mirror, I left my room and sauntered downstairs to make some parting remarks to my parents.

The coolness and smoothness of the banister rail thrilled. I felt strongly confident. This promised to be a great night that I would recall with pleasure while sweating out some far-flung hellhole of the Pacific. My reverie was suddenly interrupted by the impatient grinding of a starter, followed swiftly by the rasping grate of gears as the driver too hastily shifted into reverse. I sensed a shudder run through the house as a car raced down the driveway. Frantically I realized that my brother was escaping with the family car.

I bolted down the remaining steps, flung the front door open, leaped over the porch rail, and intercepted the car just as Jeff was manipulating his turn out of the driveway. The door handle jarred my hip as the car bucked forward, then stalled. The impact set off ripples of pain, which infuriated me. I tore the door open. My brother's eyes were wide with terror as I reached into the car to catch hold of him. He struggled to avoid my grasp and the loud rip of his suit coat startled us both. He stared at his rent coat, stunned and disbelieving, then he sprang from the car. His fists clenched and his arms flailing, he looked comically like a stumbling windmill that had somehow lost its foothold. A sob, more like a groan, escaped his lips as he caught me with one hand and struck me with the other. The crack of his fist against my cheek enraged me, and with all my strength I returned his fury. I didn't mean to hurt him, but rather only to impress him with the futility of his laboring. My blow was aimed at his chest, but in his frustration and confusion his feet became entangled and he lunged forward. As soon as the punch landed, I knew the fight was over. My fist had caught him flush in the mouth.

For a second his startled eyes met mine. He seemed surprised that I would hit so hard in so uneven a contest. His idol had feet of sand. I grabbed his arm and tried to explain that I meant only to frighten him. The sight of his mouth appalled me. He seemed to have three lips. Blood flooded his mouth and gushed from the open, jagged wound. The scarlet stream poured down his chin and dripped onto his torn lapel and stained his white shirt. His teeth were blotched with crimson and I worried that some permanent damage had been done. His sobs came in gusts and his whole body shuddered and shook from their intensity.

"I'm sorry, Jeff. Forgive me. I didn't mean—"

He writhed free of my grasp and raked me with his eyes. Blood from his torn lip splattered my face as he screamed, "Get away from me you—you bum!" He turned and ran toward the house.

My mother, who had observed the fracas, wrapped her arms around him and led him through the doorway, then closed the door behind them. She never said a word. She didn't even look at me.

My last day at home lay in ruins. I backed up the car in front of the house and then caught a bus into Elizabeth. I knew that no amount of drinking nor dancing would erase the memory of Jeff's frightened eyes or his tattered lip. I don't remember how many places I visited nor how many times I reminded myself that this was my last day at home, but the memory of his face always sobered me and a great loneliness overwhelmed me.

It was very late when I returned, for I had missed the last bus, and I had to walk most of the way home. My house was quiet and comfortingly warm when I entered, but I felt like an intruder. I'd be happy to get back to camp.

My brother's bedroom door was slightly ajar. Pausing there for a moment, I pressed my finger tip against its hard, cool surface. The opening widened silently and I edged into the room. I could see his shoes lying askew, his socks in the same position in which they tumbled from his feet, his shirt and trousers a dark shadow and a patch of white draped over the chair. Jeff's faint accent hung in the room like an invisible mist. I was about to retreat when a breeze pressed an overhanging bough away from the street light outside our house. Jeff's pale face was lit with a vague, inexpressible radiance. This reflection was marred only by the livid gash in his lip and a perceptible puffiness under his right eye, which had somehow been blackened. I yearned to wake him and to appeal once more for his forgiveness, but the unpredictability of his reaction held me motionless. I promised myself that I would speak to him in the morning . . . everything would be all right in the morning.

The warmth and brilliance of sunlight splashing across my face warned me it was already late when I awoke. I leaped from the bed carrying half the sheets and blankets with me, and raced downstairs. I was both embarrassed and ashamed that I had squandered my last morning at home indulging myself with sleep when I knew how very much my parents wanted to chat. My mother guessed that I wanted to "mend fences" with Jeff and answered my unspoken question. "Jeff went to Mary's. They took a taxi last night."

"Did he say anything before he left?"

"Only that he was sorry he spoiled your last night home."

I waited around the house longer than I should have. If my train hadn't been late, I would have been A.W.O.L. My farewells with my parents were repeated several times. Each time I heard a door slam or footsteps on the porch my pulse quickened and I felt a strange elation, but Jeff didn't come home until after I left.

I never saw my brother again. On some forgotten, unimportant slope in Okinawa a month before the war ended, my brother bled for the last time. "Proud words wear long boots and you can't call them back."

—Eugene N. Doherty

1. What hints are there early in the selection that the narrator is a soldier?

_____

_____

2. Read the sentence in paragraph 1 that tells the topic of the selection.
3. Read aloud several images that mention colors, that describe actions, that name sounds or sensations of touch.
4. How did the narrator learn the meaning of pride? How does the sentence beginning "On some forgotten, unimportant slope . . ." in the last paragraph add a special tragedy to the moment Mr. Doherty describes?

_____

_____

5. Which picture of Jeff do you find most memorable? Why?

_____

_____

REACHING HIGHER

Step 1. Art as Definition. Look at the photograph on p. 413. Write a paragraph which explains what you think is the painter's definition of the words he uses as the title of the picture.

Step 2. A Photo Essay as Definition. Select any *five* abstract terms (ten possibilities are listed on p. 423), and from magazines and newspapers cut out and mount a face, a scene of action, or a place that you think illustrates each abstraction. Or, you might wish to take your own photographs of scenes or people, photographs that would show in concrete terms what you mean by some abstract word like *fear, love, happiness, hatred,* or *sorrow*.

On the back of each mounted picture, write a sentence which names the word you are defining and explains why you represented it by the picture you selected.

part III

A MINIBOOK
OF THIRTEEN SPECIAL SKILLS

1. Improving Spelling
2. Learning Vocabulary
3. Reading a Dictionary Entry
4. Using a Thesaurus
5. Writing Simple Footnotes
6. Preparing a Bibliography
7. Using the Reader's Guide
8. Quoting from Books
9. Business-Letter Format
10. Taking Notes
11. Writing a Summary
12. Answering Essay Examination Questions
13. Making a Simple Outline

1. IMPROVING SPELLING

Whether it is fair or not, people judge our intelligence by the way we spell. Although poor spellers are not necessarily low on thinking ability, the business and academic communities put a high value on spelling skills. With that in mind, you need to reapproach your own problems in spelling. If you don't want others to think of you as unintelligent, you need to make a conscious effort to improve your spelling, no matter what it takes. In many instances students have improved their spelling remarkably simply by deciding that they would make a stronger effort to build up skills. Once you make up your mind that you no longer want to spell poorly, follow these steps for improvement:

HOW TO BE A BETTER SPELLER

1. Keep a list of the words you usually have trouble with: write the word correctly spelled; underline the troublesome letters; and make up some way of remembering the word. Start your list on p. 459 after you examine the sample.
2. Write troublesome words several times, saying the letters aloud.
3. Trace the letters with your fingers after you think you know the spelling.
4. Use the dictionary to find correct spelling. Note the syllables.
5. If you cannot find a word in the dictionary, don't assume that the dictionary left out the word you are looking for. Try as many possible letter combinations as you can. For example, let us imagine that you had real trouble spelling *conscious*. You look first under the letter *k* (it often makes the same sound as *c* at the beginning of a word), but when you find no *kon* combination, you have to look for another possibility: *con* starts many words. If you had trouble with letters after *con*, you might look next at *sh* (it makes the same sound as *sci* here). But when you find no *consh*, you need to think of other possibilities: maybe even *consch*. If you follow these suggestions you will often locate the correct spelling. When you find the spelling that looks right to you, *read the definition* to make sure that the spelling offered is the correct one for the word you want.
6. Learn the spelling demons, words most frequently misspelled by many people. One hundred and fifty appear below.
7. Learn spelling rules for the most difficult problems.

Spelling Demons: Group A

1. *abundance* : Have <u>a</u> <u>bun</u>; then <u>dance</u>.
2. *accommodate:* two <u>c</u>'s, two <u>m</u>'s
3. *achievement:* <u>i</u> before <u>e</u>
4. *adolescence:* -<u>scence</u>
5. *allowed:* Look for <u>all</u>.
6. *analyze:* -<u>yze</u>
7. *apparent:* double <u>p</u>; -<u>ent</u>

8. *appreciate* : double p; iate
9. *arrangement* : Don't drop the e.
10. *attendance* : Two t's; end in dance.
11. *available* : Ail is in this word.
12. *becoming* : Drop the e in become; one m only.
13. *benefited* : Look for the fit after bene.
14. *business* : The bus is in so add -ess.
15. *category* : an e between cat and gory
16. *cigarette* : two t's surrounded by e's
17. *competition* : Make the last e in compete an i; add -tion.
18. *conscious* : sc + ious
19. *cruel* : u + e
20. *dependent* : -ent ending
21. *dilemma* : Emma has a dilemma.
22. *discipline* : -sci
23. *eliminate* : e + lim + i + nate
24. *environment* : nm combination
25. *exaggerate* : two g's
26. *existence* : exist + ence
27. *familiar* : The word liar is in familiar.
28. *grammar* : **Hint:** ram and mar are the same letters reversed.
29. *guiding* : Drop the e in guide.
30. *hoping* : only one p in hope
31. *independence* : -ence at the end
32. *jealousy* : Jealousy is lousy!
        i
33. *loneliness* : lonely + ness
34. *management* : Add ment to manage.
35. *mischief* : The Indian chief does mischief.
36. *organization* : Drop the e in organize; add -ation.
37. *particular* : i c u are particular.
38. *persuade* : Add -suade to per.
39. *precede* : pre + cede
40. *presence* : If you are present make your presence known.
41. *proceed* : The church needs the proceeds.
42. *receive* : i before e except after c
43. *rhythm* : rhy + thm
44. *satisfied* : -fied
45. *separate* : Separate means part.
46. *sincerely* : Keep the last -e.
47. *succeed* : two c's, two e's
48. *thorough* : a rough word to spell
49. *thought* : -ought
50. *unnecessary* : two n's, two s's

Step 1. Practice with Group A Words. Fill in the blanks to complete the following words.

1. Since the new man____ment took over, the bus____ess has ben____fi____d greatly.

2. Paul was ho____ng to rec____ve the award for highest ach____ement.

3. Our ex____t____nce is depen____nt on our ability to cope with our env____r____ment.

4. The organ____tion tried to el____m____ate their compe____ion.

5. It was soon ap____ent that the restaurant was too small to ac____o-____odate all the people.

6. John was unable to per____de his parents to give him greater ind____-p____nd____nce.

7. Tom would never dare to smoke a cigar____e in the pre____ce of his parents.

8. The period of adol____c____nce is often a time of great lon____ness.

9. After giving the situation some serious th____ght, Bill was sat____-f____ed that he would soon suc____d in solving his dile____a.

10. Gail was not con____ous of the cr____l thing that she had done.

Spelling Demons: Group B

1. *acceptance:* accept + ance
2. *accompanied:* two c's + -ied
3. *acquaintance:* ac + quaint + ance
4. *advertisement:* tise
5. *all right:* two words like "all wrong"
6. *annually:* double n
7. *appearance:* An ear is part of your appearance.
8. *approach:* a double p before the roach
9. *article:* -le ending
10. *attitude:* double t
11. *basis:* ends in is
12. *behavior:* Don't forget the i.
13. *breathe:* We breathe to take a breath.
14. *career:* two e's

15. *certainly:* <u>cer</u>-<u>tain</u>-<u>ly</u>
16. *coming:* Drop the <u>e</u> in <u>come</u>.
17. *condemn:* Don't forget the silent <u>n</u>.
18. *convenience:* <u>con</u> + <u>ven</u> + <u>ience</u>
19. *deceive:* <u>i</u> before <u>e</u> except after <u>c</u>
20. *description:* <u>des</u>
21. *disappoint:* <u>dis</u> + appoint
22. *discussion:* discu<u>ss</u> + <u>ion</u>
23. *embarrass:* two <u>r</u>'s, two <u>s</u>'s
24. *equipment:* Look for the quip.
25. *excitable:* Drop the <u>e</u> in excite; add -<u>able</u>.
26. *experience:* -<u>ence</u> at the end
27. *fascinating:* <u>sc</u> after the <u>a</u> and before the <u>i</u>
28. *guaranteed:* <u>guar</u> as in <u>guard</u>; two <u>e</u>'s at the end
29. *height:* -<u>ei</u> in the middle
30. *hungrily:* Make the y in hungry an <u>i</u>; add -<u>ly</u>.
31. *intelligence:* Can you <u>tell</u> he has intelligence?
32. *knowledge:* Did you <u>know</u> the <u>ledge</u> was there?
33. *losing:* Drop the <u>e</u> in lose.

        i
34. *marriage:* marr~~y~~ + age
35. *morale:* <u>Ale</u> will lift a soldier's morale.
36. *parallel:* Are <u>all</u> lines par<u>all</u>el?
37. *peculiar:* A <u>liar</u> is pecu<u>liar</u>.
38. *pleasant:* Drop the <u>e</u> in pl<u>ease</u> and add an <u>ant</u>.
39. *preferred:* Start with <u>pre</u>; double -<u>r</u> at the end.
40. *principle:* A principle is a <u>rule</u>.
41. *psychology:* <u>psy</u> to open
42. *recommend:* one <u>c</u>, two <u>m</u>'s
43. *ridicule:* <u>rid</u> + <u>i</u> + <u>cule</u>
44. *schedule:* <u>s</u> + <u>ch</u>
45. *significance:* -<u>ance</u>
46. *studying* study + <u>ing</u>
47. *surprise:* no <u>z</u> in this word
48. *tragedy:* no d before the <u>g</u>
49. *valuable:* Drop the <u>e</u> in value; add <u>able</u>.
50. *weather:* I can't <u>bear</u> the w<u>ea</u>ther.

Step 2. Practice with Group B Words. Unscramble the following list of jumbled letters in order to spell correctly these words that are taken from the above list. (Hint: The first letter of each word is in boldface; the second letter is underlined.)

1. **g**<u>o</u>minc

2. **r**<u>o</u>mela

_____   _____

3. ne̱ctpacec**a**

_____

4. so̱lgin

_____

5. teebha̱r

_____

6. cs̲oylgphoy

_____

7. aio**b**hvre̲

_____

8. etigne̲lenli̲c

_____

9. pise̲d**d**roctin

_____

10. c̲eehuld**s**

_____

Step 3. More Group B Practice: Looking for Smaller Words. In the above list, there are many words that contain another word of five letters or more. Write nine of these words below and underline the smaller word contained in each.

Example:
1. acceptance
2. _____
3. _____
4. _____
5. _____

6. _____
7. _____
8. _____
9. _____
10. _____

Spelling Demons: Group C
1. *accidentally:* two c̲'s, two l̲'s
2. *accustom:* double c̲
3. *admittance:* two t̲'s
4. *aggravate:* two g's
5. *amateur:* ₑ e u r̲
6. *apologized:* Look for the lo̲g; add i̲ z̲ e̲ d̲
7. *applying:* two p's. Don't drop the y at the end!
8. *argument:* Drop the e̲ in argue.
9. *athlete:* Don't forget the e̲ in "let." No e̲ after h̲.
10. *audience:* At such a bad show the au̲di̲ence almost di̲ed.
11. *beautiful:* y in beauty changes to i̲
12. *believe:* Don't beli̲eve a li̲e.
13. *brilliance:* two l̲'s + ia̲nce
14. *carried:* double r̲.
15. *changeable:* Leave the e̲ in cha̲nge.
16. *committee:* two m̲'s, two t̲'s, two e̲'s
17. *conscientious:* A sci̲entist is consci̲entious.
18. *criticize:* -c̲ize

19. *definitely:* Look for the <u>finite</u>.
20. *difference:* two <u>f</u>'s; <u>ence</u>
21. *disastrous:* no <u>e</u> between the <u>t</u> and <u>r</u>
22. *efficient:* -<u>ient</u> after <u>c</u>
23. *emphasize:* Does it emph<u>size</u> your <u>size</u>?
24. *especially:* This word has something <u>special</u>: double <u>l</u>.
25. *exercise:* no -<u>z</u> here!
26. *extremely:* The <u>m</u> stands between two <u>e</u>'s.
27. *genius:* -<u>ius</u> not <u>ious</u>
28. *guidance:* Put <u>gui</u> before <u>dance</u>.
29. *heroes:* Add <u>es</u> to hero.
30. *ignorance:* He <u>ran</u> in igno<u>rance</u>.
31. *interest:* in + <u>ter</u> + est
32. *leisure:* -<u>ei</u>

                         i
33. *magnificent:* magnif̸y + -cent
34. *miniature:* <u>mini</u> + <u>a</u> + <u>ture</u>
35. *noticeable:* Was <u>not</u> <u>ice</u> <u>able</u> to freeze the lock?
36. *paralyze:* -<u>yze</u>
37. *performance:* -<u>ance</u> after perform
38. *possession:* two double <u>s</u>'s
39. *prejudice:* Look for the <u>dice</u>.
40. *privilege:* priv<u>ile</u>ge
41. *pursue:* two <u>u</u>'s
42. *relieve:* <u>Lie</u> down to rel<u>ie</u>ve your pain.
43. *sacrifice:* sacrifice
44. *seize:* The -<u>e</u> comes before the -<u>i</u>.
45. *similar:* <u>.</u>ilar (no u in this word)
46. *sufficient:* double <u>f</u>; -<u>cient</u>
47. *transferred:* two <u>r</u>'s
48. *unusually:* three <u>u</u>'s all in one word
49. *villain:* The vill<u>ain</u> had <u>lain</u> on the street.
50. *writing:* Drop the <u>e</u> in write.

Step 4. Group C Practice.   In each of the following sets of words, one is misspelled. Write that word correctly spelled in the space provided at the left.

_____	1. efficient	commitee	genius	pursue
_____	2. differance	especially	villain	seize
_____	3. unusually	relieve	sacrifice	beleive
_____	4. paralize	writing	brilliance	definitely
_____	5. disastrous	leisure	transfered	athlete
_____	6. accidentally	carried	minature	similar

	7. extremely	guidance	noticeable	heros
_____	8. changeable	exercize	sufficient	privilege
_____	9. possesion	prejudice	magnificent	interest
_____	10. emphasize	performance	applying	amateur

Step 5. Mastering Spelling Demons. Fill in the blanks to complete correctly the words (taken from Groups A, B, and C) in the following phrases.

1. the b____is for ac ____vement

2. to anal____e the ar____ment

3. unable to acco____date the aud____nce

4. an amat____ ath____te

5. a successful b____iness car____r

6. appl____ng the princip____

7. a be____t____ful des____iption

8. to criti____e the commit____e

9. to exa____erate the d____le____a

10. a d____ast____us exper____nce

11. to el____m____ate compet____ion

12. the p____chology of human behav____

13. to s____ze val____ble gems

14. the man____ment of an organ____tion

15. a cr____l ex____t____nce

16. a fa____inating per____m____nce

17. to rid____le pre____dice

18. her magn____cent appe____nce

19. must have suff____ent exer____e

20. an eff____ent sch____d____le

21. a pecul____r vill____n

22. to surp____e her ac____dent____y

23. pl____sant w____ther

24. a di____us____ion about mar____age

25. the e____pment is gu____ant____ed

26. the pr____v____lege of his
  a____uaint____nce

27. It was cert____nly a great tr____edy.

28. to p____sue knowl____e

29. con____entious stud____ing

30. a cigar____te advert____ement

31. to rec____ve their
  indep____nd____nce

32. the lon____l____ness of
  adol____c____nce

33. to proc____d with the
  ar____ang____ment

34. an ext____mely good
  env____ro____ent

35. hop____ng to suc____d

36. to sac____f____ce his
  pos____e____ion

37. They are def____nit____ly
  sim____l____r.

38. a chang____ble a____itude

39. We conde____ his j____lo____sy

40. He al____o____ed them to
  sep____r____te.

41. sat____sf____d with his grades in
  gra____r

42. very cons____ous of his wri____ng

43. A gen____s has great intel____gence.

44. His at____nd____nce is

esp____c____ally poor.

45. I ap____re____ate his pre____nce.

46. Th____ough di____ip____ine is
needed.

47. Don't bel____ve his g____d____nce.

48. His int____est is in min____ture
trains.

49. Her____s are unus____al____y brave.

50. The troops are lo____ng their

mora____.

SOME SPELLING RULES FOR DIFFICULT PROBLEMS

Rule 1. Solving *-ie* Headaches

1. *i* usually becomes before *e*.

   Examples: field   yield   achievement   believe

2. If the letter immediately before the *-ie* combination is *c*, the *e* usually comes before the *i*.

   Examples: deceive   receive   conceive

3. The *e* also comes before the *i* if the combination of letters sounds like the *a* in *say* or *clay*.

   Examples: neighborhood   weight   eight

   [This sounds like *a* in *say* so the *e* comes before the *i*.]

EXCEPTIONS: FOR YOU TO MEMORIZE

either	leisure
foreign	science
seize	height
neither	efficient

The following jingle will help you to remember the above rule:

i before *e* except after *c*,
or when sounded like *a* as in *neighbor* and *weigh*.

Step 1. Using *-ie* Correctly.   Fill in *ie* or *ei* in the words below.

1. rec____ve

2. dec____ve

3. conc____ve

4. bel____ve

5. perc____ve

6. w____gh

7. n_____ther

8. sc_____nce

9. th_____f

10. misch_____f

11. l_____sure

12. exper_____nce

13. n_____ghbor

14. sh_____ld

15. f_____ld

16. aud_____nce

17. rel_____ve

18. r_____gn

19. sl_____gh

20. for_____gn

Rule 2. Changing *y* to *i*

1. If a word ends in *y* and the *y* is directly preceded by a consonant (any letter other than *a, e, i, o,* and *u*), the *y* is changed to *i* before an ending (suffix) is added.

   Examples: fly + *es* = flies   carry + *ed* = carried
   [The *y* is preceded by   ⟍[This is the new ending.]
   the consonant *l.*]

2. However, when the ending begins with *i* as in *-ing,* the *y* is *not* changed.

   Examples: study + *ing* = studying   try + *ing* = trying

EXCEPTIONS: FOR YOU TO MEMORIZE

lay + *ed* = laid   say + *ed* = said   pay + *ed* = paid

Step 2. Adding to Words That End in -*y*.   Using the above rule, add the suffixes indicated to the following words.

	-*ed*	-*ing*	-(*e*)*s*
1. reply	_____	_____	_____
2. accompany	_____	_____	_____
3. bury	_____	_____	_____
4. annoy	_____	_____	_____
5. dry	_____	_____	_____

Step 3. More Practice.   Add the indicated endings to the following words.

1. carry + *ed* _____

2. destroy + *ed* _____

3. apply + *ing* _____

4. lonely + *ness* _____

5. country + *s* _____

6. beauty + *ful* _____

7. satisfy + *ing* _____

8. portray + *ed* _____

9. hurry + *ing* _____

10. deny + *al* _____

Rule 3. Words That Drop the Final *e*

1. Words ending in silent *e* usually drop the *e* before a suffix beginning with a vowel.

    Examples: use + -*ing* = using   use + *able* = usable

2. However, the silent -*e* usually remains before a suffix beginning with a consonant.

    Examples: use + ful = useful   use + less = useless

EXCEPTIONS: FOR YOU TO MEMORIZE

argue + *ment* = argument   change + *able* = changeable
judge + *ment* = judgment   courage + *ous* = courageous
true + *ly* = truly   canoe + *ing* = canoeing
notice + *able* = noticeable

Step 4. Working with the Final -e.   Using the above rule, add the suffixes indicated to the following words.

	-*ing*	-*ment*	-*able*
1. arrange	_____	_____	_____
2. achieve	_____	_____	_____
3. move	_____	_____	_____
4. manage	_____	_____	_____
5. excite	_____	_____	_____

Step 5. More Practice.   Add the suffixes to the following words:

1. describe + *ing* = _____
2. true + *ly* = _____
3. care + *ful* = _____
4. receive + *ing* = _____
5. entire + *ly* = _____
6. notice + *able* = _____
7. have + *ing* = _____
8. write + *ing* = _____
9. argue + *ment* = _____
10. arrive + *al* = _____
11. lone + *ly* = _____
12. love + *able* = _____
13. judge + *ment* = _____
14. become + *ing* = _____
15. safe + *ty* = _____
16. courage + *ous* = _____

Rule 4. Doubling the Final Consonant

1. When adding a suffix to a word, the final consonant of that word is doubled if the following are true:

The suffix begins with a vowel.
  Examples: rot   -*ing* = rotting
The word is one syllable *or* is accented on the last syllable.

  Examples: sit -*ing* = sitting
  (This word is one syllable.)
  control (con-trol) ed = controlled
  (The accent is on the last syllable.)
  offer (of-fer) ed = offered
  (The accent is *not* on the last syllable and so the final consonant is *not* doubled.)

Step 6. Doubling Practice.   Add the indicated suffixes to the following words.

1. quit + *ing* = _____
2. prefer + *ed* = _____
3. occur + *ed* = _____
4. begin + *ing* = _____
5. differ + *ence* = _____
6. forget + *ful* = _____
7. swim + *ing* = _____
8. big + *est* = _____
9. profit + *able* = _____
10. listen + *ing* = _____
11. plan + *ing* = _____
12. benefit + *ed* = _____
13. admit + *ing* = _____
14. whip + *ed* = _____
15. stop + *ed* = _____
16. compel + *ed* = _____
17. beg + *ed* = _____
18. transfer + *ing* = _____
19. win + *ing* = _____
20. forbid + *en* = _____

Step 7. Mastering the Spelling Rules.   Test your mastery of the preceding spelling rules by adding the indicated suffixes to the following words. The numbers in parentheses refer to the spelling rule that applies to that word.

1. study + *ing* _____ (2)
2. judge + *ment* _____ (3)
3. occur + *ed* _____ (4)
4. manage + *ing* _____ (3)
5. differ + *ence* _____ (4)
6. accompany + *ed* _____ (2)
7. benefit + *ed* _____ (4)
8. forbid + *en* _____ (4)
9. deny + *al* _____ (2)
10. safe + *ty* _____ (3)
11. whip + *ed* _____ (4)
12. try + *ing* _____ (2)
13. defer + *ed* _____ (4)
14. use + *ing* _____ (3)

15. lonely + *ness* _____ (2)

16. commit + *ing* _____ (4)

17. move + *able* _____ (3)

18. annoy + *ed* _____ (2)

19. argue + *ment* _____ (3)

20. dry + *es* _____ (2)

21. portray + *ed* _____ (2)

22. offer + *ed* _____ (4)

23. notice + *able* _____ (3)

24. profit + *able* _____ (4)

25. destroy + *ed* _____ (2)

26. transfer + *ed* _____ (4)

27. entire + *ly* _____ (3)

28. arrange + *ment* _____ (3)

29. prefer + *ed* _____ (4)

30. receive + *ing* _____ (3)

31. lay + *ed* _____ (2)

32. write + *ing* _____ (3)

33. admit + *ing* _____ (4)

34. true + *ly* _____ (3)

35. forget + *ful* _____ (4)

36. apply + *ing* _____ (2)

37. care + *ful* _____ (3)

38. equip + *ment* _____ (4)

39. excite + *ing* _____ (3)

40. bury + *ed* _____ (2)

Fill in *ie* or *ei* in the words below. To check your spelling, refer back to rule 1.

1. f____ld

2. aud____nce

3. n____ghbor

4. l____sure

5. rec____ve

6. bel____ve

7. sl____gh

8. dec____ve

9. s____ze

10. w____gh

YOUR OWN DEMON LIST: WORDS YOU MISTAKE

Fill in the columns, as indicated, with your own troublesome spelling words. Study the examples. Continue your list, if necessary, on your own paper.

Word Correctly Spelled	Confusing Letters Underlined	A Way to Remember
You're accommodate	You're accommodate	You're = you + are double c, double m

2. LEARNING VOCABULARY

The following steps will help build your vocabulary.

1. Look up new words in a reliable dictionary.
2. Read definitions carefully. Pick only definitions which explain words as you want to use them or as they are used in what you have read.
3. Write each word on small index cards. Put definitions on the other side.
4. Study words in related groups: *size* words, *liberation* words, *space-age* words, etc.
5. Study words briefly on several occasions rather than for long periods on few occasions.
6. Say the word and meaning aloud.
7. Make up sentences for the word.
8. Add words to your speaking vocabulary.
9. Use words in writing sentences.
10. In reading, if you see an unfamiliar word, try to figure out its meaning from

    the way it is used in a sentence

    the prefix, root, or suffix that you see

    the words that may be put together to make up the new word

    a smaller word you recognize within the new word.

Step 1. Predicting Meanings.   Try to determine the meanings of the words below in any way you can. Write definitions in the blank space.

1. overanxious _____

2. unambitious _____

3. spittoon _____

4. keepsake _____

5. oceanside _____

6. blessedness _____

7. transport _____

8. extramarital _____

9. The professional worker showed the *neophyte* very slowly just what had to be done. _____

10. With his arms *flailing* wildly, the boy screamed, "I'm drowning! I'm drowning!" _____

3. READING A DICTIONARY ENTRY

Most instructors encourage you to use dictionaries to check meanings and spellings even when you write a test or essay in class. Although pocket dictionaries give simplified entries for words, you still need to understand the several parts of each entry. Here are samples from the *New Merriam Webster Pocket Dictionary* (New York, 1964):

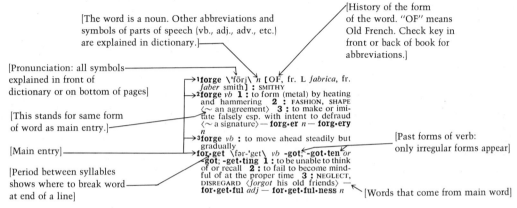

[The word is a noun. Other abbreviations and symbols of parts of speech (vb., adj., adv., etc.) are explained in dictionary.]

[History of the form of the word. "OF" means Old French. Check key in front or back of book for abbreviations.]

[Pronunciation: all symbols explained in front of dictionary or on bottom of pages]

[This stands for same form of word as main entry.]

[Main entry]

[Period between syllables shows where to break word at end of a line]

¹**forge** \'fōrj\ *n* [OF, fr. L *fabrica*, fr. *faber* smith] : SMITHY
²**forge** *vb* **1** : to form (metal) by heating and hammering **2** : FASHION, SHAPE ⟨~ an agreement⟩ **3** : to make or imitate falsely esp. with intent to defraud ⟨~ a signature⟩ — **forg·er** *n* — **forg·ery** *n*
³**forge** *vb* : to move ahead steadily but gradually
for·get \fər-'get\ *vb* **-got**; **-got·ten** *or* **-got**; **-get·ting 1** : to be unable to think of or recall **2** : to fail to become mindful of at the proper time **3** : NEGLECT, DISREGARD ⟨*forgot* his old friends⟩ — **for·get·ful** *adj* — **for·get·ful·ness** *n*

[Past forms of verb: only irregular forms appear]

[Words that come from main word]

Step 1. Understanding Dictionary Entries. Using the *New Merriam Webster Pocket Dictionary* or some other handy pocket dictionary, look up the word *foreign*. Write the answers to the following questions.

1. What languages did the word come from? _____

_____

2. What syllables make up the word? _____

_____

3. What part of speech is the word? _____

_____

4. How is the word pronounced? _____

_____

5. How many definitions appear? _____

_____

6. Which definition is new to you? Write it here. _____

_____

4. USING A THESAURUS

A *thesaurus* is a dictionary of synonyms. You can look up a word like *humorist* (given below), for example, and find fifteen or twenty words which are in some way related in meaning to that word.

WHEN TO USE THE THESAURUS

when you repeat the same word too often

when a word does not sound right in your sentence

when you write slang or substandard expressions and you want more formal language

when you learn new words and you want to see other words used in a similar way

---

Two Hints for Thesaurus Use:

1. Different methods of organization are used in preparing a thesaurus. One thesaurus groups synonyms according to ideas or subject categories. There, you look up words in the back of the book, find the section numbers in which the word you want appears, and then turn to a specific section which gives the synonyms that interest you. Others are alphabetically arranged, like dictionaries.

2. Not all synonyms listed for any word have the same meaning. And the thesaurus rarely tells the difference in shades of meaning (see p. 261) among the synonyms offered. Therefore, know definitions of any words you select. Don't pick words just because they are unusual, impressive in length, or new to you. Use a dictionary to check out differences in meanings.

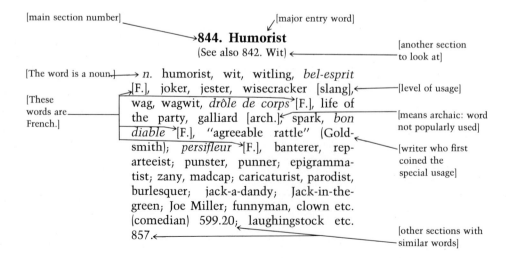

[main section number]

[major entry word]

844. Humorist

(See also 842. Wit)

[another section to look at]

[The word is a noun.]

n. humorist, wit, witling, *bel-esprit* [F.], joker, jester, wisecracker [slang], wag, wagwit, *drôle de corps* [F.], life of the party, galliard [arch.], spark, *bon diable* [F.], "agreeable rattle" (Goldsmith); *persifleur* [F.], banterer, reparteeist; punster, punner; epigrammatist; zany, madcap; caricaturist, parodist, burlesquer; jack-a-dandy; Jack-in-the-green; Joe Miller; funnyman, clown etc. (comedian) 599.20; laughingstock etc. 857.

[These words are French.]

[level of usage]

[means archaic: word not popularly used]

[writer who first coined the special usage]

[other sections with similar words]

Step 1. The Thesaurus for Forceful Words. Look up the word *beautiful*— a popular but very overused word in our language—in a thesaurus. Select five words that give the same meaning as *beautiful* but provide a fresher, sharper, more vivid description. Write the words below; and look up in a dictionary any words whose meanings you do not know.

1. _____

2. _____

3. _____

4. _____

5. _____

5. WRITING SIMPLE FOOTNOTES

Sometimes you need to tell in footnotes the source for each quotation you use. Each quotation or paraphrase in an essay with such requirements, then, should be consecutively numbered slightly above the line and at the end of the statement you are borrowing from someone else's writing. At the bottom of the page or at the end of the essay, give the information about your source for each numbered quotation.

If your quotation comes from a book, write your footnote this way:

[the author: first name, then last name]   [means "page"] [period (after abbreviation)]

[comma]   [title (Underline it!)]   [parenthesis]   [comma]   [page number]

Robert Karlin, <u>Teaching Reading in High School</u> (Indianapolis, 1964), p. 29. ← [period at end]

[city of publication]   [date of publication]   [close parenthesis]

If your quotation comes from an article in a magazine or in some other periodical, write your note this way:

[author]   [comma]

Jack A. Holmes, "Personality Characteristics of the Disabled Reader,"

[title of article (use quotation marks)]   [comma inside]

[comma]   [volume]   [comma]   [year of publication]   [page number]

<u>Journal of Developmental Reading</u>, 4 (Winter, 1961), 112. ← [period at end]

[title of periodical (Underline it!)]   [parenthesis]   [season or month of publication]   [close parenthesis]

If you quote from a book or article and the very next quotation you use in your paragraph comes from the same book or article, do this:

[This means *pages.*]

[period]   [the page numbers]

Ibid., pp. 29–30. ← [period at end]

[comma]   [period]

[This is an abbreviation for the Latin *ibidem*, meaning *in the same place.*]

If you quote again from a writer's book or article that you have described in an earlier footnote but not in the immediately preceding footnote, do this:

Karlin, p. 29. ← [page from which quotation comes]
[author's last name]
[comma] [period]

Step 1. Understanding Footnotes. Look at the footnotes at the bottom of the paragraph on pp. 466–467. Explain the reasons for each of the entries.

6. PREPARING A BIBLIOGRAPHY

Footnotes are only the first part in noting the materials you have used in an essay or term paper. A *bibliography* — an alphabetical list of the sources you have consulted or quoted from in your paper — is often required.

GUIDELINES FOR BIBLIOGRAPHIES

1. The bibliography appears on a separate page at the end of the paper.
2. Items are *not* numbered but are listed alphabetically according to author's last name.
3. Write author's last name first, then first and middle name.
4. List alphabetically according to title other works by same author, directly under first entry for his name.
5. For works by more than one author, list the entry under last name of first author, giving other writers' names in regular order (first name, middle, last).
6. List works with no authors alphabetically according to the first important word in the title.
7. Do not mention pages for books. Do tell pages on which essays and articles in periodicals, encyclopedias, and newspapers appear.
8. The first line of each bibliography entry starts at the left-hand margin. Indent all other lines.
9. Single-space all entries but separate one entry from another by double-spacing.
10. *a.* Here is a sample bibliography entry for a book (see how it compares to a footnote entry for the same book by turning to p. 463).

[author's last name first] [title (Underline it!)] [period]
Karlin, Robert. Teaching Reading in High School. Indianapolis: Bobbs-
[period] [city of publication] [colon] [publisher's name]
Merrill Company, 1964. ← [period]
[comma] [date of publication]

b. Here is a sample bibliography entry for an article that appears in a periodical (see how it compares to a footnote entry for the same book by turning to p. 463).

[author's last name first] [title of article (in quotes)]
Holmes, Jack A. "Personality Characteristics of the Disabled Reader." Jour-
[title of periodical (Underline it!)] [volume] [comma]
nal of Developmental Reading, 4 (Winter, 1961) 111–122. ← [period]
[season or month of publication] [date] [pages on which article is found]

Step 1. A Bibliography Exercise. Using the resources of your college library, prepare on a separate sheet of paper a bibliography of *five* entries for one of the topics below. Make sure that at least one of your entries is for a periodical.

1. The origin of money
2. Teen-age drug use in an urban ghetto
3. A nurse's training in the 1970s
4. The Greek community in New York
5. Computers and high school education

7. USING THE READER'S GUIDE

The Reader's Guide to Periodical Literature is a semimonthly report giving the names of authors and the titles of articles in many important magazines like *Time, Life,* the *Atlantic, Saturday Review, Harper's,* and the *New Yorker.* The reports are bound together in volumes each year.

HOW TO USE THE READER'S GUIDE

1. To find articles on any given subject, look up the subject in the index. Several authors, titles, and names of the magazines in which they appear are listed.
2. To find an article written by an author whose name you know, look up the author's last name in the index.

Sample Subject Entry

FOOD, organic
  \[the subject of the article]   /[title of the article]   [article continued on later pages]\
Health is busting out all over; health food restaurants. Vogue 157: 57+
F 1, '71   [the name of the   [volume↑   ↑
  \[date of issue   periodical]   number] |
  of magazine]   [the page on which
                                                     article appears]

Sample Author Entry
HARRINGTON, MICHAEL   [article has   [continued on
          /[title of article] illustrations\   later pages]\
Peace movement is using the wrong strategy. il N.Y. Times Mag: 10–11+
My 30 '71   [name of ↑   [pages of
  \[date of issue]   magazine]   article]

Hint: All abbreviations appear in a key at the beginning of the *Reader's Guide.* Look up any abbreviations you do not understand.

Step 1. Looking for Articles and Essays. For each subject below, check the latest volume or issue of the *Reader's Guide* and write one magazine reference on the line provided.

1. Space travel _____

2. Education in the Soviet Union _____

3. Jazz in America _____

4. Organ transplants _____

5. John F. Kennedy _____

8. QUOTING FROM BOOKS

1. If the passage you select to quote has fewer than one hundred words, work the quotation smoothly into your own sentences. Use a colon or a comma before the quotation. Use quotation marks at the beginning and at the end of the statement you are quoting. (Example *a* below)

2. If you quote a longer passage (three or more typed lines or more than one hundred words), block the quotation off from the rest of the text by leaving several spaces from the margin on each side. If you type, this longer quotation should be single-spaced (the rest of the paragraph or essay is double-spaced). Do not use quotation marks when you set off this longer passage (example *b* below).

3. If you want to leave out any words of a sentence in the selection you are quoting, use three dots (. . .). If you omit one or more full sentences, use four dots (. . . .). See *c* below.

Here is part of a student's paragraph on understanding reading problems. Note the correct use of quotations.

Every teacher and psychologist knows that emotional factors play an important part in the way a child reads; but specialists are still unsure of how emotional problems really affect reading skills. No one knows whether or not the problems are there to prevent the child from reading properly or if they come after the child [quotation marks] sees that he cannot learn the way others do. One teacher of reading says, "Some [comma] writers have gathered evidence to support the view that emotional upsets are [quotation mark] perhaps caused by reading failure."[1] Failure affects the way we all regard ourselves, and reading failure would have an emotional effect on a student.[2] Even if this is true, however, there does not seem to be any pattern in how personality affects reading competence. Analyzing the findings in some recent studies, a reading specialist concludes: [colon] [no quotation mark]

a.

If one hopes for consistent grade-to-grade findings in these results one is bound to be disappointed. However, and this is my first point, if one takes a *developmental approach,* one discovers that relationships between reading and personality found at the primary level become inconsistent at the intermediate and junior high school grades, and so far as the evidence is concerned, seem completely to disappear at the high school and college levels. Of course, there may be many possible explanations, such as the increased selectivity of students, the unreliability and use of different types of tests, etc.[3] ←[no quotation mark]

[single-space]

b.

But no matter how these factors work in the reading process, no one can disagree that, "Students who are . . . disturbed by major fears and anxieties should be } c. referred to persons qualified to help them."[4]

— Steve Lederman

Footnotes to show sources: see pp. 463–464.
{
[1] Robert Karlin, *Teaching Reading in High School* (Indianapolis, 1964), p. 29.
[2] *Ibid.,* pp. 29–30.
[3] Jack A. Holmes, "Personality Characteristics of the Disabled Reader," *Journal of Developmental Reading*, 4 (Winter, 1961), 112.
[4] Karlin, p. 29.
}

9. BUSINESS-LETTER FORMAT

An important on-the-job demand once you graduate from college is the writing of clear business letters. When you write you need to observe several principles agreed upon by the business world. In this letter requesting information (pp. 386–387 presents a letter of job application) the parts of the letter and some suggestions appear in the margin.

[heading
(your address)]   [no abbreviations]
[comma]   847 Ditmars Boulevard
                 Astoria, New York   10001
[date]→December 1, 1971
                                              [comma]

[inside →Office of Admissions   [no abbreviations]
address] Fordham University
             Rose Hill Campus
             Bronx, New York   10458
                        [comma]

[salutation]→Gentlemen: ←[colon]
                    [capital]

[body of letter: clear concise correct courteous complete]
{
I would like some information on the possibilities of my transferring to Fordham University from LaGuardia Community College after I complete my Associate of Arts degree this June. At LaGuardia I am a liberal arts student with the equivalent of a B- or C+ average; I would like to major in urban government at Fordham. Do you have an urban government program? If you do, would I be eligible for admission to it as a two-year transfer student?
}

[body of
letter:
clear
concise
correct
courteous
complete]

> If you have an up-to-date college bulletin,
> a schedule of tuition fees, and an application for
> admission, I should like to have that information,
> too. And any materials you could send along about
> housing and dormitories would be very helpful.

[capitalize
first word → Yours very truly,   [complimentary close]
only]   [comma]

Russel Kise   ← [signature]

Russel Kise

[name typed below
signature]

Step 1. Letter Writing. Follow the suggestions below to write a letter requesting information. Use separate paper.

1. Write to a college out of the state for a copy of the college bulletin, or for copies of campus publications.
2. Write to a local newspaper requesting a back issue that deals with drugs or pollution in your neighborhood.
3. Write to the state department of health asking for information about death rates in abortion cases.
4. Write to the chamber of commerce of a city or state you want to visit. Ask for information about hotels, amusements, places of interest.
5. Write to your state board of education for material on special programs in education for minority-group students or students in poverty areas.

10. TAKING NOTES

Few people remember accurately what they read. That is why note taking is such an aid to the college student who is frequently asked to read a great deal of material for exams, reports, and term papers.

NOTES ON READINGS: SIX STEPS TO EXCELLENCE

1. Write down the name of the author and the book, article, essay, or story you need to take notes on.
2. Take notes on one paragraph at a time.
3. Look up any words you do not know.
4. Write in your own words the main idea of the selection.
5. Write in your own words the subtopics of the selection if they are clearly stated.
6. Jot down briefly the key words, most important facts, illustrations, details, or statistics. Use the author's own words for special key ideas.

Read the paragraph below and the notes taken on the paragraph by a student.

Racism in Education

Since racism is the philosophy of the Establishment and is propagated in the institutions of higher learning and by the mass media which they control through ownership, it is not surprising to observe that "a vast majority of the white population south of the Mason-Dixon Line, and large numbers, probably a majority elsewhere, are firmly of the belief that Negroes are subhuman or only semi-human, despite the positive assertions of biology and anthropology to the contrary." (*The Rich and the Super-Rich,* by Ferdinand Lundberg).

The Black parent knows his child is "educable" in spite of all the funded programs and studies to the contrary. Dishonesty and distortions in intelligence tests are common. The literature on such tests shows that when "two groups of whites differ in their IQ's, the explanation of the difference is immediately sought in schooling, environment, economic position of parents. However, when Blacks and whites differ in precisely the same way the difference is said to be genetic." (*The Study of Race,* by Sherwood L. Washburn). There are other instances which show the prevalence of racism. Trade schools (located in all industrial centers) have a long history of excluding Blacks. However, a Black occasionally slips through the net, after which the net is thoroughly examined to see how it happened. The trustees of these trade schools include the conservative officials of craft unions which exclude Blacks from membership. A classic example involved the Sheet Metal Workers Union Local 28 in New York. There were 3,300 white members in the union, but no Blacks. Apprenticeship was reserved almost exclusively for relatives of members. Finally, the State Commission on Human Rights found the local union guilty, and the union agreed that "henceforth every applicant for membership would be judged solely on an aptitude test administered by the New York Testing and Advisement Center."

— Maude White Katz

Notes on paragraph from "End Racism in Education," by
  Maude White Katz
Main Idea: Racist beliefs make Negro appear "subhuman or only semi-human."
Subtopics and Important Details
  The Establishment, through colleges and mass media, gives racist philosophy
  Black child can be educated
    intelligence tests dishonest
    when intelligence of whites differs many reasons given as possible explanations
    when Blacks and whites differ, reason is genetic
  Other instances of racism
    Blacks excluded from trade schools
    Craft union officials keep Blacks out of schools
    Sheet Metal Workers Union Local 28 in New York has 3,300 white members, no Blacks: State Commission on Human Rights finds union guilty
                                              — Geoffrey Hunte

---

UNDERLINING DOES IT TOO

If you own the book, underlining is a very good method of note taking because it saves time. Remember these tips about underlining:

1. Underline the main points, subpoints, and the key supporting details.
2. Write notes to yourself in the margin: jot down a question; say an idea more simply than the author has, using your own words; write down an idea the author's writing makes you think about.

Step 1. Note Taking on Your Own. Reread the paragraph by Germaine Greer on p. 339. Take notes on your reading, using separate paper.

Step 2. Underlining. Read "Accidental Deaths" on pp. 179–180, underlining as you read. Follow the suggestions above.

11. WRITING A SUMMARY

Much college writing—especially brief reports and homework questions— is summary writing. A summary gives a brief idea of material you have read. It is usually a statement you write from your notes or from your underlining. Good summaries focus on main ideas, major subtopics, and only *important* details.

FOR CLEAR SUMMARIES THAT MAKE THE POINT:

1. Read carefully. Take notes as explained on pp. 469–470. Look up words you do not understand.
2. Your first sentence should state the main idea of the selection you are summarizing.
3. Use your own words in repeating details. Use the author's exact words for certain key ideas.
4. Repeat information accurately.
5. Follow the author's development in the selection you are summarizing. If information is arranged chronologically or by importance; if material is presented through comparison-contrast, narrative, several examples; your summary should reflect the author's pattern.
6. Revise your first draft so that your sentences flow smoothly. Use subordination to tighten ideas.
7. Summaries should be brief, usually not more than a third of the total number of words in the original.

Here is the summary written from the notes that appear on p. 469.

Summary of "Racism in Education"

Racist beliefs make many Americans view Negroes as "subhuman or only semi-human." The Establishment (higher education and mass media) is responsible for this philosophy. Yet Blacks *are* educable, in spite of dishonest intelligence-test results. Although valid reasons appear for intelligence differences among white children, Blacks are said to differ from whites for genetic reasons. Proof of racism in education appears in the exclusion of Blacks — through craft union officials — from trade schools. The New York State Commission on Human Rights found guilty the Sheet Metal Workers Union Local 28 because none of its 3,300 members was Black.

—Geoffrey Hunte

12. ANSWERING ESSAY EXAMINATION QUESTIONS

Midterm or final examinations in college courses usually ask — in addition to short-answer questions — that you answer some questions in *essay* form. Although the word *essay* in this sense is used loosely, it usually means some longer response to a question that requires extended thought and development.

Hint: If the exam asks you to answer more than two or three *essay* questions, a one-paragraph response is often adequate for each question.

If the exam asks you to answer only one or two questions, plan to write a four-paragraph essay to develop your responses.

MAKING THE GRADE: HOW TO ANSWER ESSAY QUESTIONS

1. Think about the question before you write. Take clues for the development of your paragraph or essay from the question itself.

   If the question says *compare and contrast*, use comparison-contrast methods of development.

   If the question says *how*, show how something is done or how something works.

   If the question says *explain, tell, illustrate, discuss*, use any method of development that uses facts, statistics, paraphrases, or quotations in order to back up your point.

   If the question says *define*, write a paragraph or essay that uses substantial details to illustrate the meaning of a word, idea, or theory.

   If the question says *list*, it is often enough just to write your answer by numbering 1 through 10, for example, and writing some fact for each number. But you can also "list" ideas in paragraph form.

   If the question asks *why*, make sure you understand what conclusion the instructor wants you to reach. Then, give as many details as you can to explain the *causes* for the result he asks you to explain.

2. Repeat the main part of the question in your topic sentence (for one-paragraph answers) or in your proposal sentences (for four-paragraph essay responses).

---

3. If you answer in a four-paragraph essay, your introduction and conclusion may be much briefer than those urged in other parts of this book. But do not abandon other requirements of the well-constructed essay.

> Make sure your proposal sentence allows you to discuss two aspects of the topic your instructor asks you to write about.
>
> Make sure the proposal sentence comes *last* in paragraph 1.
>
> Make sure to use a clear transition in the first sentence of paragraph 2.
>
> Make sure that in the first sentence of paragraph 3 you refer back to the topic in paragraph 2 and that you introduce the new aspect of the topic of paragraph 3.

4. In your conclusion, say again your main point by summarizing the topics of paragraphs 2 and 3. Then, apply your topic to some general principles, if possible (see pp. 423–427).

5. Use a number of details to illustrate or prove whatever points you make in your paragraphs. In this book you have learned how to use the following kinds of details and illustrations:

> a single moment from your life experience
> concrete sensory details
> figurative language and imagery
> statistics
> quotations and paraphrases
> illustrative moments from fiction
> cases

Step 1. Understanding Questions. These essay-type questions all come from college textbooks. Explain on a separate sheet of paper how you would go about answering these questions; tell what methods you would use in developing your paragraph or essay.

1. Compare the workings of the human eye to the workings of a camera.
2. Discuss the growth of feudalism in England.
3. List several characteristics of Marxian economy.
4. Compare and contrast Freud's view of fears with those ideas on fears held by Adler.
5. Discuss naturalism as it applies to American literature in the first part of the twentieth century.

13. MAKING A SIMPLE OUTLINE

To sort out ideas on a complicated topic, we often use the sentence outline before writing an essay. An outline allows you to see the main ideas of each paragraph at a glance; it also shows how major details (and subtopics) relate to each main idea; and it illustrates quickly just how each body paragraph relates to the proposal sentence. Writing each outline entry in a full sentence allows you to express main thoughts fully and to avoid writing fragments in the essay itself.

Hint: Outlines are designed to help you write and are useful only so long as they serve that function. Even after you prepare an outline you may change your subtopic or even main-idea sentences in the essay.

Here is a simple outline for the essay "Antonia's Strength," that appears on pp. 368–369. You will find in the margin explanations of the letters and Roman numbers.

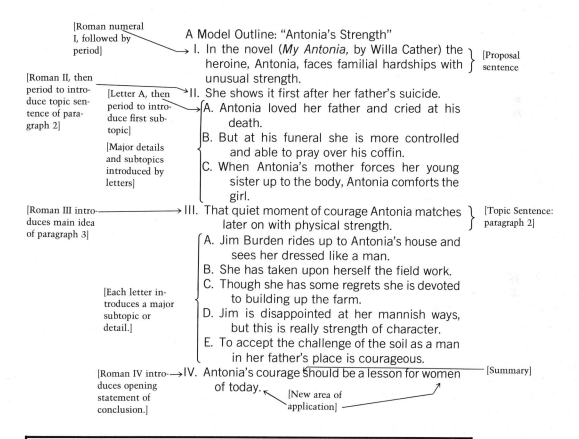

[Roman numeral I, followed by period]

A Model Outline: "Antonia's Strength"

I. In the novel (*My Antonia*, by Willa Cather) the heroine, Antonia, faces familial hardships with unusual strength. } [Proposal sentence]

[Roman II, then period to introduce topic sentence of paragraph 2]

[Letter A, then period to introduce first subtopic]

II. She shows it first after her father's suicide.

A. Antonia loved her father and cried at his death.

B. But at his funeral she is more controlled and able to pray over his coffin.

C. When Antonia's mother forces her young sister up to the body, Antonia comforts the girl.

[Major details and subtopics introduced by letters]

[Roman III introduces main idea of paragraph 3]

III. That quiet moment of courage Antonia matches later on with physical strength. } [Topic Sentence: paragraph 2]

A. Jim Burden rides up to Antonia's house and sees her dressed like a man.

B. She has taken upon herself the field work.

C. Though she has some regrets she is devoted to building up the farm.

D. Jim is disappointed at her mannish ways, but this is really strength of character.

E. To accept the challenge of the soil as a man in her father's place is courageous.

[Each letter introduces a major subtopic or detail.]

[Roman IV introduces opening statement of conclusion.]

IV. Antonia's courage should be a lesson for women of today.

[New area of application]

[Summary]

HOW TO MAKE THE OUTLINE HELP:

1. Check Roman numerals II and III to see if they clearly follow from the proposal you wrote for Roman numeral I.
2. Check subtopics A, B, C, etc. under each Roman numeral: make sure each subtopic relates to the topic sentence.
3. Leave out minor details.
4. Don't elaborate on the proposal or the introduction in the outline. You can do that in the essay itself.
5. Check to see if the transitions in the opening sentences of paragraphs 2 and 3 are clear and obvious.
6. Make sure that every entry you have written is a full sentence.

Step 1. Seeing an Outline Work. In the space provided, write an outline for "Some Disappointments," the essay by Barbara Pomerantz on pp. 364–366. Some of the entries already appear to guide you in the completion of the outline.

"Some Disappointments"

I. _____

_____

II. I realized the change in Gary one winter Saturday when I rushed excitedly into his room to talk about *The Red Badge of Courage,* a book I had just read and loved.

    A. _____

_____ .

    B. _____

_____ .

    C. I found no comfort in his dim and musty room.

    D. _____

_____ .

    E. He said with a sly smile, "I've seen the light."

    F. _____

_____ .

III. That moment in Gary's room was mild, though, when compared with the changes I saw in his temper.

    A. _____

_____ .

    B. _____

_____ .

    C. My mother asked, "Where are you going so late?"

    D. _____

_____ .

    E. Gary stormed out the door.

    F. _____

_____ .

    G. _____

_____ .

IV. _____

_____

_____.

Step 2. Putting an Outline Together. Select a topic suggested in any chapter in this book and, on separate paper, prepare an outline following the form and suggestions given above.

appendix A

VOCABULARY EXERCISES: DEFINITIONS BY CHAPTER

CHAPTER 1

A. Words to Describe Situations

1. dynamic: forceful
2. tiresome: dull, wearisome
3. frantic: wildly excited
4. tranquil: peaceful
5. intense: deeply felt
6. boisterous: noisy in an active way
7. dismal: gloomy
8. indifferent: not caring one way or the other
9. effervescent: bubbling with excitement
10. lax: not strict or tense

B. Words That Name Sounds

1. guffaw: laugh in a loud burst
2. din: loud, confused noise
3. whine: to utter a high pitched cry
4. inaudible: cannot be heard
5. erupted: blew up
6. resounded: became filled with sound

CHAPTER 2

A. Describing People

1. scowl: a lowering of the muscles of the face in displeasure
2. wilted: lost freshness; became limp
3. pious: religious
4. brute: savage, cruel
5. introvert: a person interested in his own inner self
6. rage: anger
7. disenchantment: the loss of false impressions or beliefs
8. extrovert: a person involved and interested in the world around him
9. mutter: to say indistinctly
10. gnarled: twisted and swollen

B. Showing How People Do or Say Things

1. succinctly: briefly
2. quizzically: oddly
3. sullenly: gloomily
4. limply: weakly; without firmness or strength
5. irritably: in an annoyed and angry manner
6. painstakingly: with great care
7. precariously: dangerously
8. intently: with concentration
9. jovially: happily
10. solemnly: seriously

CHAPTER 3

1. phenomenon: occasion; observable occurrence
2. dingy: dark; dirty
3. flick: strike quickly and sharply
4. bandana: colored handkerchief
5. episode: unit of action in a series of events
6. startling: causing sudden fear
7. melancholy: sad
8. burly: strongly built
9. quiver: shake slightly
10. liberate: to set free
11. rotundity: chubbiness
12. compelled: urged with force
13. grudged: reluctant
14. conviction: positive opinion
15. hover: flutter to and fro
16. illicitly: in a manner that is not permitted legally
17. unattainable: that which cannot be achieved
18. cleave: split by force
19. elect: specially selected
20. lanky: ungraceful, slim, and tall

CHAPTER 4

A. Words for Campus Personalities

1. scintillating: sparkling
2. aimless: without a goal
3. cynical: believing all actions are done for selfish reasons
4. obnoxious: offensive
5. hostile: marked by outright unfriendliness
6. stimulating: exciting
7. erudite: scholarly
8. egotistical: involved in self-interest
9. perceptive: aware of things without any formal learning or explanation
10. dedicated: devoted

B. Words for Contrasting Moods

1. rapturous: filled with ecstasy
2. confident: assured
3. affectionate: loving
4. serene: peaceful
5. magnanimous: noble and generous
6. irate: angry
7. depressed: saddened
8. lethargic: drowsy
9. recalcitrant: stubbornly resistant to authority
10. callous: hardened

CHAPTER 5

A. Words for Automobile Facts

1. vehicular: pertaining to something that transports
2. definitive: conclusive
3. sustain: to stand up under; to suffer or experience (as injuries)
4. statistically: pertaining to data or facts
5. autopsy: examination of a dead body to find cause of death
6. protrusion: something that sticks out
7. chronic: something that happens over and over
8. allude: refer to indirectly
9. graphic: vividly described
10. emission: that which is given off

B. -ing Verbs for Liveliness

1. wheezing: breathing hoarsely
2. sputtering: speaking in an explosive way
3. asserting: claiming
4. elucidating: making clear
5. assenting: agreeing
6. reiterating: saying again
7. lauding: praising
8. intervening: stepping in to settle or stop
9. brandishing: threatening
10. lamenting: crying out in grief

CHAPTER 6

A. Sharpening the Senses

1. savory: something with special flavor
2. rancid: rotten smell or taste
3. musty: moldy; smelling or tasting of dampness
4. pungent: sharply stimulating
5. medicinal: relating to medicine
6. supple: able to bend easily without breaking
7. clammy: damp, sticky, and cool
8. gossamer: thin, sheer fabric
9. furrowed: filled with wrinkles or grooves
10. sinewy: physically strong

B. Energetic Verbs

1. totter: tremble as if about to fall
2. trudge: walk steadily with effort
3. deplore: regret strongly
4. glare: shine with a dazzling light
5. grimace: express disapproval with the face
6. sprint: run at top speed
7. saunter: stroll
8. swagger: walk conceitedly
9. clasp: to fasten or embrace
10. spurn: to reject with scorn

CHAPTER 7

A. Words for Size and Shape

1. vast: very great in size
2. minute: tiny
3. towering: noble; reaching high intensity
4. corpulent: excessively fat
5. squat: low to the ground; short and thick in stature
6. oblong: a four-sided figure—opposite sides parallel—that is longer in one direction than in the other
7. illimitable: boundless
8. amorphous: without definite shape
9. rectangular: four-sided
10. symmetrical: in balanced arrangement

B. Exact Words for Exact Meanings

1. obscene: anything that offends morality or decency
   fetid: having a bad smell
   squalid: filthy through neglect or poverty
2. alluring: attracting with charm

   stunning: exceptional in a striking, attractive way
   provocative: stimulating to anger; arousing
3. uncluttered: not heaped in a disorderly manner

ample: enough; sufficient

copious: extensive; abundant; large in quantity

4. impersonal: without any personal connection

inimical: unfriendly; having a negative effect

antagonistic: acting in opposition

5. serene: peaceful; calm; tranquil

hushed: silent

muffled: deadened; made quieter by wrapping or by some other way preventing the occurrence of noise

CHAPTER 8

A. Words in the Woman's Struggle

1. feminist: one who believes women's activities should be extended in social and political life
2. suffragette: a woman who believes women should have the right to vote
3. chauvinist: anyone who has blind devotion to any cause
4. hormonal: relating to substances given off by certain organs in the body
5. puberty: sexual maturity; the age at which a person is able to have children

6. mortality: the condition of being subject to death
7. inferiority: the state of being lower in rank
8. stereotype: a fixed idea about a person or thing based upon oversimplified points of view
9. degradation: the state of being lowered in quality or estimation
10. discrimination: a distinction or preference in favor of or against some thing or person

B. More Words in the Struggle for Equality

1. enslavement: the state of being a slave
2. repression: the state of being kept under control
3. oppression: the use of power over others in a cruel way
4. downtrodden: trampled upon; ruled over severely
5. prejudice: an unfavorable opinion formed beforehand, without knowledge

6. exploitation: using selfishly for individual profit
7. emancipation: the act of setting free
8. enfranchisement: the act of being made a citizen who can vote
9. activist: an especially enthusiastic worker in a political cause
10. revolutionary: one who works to change something drastically

CHAPTER 9

Words to Name Relationships among People

1. peer: an equal; someone of the same rank
2. contemporary: living at the same time
3. familial: pertaining to a family
4. sibling: brother or sister
5. cohort: a companion or accomplice
6. crony: an intimate friend

7. fraternal: brotherly
8. conjugal: pertaining to marriage or to the mutual relations between husband and wife
9. paternal: fatherly
10. maternal: motherly

CHAPTER 10

Some Words for the Business Scene

1. escrow: in law, something held until some terms or conditions are met
2. correspondent: someone who communicates by letters
3. liabilities: debts; any disadvantageous things
4. dynamo: an individual with unusual force or energy
5. laissez-faire: the theory that says government should not interfere in economic affairs
6. entrepreneur: one who enters business deals without hesitation or fear of danger
7. assets: resources or earnings of a person or business
8. collateral: security pledged for the payment of a loan
9. productivity: ability to produce
10. insolvency: the condition of being unable to pay creditors

Words for the Job Situation

1. initiative: introductory act or step which leads to further action
2. probity: honesty
3. promptitude: being on time
4. compliance: the act of giving in or yielding
5. assiduity: constant or close application of oneself to work or to a job
6. indulgence: the act of tolerating someone's wishes or whims
7. amity: friendship; harmony
8. generosity: readiness to give liberally
9. inspiration: a stimulating influence or suggestion
10. compassion: a feeling of sorrow or pity for the sufferings of someone else

CHAPTER 11

A. Roots for Definitions

1. moribund: on the verge of dying
2. tangible: able to be touched
3. loquacious: talkative
4. evoke: to call up or produce memories
5. remit: to put back to a previous condition; to send (money, etc.) to a person or place

B. Prefix, Suffix, Root in Combination

1. submitter: one who gives in
2. circumlocution: a roundabout way of speaking
3. inversion: the act of reversing in position; turning upside down
4. subversion: act of overthrowing or undermining; destruction
5. comportment: behavior; bearing
6. intangible: unable to be touched
7. exposedness: state of being left without protection
8. invisible: not able to be seen
9. disposal: act of putting something away in its place
10. introspection: act of looking into one's self and examining one's own mental state

appendix B

THEME PROGRESS SHEET

After your essays and paragraphs are returned graded by your instructor, count up and enter the number of errors you make in each category listed on top of the chart. Enter your theme title in the space provided. Before you write each following composition, study this sheet so that you know where you usually make errors and so that you can avoid them in your writing.

Date	Title of composition	Run-on sentences	Sentence fragments	Spelling	Word usage	Quotations	Subject-verb agreement	Misused sentence openers	Capital letters	Commas	Other punctuation	Levels of language	Pronouns	Abbreviations	Possession	Tenses	Placement of words	Parallel structure	Logic	Details

appendix C

**RECORD OF TEACHER-STUDENT CONFERENCES
ON COMPOSITIONS**

Date	Discussion points	Follow-up assignment

INDEX

INDEX